DEBATING MORAL EDUCATION

Rethinking the Role of the Modern University

EDITED BY
Elizabeth Kiss and
J. Peter Euben

Duke University Press   Durham and London   2010

© 2010 Duke University Press

All rights reserved

Printed in the United States of
America on acid-free paper ∞

Typeset in Arno Pro by Keystone
Typesetting, Inc.

Library of Congress Cataloging-in-
Publication data appear on the last
printed page of this book.

CONTENTS

This volume originated through a series of conversations occasioned by a conference held at Duke University, conversations which have been sustained by continued discussion among contributors and colleagues. It is the third in a series of books from the Kenan Institute for Ethics that address core questions of moral life today. The first volume focused on issues of nationhood and citizenship and the second highlighted key problems in talking about evil today. This volume takes aim at the notion of moral education and the purposes of a university.

As an edited volume, *Debating Moral Education* extends what Alasdair MacIntyre called "an admirable tradition of collegial friendship among those in Duke's various departments and schools" to encompass many long-time colleagues and friends at other institutions. That tradition and those friendships have been nurtured by the coeditors of this volume, Peter Euben, the Kenan Institute for Ethics' Distinguished Faculty Fellow, and Elizabeth Kiss, the Institute's founding director and now president of Agnes Scott College.

Debating Moral Education builds on Euben's and Kiss's shared concern to advance the teaching and practice of ethics and moral education in the university. Equally important, it exploits their differences in ways that open up, rather than close down, discussion about the risks and pitfalls of such an enterprise. They accomplish this dual purpose by bringing into conversation a range of contributors from different disciplines as well as proponents, skeptics, and critics of the "turn to ethics" in higher education.

As a result, this book speaks to a wide range of audiences: faculty who are either committed to or troubled by the resurgence of moral education in the modern university; academic administrators pondering whether to launch an ethics center or add ethical reasoning to their curricular requirements; student affairs professionals wrestling with what the editors call the "hidden curriculum" of campus policies, practices, and norms; members of the community at large who are concerned about the role universities play in character development and the formation of citizens; and, perhaps most of all, students who wonder just what they've gotten themselves into once past the gates of the admissions office.

As this manuscript moved from conference papers to completed volume, I tried out a variety of these chapters in the classroom, supplemented by documents from Duke's own history: the founding indenture and updated mission statements, faculty jeremiads, presidential convocation addresses and sermons by religious leaders, student opinion pieces and student affairs' statements of philosophy and practice, and internal and external assessments of and recommendations for changing curricula and campus culture.

Uniformly, I found that this volume enabled my students to read these statements and assessments with new eyes and to assess where *their* school has been, and claims to be going, with regard to questions about the meaning of autonomy and the formation of character, the nature of self-government and the role of community, and the relationship between politics and education. Call it a guide for the perplexed undergraduate to a singularly important and yet often little discussed part of his or her college years and future life as a parent, professional, and citizen.

Modern university life is often described as striking to the degree that it refuses to self-consciously attend to these questions. The political commentator David Brooks laments the fact that universities "do not go to great lengths to build character, the way adults and adult institutions did a century ago." Rather, he writes, "the job of the university is to supply the knowledge that students will need to prosper, and, at most, to provide a forum in which they can cultivate character on their own." This, of course, is precisely what Stanley Fish celebrates in his contribution to this volume and wishes only that it were more true. And in her contribution, Julie Reuben casts an historian's eye on the complex countercurrents in which universities often urge students to become more morally engaged while also telling them that they don't want to limit their freedom of choice.

I asked my students to analyze whether colleges and universities have moved toward a more tolerant, meritocratic, and essentially characterless model of higher education that Brooks identifies, and, if so, what has been gained and what has been lost. Did they think universities should return to an older model of character education—or at least use that model as a guide for revising the current one? Alternatively, did they think it is possible, and desirable, to create new models focused on the moral claims that underpin current campus-wide efforts to protect the environment, secure human and social rights, and promote tolerance? Or did they want to stand fast against any such initiatives and defend universities for having quit the business of explicit efforts to shape the moral and civic lives of students?

In answering these questions, students had to contend with the voices in this volume that challenge the moral grounds on which they would respond. Stanley Hauerwas, for instance, argues that any attempts to shape culture and character in modern, pluralistic universities are doomed by the lack of a shared ability to participate in public debate, shared standards of justification, and a shared view of the past. By contrast, Don Moon suggests that we can establish stronger conditions for a shared life by identifying "common bads" and by providing the knowledge and skills for students to join a conversation about a shared life.

Arguments like these, supplemented by readings specific to my own institution, propelled my students into the debate over moral education in the modern university with a newfound depth and an increased awareness of the stakes. They engaged the issues not as a set of abstract propositions but as a matter of significant meaning to their own lives and futures. *Debating Moral Education* pressed them to entertain the core questions of what a university is for and why they were part of one. As any teacher will tell you, generating serious analysis and discussion of these two issues, especially analysis and discussion informed by philosophical, educational, and historical context, is itself at the center of a truly liberal education. So, having road-tested this book, I commend it to you for doing just that.

In closing, I also want to mark the passing of one of the volume's contributors, Wilson Carey McWilliams, a scholar and teacher who lived the life of fraternity and community that he wrote about so eloquently. We are fortunate that his daughter, Susan McWilliams, could complete his unfinished essay. Their essay combines a shrewd skepticism about a turn to ethics in a land defined by self-interest and pluralism with a call for educators to "articulate the second voices of American political culture— those voices which see human beings as born not free but subject, which privilege sociability over individualism, which emphasize obligation rather than self-preservation, and which speak the language of the spirit instead of the language of self-interest." This combination of skepticism and commitment captures both the complexity and the urgency of the debate over the future of moral education in the modern university. In doing so, it reinforces the editors' invitation to all readers to join that debate.

ACKNOWLEDGMENTS

This book started out as a working conference at Duke University that tackled the "why, whether, and how" of moral education in colleges and universities today. We wish to thank the participants whose wisdom and lively engagement helped shape the project and contributed much to whatever merits it may have. In addition to the volume's contributors they included Eva Brann, Geoffrey Harpham, Josina Makau, Darcia Narvaez, Gary Pavela, and Bill Taylor, as well as Duke colleagues Evan Charney, Troy Dostert, Nan Keohane, Fiona Miller, Noah Pickus, Kathy Rudy, Tom Spragens, and David Wong.

While he was unable to participate in the original conference, we owe special thanks to Stanley Fish, whose bracing critique of moral and civic education provoked us to think more deeply about its value and purposes. One of the most provocative voices at the conference itself was that of Carey McWilliams, whose untimely death robbed all of us of a memorable and insightful colleague. We are grateful to his daughter Susan McWilliams for joining our conversation and completing her father's unfinished chapter.

The Kenan Institute for Ethics provided funding for the conference and a supportive intellectual home for our efforts to bring teachers and scholars from widely varying disciplines and perspectives together to engage ethical issues at the heart of the educational enterprise. We are grateful for that support and for the superb research assistance it made possible from Bill Curtis, Dave McIvor, and Andrew Terjesen. Dave especially offered invaluable help for the one of us (it is not Elizabeth) who is technologically challenged.

We wish to thank the contributors for their patience and good will in responding to various suggestions for revisions, and Courtney Berger, our editor at Duke University Press, as well as our outside readers for the time and effort they put into making this book much better than it would have been without them.

We were going to thank each other but thought better of it, not only because it seems self-indulgent but because neither of us thinks the other deserves it. This book is the fruit of our own debates over ethics and education, debates that have defined and enriched our friendship as they have our understanding of the subject. We offer this volume as an invitation to join us and our contributors in sustaining this invigorating conversation.

Introduction

WHY THE RETURN TO ETHICS? WHY NOW? I

Elizabeth Kiss and J. Peter Euben

DEBATING MORAL EDUCATION   *An Introduction*

The past two decades have witnessed a substantial turn, or more precisely a return, to ethics in the American academy.[1] While this trend remains incomplete and contested, it is visible in the recent establishment of over one hundred ethics centers and programs;[2] the creation of numerous undergraduate and professional school courses in practical or applied ethics; and increased interest in normative questions in a variety of academic disciplines. New national associations have emerged that promote ethics in higher education, including the Association for Moral Education (founded in 1976), the Association for Practical and Professional Ethics (founded in 1990), Campus Compact (founded in 1985), and the Center for Academic Integrity (founded in 1992). A small but growing number of schools have made the study of ethics part of their core curricula and have emphasized the ethical dimension of courses more generally.

Nor is the burgeoning interest in ethics confined to the classroom. Efforts to promote academic integrity, respect for diversity, and civic engagement reach beyond the classroom to encompass student life, campus policies, and university-community relations. A number of ethics centers, including one, Duke University's Kenan Institute for Ethics, with which we are or have been affiliated, pursue a broad university-wide mission that seeks to infuse ethical concerns and conversations across the curriculum, in everyday campus life, and in institutional practices and priorities.[3]

This growing interest, and the educational vision that animates it, has not gone unchallenged. For example, when the distinguished political scientist John Mearsheimer delivered the annual "Aims of Education" address in 1997 to the incoming first-year class at the University of Chicago,[4] he argued that the purpose of a university education is to help students think critically, to broaden their intellectual horizons, and to promote greater self-awareness. What the university does *not* do, he added, is "provide you with moral guidance. Indeed, it is a remarkably amoral institution." The university does not, and should not, offer courses "where you discuss ethics or morality in any detail," nor should it see it as part of its mission to help students "in sorting out" the ethical issues they will face in their lives.[5]

As the essays in this book indicate, Mearsheimer is not alone. Many colleagues with very different political, methodological, and theoretical commitments are indifferent to, if not actively hostile to, the language of ethics and morals. To complicate matters further, they often mean different things by the terms "ethics" and "morals" and have very different conceptions of the relationships between ethics and morality, moral and civic education, or ethics and politics. For example, Bernard Williams insists on a clear distinction between ethics and morality, preserving the broader Greek meaning of the former from modern attempts at co-optation and linking the latter with what he regards as a peculiar, and fundamentally flawed, Western Enlightenment tradition of ethical thought focused on obligation.[6] While Lawrence Hinman regards ethics as systematic reflection on moral issues, John Caputo is critical of both ethics and morality.[7] In this volume, Patchen Markell, George Shulman, and Romand Coles are all leery about what is elided by the very language of morality and moral education. Markell argues that morality (probably unlike ethics) "risks flattening a rich field of questions about conduct into a single register of law, dutiful obedience, and righteous punishment," all of which risk reducing politics and citizenship to matters of individual virtue. Similarly, Shulman emphasizes the way practices of morality constitute forms of power, and Coles argues that ethical education as generally conceived and practiced in universities obscures urgent questions of systematic injustice. As to the idea of civic education, some regard its aim as civility while others draw on a more politically rigorous tradition of civic republicanism. We have not insisted that our contributors use these terms consistently, since their very inconsistencies attest to the underlying debates this book seeks to explore.

Even when there is broad agreement on the desirability of teaching ethics there is vigorous disagreement about what this means. For instance, should the aim of moral education—or of education in general—be to make people more ethical? Or should it aim to avoid corrupting what Ruth Grant (following Rousseau) calls "ordinary goodness"? And what sense can we make of the idea of ordinary goodness given the prevalence in our world of ordinary evil?[8] Can moral education, for instance, help us to prevent another Auschwitz, Rwanda, or Darfur? Closer to home, can moral education prevent, or at least discourage, our students from acting in boorish, racist, sexist ways?

Advocates of moral education also differ on what those who teach ethics should actually *do*. Should we teach critical interpretation of texts that raise ethical issues, introduce students to traditions of ethical thought, teach moral reasoning or deliberation or judgment, cultivate the moral imagination so students can see the world from other points of view, or some combination of these? What is the role and place of experiential approaches to the teaching of ethics, from service-learning to student-run honor systems? How can we integrate such learning with more traditional academic purposes so that each informs the other? If, as Aristotle argued, being ethical requires the reciprocity of habit, character, and action, how do universities create contexts for moral growth?

Our aim in this volume is to explore and participate in the debate over moral education. We want to engage the substantive question of what it means to teach ethics and what moral education worthy of the name might look like in today's colleges and universities. To this end we have gathered a group of scholars and teachers from different disciplines and institutions who offer strong, divergent views on these questions. But while we consider ourselves participants in the "return to ethics" and respect the moral ambitions of those who champion it, we have also invited critics and skeptics to join the conversation and indeed to contest its terms. In this sense we want to debate the debate: to read the return to ethics (and rejections of it) symptomatically as well as substantively. Thus we ask why the growing preoccupation with ethics (insofar as there is one) appears when it does, where it does, and as it does.

But before we can approach any of these aims, we need to develop a deeper understanding of today's "return to ethics." To that end, we offer a historical narrative of the decline of ethics and of changing perceptions of its relationship to fundamental issues of higher education.[9] It is this larger narrative that sets the stage for the terms of today's debate. In telling our story, however, we acknowledge that every narrative of decline is both less and more than it seems.

Educators in the American colonies and the young United States embraced a tradition going back to Aristotle and the Greeks that linked liberal education with the development of moral and civic virtue.[10] A concern for character formation and citizenship, intertwined with Christian and civic republican conceptions of duty and virtue, dominated American higher education throughout the nineteenth century. Ethics "furnished an integrating principle for the entire curriculum," most notably through a capstone course in moral philosophy required of all seniors at many institutions.[11] The abrupt demise of this curricular emphasis occurred around the turn of the twentieth century.[12]

Recent work by Sloan, Julie Reuben, and Edward McClellan traces the complex cultural, intellectual, and institutional factors that led to the marginalization of ethics in the twentieth-century academy.[13] These included the creation of the research university with its specialized disciplines and professional norms centered on research; the rise of the ideal of "value-free" inquiry in the social sciences; the increasing secularization of intellectual life; the precipitous decline of normative ethics that accompanied the rise of analytical philosophy; growing suspicion about the status of ethical claims fueled by otherwise disparate intellectual movements such as logical positivism, behaviorism, and postmodernism; an emphasis on vocational and technical training in professional schools and in the state universities and community colleges that enroll the majority of America's college students; a rising culture of consumerism within and about higher education; and a new and widening division of labor between academic and student affairs that led faculty to limit their student interactions to the classroom, leaving all other aspects of students' lives to other campus professionals.[14]

Of course, the reality was more complicated than this relentless story of decline suggests. For one thing, institutions of higher education, then as now, often embraced contradictory aims which could safely be espoused by various factions as long as no one insisted that they be reconciled. For another, the modern research university was initially conceived as a vehicle for *renewing* the moral and civic mission of higher education by equipping citizens with the moral ideals and specialized knowledge needed to solve the problems of an increasingly complex society. The new social sciences were supposed to "embrace the ethical tasks of their moral philosophical heritage, but fulfill them in ways appropriate to the modern world." Still, within just a few years, this vision of the social sciences and of the new university had been largely abandoned in favor of an ideal of professional researchers pursuing "value-free" inquiry within narrowly defined disciplinary boundaries.[15] The cataclysmic events of the Holocaust and World War II did inspire some powerful scholarship informed by a normative agenda, such as Hannah Arendt's analysis of evil, the critical theories of Herbert Marcuse, Max Horkheimer, and Theodor Adorno,[16] and Stanley Milgram's controversial experiments on obedience.[17] But by and large, the study and teaching of ethics was relegated to a few specialized courses in religion and philosophy and increasingly marginalized even within these disciplines.

Consider developments within philosophy. Anglo-American philosophers at midcentury were, by and large, uninterested in or even contemptuous of the approaches taken by critical theorists, opting instead for a focus on meta-ethics that delegitimated philosophical concern with practical ethics and with the most perplexing moral issues of modernity. While the rise of analytical philosophy has often been portrayed as a victory for logical clarity and precision, recent scholarship has suggested that the shift away from socially and ethically engaged forms of philosophy was prompted, at least to some degree, by Cold War pressures in the era of McCarthyism.[18] But whether prompted by political anxiety or intellectual commitment, many academic philosophers in the 1950s and 1960s came to regard moral judgments as nonrational expressions of personal preference. However, while these views may have been a breath of fresh air compared to some of the excesses of neo-Hegelianism, the dry, deflationary accounts of moral life offered as alternatives by theories like emotivism ultimately failed to illuminate moral life and generated little intellectual excitement on campus. The author of an article in *Liberal Education* in 1964 on the role of philosophy in the undergraduate curriculum noted that at his own institution of 12,000 students the enrollment in ethics courses averaged eleven students per year.[19]

Meanwhile, in law and medical schools, traditional emphases on developing a rigorous professional ethos were replaced by a focus on technical expertise that ignored, or on occasion was actively hostile to, ethical considerations. A memorable example was offered by former Harvard president Derek Bok, whose efforts in the 1980s to establish a program on professional ethics were opposed by some senior faculty of the Harvard Law School, one of whom patiently explained to Bok that the goal of legal education was precisely to "anesthetize" students' moral judgments.[20] Oscar Wilde had once quipped that "a preoccupation with matters of right and wrong in conduct is a sign of arrested intellectual development,"[21] and the twentieth-century American academy was inclined to agree.

To be sure, traditional moral and civic themes continued to be invoked in commencement addresses and college and university catalogues, where, as David Hoekema points out, "the language of character, citizenship, and moral community is laid on with a trowel." But the reality behind the rhetoric, he adds, "might be summarized thus: 'We hire excellent scholars for our faculty, maintain a good library, and fill the flower beds for parents' weekend; and we sincerely hope that the students will turn out right.' "[22]

Ironically, the events that began to revive interest in ethical questions on college and university campuses are precisely those that conservatives frequently cite as catalysts for moral decline. As Edward McClellan notes, "The very events that brought disorder to the campus—the civil rights movement, the war in Vietnam, concerns about the environment—also gave birth to a new vigor in moral discourse."[23] Indeed, for better or for worse, the political movements of the sixties and early seventies were driven by a sense of moral outrage at the hypocrisies of American democracy and a desire to reexamine the relationships between ethics, politics, and power. The rise of "practical" or "applied" ethics owes a great deal to the movements demanding power and respect for African Americans, women, the poor, and other subordinated and marginalized groups, movements that powerfully posed and reframed questions about justice and the good society and about norms of personal conduct between women and men, whites and blacks, gay and straight people.

A second and distinct source of the campus ethics revival is public concern about a decline in ethical standards and commitment in personal, professional, and public life, fueled by a wave of scandals stretching from Tuskegee and Watergate to the Lewinsky affair and Enron, as well as by broader social trends, from rising rates of crime, drug use, cheating, and divorce, to rampant materialism and civic apathy. Together, these clusters of events have fueled inquiry into public goods and private virtues and the social and educational conditions that sustain them. Influential scholarship on ethical theory and moral development by such diverse scholars as John Rawls, Lawrence Kohlberg, Bernard Williams, Alasdair MacIntyre, and Carol Gilligan reflected and inspired this inquiry—and made ethics academically respectable again. A growing number of educators argued that questions about right and wrong, justice and injustice, virtue and vice were essential elements of a good education. In the words of a pioneering Hastings Center report in 1980, "A 'higher education' that does not foster, support, and implement an examination of the moral life will fail its own purposes, the needs of its students, and the welfare of society."[24]

Yet this story, like the previous ones, is also too one-dimensional. Like its decline, the ascent of ethics in the academy has been a complex affair. For example, MacIntyre's critique of Rawls, like Gilligan's critique of Kohlberg (and subsequent critiques of *both* MacIntyre and Gilligan by feminist theorists like Marilyn Friedman) helped to drive and shape the return to ethics.[25] Then there are the obvious tensions between ethics initiatives that are primarily concerned with contesting unjust structures and those that stress individual moral reform, what James Joseph has called the difference between "macroethics" and "microethics."[26] But while it may be tempting to associate "macroethics" with the right and "microethics" with the left, the reality is more complicated. Take, for example, the dramatic revival of virtue ethics as a basis for moral education in both K-12 and university contexts. The new emphasis on virtue arose as a reaction against the rationalism of neo-Kantians like Rawls and Kohlberg, but was motivated by a wide array of concerns, from traditional conservatism to neo-Aristotelianism to feminism and radical social activism. Its models range from Mother Teresa to Nelson Mandela. The "return to ethics" is thus not a product of either the political left or right but a complicated and often surprising interweaving of progressive and conservative convictions and concerns.

By way of summary and anticipation, we want to identify twelve trends that characterize the return to, and debate over, moral education today.

First, normative questions have acquired new intellectual legitimacy as a core dimension of inquiry across a range of disciplines, from philosophy to literary theory to the natural sciences. Lively debates are taking place over such issues as moral relativism and pluralism, cosmopolitanism and universalism, bioethics and environmental justice, abortion and surrogate motherhood. In fields ranging from laboratory science to ethnography, core competencies are being revised to include ethical components.[27]

Second, while it is already clear that the return to ethics is not a monolithic movement, there is considerable agreement over what the major points of *disagreement* should be. For example, as Geoffrey Harpham has put it, should ethics be regarded as an essentially *critical* enterprise—a process of "relentless and skeptical scrutiny"—or does it need to be practical and action guiding?[28] Must moral education be grounded in substantive ethical truths, or is the search for firm foundations a fool's errand to be abandoned in favor of efforts to ground ethics in open-ended dialogic or democratic processes?[29] And should moral education confine itself to the intellectual virtues essential to teaching, learning, and research,[30] or should it focus more broadly on personal, civic, and political virtues?[31]

Third, while the capstone courses of the nineteenth century were characterized by moral confidence, today's return to ethics confronts a hermeneutics of suspicion. Such a hermeneutics, because it challenges appeals to authority, helps put the issue of moral and cultural relativism on the intellectual agenda. To be sure, attitudes to relativism differ widely. For some, it is a symbol and symptom of moral collapse, while for others the acceptance of some form of moral relativism, or at least of a strong version of moral pluralism, is a sign of ethical maturity and wisdom.[32]

Fourth, there is a reemphasis on higher education's responsibility to prepare women and men for democratic citizenship, though there is considerable disagreement over what sort of democracy we mean and thus what sort of citizens we want to "make." For some, citizenship is a minimal legal status largely fulfilled by paying taxes and obeying the law. Others affirm more robust visions of citizenship focused on patriotism and public service that require a willingness to serve collective ideals. Still others emphasize the role of moral education as a vehicle for the formation of deliberative citizens capable of thoughtful judgments about such issues as biotechnology, globalization, abortion, gay marriage, immigration, and terrorism and able and willing to engage in protest when the situation requires.[33]

Fifth, a more complex understanding of moral development has led to a tendency to replace a singular emphasis on moral reasoning with models of moral education that combine cognitive, affective, volitional, and behavioral capacities.[34] For instance, recent work by Colby, Ehrlich, Beaumont, and Stephens emphasizes understanding, skills, and motivation as essential components of moral development.[35] This trend, which reflects the emergence of a focus on virtue, character, community, and emotion as intellectual counterpoints to the Kantian-utilitarian debate, has also prompted renewed interest in previously ignored traditions of moral wisdom, including philosophy, theology, and literature from "non-Western" cultures.[36]

Sixth, ethics educators are increasingly respectful of a range of curricular approaches relevant to their enterprise—from training in systematic moral theory to discussions of case studies to films and novels to service-learning and community-based research—and some are beginning to explore how we might assess their comparative strengths and weaknesses as vehicles of moral education.[37]

Seventh, experiential approaches that bridge action and reflection deserve special mention because of their prominence within today's return to ethics. A growing number of colleges and universities are embracing service-learning, community-based research, student-governed honor codes, and other experiential pedagogies.[38]

Eighth, an emphasis on pedagogy extends to a growing awareness of the performative dimensions of teaching. How does a teacher help students cultivate analytical skills, a refined moral imagination, and virtues like empathy, courage, nobility, and common sense? If a focus on ethical questions in the course syllabus does not guarantee an appreciable impact on students' moral sensibilities, what would have such impact? How much does such impact depend upon the character of the teacher and the dynamic of the classroom he or she helps to create?[39]

Ninth, this focus on the teacher's character and performance has led to efforts to stake out a middle ground between the extremes of moral indoctrination and value-neutrality, neither of which takes into account the power of faculty as role models or the kinds of professorial stance best suited to helping students develop capacities for moral judgment and commitment.[40]

Tenth, there is a growing acknowledgment of the need to make room for spiritual exploration as a part of moral education, since it is the realm of religion and spirituality, in its less doctrinaire forms, that engages many students' deepest questions and strongest convictions about how to live an ethical life.[41] But this renewed interest in spirituality and its links to moral education makes many in the academy deeply uneasy.

Eleventh, there is a recognition of how the "hidden curriculum" of campus policies, practices, and norms contributes to student learning and development. In some ways this trend represents an attempt to reconnect elements of the academic enterprise that became fragmented by the forces of specialization over the course of the twentieth century. But it also reflects a new willingness to turn a critical eye on how colleges and universities, as powerful corporate entities, succeed or fail in setting high standards for their internal conduct and external relations with local, national, and international communities. Thus Derek Bok argues that universities should be "more alert to the countless signals that institutions send to students" and strive to make these signals "support rather than undermine basic norms,"[42] and Gary Pavela and Patricia King urge campuses to provide students with more opportunities to exercise moral responsibility and leadership.[43]

Finally, there seems to be a trend toward embracing Aristotle's dictum that the aim of ethics is not just theoretical knowledge but practical wisdom: "For we are inquiring not in order to know what virtue is, but in order to become good, since otherwise our inquiry would have been of no use."[44] As Robert Coles put it in an influential essay in the *Chronicle of Higher Education*, faculty need to affirm the importance of the link between moral reasoning and action and to acknowledge that purely intellectual approaches to the teaching of ethics may reward students who, while clever, are also "smug, ungenerous, even cruel."[45] In 1994 a Hastings Center report on ethics education exemplified this trend by explicitly moving beyond the Center's own study in 1980 on the same subject. The earlier study had concluded that, while the teaching of ethics was essential to higher education, influencing student behavior was a "doubtful" goal.[46] Fifteen years later, however, a follow-up study evinced far more "interest in and support for" moral education that encompassed efforts to promote behavioral change. The authors of the later study emphasized that this new trend was not an ideological swing either to the right or the left but rather came "from within the liberal arts tradition itself and from the identity of the campus as a community of critical reasoning, inclusive dialogue, and the quest for truth."[47] On this view, colleges and universities should strive to provide students with practical tools for ethical life and take seriously their role in the "moral formation" of young people.

While our account of the decline and revival of ethics highlights many contested issues, it does not give voice to those who read the return to ethics symptomatically or regard the moral education debate as too unaware of its own presuppositions and too willing to endorse platitudes. As we mentioned earlier, many of our colleagues are indifferent to, or suspicious of, the language of ethics, and those who harbor these deeper suspicions represent a wide array of political, theoretical, and methodological commitments. For instance, many of those who identify themselves with postmodernism regard the enterprise of ethics as a mode of policing and normalization.[48] A number of liberals are uneasy about any moral project that issues from an institutional authority, be it a state or a university.[49] Social scientists look askance at an effort to emphasize the normative components of their work, which they regard as inimical to their scientific aspirations. Communitarians and theologians worry that the language of ethics quickly becomes the language of secular liberal individualism, while radical democrats worry that a preoccupation with moral questions underplays the role of power in shaping what those questions are and who gets to pose them. Finally, those who regard themselves as realists believe that, as a matter of principle and survival, moral considerations have no place in political life, particularly in the international sphere.

It is crucial for the kind of volume we want this to be that we take these criticisms and this skepticism with the utmost seriousness. While we respect—indeed share—the moral ambitions of those applauding the return to ethics, we also want to move outside the celebratory discourse that often frames it. Thus we join the critics of the return to ethics by reading that return symptomatically as well as substantively.

We need to emphasize, however, that reading the return symptomatically does not mean we simply endorse such skepticism. For example, while we recognize the ways in which the language of ethics is a normalizing discourse and acknowledge that a preoccupation with morality can turn into a narrow moralism, we do not believe such acknowledgment justifies rejecting the enterprise as a whole. To begin with, all normalizations are not created equal. It is appropriately a function of ethics to draw lines between acceptable and unacceptable behavior (even while it is another, equally important, function of ethics to subject such lines to debate). Moreover, since the teaching and learning of ethics goes on whether we like it or not, the question is not whether it should be taught but how, when, and by whom. Aristotle argued that every association—he would surely have included universities—is defined by a conception of the good. That good is manifest in the people, acts, achievements or events, and traits of character it honors most highly and in the stories it tells about itself. While it is "natural" that every society and association should establish practices that reproduce it, it is equally "natural" that the moral and civic education which accomplishes these tasks should itself become subject first to recognition and then to either reaffirmation or critique. In these terms, moral education includes educating citizens to participate in shaping the conditions that had conditioned them.

We would offer a similar response to the concern voiced by some liberals about the dangers of moral education as a form of centralized political and moral power. That concern has a distinguished history and an important legacy which we have no wish to deny. But those who worry that any pursuit of moral education by universities will threaten students' creative autonomy should remember that the absence of such university efforts does not mean the absence of power in students' lives but rather the sway of whatever forms of economic and cultural power happen to be dominant. Thus, in a media-saturated culture rife with messages promoting individualism, materialism, and consumerism, university efforts to promote moral reasoning and imagination are not the uniquely dangerous coercive forces that some liberal critics fear.

As to the worry expressed by some social scientists that normative concerns are either irrelevant to their work or, worse, that they compromise the scientific status of their findings, we are skeptical of the distinction between the normative and the empirical as it is usually made.[50] Indeed, it seems to us that social science research is ineluctably entangled in normative assumptions and purposes. The very choice of a subject to study (say, voting) assumes its value as an object of study. Just think, as

Peter Winch invited us to do some years ago, of what must be assumed for someone to distinguish between making a mark on a piece of paper and voting.[51] As is evident from the free-rider egoism of many versions of Economics 101 and the uncritical Marxism of many versions of Sociology 101, social science is all too often characterized not by an absence of normative concerns but by strong, but unexamined, moral assumptions.

Communitarians and theologians are partly right when they assert that the language of ethics is dominated by liberal individualism and that such individualism tends to dismiss a wide range of views as nonrational and to underestimate the degree to which people are already and always implicated in the lives of others. But this does not warrant a wholesale rejection of the return to ethics, for two reasons. First, the moral language of liberal individualism remains crucial for our understanding of moral responsibility, judgment, and action. And second, as we have already suggested, today's moral education debate provides ample room for, and indeed has been shaped by, perspectives and voices from many traditions.

Penultimately, while radical democrats are right to worry about the language of moral education obscuring the presence of power in shaping what counts as moral, one cannot reduce ethics to politics even if, as Aristotle insisted, they are mutually implicated activities. Finally, the realist claim about moral considerations is misleading if not tendentious even in such foundational "realist" thinkers as Thucydides and Machiavelli.[52] Realist skepticism about ethics, like that grounded in social science more generally, is persuasive only insofar as its own normative assumptions remain unexamined.

While we are skeptical of the skeptics, we respect the significance of the questions they pose. For example, why are we seeing a new preoccupation with ethics? Why does it appear now in the form it does and where it does? What cultural anxieties or economic forces does it address or respond to, and what social ideals or political agendas does it promote, either explicitly or implicitly? Is the proliferation of ethics centers a symptom of a sense of moral crisis or decline, signifying that something has gone terribly wrong with the project of modern capitalism, with America as a quintessential expression of that project, or with our society's professions and institutions? Is it a revolt against the casual mendacity of our public and professional life? Or is it after all a return driven by positive commitments to individual virtue or social justice? These questions matter and their pursuit can help deepen the moral education debate. But none of them vitiates the ultimate need to confront Socrates's question of "how we ought to live."

Reading the return to ethics symptomatically reveals issues that are too often overlooked. For example, much of the literature on moral education has concentrated on America, been written by scholars at elite four-year institutions, and taken eighteen-to-twenty-two-year-old students as the norm.[53] But the increasing professionalization of ethics as an academic subject and an area of expertise holds real dangers of excluding "ordinary folks" from the conversation and, as with all specialization, of narrowing the terms of the debate. Moreover, a concentration on ethics may displace other models of inquiry and curriculum. And what of the nontraditional student? We believe that moral education involves a different dynamic when the student is a forty-year-old woman who has raised two children, is working twenty hours a week, and whose sense of the world may be far richer than that of the person teaching her. Finally, we are concerned whether a stigma might attach to those who attend or work at institutions that are not engaged in "serious" debate over moral and civic education, for this would have the effect of inscribing new forms of inequality based on the extent to which institutions and students honor and study ethical issues. Given how easily a concern for morals can lapse into moralism and self-righteousness, it is important for the moral education movement to be alert to these dangers.

A growing emphasis on ethics expertise poses another danger: it can obscure recognition of the fact that our students are also our fellow citizens, and that in a democracy educational authority takes place in the context of a commitment to legal and political equality. This may mean that democracy requires distinctive forms of teaching and learning ethics. When Socrates was accused of corrupting the young he replied that either he did so inadvertently, in which case he should be admonished but not punished, or he did it on purpose, in which case he was extremely stupid. For why would anyone be so foolish as to corrupt those with whom he lived his life? If we take him at his word, then colleges and universities should not only encourage students to be active citizens but actively promote the skills and knowledge that enhance the quality of public deliberation and judgment. But, as Socratic gadflies continue to remind us, we should strive to keep talk about moral and civil education from dissolving into pieties about democracy, citizenship, critical thinking, and virtue which blunt rather than invigorate moral imagination and political reflection.

What, then, might a moral education worthy of the name actually look like? While we cannot answer all of the questions we have raised in this introduction, nor confront the full dimensions of the moral education debate, we can outline some key features of moral education in our own time and place. What follows reflects our own conversations and disagreements as coeditors and reveals both the common ground we have come to occupy and the divergent commitments we continue to bring to the moral education debate.

As we suggested earlier, the question is not *whether* colleges and universities should pursue moral education, but *how*. Moral (or perhaps immoral) education goes on constantly, if not always self-consciously. As we saw, Aristotle captured this insight when he argued that every association has a moral end, a hierarchy of values, which is cultivated through its everyday norms and practices. Colleges and universities, too, have such moral ends and purposes, expressed not only through institutional mission statements and curricula but also, and often more powerfully, through the hidden curriculum of everyday campus life. The more these commitments remain unarticulated the less they can be subject to scrutiny and the more ignorant we remain of the ends that animate our actions and lives. One task for moral education in the modern college or university, then, is to articulate and scrutinize the moral ends of our shared enterprise. Truth seeking, a willingness to think deeply about alternative positions and arguments, to be swayed by evidence and argument, to acknowledge our intellectual debts to others, and to judge others on the quality of their work and not their family background, skin color, or political affiliation: these are a few of the moral commitments central to academic life that we need to articulate and explore. Other moral ends and commitments may be specific to particular institutions, as Stanley Hauerwas reminds us. But the task of critical self-reflection and appreciation remains the same, as does the importance that students experience higher education as an enterprise committed to high ideals, thoughtfully pursued.

This suggests a deeper point about moral judgment. It is a commonplace today for students (and faculty) to exclaim "Who am I to judge?" But of course that, too, is a moral judgment. We make normative judgments all the time, so the question again is not whether to make them but on what basis or grounds we do so. If we cannot offer such grounds, then we may be making judgments, or acting, in ways that contradict our most basic moral commitments and ends. A second task for moral education, then, is to challenge moral evasions, whether in the classroom or the streets, and to teach the practical wisdom that enables us to discern and explore the grounds of the judgments we are making.

It is important to recognize that argument and debate play a key role in pursuing both tasks we have outlined so far. Critics of moral education contend that ethics cannot be central to the university's mission because this would require a substantive moral consensus that is contrary to critical inquiry and academic freedom.[54] Yet these same critics acknowledge that universities pursue intellectual excellence not by deciding in advance which of the competing views of such excellence is right but by continuous argument over what's true, right, and persuasive, including argument over what the standards should be for good intellectual work. Similarly, argument about and over ethics, and about the ethical ideals and norms we should teach and promote, is not inimical to, but actually helps constitute, the pursuit of moral education.

Indeed, arguing over what's right, fair, and just is one of the central ways in which human beings "do ethics." This reaches across cultures and religions, from traditions of ethical argument expressed in Talmud, in the Islamic *ulama*, or in the common law, as well as in fundamental moral confrontations such as those between Socrates and Thrasymachus in Plato's *Republic*. We enact new forms of this tradition when we invite students to engage debates and controversies, asking them, for instance, to argue for or against human rights, stem cell research, or the International Criminal Court, or to assess different interpretations of *Antigone*, or weigh alternative approaches to educational policy.

But rigor and argument are not enough. Ethics cannot be reduced to analytical argument but needs to be attentive to the broader variety and complexity of moral life. Argument alone does not capture the moral insights of great literature, nor does it yield the lessons present in a work like Hannah Arendt's *Eichmann in Jerusalem*. Arendt argues that Eichmann was thoughtless; that he was unable to put himself in another person's shoes. What Eichmann lacked was moral imagination, which in Arendt's terms requires the ability and willingness to go visiting another.[55] You do not move in with them, or stand in their place, but next to them. The prominence of the Golden Rule in so many moral and religious traditions points to the centrality of moral reciprocity and the qualities of curiosity, compassion, and imagination it requires.[56] The cultivation of a capacious moral imagination is a fourth task for moral education.

But ethics is more than a set of questions to debate or even of imaginative perspectives to adopt. It is also, as Will Willimon notes, a "body of commitment."[57] To take ethics seriously requires us not only to engage in ethical critique and debate but to come to moral judgments, to take a stand. If cultivation of the capacity for ethical commitment is a fifth task of moral education, then we need to focus on the interplay of principles and actions, both for our students and ourselves. But what constitutes a moral commitment? The great moral teachers have generally insisted on certain truths of moral life. Socrates, for instance, professed that it is better to suffer injustice than to commit it, that virtue is knowledge, and that what you do to others you do to yourself. But justice, knowledge, and truth did not function as "shut up words" because he was also willing to acknowledge that the truths for which he was willing to die might be shown to be faulty in the next dialogic encounter; that he might have missed something in the world or the argument that would force him to modify what he had come to believe with such conviction. Socrates is a valuable exemplar because he showed what it means to combine a capacity to be self-critical with a willingness to affirm moral commitments and stand up for them. It is by navigating that tension ourselves that we can do our best as teachers of ethics.

What are the implications of these four tasks for *how* we should teach ethics in colleges and universities today? We applaud the pedagogical pluralism that characterizes the return to ethics and see a valuable role for a variety of curricular and co-curricular approaches, from the interpretation of canonical texts and popular culture to case studies to service-learning to student-run honor codes. An appreciation for the role of ethical reflection, deliberation, imagination, and practice is both a key contemporary insight and a welcome revival of cultures and traditions of ethical argument such as those expressed in the Talmud. A plurality of approaches does not, however, imply that any pedagogical technique is as good as any other in achieving each of the aims of moral education. Different pedagogies have particular strengths and characteristic weaknesses. Take, for example, the conventional "Introduction to Moral Philosophy" course. It has the great advantage of providing students with systematic frameworks for assessing moral judgments. But its focus on critique can leave students with a dizzying and potentially demoralizing sense that there are no defensible moral positions, or that ethics has to do with canonical debates but not with their own lives. Conversely, the case study method, or a conventional service-learning course, will expose students to a variety of powerful practical moral issues and dilemmas, from questions of personal motivation and virtue to issues of organizational ethics, politics, and policy. All too often, however, such courses can leave students floundering in aimless exchanges of personal opinion without providing them with ways to organize and assess their judgments. What's needed are integrated approaches that combine theory and practice, imagination and justification.

We also believe that moral education—whether in a philosophy classroom, a judicial affairs hearing room, or a sociology service-learning class —should be dialogical, by which we mean that there should be a degree of reciprocity between students and teachers, a sense of shared vulnerability in the pursuit of an ethical life. This does not mean that every view is entitled to an equal hearing: students have to make arguments, offer evidence, show they are listening to others and reading the texts with care. But without such reciprocity the enterprise of moral education lacks vigor and seriousness. The centrality of dialogue to moral education in democracies acknowledges the degree to which ethical life is necessarily collective and enhances moral imagination by enabling student and teacher alike to see the world from one another's point of view.

This emphasis on taking a dialogical, rather than didactic, approach to moral education does not mean that universities, or individual faculty, cannot profess moral commitments. The vexed issue of whether teachers of ethics should reveal their own moral commitments to students or adopt a neutral stance to moral questions seems to us wrongly posed. For one thing, genuine moral neutrality is both devilishly difficult to achieve and counterproductive for moral education: what, after all, are students likely to learn about moral stances from someone who claims that, for the purposes of the classroom, he or she has none? At the same time, a general expectation that one will confess one's moral commitments is hardly more attractive (for one thing, it is likely to leave out those deepest convictions that cannot be easily articulated, since most of us remain to some degree mysteries to ourselves). The issue seems to us to be primarily pedagogic: what creates a classroom atmosphere in which students are encouraged to think deeply, to pose tough questions, and to vigorously disagree with the teacher and with their fellow students? We suspect that respect and humility, humor and friendship, curiosity and collaboration play key roles in creating such a classroom.

This brings us, finally, to the question of what makes someone a good teacher of ethics. Here, we are inclined to believe that there is an important relationship between who we are, what we teach, and how we teach it. In other words, both the character of the teacher and the performative dimensions of his or her teaching are central rather than marginal aspects of moral education. We all have colleagues who teach in a way that undermines the arguments they make, as when a teacher of democratic education teaches in a thoroughly authoritarian way. But unlike Tolstoy's quip about happy families all being alike, we suspect there is no single model of excellence among teachers of ethics but rather a cluster of traits that good teachers of ethics exhibit to varying degrees. We are unsure, however, if these traits can be taught as a pedagogic practice, or if they are fundamentally idiosyncratic. But these questions, however difficult, must remain central to any debate about moral education.

In the end, the value of today's return to ethics will rest on whether it serves to reveal important questions and possibilities that have otherwise been ignored or have gone unrecognized. On this score, it appears to have had some success, for it has made us more aware of how moral teaching and learning occur and has revived the perennial question of what the aims of moral education, and indeed of all education, should be.

It is probably not difficult to discern several voices in the ways we have sketched these questions and aims. This polyvocality reflects our own divergent moral commitments and vocabularies, as well as our commitment as coeditors and friends to learn from one another. We hope it serves to anticipate and illuminate the book that follows.

We divide the book into four parts. Except for Julie Reuben's essay, which, as its title indicates, is a historical overview of the place of ethics in American higher education, we have organized the book in a way that emphasizes the differences between the contributors and highlights the "debating" part of our title. We do this in the hopes both of inspiring others to join the debate and of dramatizing the variety of sensibilities, preoccupations, and approaches which inform it.

Our effort to encourage debate is perhaps most obvious in part 2, which is prompted by and organized around some recent writings by Stanley Fish. However much we may disagree with him, Fish's essays—including the one in this book—have raised fundamental questions about what universities are for and whether moral education should even be on their agendas let alone be an animating aim or organizing principle for them. Thus part 2 raises the question of whether universities should be engaged in moral education at all.

The essays in part 3 examine the challenges and opportunities that contemporary politics and culture present to moral education today. They do so by exploring what "moral" means (and hence what we should think about the current preoccupation with "moral talk") and by unpacking the relationships between morality, ethics, politics, and power. The authors in this section offer dramatically different visions of the prospects for moral education in our world, given its cultural pluralism, extremes of wealth and poverty, and struggles over race and civic identity.

Finally, part 4 focuses on the virtues and character traits that a moral education worthy of the name should aim to foster, and the means available for their pursuit on today's campuses. Should colleges and universities focus solely on nurturing intellectual virtues, or are civic and political virtues equally important? Do faculty and student affairs staff need to overcome their reluctance to offer practical guidance to the young, or would it be better for them to acknowledge the limits of their didactic power and to focus on addressing their own professional and institutional moral failings, instead? And are the most influential vehicles for moral education found in the classroom, or should we look to the norms, rituals, and reward systems of sports and campus life?

While they differ in tone and argument, the essays gathered in this volume do share one purpose: to engage us with the question of the fundamental goals not only of moral education in the modern university but of higher education itself.

Notes

1. We borrow the phrase from the title of a recent book that explores the emerging interest in ethics across disciplines in the humanities and social sciences, Garber, Hanssen, and Walkowitz, *The Turn to Ethics*.
2. The Association for Practical and Professional Ethics currently has 117 ethics centers and programs as institutional members, the majority of them founded during the past decade.
3. See http://kenan.ethics.duke.edu. Both the Carnegie Foundation for the Advancement of Teaching and the John Templeton Foundation recently launched major projects to encourage colleges and universities to pursue such comprehensive efforts in moral education (see Colby et al., *Preparing America's Undergraduates*; and www/collegeandcharacter.org/guide).
4. The annual "Aims of Education" speech series began at Chicago in 1962 and is patterned after the "Aims of Education" speech delivered by Alfred North Whitehead in 1912 to the International Congress of Mathematicians and subsequently published in his book *The Aims of Education and Other Essays*.
5. Mearsheimer, "The Aims of Education."
6. Williams, *Ethics and the Limits of Philosophy*. The original Greek meaning of "ethics" ranges from custom, habit, and the usual practices that distinguish a people to the animating principles that actively and reflexively inform their beliefs and actions.
7. Hinman, *Ethics*; Caputo, *Against Ethics*. For other examples of efforts to distinguish and critique the terms "ethics" and "morality," see Connolly, *The Ethos of Pluralization*; Bennett and Shapiro, *The Politics of Moralizing*.
8. Arendt, *Eichmann in Jerusalem*; Browning, *Ordinary Men*; Glover, *Humanity*.
9. For a fuller account of this history, see Julie Reuben's chapter in this volume.
10. Nussbaum, *Cultivating Humanity*.
11. Sloan, "The Teaching of Ethics in the American Undergraduate Curriculum, 1876–1976," 5.
12. Douglas Sloan vividly illustrates this shift with the case of Amherst College. Amherst's 1895 catalogue opened with a lengthy description of the ethics course taught by the college president to the senior class. By 1905, ethics had been demoted to one among several elective courses for sophomores offered by the philosophy department. Ibid., 9.
13. Reuben, *The Making of the Modern University*; McClellan, *Moral Education in America*.
14. King, "Why Are College Administrators Reluctant to Teach Ethics?"; Reuben, *The Making of the Modern University*.
15. Bourdieu, *Homo Academicus*; Ross, *The Origins of American Social Science*;

Sloan, "The Teaching of Ethics in the American Undergraduate Curriculum, 1876–1976."

16. For insightful historical analysis and critical appreciation of "critical theory," see Geuss, *The Idea of Critical Theory*.

17. Milgram, *Obedience to Authority*.

18. McCumber, *Time in the Ditch*.

19. Moulds, "The Decline and Fall of Philosophy," 41.

20. Derek Bok recounted this story at the tenth-anniversary celebration of the Harvard Program on Ethics and the Professions (1997). Note that some lawyers would argue that their profession requires a moral division of labor which demands that defense attorneys, for example, refrain from morally judging their clients. But of course this division of labor itself, and the justifications for it, would be the proper subject of inquiry at a center for ethics and the professions.

21. "Phrases and Philosophies for the Uses of the Young." Wilde's piece, which appeared in the first and only issue of the Oxford journal *The Chameleon*, has been widely published and anthologized.

22. Hoekema, *Campus Rules and Moral Community*, 126–27.

23. McClellan, *Moral Education in America*, 101.

24. Callahan and Bok, *Ethics Teaching in Higher Education*, 300.

25. Friedman, "Beyond Caring" and *Feminism and Community*; Gilligan, *In a Different Voice*; MacIntyre, *After Virtue*.

26. Joseph, "Public Values in a Divided World," 6.

27. For a good example from the natural sciences, see National Academy of Sciences, *On Being a Scientist*. For ethnography, see American Anthropological Association, *Statement on Ethnography and Institutional Review Boards*. See also French and Short, eds., *War and Border Crossings*.

28. Harpham argues that this is a defining tension of ethics. "What is ethical discourse?" he asks, "A relentless drive toward the necessary answer, conjoined with the equally relentless generation of yet more preliminary questions." Harpham, *Shadow of Ethics*.

29. James Davison Hunter provides a strong example of the former position in his *The Death of Character*. Richard Rorty and Martha Nussbaum, in very different ways, embrace a form of the latter; see Rorty, *Contingency, Irony, and Solidarity*, and Nussbaum, *Cultivating Humanity*.

30. See, for example, Stanley Fish's and James Murphy's chapters in this volume.

31. See, for example, the chapters by Shulman and Coles, as well as our own chapter.

32. A good example is Hunter, who argues that concerns about diversity and democratic process have derailed moral education. Recent work by a wide

range of normative theorists, from Rawls's *Political Liberalism* and *Law of Peoples* to MacIntyre's *Whose Justice? Which Rationality?* to Nancy Fraser's *Justice Interruptus* to Michael Perry's *The Idea of Human Rights* all focus to a considerable extent on questions of universalism, particularity, and diversity.

33. For a good example of this trend, see the American Association of Colleges and Universities, *Statement on Liberal Learning* (www.aacu.org/about/state ments/liberal_learning.cfm).

34. It's important to note, however, that some critics of "moral reasoning" approaches have ignored some of the most interesting ideas advanced by Kantian theorists. An example is Lawrence Kohlberg's "just community" approach to education, which encourages not only discussion of moral issues but also a culture of community building through the democratic establishment of rules and a climate where students and teachers can act on their moral decisions.

35. Colby et al., eds., *Educating Citizens*.

36. Jennings, Nelson, and Parens, "Values on Campus"; Kupperman, *Character*; Wong, "Is There a Distinction between Reason and Emotion in Mencius?"

37. Ozar, "Learning Outcomes for Ethics across the Curriculum Programs."

38. Battistoni, *Civic Engagement across the Curriculum*; Colby et al., eds., *Educating Citizens*; Ehrlich, ed., *Civic Responsibility and Higher Education*; Ozar, "Learning Outcomes for Ethics across the Curriculum Programs."

39. Grant, "The Ethics of Talk"; Rich, "Toward a Woman-Centered University."

40. On faculty as role models, see Bill Taylor's powerful "Integrity: A Letter to My Students."

41. Pavela, "A Renewed Focus on Student Ethical Development." The spiritual lives of college students, and the extent to which institutions of higher learning are providing students with opportunities to examine them, is now the subject of a major research initiative led by Alexander and Helen Astin of the Higher Education Research Institute and funded by the John Templeton Foundation.

42. Bok, *Universities and the Future of America*, 97.

43. King, "Why Are College Administrators Reluctant to Teach Ethics?"; Pavela, "A Renewed Focus on Student Ethical Development"; Pavela, "Fifteen Principles for the Design of College Ethical Development Programs." Examples include renewed interest in honor codes, decisions by university leaders to treat student activism as an invitation for moral deliberation and institutional decision-making (Kiss, "The Courage to Teach, Practice, and Learn"), and "engaged university" projects that seek to mobilize the intellectual, social, and financial resources of colleges and universities to promote civic renewal, economic development, and other public goods. This emphasis on the way institutions engage in moral education beyond the formal curriculum has

been embraced in recent years by a number of national foundations and educational associations, including the Carnegie Foundation for the Advancement of Teaching, the Kellogg Foundation, and the Templeton Foundation, the American Association of Colleges and Universities, the Center for Academic Integrity, and Campus Compact.

44. Aristotle, *Nicomachean Ethics*, 1103b27–28.
45. Coles, "The Disparity between Intellect and Character."
46. Callahan and Bok, *Ethics Teaching in Higher Education*, 64–72.
47. Ibid., 110.
48. Caputo, *Against Ethics*; Foucault, *Discipline and Punish*, and *Power/Knowledge*.
49. Flathman, "Liberal versus Civic, Republican, Democratic, and Other Vocational Education."
50. Latour and Woolgar, *Laboratory Life*; Taylor, "Neutrality in Political Science"; Topper, *The Disorder of Political Inquiry*.
51. Winch, *The Idea of a Social Science and Its Relation to Philosophy*.
52. Lebow, *The Tragic Vision of Politics*.
53. There are exceptions, however. *Educating Citizens*, the influential book by Anne Colby, Thomas Ehrlich, Elizabeth Beaumont, and Jason Stephens, includes in its reference group of twelve institutions two community colleges (Kapi-olani in Hawaii and Turtle Mountain on the Chippewa Indian Reservation in North Dakota), as well as a large public institution, Portland State University.
54. Fish, "Aim Low"; Mearsheimer, "The Aims of Education."
55. Arendt, *The Life of the Mind*.
56. For examples from a wide array of religious and cultural traditions, see Wilson, *World Scripture*, and the websites ReligiousTolerance.org and Teaching Values.com. To be sure, the Golden Rule has its critics, including Immanuel Kant, though they generally critique its limitations as a principle of reciprocity rather than rejecting the moral value of reciprocity itself (Kant, *Groundwork of the Metaphysics of Morals*).
57. Willimon, "Old Duke—New Duke."

THE CHANGING CONTOURS OF MORAL EDUCATION
IN AMERICAN COLLEGES AND UNIVERSITIES

"New England's First Fruits," a pamphlet published in England in 1643, proudly portrayed Harvard College, leaving no doubt that its central mission was religious and moral. It detailed the ways Harvard insisted its students understand and live according to Christian principles. Harvard accomplished this through a prescribed curriculum and careful supervision of students' daily behavior. Although Harvard realized its purpose through its influence on individual students, it conceived of its mission in social terms. The pamphlet explained that the College was founded to "advance *learning* and perpetuate it to posterity; dreading to leave an illiterate Ministry to the Churches, when our present Ministers shall lie in the Dust." Harvard was created not just to save individual souls, but to sustain a righteous community.[1]

When I assign "New England's First Fruits," my students at Harvard today find seventeenth-century Harvard incredibly foreign. The first comment in class discussion is invariably "I had no idea how religious Harvard originally was." Then they usually marvel about how many rules students had to follow, and talk about how central moral formation was in the mission of the College. In these discussions, my students quickly formulate one interpretation of the history of morality in higher education—decline. They note that moral concerns once so central to higher education are now absent.

They also relate this decline to another change, secularization. Harvard College's moral education was embedded in its ties to a particular church; so, my students reason, perhaps when it cut its ties to the church, it also abandoned moral education. This interpretation is easily inverted and told as a story of progress. Depending on one's perspective, American higher education has either regressed from a clearly defined, religiously based, moral education to a relativistic, unmoored, amoral education; or it has progressed from an authoritarian, church-controlled, narrow education to an open, inclusive, inquiry-based education.[2]

As the class discussion continues, however, some students inevitably challenge this narrative. They point out continuities—aspects of the old Harvard that survive in contemporary liberal arts colleges' rhetoric about shaping the whole student and preparing future leaders. They talk about the ways colleges try to inculcate values, such as tolerance and appreciation for cultural differences. They note that colleges are still concerned with students' lives outside the classroom—although the elaborate rules have been replaced by resident assistants and programs promoting healthy behavior and constructive peer relations. Typically, at this point, a debate ensues between a group of students who maintain that the similarities between the Harvard of today and that of the seventeenth century are most salient and those who continue to view the old College as foreign territory. My students do not resolve this debate, except perhaps to agree that the issue is more complicated than it initially appeared.

My students' discussion reveals two seemingly contradictory features of the history of morality in American higher education—the long-term attenuation of moral purposes and the constancy of this aspiration. Over the centuries since Harvard was founded, dominant forms of moral education have been repeatedly challenged and reconstituted in new forms. This pattern of renewal, however, did not produce stability over the long run. Instead, changes in knowledge production and the greater diversity of society made it increasingly difficult to establish the authority necessary to sustain vigorous forms of moral education. As a result, universities that embraced research and/or served diverse constituents have struggled to maintain a modest commitment to the moral formation of their students. Only colleges that continued to serve a subsection of the population, typically defined by religious identity, have kept morality at the center of their curricular and community life, and these have faced the opposite battle, establishing their legitimacy as educational institutions.

The Colonial Colleges

In its early decades, the Congregational Churches of Massachusetts provided clear intellectual and moral authority for Harvard College. They helped determine the content of students' education and the norms of behavior expected of students and faculty at the college. The authority of the church over the college was reinforced by the authority of the church in the larger society, particularly its ability to produce a homogeneous population in which groups that did not recognize the authority of the church, such as native peoples and religious dissenters, were driven out and/or relegated to a subordinate position within society. Under these conditions, the moral purposes of the College were dominant and uncontested.[3]

Other colleges created in the colonial period followed the same model as Harvard—established authority based in a particular church and serving a relatively homogeneous, socially and politically dominant group. For example, the College of William and Mary was connected to the Anglican Church; the College of New Jersey (later Princeton) was associated with the Presbyterian Church; Rhode Island College (later Brown) was initially tied to Baptists. However, the hegemony of the Congregational Church in early Massachusetts Bay colony was not replicated in most of the other colonies (or sustained in Massachusetts over the course of the eighteenth century). The population of most of the colonies became, in varying degrees, religiously diverse. Although colleges, as elite institutions, could maintain ties to a single church if that group was politically powerful, religious diversity inevitably weakened churches' control of colleges, which in turn could challenge the authority of the moral education they provided. Internal divisions within churches were an additional source of instability. They could lead to the creation of a rival college—as in the case of the creation of Yale College, a second Congregational college in New England—or to competition for control over existing colleges. The effect of internal divisions was similar to that of denominational diversity—they damaged the institutional foundation for the moral truths taught at a particular college.[4]

Colleges responded to religious diversity and internal divisions in two ways. The first was to seek ways to strengthen the position of the established church and protect current practices from outsiders. The second was to broaden the religious base to be more inclusive. Both impulses were evident in the colonial period. For example, colleges began welcoming students from various churches and did not administer religious tests for students. The former strategy, however, predominated. The only institution that attempted to be independent of a particular church—the College of Philadelphia (later University of Pennsylvania)—quickly succumbed to denominational infighting and was taken over by Anglicans. At the end of the colonial period, all of the existing nine colleges had clear church affiliations that determined who taught and, at least in some measure, the content of students' education. It ensured that moral education was central and was achieved in the context of Christian teaching. This teaching fit comfortably with the rest of the curriculum, which was based in Latin, Greek, mathematics, and natural and moral philosophy, and was largely common to the various colleges irrespective of denominational affiliation.

The Triumph of Pan-Protestantism, 1780s–1870s

The Revolution, however, increased support for the second option—a more inclusive moral education independent of a particular church's teaching. Influential revolutionary leaders, most notably Thomas Jefferson and Benjamin Rush, argued that the survival of the new nation depended on new forms of education, tailored to prepare citizen-leaders of the next generation. Jefferson's ideas were articulated in the context of his campaign to reform the College of William and Mary (and later in his plans for the University of Virginia) and Rush's in his proposal for a National University. They argued that the existing college course was rooted in the preparation of ministers, but the nation needed secular leaders—future politicians, engineers, doctors, lawyers, and merchants. To meet this need, they advocated more freedom for students to select their course of study and for the introduction of more practical and scientific subjects into the curriculum. They opposed church control of colleges and sought to bring faculty and students together across sects and regions in order to transcend existing social divisions. While Rush and Jefferson viewed their ideal education as broadly Christian, they both emphasized classical republican notions of virtue and reason rather than revelation. Although moral education was central to both Jefferson's and Rush's vision of higher education, the reforms they promoted, such as electives, the introduction of technical subjects, and greater freedom for students, could diminish the relative importance of moral education in students' overall education. For this reason, as well as their positions on church control, opponents of their reforms branded them immoral and irreligious.[5]

Neither Jefferson's plans to reform William and Mary nor Rush's proposal for a National University succeeded (although Jefferson's efforts would come to fruition in the University of Virginia, which for a brief period would operate according to his Enlightenment ideals). But their ideas would animate numerous battles over the orientation of collegiate education in the early nineteenth century. One of the most famous of these involved Dartmouth College. In response to pleas by John Wheelock, the president of Dartmouth College who had been fired by the board of trustees in 1815, the New Hampshire legislature took control of the College by enlarging the board of trustees and appointing new members. The new board introduced reforms similar to those Jefferson promoted, such as a broader, more practical curriculum. While the case was complicated by personality conflicts, it represented part of the larger struggle over the purposes of higher education—service to the "public" broadly conceived or fidelity to the religious belief of a church that had come to represent only a portion of the population. The original trustees refused to accept the legislatures' actions and operated their own college in competition with the reformed "University" created by the new board. They also turned to the courts to restore Dartmouth to their control. They lost in state courts but eventually won before the U.S. Supreme Court, which argued that although the state had chartered and partially supported the college, it was created to serve the particular charitable purposes of its founders and the state could not alter that. The case supported the first solution to the problem of religious diversity—many colleges serving particular segments of the population.[6]

The Dartmouth case strengthened denominational control, but it did not end the battles over collegiate reform. A decade after the New Hampshire legislature tried to transform Dartmouth, the Connecticut legislature threatened to do the same to Yale College. In response, the president of Yale, Jeremiah Day, produced a remarkable defense of the traditional college curriculum, in a document that came to be known as the Yale Report (1828). Day switched the emphasis of the curriculum away from its content to its value as mental training, or in Day's words, from the "furniture" of the mind to the "discipline" of the mind. The standardized curriculum, he argued, was essential for thorough and effective mental training.

Each subject in the course of study was uniquely suited to training each of the student's mental powers equally and in association with the others. By evoking the concept of mental discipline, Day defended the traditional curriculum which required all students to study a broad range of subjects and did not concede that practical subjects also deserved a place in the curriculum. The study of these subjects, he argued, properly followed the completion of the college course after students' mental capacities were well developed. Day argued that this broad mental discipline was as valuable for the future farmer and engineer as it was the minister. He maintained that the classical curriculum was helpful—it would benefit men in various lines of work—and patriotic—these men would promote the material, intellectual, and moral development of the nation. By defending the classical curriculum in modern terms, Day successfully deflated the momentum of collegiate reform and helped keep moral education firmly within a Christian framework.[7]

Although traditional forms of college education survived the reform impulse coming out of the Revolution, changes in American society helped produce a compromise between the two visions of higher education. During the late eighteenth century and the early nineteenth, new intellectual developments, particularly the increasing influence of both pietism and rationalism, helped colleges develop new models of moral education, better suited to the religious diversity of North America and the political realities of the new United States. Pietism decreased the importance of theological distinctions dividing different denominations. This encouraged interdenominational cooperation and led to the flourishing of several broadly Protestant reform movements in the first half of the nineteenth century. In higher education, a number of denominations cooperated in founding colleges and funding the education of future ministers. Within the colleges, the curriculum shifted from basing moral education on theology to relying primarily on instruction in natural theology and moral philosophy. These subjects, which relied on human reasoning to address questions about the existence of God, the nature of humanity, and the requirements of living a Godly life, provided moral education that was better suited to a religiously diverse society. William Paley's *The Principles of Moral and Political Philosophy* (1785) was commonly assigned in American colleges in the first decades of the nineteenth century. It was gradually replaced by American texts, particularly Francis Wayland's tremendously popular *Elements of Moral Science* (1835). These texts created a national moral education, palatable to a diversely Protestant student body, while still allowing professors to adapt denominational and regional differences on particular issues.[8]

College officials also faced challenges to their moral authority from students. On a small scale, students resisted the colleges' moral authority by simply ignoring the elaborate rules designed to ensure upright behavior on their part. By the early nineteenth century, individual resistance coalesced into group rebellion at numerous colleges. In all these cases, colleges refused to reduce their oversight over students' lives. Even when they had to expel large numbers of students, colleges remained firmly committed to regulating student behavior in the name of morality. Students gained greater freedom only when overcrowding forced colleges to allow students to live outside dormitories in local boarding houses. Although unable to supervise students' daily lives, colleges still expected these students to participate in daily prayers and to follow strict codes of personal conduct. Just as college leaders rejected educational reforms that they believed would weaken the Christian basis of the curriculum, they also reasserted their right to shape students' character by regulating their behavior.[9]

Moral Education in the Age of Freedom, 1880s–1940s

This pattern of moral education dominated American higher education until the 1880s, when new intellectual developments energized a fresh generation of educational reformers. These reformers challenged the authority of deductive reasoning that sustained the classical curriculum. In a wide-ranging attack on contemporary higher education, reformers promoted "freedom" as the defining value of the "true" university. As an ideal, it was a fortuitous choice. Freedom carried considerable rhetorical power, referring directly to practice of academic freedom in German universities, then considered the best in the world, while also evoking more generally the success of American democracy and the glory of the Protestant tradition. Freedom also served as a broad platform from which the modernizers could justify numerous specific educational reforms, from the formal secularization of institutional governance to changes in the criteria for selecting faculty and the introduction of electives in the curriculum. Waving the banner of freedom, these educators introduced practices that would create the American research university and would eventually be exported, at least partially, to all other institutions of higher learning in the country.[10]

In elevating freedom to the core value of the university, these educational reformers did not intend to abolish religion and morality from higher education. On the contrary, they hoped to strengthen the moral mission of the university by modernizing it. But their reforms had unintended consequences and over the following decades universities would pursue a number of unsuccessful strategies to provide a modern form of moral education. Educational reformers believed that universities could offer their students a modern form of religious education by promoting the scientific study of religion. The scientific study of religion, its advocates projected, would integrate religion into modern intellectual life. Educational reformers and intellectuals wanted a "modern reconstruction of religion" which would develop "a new conception, a new expression, a new administration of religion, fitted to the modern-world and the current need." Educators hoped that the scholarly study of religion would help define this modern religion.[11]

The science of religion was the first attempt to modernize moral education. By the early twentieth century, however, this effort was clearly failing. Scientific studies of religion, instead of integrating religion into modern intellectual life, ended up concluding that factual knowledge and religious "truth" were essentially separate and distinct. Most scholars wanted to demonstrate that religion had an important role in modern, scientific culture. They believed they could show this by studying religion's psychological and social function. This functional approach did not, however, produce modern religious beliefs. In addition students showed little interest in the new courses on religion and, in many major universities, the science of religion languished for lack of interest.

When efforts to create a science of religion failed to provide a new form of moral education, educators turned to science itself. In the late nineteenth and early twentieth centuries, American intellectuals commonly viewed science as a potent source of moral guidance. They believed that scientific inquiry encouraged good personal habits, consistent with those promoted by liberal Christianity. They conceived of the progress of scientific knowledge in utopian terms. Scientists confidently expected to produce grand unifying theories that would explain everything from the simplest physical process to the complexities of advanced human civilizations. They assumed that scientific knowledge would easily translate into guides for action, and spoke of the scientific method as a key that would open the door of unlimited personal and social progress.

Proponents of the biological and social sciences assumed that these new fields would provide answers to moral problems. They addressed the nature of life and human society and therefore touched on the central moral question, what is the best way to live? Biologists and social scientists believed their research would help answer this question. For example, ethically minded scientists thought biology contained lessons for personal behavior. "It is a very significant fact that the rules of conduct for the best development of men, discovered first by the experience of the human race, and afterward formulated as religious precepts, have now been established as laws of biology," wrote John Coulter, a botanist at the University of Chicago. In addition, most social scientists were involved in contemporary social or political movements either as activists, advisors, or publicists. Like biologists active in eugenics and hygiene reforms, social scientists involved in campaigns to address problems in municipal government, labor conditions, urban housing, rural schooling, immigration policies, race relations, and a myriad of other issues saw their activities as a natural component of their duties as scientists.[12]

The assumption that science had moral value dominated the discourse about scientific inquiry in the late nineteenth century. As a result of these views, university officials in the early twentieth century looked to the biological and social sciences to provide modern moral education. In the first two decades of the century, university educators tried to increase the influence of science by developing "general" science courses. Universities increasingly required or strongly encouraged students to take these new introductory courses in the biological and social sciences. Several universities introduced requirements in evolutionary biology and many more created freshman surveys in the social sciences. These courses reflected the belief that the university could best fulfill its duty to society and students through research and instruction in the social sciences.

But the plans of university educators to use the biological and social sciences as the source of modern moral education, and the intellectual developments in biological and social science disciplines, moved at cross-purposes. In the twentieth century, scientists became uncomfortable with utopian visions of science and began to make more limited claims for their subjects. They embraced specialization and eschewed efforts to unify all knowledge. They maintained that their disciplines would yield useful, "practical" information. But the meaning of "practical" and "applied" was flattened out to include material and vocational utility but not moral value. These changes were first evident in the biological sciences, where younger biologists pursued experimental research agendas and began to purge larger philosophical issues from their professional work. Similar changes followed in the social sciences, when, beginning in the teens, a new generation of scholars advanced a more narrow notion of science with particular vigor. Like biologists, these social scientists emphasized the importance of carefully controlled research and the collection of empirical data. They advocated the use of statistics and other research techniques, such as case studies and surveys, to standardize and increase the reliability of their work. They thought that by eliminating moral and philosophical questions from their professional discourse, they could end long-standing disputes within their disciplines. They maintained that true science was "objective" and "value-free" and that social scientists should avoid moral commitments that might corrupt the scientific standing of their research.

University reformers initially used the ideal of freedom to guide changes in practices governing students' lives as well. They argued that freedom would encourage responsibility and maintained that students needed to choose their own courses, choose whether and where to attend chapel, and choose whom to associate with, in order to develop into independent adults. University reformers, interested in developing the academic re- sources of their institutions, stopped building dormitories, allowing an even larger percentage of students to live on their own. They allowed these newly independent students to form their own organizations, and an array of extracurricular activities from humor magazines to football teams flour- ished without much direct supervision from college officials. They also encouraged the size of the student population to grow rapidly, in some cases admitting women and a more economically and ethnically diverse group of students than had ever attended college before.

Once again, reforms did not produce the results that its advocates had predicted. The new array of extracurricular activities kept students out of certain kinds of trouble but provided opportunities for new kinds of trouble. At first university leaders tried to ignore the less than wholesome activities around them and continued to extol the benefits of freedom. But a number of muckraking journalists took aim at universities, writing exposés on the underside of collegiate athletics and other aspects of student life. These unflattering portraits were confirmed by a spate of college novels, such as F. Scott Fitzgerald's *This Side of Paradise*, depicting the main preoccupations of university students as sexual experimentation, excessive drinking, immature pranks, and improving their position in the hierarchical campus social structure.[13]

No longer able to avoid these problems, university officials in the teens and twenties set out to rein in students' freedom and use extracurricular activities as a positive source of moral guidance. Institutions took over formal control of activities that had been run by students and alumni and hired professional staff to oversee these activities. In those decades, university leaders began to raise money to build dormitories. Once students were housed on campus again, educators instituted tighter restrictions on their personal lives. They also tried to institute similar oversight of fraternities, sororities, and other forms of off-campus housing. In addition, elite institutions moved to restrict the diversity of their students by limiting the size of incoming classes and introducing quotas on the numbers of Jewish students. These new regulations followed conventional moral norms and required little justification other than appeal to the common values of honesty, loyalty, fraternity, self-control, and sexual restraint.

Colleges adopted the reforms associated with the ideals of freedom at different points. Colleges with ties to clearly defined ethnoreligious communities, which provided students and financial support, generally ignored reforms until social change disrupted these communities and forced them to seek more diverse forms of support. These colleges were also pushed into adopting reforms by numerous new organizations, from philanthropies to professional associations, formed in the early twentieth century. For example, the Carnegie Foundation for the Advancement of Teaching, created in 1905, offered faculty pensions to colleges and universities. However, this financial support was not available to institutions under denominational control. In addition, a system of regional accreditation associations was developed in this period. These relied heavily on the example of reform-oriented universities as they established "standards" for what constituted collegiate education.[14]

Nonetheless, some institutions actively sought ways to create alternatives to the dominant pattern. Most of these were religious institutions, seeking ways to keep moral education firmly grounded in religion. Among the most successful were Catholic colleges and universities. Through the early twentieth century, Catholic institutions retained a required curriculum based on the classics, modeled on the *Raticio Studiarum*, a seven-year curriculum developed by the Jesuits in 1599. When increasingly powerful accreditation associations refused to acknowledge this as a legitimate form of higher education, Catholic institutions sought to modernize without becoming like their secularized Protestant counterparts. Drawing on a neoscholastic revival among Catholic intellectuals, Catholic colleges developed a new required curriculum consisting of series of philosophy courses, based on "classic" texts, and theology courses designed to ensure students were knowledgeable about Catholic doctrine. Aside from these new courses, colleges adopted forms standard at other institutions, such as four-year programs, and a system of electives and majors in modern academic disciplines and professional subjects.[15]

Some secular colleges also rejected the dominant patterns and sought forms of education that overcame the split between the value-free curriculum and the extracurricular, which was supposed to be the locus of community and personal development. These included a number of small colleges, among them Bennington, Black Mountain, and Reed. Although they offered diverse programs, these colleges shared a common concern with the "whole student," including his or her psychological well-being, character, creative expression, and connections to others. Often referred to as "experimental colleges," many were influenced by progressive educational philosophies associated with John Dewey. They emphasized the integration of academic learning with experience, the artificiality of divisions of knowledge along disciplinary lines, and the importance of personal and social relevance to learning. These colleges were frequently "countercultural," in that they intentionally challenged conventional social and cultural norms and typically attracted a small group of students from families with liberal political views.[16]

The Crisis of Democracy and Renewed Interest
in Citizenship Education, 1940s–1960s

Moral education became a pressing issue for mainstream institutions once again in the post–World War II period. Despite having just won the war to "preserve democracy," Americans entered the armistice with a sense of the fragility of the "free society" they had fought to protect. The possibility of the return of the Depression with its widespread hardship and threats of social conflict; the increased information about the horrors of the Nazi regime and the attendant confusion regarding how such occurrences were possible in a "civilized" nation; the atomic bomb with its threat of future world destruction—these and other hazards fostered feelings of a more pervasive danger, a danger that could not be addressed by technical fixes or government policies. This broader peril could only be averted by strengthening the nation from within, by ensuring that citizens understood, cherished, and acted to protect the principles of democracy.

A series of reports and books published in the second half of the 1940s examined how universities and colleges could help mold students into the kind of citizens that would strengthen democracy. Prominent among these were *Higher Education for American Democracy* (1947), the report of the first commission on higher education appointed by a U.S. president; *Democratic Education* (1945), a passionate plea for the reorientation of American higher education by Benjamin Fine, the education writer for the *New York Times*; and *General Education in a Free Society* (1945), a report of a committee of Harvard University professors in a variety of academic disciplines and from the Graduate School of Education assessing secondary and higher education in the United States in order to recommend a program of general education. These three books were widely read and debated and were joined by many other books and articles that critiqued, elaborated, applied, and evaluated related ideas. This vast literature converged on two points: first, in the postwar period, higher education must accept its responsibility for the education of citizens; second, citizenship education was largely the province of "general education," a part of the higher education curriculum that had been neglected and needed to be developed. Beyond this, there was plenty of disagreement.[17]

Proponents of general education fell into three broad camps, all with roots in the prewar period. One group, not surprisingly, argued for a revival of religious education. They drew on a long tradition that linked citizenship to Protestant morality and maintained that strengthening the nation required strengthening Christian values. This approach, however, contradicted important elements of the postwar understanding of democracy, particularly a new awareness of the dangers of religious prejudice and a desire to unite Americans across the boundaries of Protestant, Catholic, and Jew. General education based in a particular religious tradition seemed an oxymoron in this context. Nonetheless, many higher education leaders were sympathetic to arguments about the importance of religion, and the science of religion, now called religious studies, experienced a revival in mainstream institutions. Between 1945 and 1960, the number of undergraduate programs in religious studies nearly doubled, and the number of doctorates in religious studies tripled over the course of the 1950s. The field, though, was beset by similar tensions that had plagued its earlier incarnation—conflicts between established scholarly norms and devotional purposes and difficulties transcending its Protestant roots.[18]

The second group shared the progressive philosophy of the experimental colleges. Educators in this group emphasized the importance of general education that was relevant to students' lives and the political problems of the contemporary world. The most influential statement of this position was the President's Commission on Higher Education, *Higher Education for American Democracy*. The report used the jargon of the progressive education movement and spoke about the aims of general education in terms of "adjustment"—particularly the adjustment of the individual to social norms that the Commission saw as necessary to a healthy democracy. It also advocated direct forms of political education, in which students learned about pressing national problems such as racial inequality. The report emphasized the importance of preparing students to be citizens not only of the nation but also the world and recommended required courses in which students learned about international affairs and internationalist organizations such as the United Nations. These courses were supposed to encourage students to develop a particular moral stance toward national and world affairs—engagement with public issues, a sense of personal responsibility for ensuring justice for all, and respect and acceptance across religious and racial differences.

Initially, this group seemed poised to set standards for general education. In addition to the support of the Presidential Commission, most of the researchers in the emerging field of higher education advocated this model of general education. These researchers worked to define the aims of general education in terms of clearly defined outcomes, including modes of thinking, and to develop instruments that could assess the extent to which students conformed to the desired outcomes. However, this model of general education came under increasing public attack as the Cold War heated up. Progressives' focus on adjustment and measurable outcomes was labeled indoctrination and viewed as parallel to the kind of political education offered in fascist regimes or in the Soviet Union. The curriculum they advocated involved teaching controversial political topics. Internationalism and government activism—both principles that progressives wanted taught in general education—were viewed as signs of communist sympathies by conservative critics. Faculty who actively promoted these ideas were targeted as dangerous radicals. In this context, universities wanted those subjects taught, if at all, to small numbers of students specializing in the social sciences—certainly not to all incoming freshmen.[19]

As a result, a third model, derived from the Great Books movement of the 1930s, became the norm for postwar general education. Associated with Robert Hutchins of the University of Chicago, Mortimer Adler of Columbia, and the refounding of St. Johns College, the Great Books movement initially focused on the training of students' intellect rather than their character. However, during the war, Hutchins recast the justification for a Great Books curriculum in terms of the preservation of democracy and the education of citizens. Hutchins argued that students, by studying the great books, would gain a "rational" and "true" conception of human nature and the good society. And only with this knowledge could they appreciate why democracy is the best form of government or have any standard for seeking social improvement. He asserted that defending democracy in pragmatic terms—such as efficiency—was inherently weak because other forms of government, such as fascism or communism, might be more efficient. Hutchins also argued that an intellectual understanding of these political principles was more trustworthy that ones based on emotion and habit because the intellect, in his view, controlled the will.[20]

The Great Books curriculum, however, held certain problems for mainstream academics, who viewed it as dogmatic and antimodern. This view was strengthened by the similarity Great Books curriculum held to the philosophy core adopted by Catholic colleges and universities. It therefore had to be modified before it could be widely adopted. The most influential modification came from the Harvard Committee on General Education. The Harvard Committee took the idea of a general education based on great books of Western civilization and historicized it. So, unlike Hutchins, who wanted to teach texts as sources of eternal rational truths, the Harvard Committee placed the texts into the context of a course on the development of modern civilization, which by its structure "could capture the spirit of innovation and change" which they saw as a "fundamental part of Western culture." The class that the Harvard Committee placed at the center of general education, "Western Thought and Institutions," was designed as a "selective" history of the "West"—focusing on those periods in the past most relevant to the "great questions" of democracy in the present. The texts, beginning with Plato and Aristotle and continuing through Bentham and Mill, would be read "not simply as great books, but as great expressions of ideas which emanated from certain historical backgrounds." [21]

The course would include a lecture which would provide a narrative, communicating the proper balance between continuity and change, tradition and innovation. But the core of the course was supposed to be discussion of the texts. The Committee wanted these texts discussed in ways that would encourage each student's personal reading and questioning—a pedagogy designed to ensure "the quality of alert and aggressive individualism" which the committee saw as "essential to good citizenship." Through this combination of lecture and open discussion, the Committee hoped to create a pedagogy that struck the proper balance between the need to inculcate certain values and to encourage freedom and independence and would also encourage in future citizens the proper balance of "liberty and loyalty"—both qualities that they saw as essential in a democracy. The Harvard Report became the most influential of the various books on general education in the postwar period, and the Western Civilization course became the most common form of general education. [22]

Western Civilization courses provided an indirect form of political education—they aimed to instill certain political values without directly engaging students in contemporary social and political debates. As concern over college student apathy grew in the late 1950s, this form of citizenship education came to be seen as insufficient. Within higher education, college administrators and social scientists began to look for ways to have a larger influence on students' moral values and their social engagement. Once again, reform-oriented educators began to call for ways to make college education more personally and socially relevant. This stimulated interest in programs such as independent study, freshman seminars, residence-based courses, and experimental colleges. But advocates of these reforms struggled to receive an audience among administrators preoccupied with managing and exploiting growth.[23]

The 1960s, however, brought a new group into the debates about college curriculum—students. In the first years of the sixties, small groups of students formed on American colleges and universities to encourage political activism among their peers. Inspired by the sit-in movement led by students at black colleges in the South and disturbed by the general apathy that reigned on their campuses, these students analyzed the insularity of student life and blamed the colleges and universities they attended for the complacency of their fellow students. They argued that the nature of university education—its abstract curriculum that ignored contemporary social issues; its devotion to the ideal of objectivity and distrust of commitment and engagement; its authoritarian style of instruction that encouraged passivity rather than participation on the part of students; and campus rules that unnecessarily restricted students' freedom—produced uninvolved, self-centered students and graduates.[24]

Student activists faced a dilemma: they wanted to transform the curriculum but they had no control over the content or structure of the courses offered at their universities. The Vietnam Teach-Ins, organized by students and faculty at a number of universities in 1965, offered a potential solution to this problem—alternative political education outside the regular course of study. Over the next few years, students at hundreds of institutions across the nation founded "free universities." Intending to "destroy the irrelevant university," students designed their free universities to challenge academic practices that they thought promoted passivity among students. Free universities allowed students to control their own education. Organizers of free universities sought to decrease the authority of the instructor. They encouraged faculty to think of themselves as facilitators and to use pedagogical techniques that promoted active learning and relied on students' experiences. Although regular faculty could teach at free universities, organizers welcomed students, community activists, and others as instructors. Organizers of free universities also rejected the model of political neutrality. Although most accepted courses presenting any ideological position, political courses were designed to engage students in a cause, not simply offer a dispassionate analysis of events. Free universities eschewed grades and other mechanisms of evaluation that student activists thought were irrelevant to learning and encouraged competition and conformity.[25]

Student activists, however, were not content creating alternative institutions—they wanted to transform existing colleges and universities. Students demanded new programs in black studies, women's studies, environmental studies, ethnic studies, and peace studies to introduce political causes and alternative viewpoints into the curriculum. These programs, students hoped, would reject models of "objective" scholarship and instead encourage moral commitment and political engagement. They wanted these programs to institute the pedagogical practices developed in free universities. They also pushed to share authority with faculty over the development of these programs and other aspects of higher education curricula. Student activists found some allies among the faculty, who joined the critique of universities, drawing attention to the type of research they produced. Faculty activists charged that the values and structure of the university distorted the production of knowledge. They argued that the university espoused the values of objective and neutral scholarship—values that were both wrong and false. These ideals were wrong because, to the extent that they were achieved, they produced meaningless knowledge; they were false because the knowledge produced by the university was not objective and neutral but in fact served the interests of the elite. Under the guise of objectivity, universities and disciplines came to favor a certain style of research, dispassionate and aloof. But this style did not guarantee "truth" and indeed often prohibited important truths from being spoken.

Activists saw themselves as reorienting the social function of the university from power to justice and therefore reviving its moral mission. The university, they believed, served a system that benefited the interests of the few at the expense of the exploited masses. Although they were relatively privileged (most activists came from prosperous, middle-class homes), students came to see themselves as victims of this system. As the student movement merged with the counterculture, activists developed a cultural critique of the middle-class life. They argued that students were being channeled into stifling futures, pushed to assume inauthentic identities and to alienate themselves from their true emotions and desires. This critique gave larger meaning to another activist cause—the fight against *in loco parentis* regulations. Initially activists targeted *in loco parentis* for tactical reasons. They thought most students resented restrictions on their personal freedom such as dress codes and parietal hours and would therefore be attracted to activists if they fought to revoke these restrictions. In addition, *in loco parentis* restrictions justified a system of discipline that, on a number of campuses, was used to discourage political engagement by punishing activists. The counterculture, however, gave issues of personal freedom greater political and moral significance. The length of one's hair, the clothes one wore, the food one ate were no longer viewed as matters of taste or manners but reflections of a larger philosophy of life.

Activists were able to successfully challenge *in loco parentis* in part because they found sympathetic allies in the faculty and administration, in part because they could mobilize large numbers of moderate students around these issues, and in part because they won support of the courts for greater civil liberties on campus. As a result, by the early seventies, institutions revamped their disciplinary systems, replacing broad proscriptions against "behavior unbecoming to students" or "damaging to the institution" with much more narrowly tailored rules forbidding actions that disrupted the educational process or harmed other members of the campus community. In addition, standard procedures for discipline replaced the personal discretion of deans. Dress codes, curfews, requirements for chaperones, and other personal restrictions were revoked. Students were given more control over publications and artistic performances, speaker bans were eliminated, restrictions on student groups were removed. Students successfully dismantled the main form of moral oversight in higher education in the twentieth century—regulation of student behavior.

Activists were only partially successful at institutionalizing other educational reforms. Many colleges and universities established new programs, such as black studies and women's studies. These programs introduced information about important social and political issues into the curriculum and provided positions for at least some faculty who conceived of their teaching and scholarship in activist terms. However, activists' educational ideas were never fully accepted, and universities frequently rejected or downplayed features that most challenged conventional practices, such as hiring faculty without traditional academic credentials or programs for community involvement. Other reforms advocated by students, such as abolition of grading or democratic pedagogical practices, were never adopted on a large scale. Universities and colleges were particularly resistant to the idea of "student power." The most common response to activists' demand that students have a significant voice in education policy was to give students more freedom. At end of the 1960s and beginning of the 1970s, many universities dropped general education requirements. Administrators elected to give students more "control" over their education through individual choice rather than through mechanisms that would give students corporate authority within the institution. This change, which paralleled the elimination of *in loco parentis* rules, removed a source of dissatisfaction among students and made it more difficult for activists to mobilize their less political peers around educational issues. It also effectively ended colleges' post–World War II commitment to educating their students for democratic citizenship.

Similar changes occurred at Catholic colleges and universities, although for different reasons. The Second Vatican Council, convened in the early 1960s, initiated profound changes in American Catholicism. Following Vatican II, many men and women left religious orders, and the number of young people entering dropped significantly, forcing a long-term trend toward the secularization of faculty and administration at Catholic colleges and universities. In addition, many Catholic colleges and universities undertook a number of structural changes. They released themselves from the formal authority of religious orders and created lay governing boards, and they adopted management strategies similar to those of their secular counterparts. Many Catholic institutions hired a greater proportion of faculty from leading research universities and either dropped or significantly reduced required courses in philosophy and theology. In addition, like other colleges, they gave their students more personal and academic freedom. The secularization of mainstream Protestant colleges, which began much earlier, continued in this period. As a result, only colleges associated with the fundamentalist wing of American Protestantism continued to enforce a strong religious orientation among their faculty and vigorous oversight of their students' behavior and beliefs.[26]

Retreat and Renewal, 1970s to the Present

Campus activism of the 1960s produced greater tolerance for politics in universities—restrictive regulations on student political activity were dropped and new courses dealing with political issues were added. But the decades that followed did not witness a renaissance of social engagement on the part of students or universities. On the contrary, economics became the overwhelming preoccupation of higher education. This manifested itself in several ways, including institutional policies, student attitudes, and the curriculum. Since the 1990s, there have been efforts to reverse this trend and reinvigorate moral and civic mission of higher education. These efforts faced familiar problems, including conflicts over values given the diversity of the society and the limits of existing ideas about knowledge, as well as the increased materialism of students and institutions.

The seventies began with the threat of severe economic recession, marked by rising costs, shrinking numbers of traditional-age students, and reductions in public aid, triggered in part by legislative disapproval of campus activism. While the worst predictions for the decade did not materialize, the rapid expansion of resources seen in previous decades slowed, and leaders of higher education responded by seeking new models of revenue and adopting new "management" practices imported from the corporate world. As government support for research declined, universities sought new alliances with the corporate sector. These efforts were aided greatly by the Bayh-Dole and Stevenson Wydler Acts in 1980, which allowed universities to obtain patents for research conducted in their laboratories even if the research had been supported with funds from the federal government. These acts encouraged universities to license technologies to firms and permitted universities to retain equity in companies begun by staff and students. The National Science Foundation (NSF) also devoted a larger proportion of its shrinking budget to research on projects with commercial applications. The notion that universities were valuable because they contributed to economic growth through technological innovation began to dominate public discourse about higher education. Universities created "technology-transfer" offices to encourage the commercialization of faculty research and to develop lucrative contracts with corporations.[27]

At the same time, universities and colleges revamped admissions by adopting "enrollment management" techniques, which adopted more aggressive marketing strategies, aimed at recruiting particular types of students, such as those who could afford full tuition or whose SAT scores improved the academic reputation of the institutions. The development of popular college rankings, such as those published by *U.S. News & World Report*, which used measures such as the number of applicants, the percentage of applicants admitted, and the test scores of enrolled students, intensified competition for the "right" kind of students. Institutions developed new programs such as merit scholarships, discounted tuition, and early admissions to attract students.[28]

These practices brought in new revenue but also drove up expenses. Building research facilities, attracting faculty in fields with commercial promise, and maintaining the administrative offices necessary for licensing intellectual property were all costly, while the payoffs from such investments were uncertain. Some institutions had very lucrative programs, but many institutions were not as lucky. However, institutional competition made it difficult for research universities to abandon these efforts. Instead, the general pattern has been an expansion and intensification of this kind of applied scientific research. Competition for the "right" kind of students has also created new expenses. To attract students, colleges and universities have tried to become more consumer-friendly, building new recreational facilities and more luxurious dormitories and expanding various kinds of student services. Colleges with greater resources have been better able to provide amenities that attract students. As a result, over the past decades, the gulf between elite schools and the rest of higher education has grown larger. But even for wealthy universities, the constant need to expand services has proven burdensome. Leaders of both rich and poor institutions have to constantly focus on material needs, leaving little time to deal with substantive questions about the purposes of education.[29]

While the institutions they attended engaged in more aggressive efforts to obtain greater and greater resources, students themselves also increasingly defined education in economic terms. Just as stimulating economic growth has come to be viewed as the primary social benefit of higher education, its value to individuals has come to be defined primarily by earning potential. Economists have documented growing income differential between college graduates and high school graduates (due primarily to the decline in industrial jobs), and these facts have received extensive coverage in the media. Not surprisingly, students report that their primary motivation for going to college is entry into a professional career. In addition, over the past decades, more students have identified financial success as a primary aim in life. Since 1966, Alexander Astin and his colleagues at the Higher Education Research Institute have surveyed incoming freshmen regarding their attitudes about various issues. One of the most striking changes has been what students identify as important in life. In the late sixties, students selected "developing a meaningful philosophy of life" as their highest value, with 80 percent of freshmen labeling it "very important" or "essential." At the same time, only 45 percent of freshmen viewed "being very well off financially" as "very important" or "essential." But in the 1970s, student priorities began to shift, and since the late 1980s the relative support for the two values has been inverted.[30]

At the same time that students' values were shifting, colleges' curricula were also becoming increasingly vocational. When colleges reduced general education requirements in the late sixties and early seventies, students replaced these courses with vocationally oriented subjects. Traditional academic courses became a smaller percentage of students' overall course of study. Over the seventies and eighties, the range of vocational programs offered by institutions of higher education expanded dramatically. Majors in practical fields such as business administration and communication eclipsed traditional favorites such as English, economics, and history. Only the most selective colleges maintained a strong liberal arts orientation. These schools could resist the trend toward vocational degrees because most of their students intended to apply to graduate programs in law, medicine, and business.[31]

Although many faculty and administrators have expressed concern over these trends, they have had difficulty reversing them. Efforts to reinvigorate general education have faced numerous challenges. Developing a critical mass of support for new general education requirements has always been difficult given that many students favor flexibility in their course selection, and faculty often prefer to teach specialized courses in their disciplines. In addition, establishing consensus that certain subject matter is essential for all students has become increasingly difficult as the boundaries of knowledge expand. Furthermore, political conflict over the past decades has contributed to challenging plans for general education. In the late 1980s, several universities sought to reestablish a core curriculum for undergraduates. When faculty tried to include recent scholarship on race and gender, critics responded with a contentious public attack. One of the most sensational cases occurred at Stanford University, where Secretary of Education William J. Bennett garnered a tremendous amount of media attention by accusing the Stanford faculty of undermining Western culture and succumbing to the political pressures of students when it modified the required reading list for first-year students to include a few books by women and nonwhite authors.[32]

Opposition to multicultural curricular reform was intertwined with attacks on other university policies, such as affirmative action, speech codes, and residence hall programs on date rape and AIDS prevention. Although each of these programs garnered its own critique, opponents maintained that together they proved that universities had been politicized by the left. This charge of politicization, although ironic given the way conservative politicians like Bennett exploited campus controversies, was at least partially true. These programs did have their roots in protest movements of the 1960s. However, they also should be viewed as part of the long interest of colleges in the moral formation of their students. In this case, the virtues that advocates hope to inculcate emphasized empathy with others, tolerance, and justice.[33]

While these political battles slowed the process of curricular reform, they did not completely derail them. Over the last two decades, numerous colleges and universities have adopted measures to strengthen general education, including multicultural distribution requirements. These efforts have been led by the American Association of Colleges and Universities (AAC&U), which has sponsored several initiatives aimed at developing model general education curricula and revitalizing liberal arts education. Part of the AAC&U's success has been its realistic attitude toward the material orientation of contemporary college students. Instead of decrying the dominance of vocational majors, it has sought to work with colleges to find ways to infuse the values of liberal education, such as critical thinking, into such programs.[34]

Concerns over the materialism and apathy of college students have also prompted new programs to promote civic engagement among college students. One of the most successful of these has been "service-learning," the integration of community service into regular academic courses at colleges and universities. Service-learning has been promoted by a number of organizations, particularly Campus Compact, which was created by several prominent university presidents in 1985 to encourage volunteerism among students. Over the 1990s, Campus Compact expanded dramatically (to more than nine hundred member institutions by the beginning of the new century) and initiated several programs to deepen colleges' commitment to student community involvement. In the past few years, new initiatives related to the civic education of colleges students have been undertaken by prominent professional associations, including the AAC&U and the American Council on Education (ACE). In addition, a number of individual colleges and universities have developed innovative programs, including special centers dedicated to moral and civic education, new curricular initiatives, and student-life programs.[35]

During this same period, colleges and universities with religious affiliations also took steps to reinvigorate their religious and moral mission. In 1990, Pope John Paul II issued *Ex Corde Ecclesiae*, a document aiming to strengthen the connection between the Catholic Church and Catholic universities. It called on Catholic universities to hire a majority of Catholic professors, select Catholic presidents, and maintain boards of trustees with Catholic majorities. It also required that faculty teaching theology receive a "mandate" from their bishop certifying their adherence to Church doctrine. Leaders of American Catholic institutions initially resisted the demands of *Ex Corde*, but over a decade they began to seek distinctive ways to strengthen their Catholic identity. Some colleges forbade student activities that contradicted Church doctrine, such as groups advocating abortion rights, while others sponsored programs to engage students in the social justice traditions of the Church. At the same time, the Lily Endowment sponsored a program on religion and higher education to strengthen Christian education—defined broadly—at both Catholic- and Protestant-affiliated colleges. Several colleges and universities founded centers to promote religious scholarship and religious teaching as a result of this program. In addition, conservative Protestant colleges, relegated to the margins of higher education since the beginning of the century, also pushed to increase their public profile and educational legitimacy during this period. The Council of Christian Colleges and Universities (CCCU), founded in 1976, aimed to strengthen the finances, administration, faculty, and academic reputations of its "intentionally Christ-centered" members. Begun with thirty-eight members, CCCU grew to approximately one hundred institutions thirty years later, a figure which does not include some of the newer Protestant institutions, such as Liberty University or Patrick Henry College.[36]

The Future?

The developments of the past two decades demonstrate educators' continuing concern with the moral formation of college students. While their efforts have had an influence on institutional practices, they have not displaced the dominant patterns that limit the colleges' moral mission— the primacy of material interests, electives and specialization, value-neutral scholarship, and institutional caution. It is too soon to tell whether current interest in moral education will soon fade, or whether it will continue to gain strength and eventually change the broader direction of higher education, producing a new pattern of moral education. The outcome depends in large part on how well faculty, administrators, and students grapple with the hard questions raised across the history of American higher education: How to emphasize moral formation and still respect diversity? How to reconcile freedom of thought and expression with a strong moral education? How to deal with the intersection of morality and politics and morality and religion? How to balance the multiple missions of higher education? How to reconcile individual and institutional self-interest with moral demands?

Notes

I would like to acknowledge the Spencer Foundation and the Radcliffe Institute for their support of my research on the post–World War II period.

1. "New England's First Fruits" (1643) reprinted in Morison, *The Founding of Harvard College,* 433.
2. For examples of the narrative of decline, see Burtchaell, *The Dying Light,* and Marsden, *The Soul of the American University.* For a classic narrative of progress, see Hofstadter and Metzger, *The Development of Academic Freedom in the United States.*
3. Morison, *The Founding of Harvard College.*
4. On the colonial colleges, see Hoeveler, *Creating the American Mind;* Warch, *School of the Prophets.*
5. Hellenbrand, *The Unfinished Revolution;* Rudolph, ed., *Education in the Early Republic.*
6. Stites, *Private Interest and Public Gain;* Whitehead, *The Separation of College and State.*
7. *Reports of the Course of Instruction in Yale College by a Committee of the Corporation and Academical Faculty* (New Haven, 1828); Lane, "The Yale Report of 1828 and Liberal Education."
8. Meyer, *The Instructed Conscience;* Smith, *Professors and Public Ethics;* Hogan, "Moral Authorities and the Antinomies of Moral Theory." The issue of slav-

ery, of course, created distinctive patterns for moral education in the South. See Sugrue, " 'We Desired Our Future Rulers to Be Educated Men.' "

9. Novak, *Rights of Youth*; Horowitz, *Campus Life.*

10. The following section is based on Reuben, *Making of the Modern University.*

11. Votaw, "Courses in Religion," 300.

12. John Coulter, "Christianity and Science," 8–9; John M. Coulter Papers, University of Chicago Archives.

13. Fitzgerald, *This Side of Paradise*; Horowitz, *Campus Life.*

14. Leslie, *Gentlemen and Scholars*; Lagemann, *Private Power for Public Good.*

15. Gleason, *Contending with Modernity: Catholic Higher Education in the Twentieth Century*; Mahoney, *Catholic Higher Education in Protestant America.*

16. Reisman and Grant, *The Perpetual Dream*; Duberman, *Black Mountain College.*

17. *General Education in a Free Society*; Zook, *Higher Education for American Democracy*; Fine, *Democratic Education.* See also Rudolph, *Curriculum.*

18. Hart, *The University Gets Religion*; Welch, *Religion in the Undergraduate Curriculum*; Ramsey and Wilson, eds., *The Study of Religion in Colleges and Universities.*

19. Schrecker, *No Ivory Tower.*

20. Hutchins, *Education for Freedom.*

21. *General Education in a Free Society*, 39 and 216.

22. Ibid., 77.

23. Sanford and Adelson, *The American College.*

24. The following section is drawn from Reuben, "Reforming the University."

25. Lauter and Howe, *The Conspiracy of the Young*, chap. 4.

26. Elias, *A History of Christian Education*, chap. 7; Gallin, *Negotiating Identity.*

27. Slaughter and Leslie, *Academic Capitalism*; Bok, *Universities in the Marketplace*; Gould, *The University in a Corporate Culture.*

28. Duffy and Goldberg, *Crafting a Class.*

29. Ehrenberg, *Tuition Rising.*

30. Astin et al., *The American Freshman*, 16–17.

31. See the yearly *Chronicle of Higher Education Almanac* for lists of degrees earned by field.

32. Carnochan, *The Battleground of the Curriculum.*

33. Arthur and Shapiro, eds., *Campus Wars*; Aufderheide, ed., *Beyond PC*; Wilson, *The Myth of Political Correctness.*

34. For information about AAC&U's programs, see their website: www.aacu-edu .org.

35. For more information about Campus Compact, see its website: www.com

pact.org, and Hartley and Hollander, "The Elusive Ideal." For information about other efforts to promote civic engagement, see Colby et al., *Educating Citizens*.

36. Gallin, ed., *Ex Corde Ecclesiae*; and McMurtrie, "Silence, Not Confrontation, Over 'Mandatum.'" There are links to various Lily-funded centers at the Lily Endowment website: www.lilyendowment.org. For more about CCCU, see its website: www.cccu.org.

WHAT ARE UNIVERSITIES FOR? II

AIM HIGH   *A Response to Stanley Fish*

Should colleges and universities try to teach ethics and promote civic responsibility? At a time when ethics scandals have erupted in every major American social institution, including business, government, the church, the press, and the army, and the airwaves are filled with stories of student misbehavior on campus, a new debate is brewing about what role, if any, higher education should play in moral and civic education.

On one side stands a small but growing chorus of educators, such as Derek Bok, Anne Colby, and Tom Ehrlich,[1] and the hundreds of college and university presidents who have signed Campus Compact's "Declaration on the Civic Responsibility of Higher Education" or the American Association of Colleges and Universities' "Core Commitment to Educate Students for Personal and Civic Responsibility."[2] These educators assert that preparing young people for lives of moral and civic responsibility should be a central priority for institutions of higher learning. They argue that, while going to college inevitably shapes a young person's character, habits, and attitudes, what is needed are more reflective and intentional efforts to foster moral and civic development through a variety of approaches infused in the curriculum as well as in extracurricular programs and campus culture. Such efforts will help institutions reconnect with, and revitalize the pursuit of, the animating purposes of a liberal education. They will better equip college graduates with the knowledge, skills, and motivations to be thoughtful and engaged citizens in a complex democratic society. Ultimately, they may even help to reverse a troubling decline among young Americans in personal integrity, political participation, and concern for the common good.

Others in the academy have greeted these arguments with skepticism and distrust. The most forceful critic to emerge has been Stanley Fish, dean emeritus of the College of Liberal Arts and Sciences at the University of Illinois at Chicago and a brilliant and influential literary scholar. In a series of essays in the *Chronicle of Higher Education* and the *New York Times* with evocative titles such as "Aim Low," "Save the World on Your Own Time," and "Why We Built the Ivory Tower," Fish argues that it is a "bad" and "unworkable" idea for colleges and universities to embrace moral and civic education as a goal. For Fish, the university, properly understood, pursues academic purposes, not moral ones. Faculty should try to make students into good researchers but eschew any attempt to shape their students' character and lives beyond the classroom. All efforts to pursue moral and civic education are doomed to lapse into dangerous forms of dogmatism or partisanship.[3]

While its champions believe that moral and civic education can help save the academy's soul, Fish thinks it will fundamentally corrupt it. The debate between them thus engages important questions about the nature and purposes of higher education and about the relationship between the university and society.

Should proponents and practitioners of moral and civic education take Fish's concerns seriously? Certainly his arguments have reached a wide audience, both inside and outside the academy. Ironically, they have earned him friends in unexpected places, including extravagant praise from conservative gadfly David Horowitz ("I applaud Stanley Fish's lonely effort to . . . return the university to intellectual values").[4] But while becoming a resource for conservative critics may not have been Professor Fish's intention,[5] shaking things up among his academic colleagues was. Being shaken up can be a good thing, and it is worth giving his arguments closer scrutiny.

Some of Fish's points, it turns out, are very well taken. He is right to question some of the more grandiose claims made on behalf of moral and civic education. He issues persuasive and refreshing appeals for academic modesty and integrity. And when he decries the dangers of partisan scholarship and "discipleship" and worries that moral and civic commitments may prompt faculty to confuse teaching with partisan advocacy and deform core values of the academy, he raises important and legitimate concerns. In all, his essays gesture toward some of the criteria needed to develop a yardstick by which to measure the intellectual rigor and integrity of moral and civic education, to distinguish between "political" and "politicized" education.[6]

But Fish himself does not construct such a yardstick. Instead, he condemns the entire enterprise of moral and civic education, using a rhetorically powerful but logically impoverished approach that rests on sharp dichotomies between "intellectual" and "moral" learning and between "academic" and "political" activity. *No* form of moral and civic education, he insists, can ever exemplify academic virtues of rigorous analysis, attentiveness to multiple perspectives, and commitment to truth. Nor, apparently, can democratic citizenship mean anything other than partisan political advocacy. The *sole* purpose of the university is to pursue academic research and to train future researchers. Any attempt to concern ourselves with students' lives outside the classroom amounts to discipleship and indoctrination. Fish's injunction that academics "aim low" ultimately reflects not a judicious commitment to intellectual honesty and modesty but the dogmatic assertion of a cramped and compartmentalized vision of higher education that ignores an insight at the heart of the liberal arts tradition: that the abilities to listen, think and argue well, to see beyond the limitations of one's own perspective, to deliberate with others, and to come to considered and courageous judgments are as important to moral and civic life as they are to academic excellence. Professor Fish's sweeping critique has opened up some important terrain for those who want to debate and ultimately to improve moral education, but progress in traversing this terrain will depend on rejecting the terms on which Fish has framed the debate.

Let us consider Fish's arguments in more detail. His critique focuses on four closely related claims about moral and civic education: First, moral and civic education is "unworkable" because "there are too many intervening variables, too many uncontrolled factors that mediate the relationship between what goes on in a classroom or even in a succession of classrooms and the shape of what is finally a life." You "can't make [your students] into good people, and you shouldn't try" ("Aim Low").

Second, moral and civic education is a "bad idea" because it requires dangerous and intellectually bankrupt pedagogical approaches of "discipleship" designed to "determine students' behavior and values" ("Aim Low").

Third, moral and civic education is not our job. "No doubt, the practices of responsible citizenship and moral behavior should be encouraged in our young adults—but it's not the business of the university to do so, except when the morality in question is the morality that penalizes cheating, plagiarizing, and shoddy teaching" ("Why We Built").

And finally, moral and civic education violates core norms and requirements of academic work. Our job as academics is "not to change the world, but to interpret it" ("Why We Built"), to offer "precise formulations of intellectual problems and their possible solutions" ("The Same Old Song"). Moral and civic education blurs clear boundaries between the academic and the political, boundaries that must be policed if the university is to retain its integrity and ultimately its social support. Indeed, it is "immoral for academics or for academic institutions to proclaim moral views" or for any university or university official to "take a stand on any social, political, or moral issue" ("Save the World").

Fish's first point, that moral and civic education is "unworkable" because the effects of any one course, or even of an entire curriculum, are so limited and unpredictable, is at heart a call for greater academic modesty in teaching and research. Teachers, he admonishes, should acknowledge the limits of their influence on students and realize they have little chance of "determining what [students] will make of what you have offered them" ("Aim Low"). Reflecting his own discipline's tumultuous recent journey from a period of dominance by "grand theory" to the beginnings of a return to more modest and traditional textual approaches, Fish cautions against the hubris that prompts academics to widen their claims "to include everything under the sun—if you study with us your mind will be sharpened, your character will be improved, your politics will be purified, and the world will be better" ("The Same Old Song"). Instead, he embraces a "narrow" and "craftsmanlike" conception of academic work and urges faculty to teach the materials and skills appropriate to their disciplines.

All of this is in many respects appealing and wise. Proponents of moral and civic education, like other educational visionaries and reformers, need to resist the tendency to adopt inflated beliefs and rhetoric about their efforts.[7] For instance, it is tempting for each generation of educators to bemoan the moral deficiencies of the young and to offer their solution as a panacea for America's civic deficit. Fish is right to point out this danger and to argue that the modern university contributes "in unpredictable and random ways . . . to the molding of young men and women" ("Aim Low"). Curiously, though, he never mentions that the book *Educating Citizens*, one of the main targets of his critique, opens with a portrait of the education of the civil rights activist Virginia Foster Durr at Wellesley College that is acutely attentive to these limitations. As the authors put it on the book's first page, "We begin with this story not because Virginia was dramatically transformed in college but because experiences she had in college played a pivotal role in a longer process that began before her college years and continued much beyond them."[8] Virginia Durr's Wellesley education in the early 1920s had a profound but "delayed effect" on her life that emerged out of both the college's intentional efforts to "awaken intellectual excitement, challenge assumptions, and foster new ways of understanding the world" and other, more "fortuitous" influences, to eventually alter the trajectory of her life. Similarly, moral and civic education will not, according to the authors of *Educating Citizens*, leave students "transformed" but will "start students on, or move them further along on, a route that provides them with the understanding, motivation, and skills they will need to meet the challenges of engaged citizenship."[9] Fish does not contemplate this vision of education's power, its capacity to serve as a railroad switch that subtly but enduringly changes the direction of a life. Nor does he allow for the more radically transformative visions of education offered by such diverse theorists as Plato and Paolo Freire who have (for good or for ill) changed what we mean by education itself and shown us the powerful links between education and social structure.

Of course, to say that the influence faculty wield in the area of moral and civic education is limited is not in and of itself an argument against the pursuit of moral and civic education, only against inflated expectations about it. After all, Fish also believes that faculty are limited in their abilities to turn students into good academic researchers, but does not regard this as a reason for faculty not to pursue this goal. The difference is that for Fish, moral and civic education is not only unworkable, it is "a bad idea." As he puts it, "You have no chance at all (short of a discipleship that is itself suspect and dangerous) of determining what their behavior and values will be in those aspects of their lives that are not, in the strict sense of the word, academic . . . you can't make them into good people, and you shouldn't try" ("Aim Low").

The emphasis on "determining" students' behavior and values and "making" them into good people is telling: moral and civic education, in Fish's view, is designed to produce a specific kind of ethical and civic behavior. Fish makes clear his conception of the ends and means of moral and civic education by saying that "universities could engage in moral and civic education only by deciding in advance which of the competing views of morality and citizenship is the right one, and then devoting academic resources and energy to the task of realizing it" ("Why We Built").

Now this is a decidedly odd contention. Professor Fish is quite happy to acknowledge that everything in the academy is, and ought to be, contestable, and to apply that maxim to his field of study, literary theory. It is for instance common to teach Milton by having students consider, and argue over, different interpretations of Milton. But he seems unwilling to imagine a course on ethics that, in a similar way, would engage the debates and controversies, would, for instance, have students argue for or against human rights, stem cell research, or the International Criminal Court, or engage a variety of interpretations of Confucian ethics or *Antigone*, or consider different approaches to social justice or educational policy and the strengths and weaknesses of each. It is a widely held view that the goal of moral and civic education is precisely to help students become more reflective about moral and political issues, to cultivate their capacities for moral imagination and reasoning, and to provide them with opportunities to develop and defend their own judgments, including judgments that challenge their professors. This goal requires deliberative and dialogical pedagogies and literally *cannot* be pursued through techniques of discipleship and indoctrination.

Faculty who abuse their power by imposing their moral or political views on students, or who present course material in an intellectually dishonest and partisan manner, are not pursuing defensible forms of moral and civic education. Professor Fish offers several examples of such behavior, from a faculty member who "included in a course description a request that conservative students go elsewhere" to one who declared that the goal of his course was to teach "peace, freedom, diversity . . . and to challenge American unilateralism" ("Save the World"). These are deplorable actions and proponents of moral and civic education need to join Professor Fish in publicly deploring them.

It is one thing to warn against the dangers of indoctrination, however, and quite another to suggest, as Fish does, that moral education can only be pursued in partisan and ideological ways. By asserting that *no* form of moral and civic education can ever exemplify academic virtues of rigorous analysis, attentiveness to multiple perspectives, and commitment to truth, Fish forecloses an entire terrain of argument about ethics pedagogy.

Indeed, it is striking that in a series of essays on moral and civic education, Fish spends very little time discussing pedagogy, and his statements on the subject seem on occasion to be at cross-purposes with his main argument. For example, despite his claim that academic work requires an openness to "opinions pro and con" ("Why We Built"), he asserts that it is not his "pedagogical task to provoke critical thought" in his students but rather to present "materials" that will "put students in possession of a territory they did not know before" ("Aim Low"). In this process he sees nothing wrong with teachers trying to convert students to their position—so long as the position in question is related to academic or disciplinary matters, not moral ones. As he puts it in an exchange with Stephen Balch: "Anything that I teach in my classes on Milton or legal theory is contestable, but the fact that it is contestable doesn't mean that I should refrain from trying as hard as I can to persuade my students that my views are the correct ones."[10]

Just why vigorous advocacy is appropriate in a class on literature but not one in ethics is not entirely clear. The apparent inconsistency between Fish's insistence that academic work requires a presentation of multiple views and his endorsement of professorial advocacy on nonmoral matters points more generally to the need for more nuanced discussions of pedagogy in moral and civic education. For example, what does fair-mindedness and openness to multiple perspectives require in courses that raise ethical and civic issues? Does it require that faculty adopt a neutral stance and preclude them from revealing their personal moral and political commitments to their students? Or can faculty with strong commitments create an environment in which students are encouraged to develop and defend their own commitments, even when those are in strong opposition to their professor's? These are tricky and important questions. For while indoctrination clearly corrupts efforts to teach ethics, there are parallel dangers from the arguably more common professorial stance of moral detachment and ironic distance, which can convey to students the view that no value system is worth defending, reinforcing fashionable and uncritical forms of moral relativism and apathy.[11] How, ultimately, can faculty model and help students navigate the tension between critique and commitment that lies at the heart of a thoughtful ethical life—combining a capacity to be continually self-critical with a willingness to affirm moral commitments and stand up for them?[12] As proponents of moral and civic education we need to think and argue about how faculty can design courses and programs and create classroom dynamics in which competing views are fairly presented and dissenting opinions are solicited and welcomed (including dissenting opinions about the vision of education we ourselves offer). Fish's critique points to some of the dangers to be avoided but offers little positive guidance.

But isn't it nevertheless true, Fish might retort, that proponents of moral and civic education, even while proclaiming the importance of dialogical and deliberative pedagogies, have decided "in advance which of the competing views of morality and citizenship is the right one" and are seeking to deploy "academic resources and energy to the task of realizing it" ("Why We Built")? The story of Virginia Durr that opens *Educating Citizens* portrays a young white woman from a genteel and racist Southern family whose experience at Wellesley challenged her assumptions and values and propelled her along a moral, intellectual, and political journey that would eventually make her a formidable champion of black voting rights and an opponent of the poll tax. Durr's courses on economics led her to regard poverty as not a simple character defect but rather the product of political and economic structures, and the rules of Wellesley's dining hall forced her to share a dinner table with an African American student, something she at first adamantly refused to do. Did the approaches used by Wellesley faculty and staff amount to a form of narrowly partisan advocacy of the kind that Fish rightly deplores?

Here we arrive at a crucial point in debates over moral education. Does a commitment to nurture core democratic principles on campus—to encourage and on occasion even to *force* students to engage as respectful equals with people of other races, cultures, religions, and ideologies—amount to an unjustifiable form of indoctrination? Or is a liberal education, properly understood, intrinsically linked to, and undergirded by, democratic principles of equality and respect? In other words, Wellesley's insistence that Virginia Durr treat African American students as peers can be traced to the academic value that, in a community of free and disciplined inquiry, people be judged by the quality of their minds and arguments, not the color of their skin. Fish argues that democratic values and academic values are utterly distinct, and that "respect for others" and free expression, while they are legitimate democratic values, are not core values of the academy and can corrupt academic values ("Aim Low," "The Same Old Song"). On this point there is, between Fish and the authors of *Educating Citizens*, a fundamental disagreement over the nature of liberal education.

What of Virginia Durr's economics professor, who gave her, as an assignment, the task of researching household income and expenses and developing a budget for a steelworker family in her Alabama hometown? Clearly he was intent on challenging Virginia's evidence-poor assumptions about poverty. Is it an appropriate professorial goal to challenge students' simplistic assumptions, to nurture critical thinking and promote an appreciation of complexity? (Here as elsewhere, the devil is in the details, for one hopes that this professor would also have challenged students who arrived in class confidently spouting liberal welfarist or Marxist structuralist explanations to engage with the cultural and psychological complexities of cross-generational poverty.) Once again the issue revolves around pedagogy: to the extent that moral and civic education rests on certain substantive assumptions about preparing students for democratic citizenship, are the means employed in pursuit of that goal what Richard Flathman calls "impositional and indoctrinating" or do they engage students in an open-ended process of critical inquiry? Peter Euben has characterized this distinction as one between "political" and "politicized" education, where a "politicized education" "regards the 'objects' of instruction as passive recipients of knowledge which molds them according to some blueprint of the good society."[13] A "political" education, by contrast, seeks to cultivate the capacity for independent judgment, including considered judgments that challenge the beliefs and assumptions of the educator.[14]

Finally, it is important that, by her own account, faculty and staff at Wellesley did not bully or shame Virginia Durr for her racist views or prevent her from expressing them. Indeed, she was active in the Southern

Club, a student extracurricular organization that, the authors of *Educating Citizens* note, could easily have served to reinforce her previous attitudes toward race, although fortuitously it ended up doing the opposite. According to Durr, the various elements—intentional and fortuitous—of her Wellesley education served to teach her one overriding lesson: "to use my mind and to get pleasure out of it." Adds Durr: "So my Wellesley education was quite liberating."[15]

Fish appears to be left cold by such narratives. Indeed, he insists that the *only* proper professorial stance is one that seems strikingly disengaged from students' lives. He observes: "What happens to the selves of students is no doubt an interesting sociological question, but no educator should concern herself or himself with it; the fashioning of the characters of our students will occur, and what we say or do may even have an effect on the process, but we should never have it as our aim."[16] Here, as elsewhere in Fish's critique, an appropriate caution—that educators should not seek groupies or disciples and should not confuse education with therapy—gets turned into a sweeping assertion about a single standard of appropriate practice that, on its face, evinces a remarkably distanced, even inhumane, attitude toward students.

This brings us to Fish's third argument against moral and civic education: it is not our job. "No doubt, the practices of responsible citizenship and moral behavior should be encouraged in our young adults—but it's not the business of the university to do so, except when the morality in question is the morality that penalizes cheating, plagiarizing, and shoddy teaching" ("Why We Built").

Here Fish makes a point echoed by many in the academy who, when urged to promote their students' moral and civic development, exclaim in exasperation, "It's not our job! We are hired to instruct students in disciplinary knowledge and to publish scholarly research, not to be moral tutors to the next generation."

To be sure, Fish does affirm the importance of "academic virtues," which he defines as virtues that "should be displayed in the course of academic activities—teaching, research, publishing." Teachers, he argues, "should show up for their classes, prepare syllabuses, teach what has been advertised, be current in the literature of the field, promptly correct assignments and papers, hold regular office hours, and give academic (not political or moral) advice. . . . Researchers should not falsify their credentials, or make things up, or fudge the evidence, or ignore data that go against their preferred conclusions" ("Save the World"). He also approvingly cites James Murphy's work on the intellectual virtues, arguing that the only moral advocacy permitted in the classroom is the advocacy of "intellectual virtues" such as "thoroughness, perseverance, intellectual honesty" and conscientiousness "in the pursuit of truth" ("Save the World"). Thus faculty members can and should try to nurture academic and intellectual virtues among their students, through modeling high standards and holding students to them, and colleges and universities should promote academic integrity and ethics in the conduct of research.

Fish's strong appeal to academic integrity and the intellectual virtues is important and welcome. The academy has paid far too little attention to these ethical issues at the heart of its own work. Curiously, however, Fish does not regard these activities as part of the recent movement to support moral and civic education, although they are widely discussed by, for example, the authors of *Educating Citizens*.[17] Instead he aims his critique at efforts to address broader questions about "how we ought to live" that are not linked to the scholarly life, regarding these two as utterly distinct enterprises.

Yet Fish's sharp dichotomy between academic and intellectual virtues (which academics can and should teach) and other virtues (which it is *not* our job to teach) is problematic on at least two counts. First, serious discussions of a topic such as academic integrity inevitably raise questions about virtues in other areas of life. Those who teach research ethics know how quickly questions of authorship and citation bleed over into deeper moral and political issues, from norms of respect and honesty, to what people in different power positions owe one another, to how professional norms are defined, challenged, and revised. Neither the virtues themselves, nor certainly our lives as scholars, teachers, and students, are as neatly compartmentalized as Fish suggests.

Second, by insisting that the "job" of the university is "quite simply to produce and disseminate . . . academic knowledge and to train those who will take up that task in the future" ("The Same Old Song"), Fish ignores the vast and varied terrain of general undergraduate education, professional and vocational education, residential life, and extracurricular activity on America's college and university campuses.[18] His portrait of the academy also leaves little room for community colleges, "offices of cooperative extension and tech transfer,"[19] for older students seeking to improve their professional credentials, or indeed for any preprofessional program. To suggest that, say, a professor of nursing, medicine, or law must judiciously avoid any effort to influence her students' behavior beyond her classroom, since it is "not her job" to care about it, undermines one of the primary purposes of professional education.

While Fish is surely right that faculty have limited influence on students' lives, given the power of everything from families to peers to popular culture, colleges and universities nevertheless play a substantial role in students' lives at a pivotal time of ethical exploration and identity formation, especially among traditional-age college students. To eschew any concern with students' ethical development beyond the classroom, and to refuse to commit to moral virtues and ideals rooted in the liberal arts and democracy, is to abandon a sense of the value of a thoughtful life and of the academy's value to society. Such moral reticence is common in colleges and universities and indeed remains widespread even within ethics programs. But in avoiding any discussion of the good life or of ideals of personal conduct, we are, in a profound sense, abandoning our students. As David Brooks put it in a provocative article about students at elite colleges and universities, "When it comes to character and virtue, these young people have been left on their own."[20]

Indeed, it is curious that Fish acknowledges that "the practices of responsible citizenship and moral behavior should be encouraged in our young adults" but then insists that "it's not the business of the university to do so" ("Why We Built"). Residential colleges and universities, in particular, are twenty-four-hour institutions that in many cases comprise the entire social world of students for a number of years. If colleges and universities don't think about how their curriculum and climate is likely to shape student values and behavior, then who should? The undergraduate years, in particular, represent an important period of moral development and identity formation.[21] While Fish is right that there are serious limits on the influence that an institution of higher learning can have on students' lives and values, a decision to eschew any reflective and intentional effort in this area will not rob students of formative influences but leave them (or at least those who do not embrace an academic career) at the mercy of, as Peter Levine puts it, "consumerism, entertainment, and careerism."[22]

This brings us to Fish's fourth and final contention, that moral and civic education violates core norms and requirements of academic work. It is dangerous to the integrity of the academic enterprise for academics, or institutions of higher learning, to adopt moral and civic education as a goal. Fish's point is that we need to focus on the essentials of our vocation as academics. For Fish, our purpose should be "not to change the world, but to interpret it" ("Why We Built"), to offer "precise formulations of intellectual problems and their possible solutions ("The Same Old Song"). Moral and civic education blurs clear boundaries between the academic and the political, boundaries that must be policed if the university is to retain its integrity and ultimately its social support. Indeed, it is "immoral for academics or for academic institutions to proclaim moral views" or for any university or university official to "take a stand on any social, political, or moral issue" ("Save the World").

Fish is appealing here to a broader sense of academic integrity—not an injunction against cheating and plagiarism but a duty to preserve the authenticity of the academic enterprise and to protect it from external pressures that threaten to corrupt or deform it. These external pressures include "students . . . trustees, donors, politicians, parents, and concerned members of the general public" ("Is Everything Political?"), "the incursions of capitalism," and "the incursions of virtue" ("Aim Low").

Fish's reasons for "policing the boundaries," as he puts it, between academic work and everything else appear to be both strategic and principled. Strategically, we suspect he is worried, given the recent political climate in the United States, that those most likely to be in a position to shape the moral and civic mission of the university will be conservative fundamentalists demanding control of curriculum, academic standards, and hiring and firing. It is principled insofar as Fish believes that the quality of the academic enterprise depends on its narrowness and purity of purpose. Academics interpret the world rather than try to change it. They shun the seductions of relevance and political influence and focus on pursuing truth in careful and disciplined ways. Fish explicitly elevates this point to a principle: "The sharper and the more limited the focus of your labors, the more likely it is that what you produce will be useful to the larger contexts you resolutely ignore. What society needs from academics are not grand schemes and grandiose visions, but precise formulations of intellectual problems and their possible solutions." Eloquently evoking the dignity of this "fine craftsmanlike work," Fish calls on his fellow scholars to content themselves with doing a particular thing—"interpreting a poem, sequencing a gene, describing a culture, recovering a part of the past"— arguing that, if they do it truly well, they "might just . . . produce something the world will not willingly let die" ("The Same Old Song").

Fish's injunction that academics "go deep" and resist the temptations of shallow relevance speaks powerfully to the dangers of "presentism" in the contemporary academy.[23] A desire for instant "relevance" to our students' lives and our times can easily diminish or inhibit the range, subtlety, originality, and independence of a scholar's work. Fish is surely right that the norms of engagement are appropriately different for scholarship than, for instance, electoral politics. Fidelity to a vocation of truth seeking places more stringent obligations on academics: we expect scholars to be more scrupulous in their interpretations and judgments than, say, lobbyists and activists. Peter Levine, in a subtle and thoughtful critique of Fish, nicely summarizes Fish's point: "We want scholars to think somewhat differently from activists and politicians: to take a longer view, to be less influenced by immediate practical concerns, to be less committed to parties, to be more openly engaged with their intellectual opponents, to offer more complex and nuanced views."[24]

Ironically, however, Fish uses this defense of scholarly subtlety to justify a crude typology of "distinct tasks" that fails to do justice to the norms of either academe or of the social spheres Fish deploys as academe's foil. He proclaims that it is the job of academics to interpret the world, *not* to change it, and that it should never "be the design or aim of academics to play that role" ("Why We Built").

But as Levine rightly points out, there is a "large gray area" where Fish sees only black and white. Scrupulous scholars can have a desire to change the world—and indeed, one of the ways they may do so is precisely by offering new interpretations of it that support one course of public action or another. The line Fish draws between "interpretation" and "civic engagement" or "social change," like so many of the dichotomies that underlie his critique, is not as stark as he makes it out to be. The scientist researching global warming, the psychologist examining links between media violence and youth behavior, or the lawyer considering patent policy or the death penalty may seek to influence public debate and policy in responsible and scrupulous ways, and indeed regard it as a scholarly obligation to do so. Moreover, as Levine points out, "Debates in legislatures, courts, and regulatory agencies are not devoid of controversy about research methods."[25] To suggest that academics, because they are supposed to care about truth, evidence, and openness to opposing viewpoints, cannot and must not get involved in politics is thus unfair both to academics *and* politics. We do not always get politicians and government officials who care about truth and evidence or who thoughtfully consider their opponents' arguments, but our democracy is the poorer for it. Indeed, truth telling is a core democratic norm, since citizens cannot evaluate their elected officials if these officials are deceiving them.[26] And what Stephen Carter calls "civil listening"—"listening to others with knowledge of the possibility that they are right and we are wrong"[27]—is as crucial to democratic life as it is to the classroom. The many homologies between intellectual and democratic virtues show why it is not a corruption of the academy's mission to prepare students for citizenship.

Fish is perhaps at his most vehement in condemning any effort by academic institutions to take action in the public sphere on moral or political grounds. He declares that "no university, and therefore no university official, should ever take a stand on any social, political, or moral issue" and that it is "immoral" to do so ("Save the World"). He does admit one exception: "Of course [the academic community] can and should take collective (and individual) action on those issues relevant to the educational mission—the integrity of scholarship, the evil of plagiarism, the value of a liberal education. Indeed, failure to pronounce early and often on these matters would constitute a dereliction of duty" ("Save the World").

His inclusion of "the value of a liberal education" in this list is interesting, since Fish rejects efforts to link liberal education to broader social goods, insisting, for example, that it is wrong for the university to claim, as one of its purposes, in the words of David Horowitz's Academic Bill of Rights, "the teaching and general development of students to help them become creative individuals and productive citizens of a pluralistic society" ("Intellectual Diversity"). Public advocacy of academic values is, then, something that Fish is defining rather narrowly. His hero John Milton's public stance against book licensing laws in *Areopagitica* may just make the cut. Fish's insistence that "relevance to educational mission" be narrowly defined makes it unclear whether he believes the academy has a right, much less an obligation, to contribute to public debates over the balance between security and civil liberties or to condemn repressive educational policies around the world such as those that were practiced by the Taliban or by apartheid-era South Africa.

Closer to home, Fish's assertion that colleges and universities must never take stances on public moral issues overlooks the fact that many policy issues, from fair wages to parental leave policies to environmental conservation, are unavoidably implicated in university structures and practices. A university cannot avoid "taking a stand" on wages, since it sets wages for groundskeepers, cafeteria workers, and janitorial staff. It cannot avoid "taking a stand" on environmental conservation since it has to make choices on whether or not to recycle, how to allocate resources for energy, and what environmental norms to follow in new construction. Fish's attitude to students, faculty, and administrators who seek to shape university policies in these and similar areas is unequivocal: he condemns, as a "collective lapse" in judgment, "those who put pressure on universities to change practices" such as labor rules regarding the manufacture of licensed apparel, global equity in investment policy, or efforts to raise the wages or benefits of university staff ("Save the World").

In effect, Fish is arguing that academics must accept lowest-common-denominator policies in all areas of university life *other* than teaching and research. It is the duty of university officers, he says, "to expand the endowment by any legal means available," "to employ the best workers at the lowest possible wages," and to make "the athletics program as profitable as possible" ("Save the World").

Why, ultimately, does Fish insist on rejecting efforts by universities to embrace corporate social responsibility? The reasons he provides are procedural and strategic. He worries that those who seek to influence university policies for moral or political reasons are promoting positions that will not be approved by "everyone . . . in the academic community." But in the absence of universal consensus (an impossibly high standard), there are procedures that universities, faculty councils, and boards of trustees can follow for legitimate decision making. There is much room for debate over these procedures, as there is over the appropriate means advocates should employ in trying to persuade university decision makers to adopt one policy rather than another. But, as we've noted above, there is no neutral position on most of the issues Fish mentions. The university will have a policy on wages, family leave policies, investment, or athletic funding, whether it is one that has been subjected to moral scrutiny and debate or not. It is dispiriting for a prominent academic leader, in the name of truth and integrity, to denounce any effort by universities to embrace norms and restrictions that numerous for-profit corporations have done.

Fish's deeper worry may be, as we suggested earlier, that if the university takes moral and political stances, "sectors of the general public will come to regard the university as a special-interest lobby and decline to support it." In other words, universities should not only "aim low," but "lay low" to avoid controversy and possible loss of support. But beyond its depressing passivity about the academy's social role and influence, this counsel of self-protection is problematic on its own terms. It assumes, without argument, that university decisions to change wage and investment policies on moral grounds will lose, rather than gain, public support. Yet there is some evidence that the opposite is true. More ironically, a strong case can be made that Professor Fish's strategy to protect the university from outside criticism by urging it to "aim low" has backfired, since his misleading portrait of partisan moral and civic educators bent on indoctrinating America's youth has reinforced conservative stereotypes of leftist academics run amuck.

In the end, Fish offers us a cramped and compartmentalized vision of higher education that fails to do justice either to teaching or to pursuing a thoughtful ethical life within the academy. At its best, the movement for moral and civic education is not a recipe for moral indoctrination or enforced uniformity but a commitment to ensure that students have opportunities to think deeply about moral issues, that they experience scholarship and campus life as domains governed by high ethical standards, and that they are encouraged to be reflective, open, and self-critical while making moral commitments and standing up for them.

Notes

1. Bok, *Universities and the Future of America,* and *Our Underachieving Colleges;* Colby et al., *Educating for Democracy.*
2. Campus Compact, "President's Declaration on the Civic Responsibility of Higher Education," drafted in 1999, has been signed by 563 presidents to date. See http://www.compact.org (visited February 12, 2008). The "Call to Action" of the American Association of Colleges and Universities' Core Commitments project was issued in 2007 and has been signed by 169 presidents to date. See http://www.aacu.org (visited February 12, 2008).

3. The following articles by Fish are cited in this chapter. "Is Everything Political"; "The Same Old Song"; "Intellectual Diversity: The Trojan Horse of a Dark Design"; and "Why We Built the Ivory Tower."

4. Glazov, "The University Is Not a Political Party, or Is It?"

5. Indeed, Fish subsequently went on record opposing Horowitz's proposed Academic Bill of Rights. Fish, "Intellectual Diversity."

6. Euben, *Corrupting Youth*, 49–51.

7. Julie Reuben's essay in this volume provides vivid examples of this tendency from earlier educational reform movements.

8. Colby et al., *Educating Citizens*, 1.

9. Ibid., 21.

10. Glazov, "The University Is Not a Political Party, or Is It?" Fish's comment prompts Balch to note, quite rightly, that while there are many ways of being a good teacher, Fish's description of his own pedagogy would, if applied to an undergraduate course, "be something of a disservice, albeit an intellectually exciting one. There is nothing wrong with a professor imparting his own studied opinions, but in fields where subject matter is inherently complex and ambiguous, good teaching also requires conveying the extent to which reasonable thinkers can, and do, differ" (9–10).

11. For an interesting discussion of these attitudes and their prevalence in the academy, see Light, "Public Environmental Philosophy."

12. Harpham, *Shadow of Ethics*, x–xi.

13. Euben, *Corrupting Youth*, 50.

14. Ibid., 50–51.

15. Colby et al., *Educating Citizens*, 2.

16. Glazov, "The University Is Not a Political Party, or Is It?" 6.

17. Colby et al., *Educating Citizens*; see pages 230–35, 76, 78.

18. This point is also emphasized by Peter Levine in "Stanley Fish vs. Civic Engagement," May 25, 2004, http://www.peterlevine.ws (visited August 16, 2006).

19. Ibid., 2.

20. Brooks, "The Organization Kid," 53.

21. Perry, *Forms of Ethical and Intellectual Development in the College Years*.

22. Levine, "Stanley Fish vs. Civic Engagement," 3.

23. On "presentism," see Euben, *Platonic Noise*, 7–8.

24. Levine, "Stanley Fish vs. Civic Engagement," 2.

25. Ibid., 2.

26. As Shulman (among others) reminds us, the relationship between truth and politics is more controversial and complex than our argument here acknowledges. It is a relationship that has engaged theoretical and political reflection

from Plato and Aristotle to Machiavelli, Hobbes, Kant, Habermas, Arendt, and Vaclav Havel. It is not clear to what extent truth is an overriding or primary value in politics, though a certain kind of truthfulness may be necessary for democratic public life. One of the best contemporary treatments of the issue is Dietz, "Working in Half-Truth."

27. Carter, *Civility*, 139.

I KNOW IT WHEN I SEE IT   *A Reply to Kiss and Euben*

In the preceding chapter, Elizabeth Kiss and Peter Euben offer an extended critique of my insistence (in several essays) that college and university teachers should hew to the line dividing academic from nonacademic activities (I don't say "real world activities" because all worlds are real) and refrain from any kind of partisan advocacy, be it political, economic, civic, or social. Kiss and Euben make many points, but in the end they reduce to two: (1) The line I would draw is not a firm or bright one; rather, it is blurred in ways that make impossible any neat segregation of academic and nonacademic behaviors. (2) Even if the line could be drawn, the result would not be a purified academy but a diminished and impoverished one reflecting "a cramped and compartmentalized vision of higher education."

The first point is made by arguing that certain concerns and abilities are properly found on both sides of the boundary I wish to police: "the abilities to listen, think, and argue well, to see beyond the limitations of one's own perspective, to deliberate with others, and come to considered and courageous judgments are as important to moral and civic life as they are to academic excellence." The problem with this formulation is that the abilities it lists do not come in a general form such that instances of them in one precinct could be said to be equivalent to instances of them in others. Rather, the form each takes, and takes appropriately, will vary with the nature of the activity being engaged in. "Arguing well," for example, will be a quite different thing in the courtroom or the caucus room or the boardroom or the bedroom than it is in the classroom or an academic paper (like this one). You argue well as a lawyer if you throw everything including the kitchen sink into the argumentative mix as long as it has even a remote chance of helping your client's cause (in which you may or may not believe). You argue well as a politician if you demean your opponent's character on the way to (and perhaps as a substitute for) critiquing his position. You argue well in the bedroom if you manage to make your points without damaging the relationship (an almost impossible task). But if you are performing in an academic setting and make ad hominem remarks, or try anything just on the chance it might stick, or worry about hurting the feelings of those you disagree with, you will disqualify yourself in the eyes of your peers who expect you to adhere to the decorums that belong to the task you are attempting. Those decorums are not external to the task—they are not mere conventions of politeness—they are constitutive of the task, and if the task is an academic one (to describe a phenomenon, interpret a text, challenge an account, offer a correction, propose a new line of research, etc.), they demand, not as a matter of courtesy but as a matter of fidelity, a careful and nonselective marshaling of evidence, an avoidance of personal attacks, an overwhelming concern to "get it right" no matter where the effort takes you, an acknowledging of positions contrary to your own (at least those positions you take seriously) along with the reasons you reject them, and much more. Again, these demands and decorums are not incidental to academic work; they define it and by defining it they mark off academic work as a category that has its own distinctiveness.

This is what I mean by a phrase I often use: "the distinctiveness of tasks." In part the distinctiveness is a matter of logic. As the legal theorist Ernest Weinrib puts it, if a task or activity is to have its own shape, it must present itself "as a *this* and not a *that*"; it must, that is, have a "determinate content" that "sets the matter apart from other matters."[1] Otherwise, it ceases to be intelligible as an identifiable entity and is without boundaries or form. If the academic task is finally indistinguishable from the tasks of politics or character formation or nation building—if what we do in the classroom and the research essay bleeds into the world which then bleeds back—there would seem to be no rationale for giving it a room of its own, not to mention a budget and a vast machinery by which its practitioners are produced and credentialed. This is not to say that academic work touches on none of the issues central to politics, ethics, civics, and economics; it is just that when those issues arise in an academic context they should be discussed in academic terms; that is, they should be the objects of analysis, comparison, historical placement, and so on; the arguments put forward in relation to them should be dissected and assessed *as* arguments and not as preliminaries to action on the part of those doing the assessing. The action one takes at the conclusion of an academic discussion is the action of rendering an *academic* verdict as in "That argument makes sense," "There's a hole in the reasoning here," "The author does (or does not) realize her intention," "In this debate, X has the better of Y," "The case is still not proven." These and similar judgments are judgments on craftsmanship and coherence—they respond to questions like "Is it well made? and "Does it hang together?"—but craftsmanship and coherence are not the only measures of judgment and in nonacademic contexts they might not be the primary ones. You could flunk the reasoning given by a policy's supporters in your classroom and then go out and vote for it on election day; and you could do this because you felt that despite the lack of skill with which the policy was defended (an academic conclusion) it was the right policy for the country (a political conclusion). The question of whether a policy is the right one for the country is not a question to be decided in the classroom where you are (or should be) more interested in the structure and history of ideas than in recommending them (or dis-recommending them) to your students. To be sure, the ideas will be the same whether you are dissecting them or recommending them; but dissecting them is what you are supposed to do if you are paid to be an academic. Recommending them is what you do when you are a parent, or a political activist, or an op-ed columnist, all things you may be when the school day ends, but not things you should be on the university's or state's dime.

This distinction holds even when the subject of a course is ethics. Kiss and Euben wonder why I refuse to extend my approval of "vigorous advocacy" in the literature classroom, where the debate might be about which interpretation of *Paradise Lost* is the right one, to the classroom where the subject is ethics. If Fish's students "consider, and argue over, different interpretations of Milton" why is he "unwilling to imagine a course on ethics that, in a similar way, would engage the debates and controversies, would, for instance, have students argue for or against human rights, stem cell research, or the International Criminal Court, or engage a variety of interpretations of Confucian ethics or *Antigone*, or consider different approaches to social justice or educational policy and the strengths and weaknesses of each"? Well, in fact I can imagine a course in ethics characterized by the same vigorous advocacy my students and I engage in when studying Milton. In this class, however, the point would be to analyze the debates and controversies over ethical issues rather to decide that one of the positions in those debates is the right one, the one we should ourselves adopt. The Terry Schiavo case, for example, is pedagogically useful because it focuses a set of issues that have been in play at least since the beginning of the republic: the tension between procedural and substantive justice, the conflict between the "right" (as defined by philosophers from Kant to Rawls) and the good, the antimony of Natural Law and positive law. Starting with the Schiavo incident, one could first examine the many opinions handed down by several courts and then locate the philosophical and legal traditions from which those opinions emerged. One could then surface the presuppositions informing those traditions and track the different agendas that have found it useful to appropriate them (whether knowingly or not) and by appropriating them, alter them. Notice that in the course of such a sequence of investigations, the urgency felt by those directly involved in the controversy—Schiavo's husband, her parents, politicians on both sides of the aisle, newspaper columnists, clergymen—would be dissipated and would be replaced by the *academic* urgency to get it right, to provide a "thick" and persuasive account of the career of a set of ideas, an account that would include the political career of those ideas but would stop short of urging that any one of them be either taken up or rejected. That is to say, the more penetrating your analysis of the intellectual history underlying an ethical drama (and the Schiavo case certainly was that), the less you will be situating yourself in its contemporary instantiation as a participant, as someone who is trying to decide how to act. The question on the exam should not be "In this situation [details provided before the question is posed] where conflicting values vie for allegiance, what should you do?" The exam question should be "In this situation where conflicting values vie for allegiance, what would Plato, Hobbes, Rousseau, and Kant tell you to do and what reasons, drawn from what traditions with what presuppositions, would each give for so telling you?"

This does not mean that there could never be a relationship between the conclusions you come to in the course of an academic analysis and the conclusions you might reach where the question is "What should I do now?" It is just that the relationship will be a highly mediated one and far from causal. You will not resolve to do this or that in your ethical life *because* you delivered a judgment on utilitarianism or deontology in your seminar paper—someone who delivered the same judgment in a seminar might go down an ethical path wholly different from yours—although the fact that you wrote that paper might be one of the factors, along with innumerable others, that went into the fashioning of your present resolve. Kiss and Euben make much of Virginia Foster Durr's account of the effect on her later activities of her Wellesley education, but Durr makes my point when she characterizes that effect as "delayed." That is, it kicked in years later, after she had had many other experiences, and it was only way down the road, so to speak, that she reasoned backward from what she had become to the courses she took in college. What you can't do is reason *forward*, reason that if students take these courses and are taught by this method and introduced to those ideas, they will become certain kinds of persons, persons who are "more reflective about moral and political issues" and "cultivate their capacities for moral imagination and reasoning." Kiss and Euben (along with the authors of *Educating Citizens*) like the Virginia Durr story because she fought for integration and against the poll tax; it is not difficult, however, to imagine a Wellesley student who took the same courses Durr took and also developed capacities for moral imagination and reasoning (whatever they are), but came out on the other side of these political/moral questions; and one wonders if those who believe in the role of education in fashioning character would be willing to attribute *that* result to the effect of a college education. As instructors we should no more be held responsible for the students who (at least in our view) come to a moral and civic "bad end" than we should claim credit for the students who gratify us by believing what we believe and working for the causes we favor. We can (and should) be held responsible if we do not introduce our students to the relevant body of materials (relevance defined by the subject matter of the course) and equip them with the skills to analyze, describe, and assess them, which skills might be described as the skills of "critical thinking," so long as by "critical thinking" we do not intend either something mystical and ineffable or thinking that always goes in the direction of challenging orthodoxies and undoing structures of power. (Some orthodoxies are perfectly fine and structures of power are a precondition for effective action.) Virginia Durr gets it right when she describes as the fruit of her college education the ability "to use my mind and get pleasure out of it." It is both a reasonable and a responsible goal to get our students to do that, to use their minds and enjoy the calisthenics of it; reasonable because it is a goal we as teachers might actually achieve, and responsible because its achievement is something we have been trained (one hopes) to produce.

Kiss and Euben assert that I appear "to be left cold by such narratives" as Durr's. No, I warm to them as much as anyone else who shares the progressive values Durr's career displayed. What I don't warm to—am unpersuaded by—is the suggestion that a course of study could or should have been designed to produce that career or even to make its occurrence more likely. What we can design, and what we can have a chance at effecting, is the acquisition of knowledge and analytical skill. Once acquired, that knowledge and skill may play into a student's subsequent life experiences in any number of ways or in no way at all. The contingent effects of our teaching may make us happy or unhappy; but they are just that—contingent—and neither can be nor should be aimed at. Kiss and Euben report that an economics professor gave Durr the assignment of researching the household income and expenses of a steelworker family in her Alabama hometown. "Clearly," they say, "he was intent on challenging Virginia's evidence-poor assumptions about poverty." Well, it isn't clear to me—do they have evidence they do not reveal to back up *their* assumptions?—and I would think (or hope) that he was intent on supplying a defect in her knowledge about wages, budgets, household management, and the like. Whether that knowledge challenged her assumptions is again a contingent matter; it would have been just as valuable as knowledge if it confirmed her assumptions or spoke to an area in which she had none. If, in fact, her professor *was* intent on challenging (and changing) her assumptions so that they would be more in line with his political views (about the minimum wage, worker exploitation, etc.), he would have exchanged his educational efforts for ones of political indoctrination.

Kiss and Euben ask, "Does a commitment to nurture core democratic principles on campus—to encourage and on occasion even to *force* students to engage as respectful equals with people of other races, cultures, religions, and ideologies—amount to an unjustifiable form of indoctrination?" The answer is yes, and the reason for the answer allows me to speak to another of their points, that I seem to believe (in their view oddly) that "moral and civic education . . . is designed to produce a specific kind of ethical and civic behavior." Here in their question is both the proof and the pudding: respecting those of other cultures, religions, and ideologies is a particular model of ethical behavior, but it would not be the preferred model of some libertarians, free-market economists, Orthodox Jews, Amish, fundamentalist Christians, and members of the Aryan Nation, all of whom, the last time I looked, are American citizens and many of whom are college students. A university administration may believe that "principles of equality and respect" form the core of democratic life, but if it pressures students to accept those principles as theirs, it is using the power it has to impose a moral vision on those who do not share it, and that is indoctrination if anything is. (It should go without saying that such an accusation would not apply to avowedly sectarian universities; indoctrination in a certain direction is quite properly their business.) As long as respect for the culture, religion, and ideology of the other is a contested ethic rather than a universal one, a university that requires it or attempts to inculcate it is engaged not in educational but in partisan behavior.

As Kiss and Euben note, I say the same of any university effort to "take stances on public moral issues" including the issue of "repressive educational policies around the world such as those that were practiced by the Taliban or by apartheid-era South Africa." But, they demur, Fish "overlooks the fact that many policy issues, from fair wages to parental leave policies to environmental conservation, are unavoidably implicated in university structures and practices." The reasoning, I take it, is that (a) universities are situated in the world and must, for example, pay wages and manage their physical plants; (b) what is a fair wage and what is the best way to utilize energy are issues of public debate; (c) therefore universities are "unavoidably implicated" in the debates whether they acknowledge it or not. But the logic is too capacious and proves too much, for it amounts to saying that whenever anyone does anything, he or she is coming down on one side or another of a political controversy. In some municipalities, it is a political question as to whether or not a Wal-Mart should be allowed to set up shop. Yesterday my wife needed something and she purchased it at a Wal-Mart. Did she engage in a political act by doing so? I know that some people would say yes and back up the yes by reminding us that no man is an island, that in the modern economy everything is interconnected, and that therefore there is no such thing as a consumer choice that is purely economic or a matter of simple convenience. But that is to confuse and conflate two levels of understanding. On one level, reductive in the technical not pejorative sense, everything is just like everything else in virtue of some shared attribute. On another level, where the measure of difference and sameness is less general, distinctions emerge and they are real. A chair, a table, and a baseball bat might have the same molecular structure, and if molecular structure is the measure of identity, they are like one another. But if the measure is use (or cost), they are not at all alike and what you want to do is point out and honor the differences. It is true to say that by buying at Wal-Mart my wife strengthens, if only in the smallest way, the effort of that corporation to establish itself everywhere. But it was not her intention to do so (she needed a computer cable and Wal-Mart was the place where she could get it) and it is also true to say that by buying at Wal-Mart she solved a workplace problem and that's all there was to it. There must be room for a difference between a self-consciously political act (such as the one my wife performs when she refuses to purchase goods manufactured by companies engaged in or benefiting from research on animals) and an act performed with no political intention at all although it, inevitably, has a political effect (at least by some very generous definition of what goes into the political). Similarly, universities can pay wages with (at least) two intentions: (1) to secure workers, whether faculty or staff, who do the job that is required and do it well and (2) to improve the lot of the laboring class. The first intention has nothing to do with politics and everything to do with the size of the labor pool, the law of supply and demand, current practices in the industry, and so on. The second intention has everything to do with politics—the university is saying "Here we declare our position on one of the great issues of the day"—and it is not an intention appropriate to an educational institution. At the height of the debate about whether or not to invade Iraq, the provost of the University of Wisconsin at Madison said, "The University of Wisconsin does not have a foreign policy." Neither does it have a domestic policy, except in those areas—state funding, government support for research, tax exemptions for educational institutions—where the issues on the table relate directly to its health and survival.

The distinction I am insisting on—between practices appropriate to the university and practices that belong properly to a legislature or a political party—is inadvertently acknowledged by Kiss and Euben when they write, "A university cannot avoid 'taking a stand' on wages, since it sets wages for groundskeepers, cafeteria workers, and janitorial staff. It cannot avoid 'taking a stand' on environmental conservation since it has to make choices on whether or not to recycle, how to allocate resources for energy, and what environmental norms to follow in new construction." The quotation marks around "taking a stand" are a recognition by the authors that they don't really mean "taking a stand" in the usual sense—"I hereby declare myself on this side or that"—but only in a metaphorical sense; that is, they signal by the quotation marks that they mean "taking a stand" only as a way of speaking and not as a literal description of what the university is, in fact, doing. When a university sets wages, it sets wages, period (sometimes a cigar is just a cigar). The action has its own internal-to-the-enterprise shape, and while one could always abstract away from the enterprise to some larger context in which the specificity of actions performed within it disappears and everything one does is "taking a stand," it is hard to see that anything is gained except a certain fuzziness of reference. Any university I've been at decides what environmental (or disability) norms to follow in new construction not by looking into its moral heart but by consulting the city, state, and federal codes (especially the fire codes). The interest is not in anything so grand as taking a stand but in staying clear of violations that would lead to penalties and work stoppages.

At times Kiss and Euben read my strictures against university involvement (whether by individual instructors or by the institution as a corporate entity) in political/social matters as evidence of something approaching cowardice. They assert that when I say "aim low," I mean "lay low" and that what I am counseling is a "depressing passivity about the academy's social role and influence." In fact I have repeatedly faulted senior administrators for laying low when it came time to defend their universities against funding cuts, legislative intrusions, and public pressures (as applied, for example, by newspaper editorials and radio talk shows). Indeed I have urged not passivity but an aggressive and proactive stance that would have administrators playing offense rather than defense.[2] I have made the further point that universities argue from weakness when they say to a legislature or to a state board of higher education or to a congressional committee, "See, what we do does in fact contribute to the state's prosperity or to the community's cultural life or to the production of a skilled workforce." All these claims may be true, but to make them the basis of your case is to justify your enterprise in someone else's terms and that, I contend, is to be passive in the defense of the institution's core values. Better, I counsel, to stand up for those values—for intellectual analysis of questions that may never have a definitive or even a useful answer, for research conducted just because researchers find certain problems interesting, for wrestling with puzzles only five hundred people (many of them living outside the United States) in the whole world are eager to solve—and when those values are dismissed or scorned, challenge the scorner to exhibit even the slightest knowledge of what really goes on in the classroom or the laboratory; and when he or she is unable to do so, ask "Is that the way you run *your* business, by pronouncing on matters of which you are wholly ignorant?" Now this advice may not be good advice—although, God knows, the defensive strategies currently employed by administrators are spectacularly ineffectual—but it is certainly not advice to be passive or lay low. Rather, it is advice to put your best foot forward, which means, I believe, to put your *own* foot forward, and not someone else's.

By suggesting that I am counseling passivity, Kiss and Euben come close to Paul Street's contention that by my lights a German academic in the 1920s whose research "led her to believe that her homeland was heading toward a fascist-totalitarian takeover" would have been told to " 'stick to the tasks she was paid to perform,' keeping her terrible knowledge within proper academic boundaries." But Street's hypothetical academic could well have written an essay that extrapolated from the present political situation to a possible dark future and still remained within academic boundaries as long as its arguments and conclusions were couched in the terms appropriate to academic debate; as long, that is, as she examined the policies in place or under consideration and demonstrated (or claimed to demonstrate) that their logic, if followed through, would likely have undesirable consequences. Some other academic could then have written an essay in response to hers and disagreed with her analysis and the reasoning that led to her conclusion. Both would be dealing with political issues, but they wouldn't be doing politics; that is, the point of their essays would have been to make a point and not to drum up support for a specific political agenda. Of course readers of their essays might factor them into their thinking about partisan politics, and they might be cited by those who took to the streets for one side or the other (this could even happen, as I have learned recently, to essays on Milton's *Samson Agonistes*); but these would be contingent effects—they could neither be counted on nor avoided—and not the effect they aimed at, the effect of winning the day in an academic context by producing better arguments. Nothing I say bars any content whatsoever—political, religious, sexual—from the arena of academic discussion; it is just that the discussion should be, in fact, academic, stopping at the water of political activism, although academics, like anyone else, can be political activists when they are off the time-clock. And we needn't go back to the Weimar Republic and Nazi Germany for examples.[3] Professors today write pro and con essays about the Patriot Act all the time, arguing about whether or not this or that provision is an encroachment on civil liberties. Law reviews and political science journals print these essays, and invite responses to them, and one could say of a particular essay that if its analysis is correct the Patriot Act should or should not be repealed. But if the point of the essay, the reason it was written, was to issue a call for repeal (or its opposite), it would not be an academic performance but a partisan one.

When I first read Street's piece, I was puzzled by the Weimar/Nazi example and wondered why he didn't have a more contemporary illustration. Then I read a little further and realized that in his mind this *was* one: In Fish's view, "good professors are like good Germans, content to leave policy to those who are 'qualified' to conduct state affairs—people like George W. Bush and Donald Rumsfeld." As far as Street is concerned, George W. Bush and Donald Rumsfeld are today's fascist-militarists, and it should be the business of every right-thinking (meaning left-thinking) academic to teach and write about the evil of their policies so that the emergence of a new Third Reich can be nipped in the bud. Now many Americans and most academics in the humanities and social sciences share Street's political views, but does that mean that the educational experience of our students (many of whom hold opposing views) should be guided by them? Should the evil and perfidy of the Bush administration be the base-line assumption in the light of which history, literature, political theory, philosophy, and social science are taught? I think not (nor do I think that the virtue of the Bush administration should be the base-line assumption) because in a classroom like that, the gathering of evidence on the way to reaching a conclusion—the prime academic activity—would have been abandoned from the get-go; in a classroom like that, the evidence is already in (or so the instructor believes) and the conclusion—a partisan conclusion—has been reached in advance. Street, in short, is urging just the politicized academy I warn against and illustrating by his fulminations exactly how dangerous and *anti-educational* a course that would be. Later in the piece he identifies himself as "a former academic" who left the academy and now spends his time leading teach-ins and doing other politically oriented community work. He was right to leave; it was not his kind of thing. He is wrong to counsel those who remain to exchange their mission for his.

Kiss and Euben might reply, as they do in their essay, that while there may be dangers attending the blurring of the line between academic work and partisan politics (and remember, I draw no line between academic conversations and conversations centering on political issues, so long as the issues receive academic, not proselytizing, attention), there may also be dangers in the segregation I argue for: "There are parallel dangers from the . . . professorial stance of moral detachment and ironic distance, which can convey to students the view that no value system is worth defending, reinforcing fashionable and uncritical forms of moral relativism and apathy." This is an instance of the second of Kiss's and Euben's general points: that my wish to exclude from the classroom and other academic precincts the kind of activities that (I say) are more appropriately found on the campaign trail will lead to an arid experience in which values, commitments, and passion are left behind. But I do not urge detachment, moral or any other kind. In the classrooms I have in mind, passions run high as students argue about whether or not Satan is the hero of *Paradise Lost* or whether the religion clause of the First Amendment, properly interpreted, forbids student-organized prayers at football games or whether the Rawlsian notion of constructing a regime of rights from behind a "veil of ignorance" makes sense or whether the anthropological study of a culture inevitability undermines its integrity. I have seen students discussing these and similar matters if not close to coming to blows then very close to jumping up and down and pumping their fists. These students are far from apathetic or detached, but what they are attached to (this again is the crucial difference) is the *truth* of the position to which they have been persuaded, and while that truth, strongly held, might lead at some later time to a decision to go out and work for a candidate or a policy, deciding *that* is not what is going on in the classroom. Moreover, if anything is a value, truth is, and the implicit (and sometimes explicit) assumption in the classroom as I envision it is that truth, and the seeking of truth, must always be defended. To be sure, truth is not the only value and there are others that should be defended in the contexts to which they are central; but truth is a preeminent *academic* value, and adherence to it is exactly the opposite of moral relativism. You will never hear in any of my classes the some-people-say-X-but-others-say-Y-and-who's-to-judge dance. What I strive to determine, in the company and with the cooperation of my students, is which of the competing accounts of a matter is the right one and which are wrong and the reasons why. "Right" and "wrong" are not in the lexicon of moral relativism, and the students who deliver them as judgments do so with a commitment as great as any they might have to a burning social issue.

Not only is the genuinely academic classroom full of passion and commitment, it is more interesting than the alternative. Nothing is more boring than sitting around with a bunch of nineteen- or twenty-year-olds discussing assisted suicide or physician-prescribed marijuana or the war in Iraq in response to the question "What do you think?" The result is predictable: a rehearsing of the entirely canned pros and cons one hears on the nightly news; in short, a rehearsing of opinions. No instructor should be interested in his or her students' opinions (except perhaps as a springboard to serious inquiry); what you're jointly after is knowledge, and the question should never be "What do you think?" (unless you're a social scientist conducting a survey designed to capture public opinion). The question should be "What is the truth?" and the answer must stand up against challenges involving (among other things) the quality and quantity of evidence, the cogency of arguments, the soundness of conclusions, and so forth. At the (temporary) end of the process, both students and teachers will have learned something they didn't know before (you always know what your opinions are; that's why it's so easy to have them) and they will have learned it by exercising their cognitive capacities in ways that leave them exhilarated and not merely self-satisfied. Opinion-sharing sessions are like junk food: they fill you up with starch and leave you feeling both sated and hungry. A sustained inquiry into the truth of a matter is an almost athletic experience; it may exhaust you, but it also improves you.

So, to sum up, it is not the case either that the boundary line I wish to preserve is hopelessly blurred and impossible to respect or that respecting it would result in a cramped or impoverished or passionless academic experience. Nevertheless there are points in Kiss's and Euben's critique of my position with which I agree, although not always for the reasons they give in making them. They say, for example, that I ignore "the vast and varied terrain of general undergraduate education, professional and vocational education, residential life, and extracurricular activity on America's college and university campuses." Yes, I do, and the reason I do is captured in the word "extracurricular," that is, to the side of the curriculum. Although the core of a college or university experience should be the academic study of the questions posed by the various disciplines, that core is surrounded by offices of housing, transportation, recreation, financial aid, advising, counseling, student services, and much more. On any campus that is not a virtual online campus, these and other activities are necessary adjuncts to the undergraduate experience; but they are not academic, even though they support and in some instances make possible what goes on in the classroom and the laboratory. Therefore those who engage in them, either on the student side or the staff side, should not receive academic credit for doing so. I have no objection to internship programs, community outreach, peer tutoring, service-learning, and so on as long as they are not thought of as satisfying graduation or grade requirements. The exceptions one might think of do not weaken my point but make it clearer: a student who returns from an internship experience and writes an academic paper (as opposed to a day-by-day journal or a "what-I-did-on-my-summer-vacation" essay) analyzing and generalizing on her experience should get credit for it; and a student in a school of education who teaches in an inner-city school under faculty supervision should certainly get credit for that; it is part of her academic training.

Kiss and Euben also assert that my "portrait of the academy . . . leaves little room for community colleges, 'offices of cooperative extension and tech transfer,' for older students seeking to improve their professional credentials, or indeed for any preprofessional program." I'm not sure about community colleges; the ones I know are as academic at their core as any four-year school. As for preprofessional programs and professional schools, they may or may not have title to the rubric "academic," depending on whether or not what goes on in them is academic in nature or is more in the nature of a trade school. Kiss and Euben observe correctly that the "core mission" of professional education, as it is usually understood, inescapably involves influencing "students' behavior beyond [the] classroom" by putting them in possession of skills they are expected to apply directly in a specific line of work. If this is, in fact, what transpires in a particular professional school—if students are taught methods and techniques in the absence of any inquiry into their sources, validity, philosophical underpinnings, and the like—that professional school is not the location of any intellectual activity and is "academic" only in the sense that it is physically housed in a university. The question "Is it academic or is it job training?" is endlessly debated in the world of law schools, where there is an inverse relationship between hands-on training (of the kind apprentices used to receive before there were law schools) and prestige. The higher ranked the law school, the less its students will be put in touch with the nitty-gritty of actual practice and the more versed they will be in the arcana of interpretive theory, moral philosophy, Coasian economics, and even literary criticism. It is commonplace for graduates of top-ten law schools to report that the law school experience left them unprepared to deal with the tasks and problems they encountered as working lawyers. In response, a law school faculty might reply—and by so replying reinforce the distinction I have been insisting on—"We are intellectuals, not mechanics or plumbers; what we do is teach you how to think about the things we think about, and what we prepare you for is life as a law professor; that's our job, the rest you get elsewhere."

Two final (and related) points. Kiss and Euben remark that while I spend a great deal of time flagging this or that danger, I offer "little positive guidance." For example, I offer no answer to the question "If colleges and universities don't think about how their curriculum and climate is likely to shape student values and behavior, then who should?" Beats me! But I don't see why that's a question I have to answer. My argument has been about what academic activity is and what it is not; it is an argument, in short, that defines the scope and limit of the competence academics can appropriately claim and exercise, and rather than committing me to pronounce on matters outside that competence, it forbids me to do so. And as for "positive guidance," I don't think that any more is required beyond what I have given. I will, however, provide a kind of golden rule in the form of a question you can ask yourself if you are in doubt as to whether you are performing as an academic or as something else (a something else, I should add, that might be equally or even more valuable). "In saying or writing this, am I trying to get at the truth about some matter of intellectual concern or am I trying to advance my personal (no doubt deeply held and perhaps useful to society) views about character or about citizenship or about social justice or about anything (remembering always that anything, and certainly these, can legitimately be the topics of an academic discussion as long as that discussion is not politics in disguise)?" The question is at once a bit unwieldy and decidedly unhelpful if what you want is a detailed checklist of the characteristics that mark off truly academic activity from other kinds. Rather than offering any such checklist, I have been eliminating items that might be thought to appear on it. It's not content—any content can become the object of academic analysis; it's not the absence of a real-world connection—any subject matter treated inside the academy will have a relationship, indeed many relationships, to the outside; it's not detachment and ironic distance—academics are committed to the arguments they offer with much passion and no irony. What then is it and how does one recognize it? I borrow my answer from the famous pronouncement of Justice Potter Stewart: "I know it when I see it." And, I would add, so do you.

Notes

1. Weinrib, "Legal Formalism," 958.
2. Fish, "Make 'Em Cry."
3. The historian Hayden White once told me that you're going to have a bad day on the lecture circuit when the first or second question you get is about the Holocaust because then you know they are out for blood and not for knowledge.

THE PATHOS OF THE UNIVERSITY   *The Case of Stanley Fish*

Setting the Stage

There are two questions seldom asked by the faculty and administrators of universities: "What are universities for?" and "Who do they serve?" There are, no doubt, many reasons why these questions are not asked. Some may not ask these questions because they assume the answer or answers to the questions are so obvious they do not need to be raised. Moreover universities are doing so well, everyone thinks it a good thing to be educated, these questions do not need to be explored. It may also be the case that many assume that answers to these questions are so various, particularly given the multi-university, that any answer is too complex to be of much use.

Yet I think a more straightforward reason underlies the unwillingness to ask these questions, that is, we do not ask them because we sense that we, that is, those of us who administer and teach at universities, have no ready answers to give. The university may pride itself as being the place that embodies the proposition that the unexamined life is not worth living, but like most people and institutions we know that to be false. As the novelist Peter DeVries observed, the unexamined life may not be worth living but the examined life is no bowl of cherries either.[1]

Those who run and those who teach in the modern university simply have no idea how they might provide an answer to the question of what the university is for or who it is to serve. As a result we are content to comfort ourselves by repeating familiar slogans about the importance of being an educated person who can think critically. Which, as I will suggest below, means that those who have gone to universities, particularly top-tier universities, will have greater earning power.

I need to be clear: I am not blaming anyone for this state of affairs. It is just the way the world, and in particular the world of the university, has gone. But neither do I think the inability of those at universities to raise these questions or explore the answers to them is good for the health or survival of the university. When we do not know how to approach these questions—and explore the ways in which they are related—too often answers are given that tend to make universities something they should not be.

In order to show why this is so, I will explore the case made by Stanley Fish in a series of essays in the *Chronicle of Higher Education* that suggest the university does not need to answer questions of purpose or service. I do so because no one makes the case more clearly than Fish that the purpose and justification of the university is quite simply to support Stanley Fish's work as a literary critic. I focus on the case Stanley Fish makes for the university because what he has to say is so marvelously candid. Fish simply says what I think anyone should say who accepts the world in which we find ourselves, that is, a world in which there no longer exist any common judgments about the true, the good, and the beautiful. In such a world the university at best is conceived as a lovely poem that creates its own meaning. You do not need to ask what it is for or who it serves because such questions threaten its very character.

I will argue, however, that the university so understood cannot be sustained or justified. Fish's understanding of the university is betrayed by the subservience of the university to money. But money is but the medium to name the necessary service the university should perform for those who care about what universities can and should be. Which is but another way to say that universities cannot avoid questions concerning what they are and who they serve.[2]

I need to be candid about my own agenda in trying to force the question of use and service. I am trying to think through what difference it might make that a university should be in service to an institution called the church. I want to explore the difference it might make for a university that gains its purpose from a people who worship God for how knowledges are conceived and related. I hope to show Stanley Fish that given what he loves, he would be better off teaching at a university that wants him to study Milton because Milton thought God matters.

Fish's Defense of the University

In the essays Stanley wrote for the *Chronicle of Higher Education* he argues that neither the professors or administrators in the modern university should take a stand on any social, political, or moral issue.[3] In the first essay, "Save the World on Your Own Time," Fish criticizes Bob Kerrey, president of the New School, for calling for a regime change in Iraq. Fish has no objection to Kerrey taking such a position as a citizen, but he holds that if Kerrey was speaking as a university president he betrayed his role as a representative of the university.[4] He did so because, according to Fish, "it is immoral for academics or for academic institutions to proclaim moral views."

It is important to note that Fish is not suggesting that the university has no moral purpose. He quite clearly says that "it is immoral" for academics to proclaim moral views. So he is making a moral argument against those who want to use the university to support moral causes that are not intrinsic to the purpose of the university. Such purpose Fish identifies as that made in a faculty report to the president of the University of Chicago in 1967, that the "university exists only for the limited purposes of teaching and research." The report concluded that "since the university is a community only for those limited and distinctive purposes, it is a community which cannot take collective action on the issues of the day without endangering the conditions for its existence and effectiveness."

Fish argues that the university can and should take action on issues relevant to its educational mission, that is, the integrity of scholarship, the evil of plagiarism, and the value of a liberal education. But he argues against those who suggest the university must be a "free speech zone" in the interest of sustaining liberal democracies. Nor should universities use their wealth to put pressure on South Africa or Israel to be more just. The crucial question regarding any action contemplated by the university—actions such as providing places and times for controversial speakers or causes—is whether the decision to do so is justified on educational grounds.

This applies also to the classroom. The moral responsibility of professors is to teach their subjects. Their task is not to teach peace or war, to advocate nationalism or antinationalism, or to try to enlist students in their favorite causes. Such matters may be part of their teaching only if they are intrinsic to their field of study. The only advocacy appropriate to the classroom is that identified with the intellectual virtues of "thoroughness, perseverance, intellectual honesty," which are necessary for the pursuit of the truth. That is what the American public expects of teachers: to pursue truth, and if you are not in the pursuit of truth business you should not be in the university.

In a subsequent essay, "Aim Low," Fish develops his position by warning against confusing democratic values with academic ones. The task of an academic should not be to try to produce students who have a commitment to moral and civic responsibility. It may be a good thing for students to have respect for others, but the development of such respect is not and should not be the goal of academic training. Indeed Fish contends that if such a goal is made central to the work of the university, then what the university should fundamentally be about will be compromised. Even more important, however, Fish argues that the university should only try to aim for that which it *can* do. It is simply beyond the power of those who make up the university to promise to provide moral and civic education. What has to be recognized is that democratic and educational values are not the same and to confuse them can corrupt the educational mission.

Finally Fish argues in "The Same Old Song" that the argument he has been making concerning the university is but a version of the case he has made for some time in defense of the hermetic narrowness of disciplines. A discipline becomes a discipline, at least a discipline that deserves recognition in the university, by having distinct focus that allows its practitioners to prove the utility of their subject to other academics. In short, a discipline becomes important just to the extent those in the discipline represent knowledge unavailable without the narrow focus they represent.

Moreover, what is true of disciplines should be true of the university as a whole. Of course the university is under pressure from parents and politicians to achieve goals they desire, for example, higher paying jobs or conservative political positions. But the university should resist those who would demand that the university be what it cannot be. Rather the university's purpose is "quite simply to produce and disseminate (through teaching and publication) academic knowledge and to train those who will take up that task in the future." The university is in the business of the search for truth as an end in itself and fidelity to that task means the university cannot be in the business of forming character or fashioning citizens. In short, the university is a "self-consuming" artifact.

The Background of Fish's Argument Concerning the University

Fish's argument in defense of the apolitical character of the university is but a footnote to the case he makes in his book *Professional Correctness: Literary Studies and Political Change*.[5] In his book Fish takes aim at the new historicists and those in cultural studies who think their task is the study of literature in the interest of political change. In contrast Fish argues that the literary critic is not and should not be an organic intellectual (Gramsci) but rather should aspire to be "a specialist, defined and limited by the traditions of his craft, and it is a condition of his labors, at least as they are exerted in the United States, that he remain distanced from any effort to work changes in the structure of society" (*Professional Correctness*, 1).

Literary criticism must, therefore, be a distinctive enterprise. By distinctive Fish means simply that it must be what it is in itself and not something else. To be so distinctive secures autonomy for the discipline, but autonomy means simply that those engaging in literary criticism have responsibility "for doing a job the society wants done" (20).[6] Fish observes that at one time some pursued a literary life to secure a position at court, but that day is long past. Now

> literary activity is increasingly pursued in the academy where proficiency is measured by academic standards and rewarded by the gatekeepers of an academic guild. The name for this is professionalism, a form of organization in which membership is acquired by a course of special training whose end is the production of persons who recognize one another not because they regularly meet at the same ceremonial occasions (unless one equates an MLA meeting with the Elizabethan court), but because they perform the same "moves" in the same "game." That is, they participate in the same "immanent intelligibility" whose content is the same set of "internal"—not foreign—purposes. (32)

Fish acknowledges that the emergence of the profession of literary studies has been a development of the last hundred years. Moreover, there have been costs for this development, not the least being the "difficulty of connecting up specifically literary work with the larger arenas in which it was once able to intervene" (43). Some may lament this development, but Fish argues that you cannot reverse what has happened. Those in cultural studies who think they can change society by focusing their attention on television rather than poetry will only be frustrated. The new historicists' desire to substitute political agendas for the standards appropriate to the academy are simply unrealizable.

Fish does not deny that if enough literary scholars work with an eye for immediate political effect and call what they do literary criticism then literary criticism will be what they do. But Fish argues such a development would come at a great loss, that is, the skills of close reading that now give a distinctive identity to the profession of literary studies will suffer. Fish does not claim that the close reading learned from new criticism cannot be replaced by the new historicism, but such a replacement means that literary critics will no longer be doing what he does (69).

With his usual candor Fish tells us that the reason he does his work in the manner he does it is because "I like the way I feel when I am doing it" (110). He claims this is quite similar to virtue being its own reward. Like virtue, literary criticism can be difficult, but it is the very difficulty that draws Fish to engage in it. He says,

> I like being brought up short by an effect I have experienced but do not yet understand analytically. I like trying to describe in flatly prosaic words the achievement of words that are anything but flat and prosaic. I like savouring the physical "taste" of language at the same time that I work to lay bare its physics. And when those pleasures have been (temporarily) exhausted, I like linking one moment in a poem to others and then to moments in other works, works by the same author or by his predecessors or contemporaries or successors. It doesn't finally matter which, so long as I can *keep going*, reaping the cognitive and tactile harvest of an activity as self-reflexive as I become when I engage in it. (110)

Fish does not try, just as he argues that universities should not try, to provide an external justification for his work as a literary critic. The only justification is the practice of literary criticism itself. Those who might object that there must be a normative structure by which any such practice can be assessed simply fail to recognize that no such structure exists. Rather justification can only be provided within the history of the discipline. "Justification never starts from scratch, and can only begin if everything it seeks to demonstrate is already taken for granted" (113).

Accordingly, no one, Fish argues, ever chooses a profession or a discipline because of moral and philosophical considerations. You discover your life's work after many false starts by one day finding "yourself in the middle of doing something, enmeshed in its routines, extending in every action its assumptions. And when the request for justification comes, you respond *from the middle*, respond with the phrases and platitudes of disciplinary self-congratulation. . . . Justification is not a chain of inferences, but a circle, and it proceeds, if that is the word, by telling a story in which every detail is an instantiation of an informing spirit that is known only in the details but always exceeds them" (113).

Fish's arguments against attempts to justify the work of the university on grounds other than what the university can and should do is obviously an extension of his understanding of his discipline of literary criticism. He does not deny that the relationship between academic practices and social and political change is a matter of degree. For example, the introduction of noncanonical texts into the curriculum may have had an effect on students in their roles as citizens, churchgoers, parents, and so on. But the problem with such "success" is that it cannot be counted on, particularly in the United States.

Some may say so much the worse for the United States, but Fish observes that being "sequestered" in the university has advantages. Thus many academics, who, in the name of progressive causes, have recently sought increased attention by the wider society, have instead had to endure a right-wing backlash. Fish observes, therefore, that it may not be a "bad thing after all that in the United States those who operate the levers of commerce and government do not give much heed to what goes on in our classrooms or in our learned journals" (96). This, I take it, is the reason Fish argues in his essays in the *Chronicle of Higher Education* that administrators and professors should not use their positions to argue for social and political causes. He desires the university to be politically irrelevant in order to save the university from politics: that is, from having to say who the university serves and what it is for.

Money

Yet something seems missing from this picture. What I think is missing is money—a strange absence given Fish's avowal that he is a dedicated consumer. You need money to be a consumer and Stanley Fish has never apologized for being well paid. He also wants his fellow academics to be well paid. So he is acutely aware that the university runs on money, but the need for money does not seem to enter into his account of the nature of the university.

He does acknowledge that many parents send their children to the university in the hope that the education they receive will increase their ability to make money. Fish has no reason to deny that such a result may be a by-product of a university education, but he seems to object to making the making of money the purpose of the university. But it is not clear why those who think the university should be about helping their children make more money should be persuaded by Fish's justification of the university. Why, for example, should anyone pay Stanley Fish to gain such pleasure from his reading of Milton?[7]

Fish may object that his account of the university is meant to defeat such questions, but I do not think even on his own grounds he is able to do so. In his justification for the university he appeals to "the value of a liberal education" as well as the academic virtue of the conscientious "pursuit of truth." But for whom is liberal education a "value" and why is the pleasure Fish gets from his study of Milton to be identified with the "pursuit of truth"? If liberal education is a value then surely some account is needed to explain for whom it is a value. Moreover, whoever it is that values liberal education needs to sustain that education with the only measure we have of value, that is, money.

In a review of *Professional Correctness* Terry Eagleton observes that Fish's argument is "a plea for old-style New Critical textual autonomy, but one couched in the terms of the very theory such 'close readers' find most unpalatable. As such *Professional Correctness* repeats its author's customary maneuver of deploying sophisticated theory for anti-theoretical ends, wheeling up avant-garde notions to defend the status-quo."[8] Eagleton argues that this leaves Fish without any justification for his work as a literary critic. Fish has rejected the humanist case for studying literature (it makes you a better person) as well as the radical case (it aids political liberation), leaving him with what is essentially a hedonist avowal of how he feels when he does literary criticism.

In this respect Fish's adherence to close reading may be open to Frank Lentricchia's criticism of modernist poets. Lentricchia argues that modernist writers like Frost and Eliot defined themselves against the standards of the mass market by becoming champions of radical originality and makers of "a one in a kind text." But their very attempt to preserve an independent selfhood against the market, against money, was subverted by the market, not because they wrote according to popular formulas but because they gave us "their poems as delicious experiences of voyeurism, illusions of direct access to the life and thought of the famous writer, with the poet inside the poem like a rare animal in a zoo. This was the only commodity Frost and Eliot were capable of producing: the modernist phenomenon as product, mass-culture's ultimate revenge on those who would scorn it."[9]

In like manner, Fish's attempt to preserve the autonomy of the university can result in the self-deceptive strategy of hiding on the part of those who administer and teach in the university whose interests they serve even though they claim to serve none (if they are as honest as Fish) but themselves. Fish's account of the university simply avoids the reality, the reality money names, of the universities in which Fish taught and administered. James Engell and Anthony Dangerfield have, I think, named that reality in an admirably straightforward manner when they observe:

The fastest-expanding and often strongest motivation in American higher education is now money. While other aims and functions certainly persist, they are increasingly eclipsed by this ultimate goal of wealth accumulation. Money, rather than a means, is becoming the chief end of higher education. With growing frequency, the ends are not cultural values or critical thinking, ethical convictions or intellectual skills. When these goals are pursued, it is often not because they offer multiple uses and relevance but because they might be converted into cash.[10]

Engell and Dangerfield provide evidence for this development by calling attention to the implication money has had for the preferred fields of study in the contemporary university. Fish's account of the professional development of disciplines simply betrays the fact that the disciplines that flourish in the contemporary university are those that study money (economics), are the source of money (sciences), or are linked, often it seems mistakenly, to future chances of being in an occupation or profession that promises a high earning standard (*Saving Higher Education in the Age of Money*, 89). As a result, Engell and Dangerfield argue, the humanities' "vital signs are poor. . . . Since the late 1960s the humanities have been neglected, down-graded, and forced to retrench, all at a time when other areas of higher education have grown in numbers, wealth, and influence" (88).

Engell and Dangerfield observe that humanists have often been com-plicit in the loss of a central role for the humanities within the university. "Just as the cult of money was laying siege to the culture of learning, many beleaguered exponents of humanistic study divided into parties and em-barked on a series of unedifying public disputes, including ones that degraded the name, 'humanist'" (98). At the same time, many in the humanities discovered they were "interdisciplinary"—but it was an inter-disciplinarity that became even more specialized than the specializations they had purportedly left. What was lost was any attempt to show how the humanities have as one of their essential tasks to incorporate results from other areas of endeavor, not the least being science, through judgments of human value, relevance, and significance (99).[11]

Unlike Fish, however, Engell and Dangerfield argue that the university cannot survive if the purpose for its existence is disavowed. First of all, the university cannot exist as a loose aggregate of its separate parts quite simply because the university is not a capital market. The university serves other purposes which may not be inimical to the market; indeed they may even be beneficial to the market, but the university is constitutive of goods too complex to be subjected to questions of employment. Universities simply cannot avoid decisions about what forms of knowledge are most worth having.[12] Therefore it may be that the university must insist that certain disciplines be developed and taught because they are necessary for making us a better people.

Engell and Dangerfield argue that the most determinative corruption of the university that money creates is that the moral purpose of the univer-sity is lost. The power of money works, to be sure in a manner often difficult to discern, to undermine by degrees the essential goals and inde-pendent functions of the university. These are goals and functions, more-over, that other institutions either do not pursue or do not pursue nearly so well (20). Those goals and functions, Engell and Dangerfield suggest, are captured by Edward Shils's claim that "the discovery and transmission of truth is the distinctive task of the academic profession" (102).

But is that not what Fish also says? Engell and Dangerfield at least seem to differ from Fish because they think the future of democracies depends on universities producing people who can steer us, as they put it, "through these complex and perilous times." Such people must be those who have mastered language, who can put together sound arguments, who have learned from the past,

> and who have witnessed the treacheries and glories of human experi-
> ence profoundly revealed by writers and artists. The humanities can
> and should be broadly instrumental, as well as existing for pleasure and
> aesthetic pursuits. Their functions are multiple. Especially with regard
> to the uses of language, history, and ethical reflection—as well as alert-
> ing everyone to their abuses—the humanities can keep our collective
> capacities for thinking flexible, adaptable, inquisitive, tolerant, and
> open, and not only open to reasoned discourse but actively involved in
> shaping the best expression of that discourse. (2005, 103)

This may well be, however, what Fish means when he appeals to the value of a liberal education. Yet Engell and Dangerfield, in a manner unlike Fish, argue that it is not enough for the university to be about the pursuit and preservation of knowledge; it must also consider that knowledge in the light of its potential to promote the human good. They quite rightly have a chapter critical of how ethics has become another specialized discipline of the university, and they argue that "ethics" is inseparable from every subject and activity of the university.[13] Appealing to Cardinal Newman, they remind us that though Newman is often used to justify the pursuit of knowledge for its own sake, he actually sets a higher and final goal: that "all knowledge, whether applied or relished alone, is to be considered in light of ethical conduct and human good" (131).

I suspect that Fish will not find the case Engell and Dangerfield make for saving the university from the subversion of money to be an interesting alternative to the position he developed in his essays in the *Chronicle*. Engell and Dangerfield may have called attention to a subversion of the university which belies Fish's account, but Fish without contradiction can acknowledge that the university may well not conform to his "ideal." Fish can even acknowledge that Engell's and Dangerfield's suggestion that all knowledge is to be considered in the light of the human good is not foreign to his understanding of the university. He did say that it was "immoral" for academics to proclaim moral views.

Moreover, Engell and Dangerfield do not, just as Fish does not, suggest who is going to pay for the university they think is in danger of being lost. They begin their book by noting that they are not advocating "a return to some era when money exerted little or no force in higher education" (1). Indeed, one wonders if such a time ever existed, but Engell and Dangerfield do not tell us who will pay for the university they think should exist. Money is but a name for people the university is meant to serve. "What is the university for?" and "Who does the university serve?" are questions the fundraisers for universities cannot avoid.[14] Yet it is not clear whether Engell and Dangerfield have provided, in the world as we know it, any better answers to those questions than Fish has done. For in effect Fish has said that in a world in which such questions cannot be answered, it is best not to ask them in the hope that those who support and those who come to universities will let us do what we like to do. Engell and Dangerfield, however, can argue that Fish's refusal to justify the university as a moral enterprise for the societal good means that Fish can have no objection to the transformation of university curricula by money. Engell and Dangerfield believe that if the university is to be the place of truthful speech, it is important that it commit, for example, to teaching students Milton. Yet that is the kind of justification that Fish seems to want to avoid.

In contrast to Fish, Engell and Dangerfield are right to insist that the university must have a moral purpose, but it is not clear that their understanding of that purpose is an advance beyond Fish. At the very least they owe us an account of whose moral purpose the university represents. Vague appeals to the importance of the university for democracy are not sufficient. Even more important, Engell and Dangerfield need to tell us if those who represent the moral purpose they identify as the heart of the university, that is, the formation of people of truth, are willing to support that purpose with money.

Why Virtue Is Not Its Own Reward

I noted earlier that Stanley Fish defends his understanding of what he does as a literary critic on the grounds that virtue is its own reward. But Aristotle did not think that virtue was its own reward. Aristotle's account of the virtues requires that the virtuous one be recognized by the community as having attained the good life. In contrast, the Stoics thought that virtue was its own reward because the polis, which at least imaginatively informed Aristotle's account of virtue, no longer existed. Empire not polis shaped the world in which the Stoics had to think through what a worthy life might entail. Virtue had to become its own reward because there no longer existed any politics necessary to name as well as make intelligible a virtuous life. The Stoics provided the best account available for the moral formation of bureaucrats destined to serve an empire.

I am aware that the suggestion that Fish's advocacy of virtue as its own reward reflects a Stoic-like account of morality may seem far-fetched, but I am much less interested in what Fish may have meant by his appeal to virtue than the context his remarks reflect. That context I take to be the social order called America that is determinatively shaped by liberal political practice. "Liberal" names the assumption that a social order should be constituted by procedural arrangements that require no account of goods held in common. Those procedural arrangements are often articulated by "values" such as freedom and equality that are assumed to be universals that all people share. That is why America can be an imperial power without recognizing that it is so—because Americans believe that all people, if they had our money and education, would want to be just like us.

Fish, of course, has been an unrelenting critic of the epistemological conceits that have been used to justify liberal political arrangements.[15] Yet, as Eagleton notes in his review of *Professional Correctness*, the relativist Fish occasionally remembers that his position is provincially American. Eagleton suggests that Fish "represents the perilous situation of American intellectuals bleakly marooned in an extravagantly philistine, money-obsessed society."[16] Eagleton's comment, which is overly harsh, nonetheless suggests that the justification that Fish has given for the university, as well as his kind of literary criticism, in spite of his criticism of liberalism, is a reflection of as well as a reproduction of liberal theory and practice. The only way to justify reading Milton, or the other texts in the humanities, in a world that no longer believes in the God Milton believed in, is to make the text a self-consuming artifact. I need to be clear that I am not criticizing Fish for this result. What else can he do given the fact that there is no alternative?

The alternative that is missing, the alternative I suspect Fish might desire, is what Alasdair MacIntyre has called "the idea of an educated public."[17] MacIntyre notes that the primary purpose of the modern university, by which he means the university since the eighteenth century, has been to form young people to assume some social role and function that will require ongoing recruits. Its secondary purpose is to teach the young how to think for themselves. These aims depend on the purposes of the university finding articulation in the platitudes of the age as well as providing the final answer to a chain of questions of the form "For the sake of what is that being done?" (17).

MacIntyre argues, however, that these two aims, which are not necessarily incompatible, are incompatible in modernity. They are so because what modernity excludes is the existence of an educated public that represents judgments in answer to the question "For the sake of what is that being done?" According to MacIntyre, the existence of such a public depends on three conditions being met: (1) that a large number of individuals, educated into the habit and opportunity of active debate, exists to discern how the debate has implications for their shared social existence; (2) that there is a shared assent to standards by which the success or failure of any argument is to be judged; (3) that an educated community exists in which there is a shared background of beliefs informed by the widespread reading of a common body of texts which have canonical status within that particular community. The last condition requires that there is also a tradition of interpreted understanding of how the texts are to be read (19).

MacIntyre believes that eighteenth-century Scotland exemplified the kind of educated public that made intelligible the great university reforms of Scotland. However, he argues that the Scottish achievement was subverted in a manner that illumines our current situation. According to MacIntyre, the developments in philosophy of common sense resulted in a professionalization of philosophy through which the work of philosophy ceased to be intelligible to the common educated mind. Societal developments also played a role as the size of the population made it increasingly difficult for the virtues to flourish. Economic developments, in particular the specialization into different trades and professions, eroded civic virtues and diminished the degree to which individuals could understand their primary loyalties to society as a whole.

The results of these developments were magnified by the effect of economic growth on the class structure of the society in which the educated class was impotent and functionless in the face of the class conflicts between laboring and manufacturing classes. At the same time, the growth of specialization and the division of labor not only had an effect in industry but were reflected in the realm of knowledge and the curriculum of the university. The increasing professionalization made the specialized content of each discipline a subject matter that did not require knowledge of other disciplines. As a result the university could not help but become the exemplification of many different and incompatible modes of justification that made and makes it impossible for us to arrive at a common mind even about what we should be quarreling about (26–28). In short, we got the university Stanley Fish celebrates.

MacIntyre notes that someone might object that even if he has shown what brought an end to an educated public in Scotland, he has not shown that the making and remaking of an educated public is in fact presupposed by the modern educational system. He responds, however, noting that if you take away the presumption of such a public with shared standards of justification, with a shared view of the past of the society, with a shared ability to participate in a public debate, the result will be that knowledges represented by the liberal arts and sciences cannot help but be transformed into passively received consumer products (29).

One may well deem MacIntyre's account of the Scottish educated public an exercise in romantic nostalgia, but I think it provides a useful contrast to help us understand why Stanley Fish does not try to justify the university as an institution in the business of the moral formation of students. I think MacIntyre's analysis also helps us understand why Engell and Dangerfield, who believe that the knowledges of the university should be in service to ethical conduct, must leave what they mean by "ethical conduct" vague. Fish, Engell, and Dangerfield simply lack the authority made possible by an educated public to make the arguments necessary for the university to serve moral ends.

Which finally brings me to the difference it might make if a university had or may even have some relation to the church. For at the very least Christianity names an ongoing argument across centuries of a tradition which has established why some texts must be read and read in relation to other texts. Christians, for all their shortcomings, still represent an ongoing educated public, which means that they must, as MacIntyre suggests any educated public must, have agreements that make their disagreements intelligible. As a result, Christians should, if they are not intimidated by the secular academy, produce knowledges and the interconnection of those knowledges that can appropriately form students.[18]

Christians should know what their universities are for. They are to shape people in the love of God. Christians should know who their universities serve. They serve a people who must recognize that the university at its best, the kind of university Stanley Fish is willing to defend, is not the kind of university we should want. If Christians are a people with an alternative history of judgments about what is true and good, they cannot help but produce an alternative university. Which means Christians must be those who are ready to match their convictions with their money. If one of the most important questions you can ask is who a university serves, then it becomes all the more important that those who are served are also those who support the university with money.

It is not at all clear what a university supported by Christians might look like in our day. But I am convinced if Christians had the will and imagination to try to create such a university, a creation that no doubt would use the resources of universities that now claim to be Christian, we would not only surprise ourselves at how interesting such a university would be but we might also discover that Stanley Fish might want to teach at such an institution. For a university so constituted would be able to provide reasons to justify why no one graduating from the university should be ignorant of how Stanley Fish teaches us to read Milton.

Notes

1. Peter Euben pointed out to me that these questions may not be asked because those who administer and teach at universities have a profound stake in being ignorant of any answers we might find. He observes that universities tend to absent themselves from the questions they insist other institutions ask and answer.

2. That I shifted the grammar in this sentence to the plural is significant. To focus on *the* university can imply that the university has an "essence" that all universities and colleges share. I simply do not believe such an essence exists. There are no doubt family resemblances between universities that may be useful to name, but to talk about "the university" too often is an attempt to avoid questions of purpose and consistency.

3. Fish's essays appeared in the *Chronicle Careers* on January 23, 2003, May 16,

2003, and July 11, 2003. He also published an essay in the *New York Times* titled "Why We Build the Ivory Tower" on June 1, 2004.

4. Fish seems to assume that the category of "citizen" is intelligible—an assumption that certainly requires defense. Colleges and universities often claim they are educating the young to be "global citizens" but such a claim is unintelligible. Citizenship only makes sense in terms of role responsibilities correlative of a particular history and place. "Global" denotes universal pretensions that should challenge the assumptions necessary to sustain an intelligible account of citizenship. That universities use the language of "global" and "citizenship" to define their purpose is but an indication of the false consciousness that dominates university life.

5. Fish, *Professional Correctness*. Hereafter cited parenthetically by page number in the text.

6. One might wish that Fish offered a more extensive account of how disciplines are autonomous yet do a job society wants done. At the very least Fish owes us an account of the history of the development of "disciplines" just to the extent such a history reveals the quite contingent contexts that make and unmake the disciplines and the knowledges they represent.

7. Fish loves to challenge students who express admiration for Milton's poetry by pointing out that Milton did not want their admiration. He wanted their souls. Fish, therefore, insists that anyone who would understand Milton's poetry must remember that his poetry is only conflicted, tragic, paradoxical, or inconclusive if you forget that for Milton "God is God and not one of a number of contending forces" (*How Milton Works*, 14). I think Fish is right about this, but it does raise a question about his justification for his understanding of literary criticism. Why should Milton be read as a "literary" text? Milton, as Fish often does so well, should be read in the context of Christian theology. That Milton is often not read by Christian theologians is one of the reasons that Milton has become the property of English departments, but that is but a reminder of the failure of theology.

8. Eagleton, "The Death of Self-Criticism," 6. Eagleton's critique is a challenge to Fish's contention that theory has no consequences. See, for example, Fish's important essay "Consequences" in his book *Doing What Comes Naturally*, 315–41. I am quite sympathetic with Fish's argument against theory on grounds that the general can never be substituted for the local. Indeed my criticism of his defense of the university is that he fails to adequately locate the "local" that makes the university intelligible to itself.

9. Lentricchia, *Modernist Quartet*, 112–13.

10. Engell and Dangerfield, *Saving Higher Education in the Age of Money*, 2. Hereafter cited parenthetically in the text.

11. Engell and Dangerfield do not believe, just as Fish does not believe, that studying the humanities can guarantee a moral outcome. On the contrary, they observe that "like the uses of all knowledge, the uses of literature *guarantee* nothing. Its knowledge acts as an instrumentality. Like a scalpel or laser, it can heal or lance a cavity swollen with prejudice. It can also destroy, kill or justify killing. Many ss officers were well educated" (166).

12. Engell and Dangerfield quote an observation by the former president of the University of Minnesota, Mark Yudof: "The unvarnished truth is that the extraordinary compact between state governments and their flagship universities appears to be dead—or at least on life support. For more than a century, these two parties had a deal: In return for financial support from taxpayers, these universities would keep tuition low and provide broad access for undergraduates from all economic strata, train graduate and professional students, promote arts and culture, help solve local problems, and perform groundbreaking research. Unfortunately, the agreement between the states and their flagship universities has deteriorated for 25 years, leaving public research universities in a purgatory of insufficient resources—low tuition and flat appropriations" (186). I think at least one of the reasons for this development was the inability of the university to articulate for itself and for those it served the moral purpose of the university. Instead the sciences were held up to promise that the university would cure this or that disease or to give us power over "nature." But how do you provide an account of the moral purposes of the university in a social order no longer sure what its moral character is or should be?

13. In particular they argue for the importance of history. "Commercial leadership without historical imagination produces inefficiency, repetition of failed strategies, lack of situational awareness, and strategic miscalculation of long-term behaviors. When people successful in business have amassed fortunes and are prepared to aid society through philanthropy, a historical perspective helps ensure effective, meaningful gifts of lasting impact. Scientific leadership without knowledge of history of science risks unethical applications. Political leadership without historical consciousness results, at best, in blunders and ineffectiveness, at worst in fiasco and tragedy" (121).

14. Academics generally disdain the fundraising side of the university, but I have long thought that development is the most determinative form of the university's educational task. Teaching people why they should want to give money to the university is an ongoing test of the education the university provided to its alumnae. Those raising money must hope that those whom they must ask to give money were well enough educated to understand why they should want to fund an institution that teaches that making money cannot be what constitutes a good life.

15. See, for example, his wonderful response to Stephen Carter, "Liberalism Doesn't Exist," 134–38. Fish's critique of liberalism is a correlative of his attack on all forms of formalism.

16. Eagleton, "The Death of Self-Criticism," 6.

17. MacIntyre, "The Idea of an Educated Public." Hereafter cited parenthetically in the text.

18. What this means for Christians like me, who teach at secular universities, is an ongoing challenge. Such a challenge can be avoided by taking refuge in institutional arrangements, i.e., I teach in a seminary not a university. But that is far too easy an escape. That my university has a seminary is a testament to the historical background of the university as a Methodist institution. And this history should matter. But more important is the argument that Duke is a better university because the seminary is one of her educational units. That is an argument for another time. I would, however, argue that Christians in the undergraduate college should not avoid exploring what difference their convictions might make for why they do what they do. That difference will, of course, vary from subject to subject but surely such an investigation is the kind of work a university should sponsor. I obviously think that would be true of those working in other religious and nonreligious traditions. Of course, such work would make the university more conflictual, but I see no reason why that is a disadvantage.

ON THE DISTRIBUTION OF MORAL BADGES   *A Few Worries*

The notion of a *turn* to ethics in higher education should not mislead us. We shouldn't allow it to obscure either earlier assumptions about the centrality of moral education to the university's understanding of its mission, or current resistance to efforts to emphasize the moral dimension of education. There is something else it surely should not obscure: that whether or not we explicitly teach ethics or otherwise foreground morality in our curricula, we are ethical animals, always in the thick of ethical experience. This may involve something as relatively common as being called upon to decide whether an apology is in order, or as relatively rare as wondering whether or how to approach a colleague who you have good reason to believe is importuning students for sexual favors. We can't help but leave in the trail of our actions traces of beliefs or attitudes (of which we may or may not be explicitly aware) regarding what is morally allowable or unallowable, for example, or what is required or not required.

So the issue before us is not of course whether we can or should restore the moral register to our lives; it's always there, no matter how we sculpt the curriculum, no matter how many ethics committees or centers or conferences we create. The issue being debated in this volume is how much and in what ways liberal arts institutions should explicitly attend to that register. And insofar as there was a "retreat from ethics" among educators, it was not because moral experience was judged to be less central to our lives than we previously thought. Rather the retreat reflected changing understandings of the mission—or missions—

of educational institutions, changing views about the very nature of moral beliefs,[1] and perhaps the shifting influence of educational institutions (or their presidents) in the life of the nation. To the extent that the larger community turns to higher education for instruction and assistance today, how often is it to ask us to provide moral direction? Anecdotal evidence suggests, for example, that business leaders (and government officials like former Secretary of Education Margaret Spellings) don't much call upon us to help them figure out knotty moral problems but instead are much more likely to demand that we live and breathe by cost/benefit analysis. Instead of being asked to instigate and guide public reflection on, say, the fairness of wage differences between the CEOs of corporations and their average workers, educational institutions are asked why they can't provide the kinds of measures businesses rely on to demonstrate that what they offer is worth the price of admission.

Still, whether or not others appreciate it or seek it out, the question remains: what can our institutions offer in terms of moral education? We have a pretty good idea of what they can offer that other social institutions cannot—for example, certain kinds of skills, certain forms of knowledge that in general cannot (or only with considerable difficulty) be acquired elsewhere, for lack of appropriate guidance or adequate facilities. Learning history isn't merely a matter of reading what are called history books but also requires the development and exercise of critical and interpretive skills; one can't do chemistry without the right materials and equipment and training. But is moral judgment something for which colleges and universities can provide expertise? You can become a better historian on account of the instruction you get at our institutions; can you become a better moral judge, or a better moral actor?

Some institutions assert in their declared mission that they aspire to make the world a better place by educating students in the right way. (The mission statement of Smith College, for example, where I teach, proclaims that Smith "educates women of promise for lives of distinction. A college of and for the world, Smith links the power of the liberal arts to excellence in research and scholarship, developing leaders for society's challenges.") But I don't think educational institutions expect to be judged by our success or failure rate on this score. Certainly not explicitly. We don't try to entice applicants with open promises such as "Come to Magnificent U and you'll become a better person," nor attempt to snare them by offering explicit proof that graduates of Magnificent U are better people than graduates of Slacker State. When our institutions are in their peacock mode they don't claim they've won the competition to produce the best people, morally speaking; they try to justify their boasts by reference to admissions to law school, or numbers of PhDs or MDs, or ascensions to the rank of CEO, or Nobel laureates, or conference titles in football or basketball (or even more specifically their history of scholar-athletes). And even though alumni and alumnae magazines don't hesitate to use their glossy pages to feature the morally admirable works of their graduates, we do not think it appropriate to base our evaluations of students' work on how morally virtuous they are. This doesn't mean we do not assess their intellectual virtues (though yes, the distinction between intellectual and moral virtues is smudgy—a point to which I will return below). Nor does it mean that we don't reserve the right to punish students severely for certain kinds of moral infractions (e.g., dishonesty in the form of plagiarism, or sexual assault). But the best grade does not go to the most morally splendid person, except coincidentally. Nor do the best fellowships and the best jobs.

None of the above undermines the possibility that institutions of higher education can be and often are excellent places to acquire moral education —not in the form of an education for becoming moral but in terms of an education *about* morality, by way of learning about the history of debates in moral theory, or about the extent to which different cultures have or appear to have different moral underpinnings, or about the lives and works of individuals judged to be moral saints or sinners (e.g., Gandhi, Hitler). One shouldn't, of course, make too much of this distinction between learning about morality and learning to become moral, since it seems pretty clear that one of the ways people become morally virtuous, if they do, is by reflecting on what others have thought and on how others have led their lives. At the same time, we appear to hold dear the distinction between providing space for moral reflection and providing the opportunity for moral indoctrination, or, less tendentiously, for moral training of a determinate sort. We don't go so far as to say that a well-educated person must have a particular normative view, but we do go so far as to say that a well-educated person is morally reflective; that given the importance of morality in our lives, but also the complex demands it makes upon us, we need to acquire tools that can assist in such reflection.

It also must be said that even if we refuse to include any particular moral view in our portraits of the well-educated person, we do think that something must have gone wrong if a well-educated person ends up doing horrible things: think for example of the special shock accompanying the recognition that among the most energetic supporters of the Nazi regime were people with advanced degrees from reputable universities.

To the extent to which we seem dismayed, if no longer surprised, by the egregious intentional harm committed by what pass for well-educated persons, we reveal some degree of conviction that the intellectual virtues have not been adequately acquired if certain moral ones aren't there too. But what are these various virtues? In this connection we might find it useful to call upon a distinction developed by the philosopher of science Helen Longino in her discussion of the question of whether science is "value-free." Longino points out that while it is undeniable that scientific practice is governed by norms and values, there is a difference between *constitutive* values and *contextual* values. Constitutive values provide "the source of the rules determining what constitutes acceptable scientific practice or scientific method" (e.g., truth seeking prohibits the fudging of evidence to produce desired conclusions). One important question for the historian and philosopher of science is just how close such values are or should be to contextual values, that is, those values awash in "the social and cultural environment in which science is done."[2] For example, however much attention scientists think they ought to give to preventing disease, available funding may lead them to focus their research more on cure than prevention. Conversely, researchers today pay far more attention than they did in the relatively recent past to obtaining the informed consent of the human subjects used in their research, but this shift derives more from changes in broader contextual values than from values constitutive of the research process itself—although, as the example illustrates, over time changes in contextual values may reshape what is considered acceptable work within a given field.

Are the virtues we expect to find in well-educated people anything other than those necessary to perform acceptable work in one's field, those that reflect the values constitutive of one's field of inquiry? Stanley Fish appears to think that while we can try to inculcate such constitutive virtues, it would be wasted energy, or even dangerous to our constitutive virtues, and in any event beyond our professional purview, to try to encourage students to acquire other virtues, affirm other values, not so directly connected to teaching or research.[3] Kiss and Euben—with implicit support from the political commentator David Brooks among others—are worried that attention to constitutive values is not enough, and that we in effect abnegate our responsibility to students insofar as we do not engage them in discussion of values of a larger and less determinate scope of applicability, which are bound, as in the case of science, to affect the constitutive values.

Two points are in order about the very nature of this debate: First, though I introduced Helen Longino's distinction between constitutive and contextual values in the context of a discussion of the distinction between intellectual and moral virtues, the distinctions do not slice up the world in the same way. Indeed anyone who, like Stanley Fish, wishes to include virtues such as honesty and integrity as among those to be inculcated by and honored within the academy cannot be treating intellectual virtues as constitutive values of the academy and all moral virtues as dangerous contextual predators. Fish's position is more accurately described not as hostility to moral education per se but as hostility to any effort to expand the scope of moral education beyond those moral virtues constitutive of academic work, narrowly defined. Second, there seems to be no disagreement between Kiss, Euben, and Fish about at least one constitutive value of the academy: the importance of regular examination of and debate over what are or ought to be the constitutive values of the academy. That is, it seems safe to assume that neither Stanley Fish nor any other critic of the "turn to ethics" in higher education expects those to whom the criticism is directed either to ignore the criticism or to accept it wholeheartedly and foreclose further discussion. Were reflection on the constitutive values of the academy not understood to be at the center of those very values, Fish and others could not assume, as they surely do, that their provocations will be met with vigorous riposte.

Returning to the substantive question about the degree to which educational institutions can and should exclude any kind of moral education not carefully tailored to the intellectual requirements of a discipline: To the extent that we are, willy-nilly, having to make moral judgments all the time, our actions cannot help but express moral attitudes, whether or not we are trying to teach certain moral views; for no matter what we are teaching, what we are doing, we are reflecting all manner of moral judgments.

We don't expect to be called upon to make judgments that require knowledge of chemistry unless we make it our business to study chemistry. But we do expect to be called upon to make moral judgments at every turn—again, there has never been a "retreat from ethics" in this sense. Acknowledging the ubiquity of moral judgment and of contextual values might lend support to the view that whatever else students learn, they ought to be exposed to some kind of moral education—they can't get away from moral experience. Or at the very least, it may suggest that if faculty are projecting contextual values anyway, they may want to reflect more deeply on what they are doing and why. On the other hand, it also makes an exclusive focus on the moral education of *students* seem very strange.

All members of academic communities, whether faculty, administration, students or staff, are moral agents, and in the sense that there never is, never can be, a "retreat from ethics": all are always in the web of moral life. Why, then, should we focus our attention only on students? Are they the only members of the community in need of moral education? Are they the only members of the community we dare suggest are in need? Are they the only members of the community whose moral education could be within our purview? Every member of our communities is a moral agent. Why should we assume that only students need to become better at being moral agents? Do the faculty, staff, and administration have adequate training? Or only those with certain kinds of advanced degrees? When Derek Bok argues that colleges and universities should be "demonstrating high ethical standards in dealing with moral issues facing the university . . . being more alert to the countless signals that institutions send to students and trying to make these messages support rather than undermine basic norms,"[4] is he assuming that those in positions of leadership at such institutions themselves need to undergo moral education, or simply that they be more morally energetic? If they know what those high standards are and know how to live by them, is that because they got a good moral education at the universities they went to? If so, is that because there was a special effort to attend to their moral education? If not—if they learned to be capable of exercising moral leadership no matter what their majors or their interests were—then why should the universities at which they are now in leadership positions take on any special task of moral education?

It may well be that part of the "turn to ethics" is a healthy involvement of faculty and students in reflection on whether "colleges and universities, as powerful corporate entities, succeed or fail in setting high standards for internal conduct and external relations with their local, national, and international communities."[5] If that is so, why shouldn't everyone in the university community be involved in such reflection? Kohlberg's "just community" approach, as described by Kiss and Euben, involves "a culture of community building . . . where students and teachers can act on their moral decisions."[6] Why are other members of the college community out of the loop? Is the guiding assumption here that others aren't capable of arriving at or acting upon moral decisions, especially those who haven't received degrees in higher education? Or that they are capable but it is none of their business? Or that even if they like anybody else could benefit from more moral reflection, the jobs they have at the university don't require them to do that—presumably they've gotten enough moral education to be able to do their work well? But then if that is the case, why would students need any more moral education at this stage in their lives? The faculty doesn't seem to have needed anything special to acquire the moral direction they are now providing for the students, and the staff is presumed to be doing well enough, or their work assumed to be so irrelevant to the real business of the university, as not to need any attention at all.

There is another reason why limiting the "just community" to faculty and students seems odd. Decisions about the standards in accordance with which the institution conducts its internal affairs and its external relations affect all members of the community—including the trustees who oversee the institution's investments and the contractors and vendors with which it does business. Is the staff to be excluded from examination of such decisions? Or are they there mainly to execute the decisions made by others? Or to provide the setting in which the moral deliberations of those others can be carried out—not unlike, say, the chambermaids and kitchen help at the hotels in which we have our heady, heart-felt conferences about the meaning of justice? In this connection Kiss's and Euben's reference to Aristotle on practical wisdom invites a pertinent line of inquiry.[7]

As is well known, Aristotle thought that only a certain segment of the population was capable of attaining the kind of practical wisdom he had in mind; he also thought that despite their innate abilities to acquire such wisdom, it would remain out of their reach were they not free from the kind of labor involved in maintaining the material conditions of their lives. Those whose work is necessary to the existence of the polis ought not to participate in its deliberations, and those who do participate ought not to engage in the work that makes it possible. Those who do the necessary work (in Aristotle's case, of course, it was the wives of male citizens, male and female slaves, and the mass of laborers, male and female) are not without virtue, but their virtues are the limited virtues of limited people, people who are meant to be ruled by others. It is only in those people naturally meant to rule in whom we can hope to find examples of human excellence in its fully developed form. Yet if it weren't for the work of those in whom such excellence is not to be found, paragons of human flourishing—the good man, the good citizen—could not exist.

I am not of course suggesting that what Professors Kiss and Euben have in mind is a "return to ethics" that is also a return to the Aristotelian polis. But as we consider whether there are moral values, virtues or skills that ought to be embraced by and embodied in the actions of well-educated people, we have to ask whether we are assuming or gearing up to argue also for the view that such values, virtues, and skills are to be found only or mainly in well-educated people—that part of what is or at least ought to be distinctive about well-educated people is that they have (or anyway have taken the trouble to consider whether they ought to have) such values, virtues, and skills. Such a position is compatible with, even if not intended by, Kiss's and Euben's invitation to consider the possibility that moral learning requires the cultivation of analytical skills, a refined moral imagination, and virtues like empathy and courage. This hardly amounts to an unqualified endorsement of Aristotle's position about the distribution of possibilities for the acquisition of virtue. But we should examine closely to what extent the view implies a moral division of labor that reflects and helps sustain systematic inequalities elsewhere in the society.

Here, then, is the crux of my concern about Kiss's and Euben's approach. While Fish worries that explicit attention to the moral register of contextual values will corrupt the academic enterprise, my worry is that "the turn to ethics," by reinforcing the status inequalities that are already such a troubling feature of the academy and of our society, will further intensify the academy's role in legitimating and sustaining those inequalities.

In this connection we cannot fail to mention studies by Pierre Bourdieu and others to the effect that educational institutions tend on the whole to maintain and reproduce such inequalities. Given the enormous inertia of the economic, political, and social mechanisms that work to keep invidious hierarchies in place, surely we ought to be alert to ways in which the "turn to ethics" in higher education could turn out to be complicit in the creation or reproduction of a moral elite, of a special class of people who are understood to have achieved a degree of moral cultivation and refinement which is supposed to mark them as superior to, and to legitimate their social difference from, those of less cultivated, less refined sentiment.

From a Bourdieuian perspective, education is one of many societal institutions that function to produce economic capital in the form of greater wealth, social capital in the form of membership in powerful networks of people and institutions, and cultural capital in the form of distinctive and relatively rare knowledge, skills, and tastes that announce one's superior standing. One can acquire, for example, a certain kind of aesthetic sensibility and sensitivity:

> A work of art has meaning and interest only for someone who possesses the cultural competence, that is, the code, into which it is encoded. The conscious or unconscious implementation of explicit or implicit schemes of perception and appreciation which constitutes pictorial or musical culture is the hidden condition for recognizing the styles characteristic of a period, a school, or an author, and, more generally, for the familiarity with the internal logic of works that aesthetic enjoyment presupposes.[8]

Just as one's capacity to see a work of art, or hear a piece of music, depends on a certain cognitive mastery and affective cultivation and can be enhanced by working knowledge of aesthetic theory and art history, so also, from such a perspective, the ability to "read" the ethical landscape, to be attuned to the details and nuances of moral life, is enriched by a kind of acquaintance with the history of ethical thought that allows one to acquire conceptual ease with the evolving terms of debates within ethical theory—to speak easily about the difference between deontological and consequentialist views, or to hold forth authoritatively about the meaning of "virtue ethics."

Bourdieu argues that mere "technical competence" about such matters is not enough. A person might acquire "the capacity to understand, reproduce, and even produce political discourse, which is guaranteed by educational qualifications" and yet not be "socially authorized and encouraged" to be part of political deliberation and debate.[9] So, too, the achievement of a high level of aesthetic or ethical competence cannot by itself guarantee that one's voice will be sought out or listened to. There have to be ways of smoking out imposters and other incompetents—otherwise the class and status differences the possession of cultural capital is supposed to mark will lack the requisite definition.

Perhaps the remarks above about the exclusion of staff members at most institutions of higher education from moral debates on campus provide an illustration of some of the points Bourdieu is making. Typically, though mostly tacitly, part of what institutions of higher education promise is that there will be more than an economic difference between the degree-bedecked graduate and secretaries or those on the staff of the physical plant. But if secretaries and janitors and gardeners are assumed to have, or encouraged to acquire, the same cultural competence as faculty and students, that promise will appear not to have been kept.

Bourdieu's work invites the close attention of members of academic communities, especially given the growing pressure to regard higher education explicitly as a consumer good, an investment offering economic, social, and cultural returns. Indeed it is as if what in Bourdieu's own terms we are encouraged to treat as an esoteric academic understanding of certain functions of education (that is, Bourdieu's views themselves) has come back to bite the academy: what academics may treasure as insiders' carefully honed and not widely understood insight into the workings of cultural capital has become enthusiastically embraced, not sheepishly acknowledged, by consumers of education, who demand that it produce the kind of economic, social, and cultural capital Bourdieu describes (whether or not they've actually read Bourdieu).

The point of bringing up Bourdieu in this context is not to deny that some people have more moral insight than others, that some people are more honest than others, more loyal, more courageous, more fierce in their commitment to justice. But given the expectation that institutions of higher education will try to provide their graduates with a leg up in a highly competitive world, a world in which the idea of an equal playing field is still a cruel myth, we have to be very careful about how we describe the point of offering a kind or a depth of moral education not available elsewhere. We have to be very clear ourselves, and try to be as clear as possible to others, about the difference between (a) a promise that part of the cultural capital you will gain by graduating from our institutions is that you will be—or at least will be seen to be—a more morally knowledgeable and more deeply moral person, a better person, really, than those not so anointed; and (b) a recognition that there is moral learning as well as other kinds of learning, indeed that they are inextricably connected; and that educational institutions provide one of the places where moral education might be had—as much despite as because of the kinds of institutions they are.

What might it look like if colleges and universities undertook an explicit "turn to ethics" that was attentive to the dangers of distributing moral badges to an already privileged few? It would require a far more inclusive institutional culture of moral conversation and debate on campus—a conversation in which staff, for example, would be full participants. But this in turn would necessitate an honest willingness to tackle the barriers of status and vocabulary that make such conversations so difficult and rare. Doing this right would be an experiment worth trying. But I suspect it would pose dangers to the academy's comfortable self-image far more radical than even Professor Fish fears.

Notes

Warm thanks to Elizabeth Kiss and Peter Euben for their invitation to think about that contested "turn to ethics" in higher education with them and other contributors to this volume. I am also grateful to Professors Kiss and Euben, and to Monique Roelofs, for helpful critical comments on my twists through that turn.

1. A complication here is that views about the nature of moral beliefs have implications for just how central morality should be taken to be in our lives. For example, if what look to be moral decisions are really nothing much more than sophisticated cheerleading—"Root for Our Side!"—they would seem to be considerably less important than a set of guiding beliefs which can be said to be true or false.
2. Longino, *Science as Social Knowledge*, 4–5.
3. See, for instance, Fish, "Aim Low," and "Why We Built the Ivory Tower."
4. Bok, *Universities and the Future of America*, 97.
5. Kiss and Euben, introduction to this volume.
6. Ibid., note 34.
7. Kiss and Euben, introduction to this volume.
8. Bourdieu, *Distinction*, 2.
9. Ibid., 409.

THE POLITICS AND ETHICS OF HIGHER EDUCATION III

PLURALISM AND THE EDUCATION OF THE SPIRIT

We see few signs of a turn to ethics in universities, and the signs we do see are ambiguous, but we are convinced that any such turning must begin with a recognition of the limits to which we, as educators, are subject.

The great text for moral educators is the Parable of the Sower in the fourth chapter of Mark. Jesus teaches his disciples that the Word is like sown seed: some falls on the roadway and never takes root; some falls on thin soil and may spring up quickly, but the roots are shallow and the plants die at the first setback or difficulty; some is choked by weeds, strangled by the competing "cares of the world"; only a little falls on good soil and flourishes. As we all know, universities—and all schools, to some extent—get young people only after the soil of their souls has been worked on, for good or ill; the fundamentals of moral character are largely set, and whatever influence we can exert must compete with the curriculum of society at large.

There are exceptions, of course, especially since the period of university education is one of relatively intense experience, a coming into one's own that includes acquiring a vocabulary of morals and experience. Nevertheless, there are pretty severe constraints on what we can hope to accomplish.

In the days when moral education was a theme and capstone of college education, as Douglas Sloan reminds us, the parameters of that education were set by a predominately Protestant Christianity and by American democracy. Universities, then considered the cultural institution best situated to explore "'the basic questions of human existence' and cultural purpose," aspired not to convert students; rather, they aspired to convey to their students the calling to seek "truth in every domain of life."[1] Still, the concerns of the university were closely aligned with the concerns of the churches, as evidenced by their emphasis on instruction in classics, divinity, and political and moral philosophy. And college teachers along with ministers took it upon themselves to discuss the moral uses of such knowledge. Moral education offered guidance in cases of ambiguity, and especially in the task of applying principles to practice; it hoped to broaden the ethical perspective of students; a daring teacher might challenge racism or even question the inequality of the sexes.[2] Coherent moral conversations were evident on campus, though the limits of moral debate were firmly grounded and pretty strictly defined.

Then, of course, moral debate *could* be both firmly grounded and pretty strictly defined within a university that aspired to coherent moral conversation. This is no longer the case, or not nearly the case it once was—for reasons beginning well outside the control (and perhaps even the intention) of university administrators and faculty. The many technological innovations of recent decades have transformed collegiate life, checking the power of educational institutions to direct the conversations that happen within them. Technological "connectivity," to use a concept much in vogue, has more or less erased the campus's traditionally privileged separation from society at large—a separation which, Frederick Rudolph tells us, was an intentional part of the design of the American university.[3] American college founders, hoping to encourage young people toward lives of piety, operated with a kind of monastic sensibility, believing that moral character could be best cultivated within a relatively insulated community. So they built their institutions in bucolic locations, or walled them off from surrounding population centers, and embraced a residential model of higher education. Insulating college students from the din of society, they knew, would add to the focus and intensity of college life and would increase the university's power to be a moral, and not merely practical or professional, educator. Students, distanced from their earliest influences, would be compelled while on campus to look within their institution—to their teachers, and to each other—for guidance about how to live a good life.

Today, when a student begins college, one of the first things she does is connect her computer to the Internet. The overwhelming majority of students have cellular phones, those "long-distance tethers to home" that mitigate the experience of college as an independent one, or as a break from prior forces of authority in their lives.[4] The university no longer operates, in the day-to-day doings of its students, as the most powerful—or even the most evident—source of moral example and authority. Students are regularly exposed, before and during their tenure on campus, to the argument that universities, and everyone who teaches in them, have values that are dubious at best. (We think, of course, of the many popular dismissals of universities as sites of liberal or "communist" propagandizing. But we would also note that the much-lamented turn toward a "customer" metaphor in higher education, and all the practical changes in universities that this metaphor has wrought, also provide fine evidence of the erosion of social regard for the university's traditional authority.)[5] A good number of students thus approach college warily, inclined to distrust any revelations they may have there. They may go through their college years in a kind of hokey-pokey: one foot in, one foot out.

Like the society in which it exists, the university has become much more "loosely bounded," lacking the basic conditions of safety and sanctuary that encourage independent moral exploration.[6] Indeed, ever more exposed and ever less insulated, college students are reporting record levels of anxiety.[7] And because in a condition of anxiety one longs above all for security, it is not surprising that many college students seem to eschew moral questions in favor of material ones. Students worry about their postcollegiate, professional status from almost the moment they arrive on campus, directing their imaginative energies—with the assistance of the career centers that have sprung up on campuses far more quickly than have ethics programs or curricula—toward creating protected, if not particularly virtuous or decent, lives.

It may be, as the former president of Princeton University, Harold Shapiro, argues, that in a liberal, pluralist society "it is incumbent upon our universities to prepare their students to live in a society where they will have to make their own moral choices, where they will have the capacity to help shape the moral contours of the society as a whole, and where their lives will be directly affected by the moral choices of others."[8] But it is hard to see, given the present environment, why a student would be moved by even the most elegant or intelligent of ethical theories, seemingly abstracted as they are from immediate attachments, pressures, and anxieties.

Here, as it often does, considering the present returns us to the omnipresent. For moral educators, there always have been and always will be students who are content to have fallen on the proverbial roadway—who, that is, will not be swayed by moral argument or even convinced of its legitimacy in the first place. And moral educators perennially confront students who, though they may take ethical questions seriously on paper or in the classroom, are dubious about their use in what they understand to be the "real world."

We think of Crito, a good man who sees something beautiful in Socrates and evidently feels the charm of philosophy. In the dialogue that bears his name, he appears to follow Socrates's intellectual argument: we ought to follow what is right, not the opinions of the many; in doing what is right, we ought not to fear death, to say nothing of lesser privations. Crito even seems to comprehend Socrates's implied observation that, if Socrates appeared to fear death, it would suggest that he is a hypocrite, and that philosophy is—as the multitude has always suspected—only so much word-spinning. But Crito is at bottom an Athenian gentleman, one who takes ethical argument seriously but not seriously enough to rule practice. (One can hardly miss the emphasis implied in Crito's response, "I think what you *say* is right, Socrates, but think what we should *do*.")[9] If Socrates remains in prison and suffers death, it will make his enemies happy; it will deprive his family and might damage the public reputation of his friends, who will be thought to have fallen short in their devotion. There's a lot to be said for Crito's case: among other things, it has a noble element, for Crito, a good citizen, is rating the law as less important than his personal honor and his duty to his friend.

Here, however, we're concerned with Socrates as a moral educator, and hence with Socrates's recasting of his own argument specifically in terms that he thinks will command Crito's agreement, not merely to some intellectual formulation but "all the way down." It takes the form, of course, of an imagined dialogue with the Laws, which ends with the conclusion that the law has claims to override purely private right (including, implicitly, Crito's reputation and his love for Socrates). In making his argument this way, Socrates actually appeals to Crito's deep loyalties to his friends and to his teacher; he has the Laws point out that if Socrates were to leave Athens and escape his sentence, he would "appear to be an unseemly kind of person," and his friends might "themselves be in danger of exile, disenfranchisement, and loss of property."[10]

Of course, we know that Socrates would defy the law if it commanded him to violate the logos. And we also know that public appearances and material possessions—even those of his friends—are not goods that Socrates has ever sought to preserve. But in *Crito*, Socrates aims to convince Crito on not merely rational or intellectual grounds; he aims to convince him also in terms of the standard that Crito, in his noble way, holds so dear. They must in part listen to the Laws, Socrates teaches Crito, to demonstrate devotion to their friends. Socrates, that is, is engaged in moral education *within the limits of practice*—with moral education, in other words, as opposed to ethical theory.

(It is worth noting, incidentally, that Crito, a B+ student, is humanly a good deal more educable, in Plato's terms, than most ordinary Athenians. When Socrates observes, in *Protagoras*, that Athenians can do no better than to send their children to Protagoras, he is not endorsing Protagoras's claim that courage, along with the other virtues, can be taught through a kind of utilitarian calculus: he is suggesting that most Athenians—at least those who patronize sophists—could, and left to themselves would, do a lot worse.)[11]

Moral Education in Contemporary America

So, what kind of moral education is possible in contemporary America? What is possible within the limits of contemporary American practice? Evidently, American political culture, especially in its religious and moral aspects, is much more plural than it was in the past. The landmark we cherish came in 1998, when Governor Paul Celucci of Massachusetts, a fairly conservative Republican, was pressured to apologize for remarks thought to be offensive to witches.[12] In many respects, this pluralization deserves the celebration we are so often asked to give it: America today is vastly less repressive than it was in the heyday of moral education, relatively open and inclusive toward groups who even recently would have been beyond the pale. (That conservative moralists today focus on gay *marriage*, for example, marks a striking, politic retreat. It is just as notable that Mayor Richard Daley of Chicago announced that he would follow San Francisco's example in issuing licenses; his father's probable reaction could be imagined. Or, to add a final example, consider the fact that, in 2003, the Republican nominee for governor of Louisiana was an erstwhile Hindu.)[13]

As Henry Adams would have reminded us, however, multiplicity comes at a price: the diversity of faiths and morals means that in general, faith and morals lose force in the regulation of conduct.[14] Most Americans, as Alan Wolfe has indicated, continue to hold moral beliefs of a more or less traditional sort, but they see them as private preferences, choices or styles, with relatively weak claims on public life.[15] As Wolfe notes, this increasingly dominant view of morality stems directly from the awareness of moral multiplicity; for moral or religious multiplicity to function as a principle in public, all forms of faith must become essentially private.[16]

Even to the extent that there is some deeper agreement that allows the diversity of faiths and morals in America to exist, it is a kind of negative agreement; it is the agreement to *not* criticize or suppress other people's beliefs and practices. As such, it frowns on public debates cast in terms of shared morality or faith. More and more, especially in national elections, politicians are turning to the language of "personal faith," a term which suggests that one uses a moral compass, but never in the public square. In the presidential election of 2008, for instance, candidates seemed eager to concur with Senator John Edwards's assertion in an early Democratic debate that it would be wrong for "any of our faith beliefs to be imposed on the American people when we're President of the United States."[17]

Tolerance, even for people whose beliefs and ways we think wrong, is a reigning public norm, and Americans are inclined to appeal to the biblical injunction "Judge not, that ye be not judged." Of course, this appeal gets the text wrong: Jesus was arguing the Golden Rule, that one should not apply to another a standard one would not have applied to oneself; he said that one should remove the plank of dust from one's own eye before removing the speck of dust from one's brother's eye. One should judge others without hypocrisy, of course, but also with great care and clear vision; ultimately, the casting of judgment should have curative effects for all involved. Jesus expected his hearers to care for their brethren; to remove a speck of dust from another's eye is to show concern for that other person's condition and to endeavor to improve it. (Certainly, he never suggested that it would ever be appropriate to smile politely and pretend that the dirt in another's eye, and in one's own, did not exist.) Jesus was, to put it simply, articulating a standard of duty—a standard of duty rooted in an understanding of shared human imperfection and love for one's fellows.

Most Americans, by contrast, invoke Jesus's words to proclaim a soft indifference toward others. At best, they do not want to hurt their fellows; they feel for them a certain good will, a measure of liberal sympathy. But they are not greatly disposed to help their fellows, either, as their frequent public recourse to the language of "toleration" suggests. After all, when in casual conversation an American says that he is "tolerating" someone—a teenager in rebellious thrall, or a troublesome coworker—he signals that he is enduring something distasteful but ultimately of no consequence, or only passing consequence, to him. I tolerate my colleague's bad behavior: I do this because although her behavior is a nuisance, and although her behavior might hurt *her* in the long term, I do not believe that it will hurt *me* in the long term. To tolerate someone, in this sense, is to maintain a mannered distance from them. At bottom, for Americans tolerance is not a standard of duty but a standard of disengagement: polite disengagement, to be sure, but disengagement just the same.

A prevailing spirit of disengagement, or indifference toward others, is manifest in the politics of the day. Consider, for example, the broad support for President George W. Bush's successful effort to repeal the estate tax, a levy that even William Graham Sumner, the old Social Darwinist, thought an eminently proper enforcement of our obligations to political society.[18] (Though pundits were quick to credit—or blame—the repeal on the GOP's mandated shift in rhetoric, in which "estate tax" became "death tax," multiple surveys found that American aversion to such a tax remains basically strong, no matter what it is called.)[19] The more generalized American hostility toward taxes and glorification of tax evaders paints a similar picture; as Robert Putnam has demonstrated, tax hostility and evasion run high when "social capital"—a sense of reciprocity, social trust, and shared obligation—is low.[20]

Part of our problem is that the term "pluralistic ethics" is just this side of an oxymoron. When Euthyphro appealed to "what is dear to the gods," it was a simple matter for Socrates to point out that those plural deities were often in conflict, so that what one loved, another would hate. On the face of it, pluralistic ethics in the simple sense offers little security, and its most attractive aspect is the possibility of finding an ethic (to borrow

Benjamin Franklin's praise of reason's plurality) "for everything one has a mind to do."[21]

One could, of course, insist that people follow the particular god or ethic of their community, censuring any effort to adopt new norms or new communities of reference, a teaching recognizable in certain forms of identity politics. In that event, however, a political society would need to subordinate these ethical monads to some ruling public norm—minimally, the prohibition of violence—to avoid falling into anarchy. The best route away from that danger is the position that is fundamentally identical to the "overlapping consensus" of Rawls's *Political Liberalism* and, for those with longer memories, of David Truman's *The Governmental Process*.[22]

That sort of consensus is likely to support only a thin, even anorexic democracy. It does, however, establish a ruling frame or standard that sets limits to acceptable pluralism: it ordains *an* ethic, not a plurality. And, if it needs to be said, that ethic is "neutral" only in a special sense. It is neutral as among some "comprehensive doctrines," those that are compatible with the overriding obligation to tolerate others. And it hopes that such claims to truth will be compatible with civil peace, but it insists on their subordination to that peace. It instates a standard of political duty superior to all others, as in the teaching that as a matter of public doctrine, civil peace itself must be regarded as a truth outranking to any other claims: "For Doctrine repugnant to Peace," Hobbes wrote, "can no more be True than Peace and Concord can be against the Law of Nature."[23]

Interestingly, the conviction that moral plurality collapses into a single overriding ethic of peace and goodwill is evident in contemporary American practice. Most of the Americans in Wolfe's surveys tried to square the circle of pluralist ethics by asserting that true moral sectarianism actually does not exist—that, in the words of one respondent, "all religions have basically the same common good things."[24] All systems of moral belief, the argument goes, teach people to be nice to each other, and so they are fairly interchangeable. Under this assumption, any action taken in the name of faith that does not have a basically peaceful aim—we think of the many official responses to the September 11, 2001, hijackers—is based on a "misguided" or "nonrepresentative" view of faith itself.[25] As Americans increasingly understand it, all forms of belief are acceptable so long as they do not result in public violence or hostility; plural "personal" faiths are fine so long as they operate within the overriding ethic of civil peace.

A subsidiary pluralism is eminently possible, then, when it makes civil peace an overriding standard of public duty. Even so, a genuinely pluralist ethics is closer to a cessation of arms than perpetual peace. A genuinely pluralist ethics tends to mute low-level hostilities among those basically compatible "comprehensive doctrines." But in the face of deep challenges from outside the framework of that ethics—challenges from those who do not admit of tolerance as a great or even tenable virtue, from those who reject the idea of civil peace as a primary good, or from those whose convictions do not map onto the "overlapping consensus"—a regime dedicated to pluralist ethics will find that it has deep moral commitments that demand argumentation, battle, or even war.[26] And even among those who subscribe to its tenets, a genuinely pluralist ethics presumes moral contest if not mortal conflict.

The Logic of American Moral Culture

In America, this goes to the heart of things. The republic's historic "overlapping consensus"—probably best articulated in the grand ambiguities of the Declaration of Independence—has presumed an ongoing contest between truths, a continual struggle over the moral terms of political culture. This continual struggle is to be fought in and through democratic politics. What does it mean, for instance, to proclaim it a "self-evident truth" that "all men are created equal"? If it is not, to use G. K. Chesterton's words, "some crude fairy tale about all men being equally tall or equally tricky"— that is, if it is not claiming a human equality that is evident to our senses, on the surface of things—how do we articulate its meaning?[27] "That's a hard mystery of Jefferson's," Robert Frost wrote. "It will trouble us a thousand years. Each age will have to reconsider it."[28] The most basic theoretical commitments of the American republic are multiply interpretable; American political life has thus been, and must be, a site of public moral contestation.

Famously, Tocqueville saw the vitality of American life in a counterpoise between the "spirit of liberty" and the "spirit of religion," the former embodied in the laws, the latter entrenched in the "habits of the heart."[29] In the short term, Tocqueville found the mores more important than the laws, but in the long term, he expected the "spirit of liberty," better positioned to enlist public authority, to gain ground at the expense of its rival, especially given America's plurality of faith and custom. Americans, Tocqueville observed, already justified almost all their acts in terms of self-interest, a language he found somewhat misleading, since Americans often acted from what clearly seemed to be altruism or public spirit. Half amused and half horrified, Tocqueville concluded that Americans would rather honor "their philosophy"—the public doctrine that all human beings act from interest—than themselves.[30] The doctrine of "self-interest rightly understood," consequently, seemed the best hope for American ethics, a standard for moral education that offered at least some restraint on the purer language of self-interest and individualism that was silencing the older languages of obligation.[31]

Even as he articulated it, though, Tocqueville doubted the power of that doctrine to slow what he saw as the tendency of American democracy toward atomization and self-interest. Visiting a frontier outpost in Saginaw, Michigan, Tocqueville saw what he feared American democracy could become:

> Several exiled members of the great human family have met together in the immensity of the forests, and their needs are all alike; they have to fight against the beasts of the forest, hunger, and hard weather. There are scarcely thirty of them in the midst of the wilds where everything resists their efforts, but they cast only looks of hatred and suspicion on one another.

"Where," Tocqueville asked, "could one find a more complete picture of the wretchedness of our nature in a narrower frame?" Importantly, this bleak portent for the American experiment, in which American "equality" amounted only to the separate pursuit of individual self-interests, Tocqueville attributed in part to the religious plurality of the town: "Six religions or different sects divide the faith of this nascent society," he noted. "The deep lines that birth and opinion have ruled between these men by no means end with life, but stretch out beyond the tomb."[32] For Tocqueville, the condition of religious plurality increased the likelihood that Americans would turn inward, and away from each other.

It isn't hard to find contemporary evidence to support this view of the logic of American moral culture, whether one looks to Robert Bellah or Alan Wolfe or David Callahan's recently published book on the culture of cheating. ("A lot of Americans," Callahan writes, "have been inventing their own morality lately.")[33] There is much evidence, that is, that the subtle doctrine of "self-interest rightly understood" is not much understood at all, much less practiced. In a culture where Americans are quick to *say* that they "support our troops" but seem hesitant to *do* anything more than hang some yellow ribbons, it almost seems that the opposite of Tocqueville's doctrine is in force: Americans are talking much better than they walk, speaking altruistically but acting selfishly.

But that isn't the whole story: the fundamental things still apply, even if we hear them only in screams and whispers. The respondents in Wolfe's surveys regret that community is so transient and that love seems harder to find.[34] Americans—and not just young ones—yearn for the noble, for that which is not calculable in terms of reason or self-interest: witness the overwhelming popular response to Tolkien's trilogy or to the Harry Potter stories, where friendship and moral courage are every bit as important as magic. (In the latter, we are reminded that the aim of those who would live forever, who would seek to master nature out of the self-interested desire for power, is, in fact, to destroy the self rather than to free it.) In the catastrophe of September 11, 2001, Americans did not admire those who pursued their interests but those who voluntarily risked or sacrificed their lives. And just as there is considerable evidence to support Tocqueville's argument that religious needs are a constituent element of human nature, there are abundant proofs of his observation that, absent an education of the spirit, when the demands of the soul make themselves felt, they are likely to be "devoid of common sense."[35]

The Challenge of Contemporary Moral Education

The great challenge for contemporary moral educators, in universities and out, is to educate those impulses, to articulate the second voices of American political culture—those voices which see human beings as born not free but subject, which privilege sociability over individualism, which emphasize obligation rather than self-preservation, and which speak the language of the spirit instead of the language of self-interest—in their intellectual profundity and power. We think of John Winthrop's "Model of Christian Charity," and its argument that God created us with a variety of different talents to make evident our mutual dependence: "that every man might have need of another, and hence be knit more nearly together in the bond of brotherly affection."[36] We think again of Tocqueville, whose articulation of the promise and perils of American political life remain unrivaled, and who saw the need for Americans to cultivate the habits of association, fellowship, and shared sacrifice. We think of James Baldwin, of his haunting portrayal of Americans who lose love in the midst of their restlessness, even as love is the one thing that brings them calm. We think of the darkly comic voices of Mark Twain and Kurt Vonnegut, each of whose stories return again and again to the futility of projects of mastery and who see the human capacity to love and sacrifice for each other as the strongest hope for democratic life—that, in the words of the latter, "we are here to help each other get through this thing, whatever it is."[37]

These and many other voices come from deep within the American tradition. As such, they speak directly to American cultural practice, to the dominant cultural voices of self-interest and mastery, the dominant logic of unrestrained economic expansion. But they argue that freedom does not inhere in the right to be left alone, or the right to leave others alone; they say that human beings are free to the extent that they can sacrifice for and with each other. They articulate the value of inward growth as opposed to external expansion, of respecting human limitation as opposed to pursuing human mastery. They see law not merely as a means by which we may protect ourselves from each other but as a means by which we may be encouraged to help each other—a means by which we might encourage the moral and civic character upon which a robust democratic life depends.

A great challenge, too, is to present other cultures not as anthropological curiosities but as efforts to answer the human question, and in general, to treat moral argument as serious discourse about things that matter. For all the familiar reasons, the academy is to be credited for its recent efforts to pluralize the curriculum, to expose students to an ever-broader array of voices and perspectives. But it is all too easy, in teaching from a variety of cultural traditions, to spiral into the kind of moral relativism that teaches difference all the way down, and which provides students with few grappling hooks by which they can consider the enduring questions of human existence—of love, of loss, of time, of death—which they know to animate their lives.

Thus, those who aspire to moral education in contemporary America can find their surest footing in the old juxtaposition between familiar and unfamiliar—drawing students to the unfamiliar arguments within a familiar tradition, or the familiar questions within an unfamiliar tradition. As it always has, moral education begins with both safety and shamelessness; it consists in locating students where they are, and suggesting to them the new places where they might go.

There is a rhetorical dimension to this "art of turning around."[38] In the *Apology*, Socrates tells Athenians to treat him as though he were a foreigner, but he speaks Attic Greek; it was the substance of his teaching that seemed outlandish, and the more provocative because the language was familiar. Democratic moral education begins by speaking to its hearers about problems they know, in the language of everyday life. Democratic moral education presumes that the big questions—those matters that are as difficult as they are enduring—are universal questions, questions that undergird and animate every human life, and as such they can be addressed in terms that are universally accessible. Like democracy itself, its hypothesis is that, closely examined, the ordinary proves to be extraordinary, just as the common is the greatest of all political mysteries, the proposition that all of us are created equal.

Notes

1. See Sloan, *Faith and Knowledge*, 1, 41ff.
2. See Royce, *Race Questions, Provincialism, and Other American Problems*.
3. See Rudolph, *The American College and University*, 54ff.
4. See Gross, "A Long-Distance Tether to Home." Among other things, Gross interviews experts on adolescent development who say that such technology promotes dependence during years when students are supposed to be developing independent, adult modes of being.
5. See, among others, Hutton, *The Feel-Good Society*.
6. See Merelman, *Making Something of Ourselves*.
7. See Twenge, "College Students and the Web of Anxiety."
8. Shapiro, "Liberal Education, Moral Education."
9. *Crito* (Fowler, trans.), 171 [49d].
10. *Crito* (Grube, trans.), 55 [53b-d].
11. *Protagoras* (Taylor, trans.), 49 [349e].
12. See Niebuhr, "Salem Journal," A8. Celluci has not been the only major elected official pressured to apologize for such remarks; a year later, in 1999, Nebraska governor Mike Johanns was publicly condemned for his position on Wiccanism. During a press conference announcing what he intended to be a state multifaith celebration, Johanns acknowledged that he didn't know what Wicca was and, upon learning what it was, suggested that he would not sign a

proclamation supporting it. See religioustolerance.com, which awarded Johanns their first "Burning Times" award.

13. "Daley Backs Marriage for Gays in Chicago," *New York Times*, February 20, 2004, A12; Hockstader, "Surprise Front-Runner in La. Governor's Race."

14. Adams, *The Education of Henry Adams*. Adams writes, "The magnet in its new relation staggered his new education by its evidence of growing complexity, and multiplicity, and even contradiction, in life. He could not escape it; politics or science, the lesson was the same, and at every step it blocked his path whichever way he turned. He found it in politics; he ran against it in science; he struck it in everyday life, as though he were still Adam in the Garden of Eden between God who was unity, and Satan who was complexity, with no means of deciding which was truth" (377).

15. Wolfe, *The Transformation of American Religion*, 17ff.

16. Wolfe, *One Nation, After All*, 62–63.

17. Transcript of the Fourth Democratic Debate for the 2008 Presidential Election, The Citadel, Charleston, S.C., July 23, 2007.

18. Sumner wrote, "Unquestionably capital accumulates with a rapidity which follows in some series the security, good government, peaceful order of the State in which it is employed; and if the State steps in, on the death of the holder, to claim a share of the inheritance, such a claim may be fully justified." Sumner, *What the Social Classes Owe to Each Other*, 43.

19. Mayling Birney, Ian Shapiro, and Michael Graetz, "The Political Uses of Public Opinion: Lessons from the Estate Tax Repeal" (working paper, Yale University, April 2007), 8 (http://www.yale.edu/macmillan/shapiro/).

20. Putnam, *Bowling Alone*, 348ff.

21. Plato, *Euthyphro* (Grube, trans.), 11 [7a]; Franklin, *The Autobiography of Benjamin Franklin*, 28.

22. Rawls, *Political Liberalism*, 12ff.; Truman, *The Governmental Process*.

23. Hobbes, *Leviathan*, 113. Moreover, there is a slipperiness to the teaching that no "comprehensive doctrine" is sufficiently persuasive to deserve public recognition. Like most liberals—and sensible people, for that matter—Rawls thinks that Darwinism has such a claim to recognition while creationism does not, a position that can be accommodated only by the rather tendentious argument that, unlike creationism, evolutionary theory isn't really "comprehensive."

24. Wolfe, *One Nation, After All*, 63–64.

25. This theme, in fact, dominated President George W. Bush's address to a joint session of Congress less than ten days after the terrorist attacks on the World Trade Center and Pentagon. Note especially his confident assertions about the "true" content of Muslim teaching: "The terrorists practice a fringe form

of Islamic extremism that has been rejected by Muslim scholars and the vast majority of Muslim clerics; a fringe movement that perverts the peaceful teachings of Islam. . . . I also want to speak tonight directly to Muslims throughout the world. We respect your faith. It's practiced freely by many millions of Americans and by millions more in countries that America counts as friends. Its teachings are good and peaceful, and those who commit evil in the name of Allah blaspheme the name of Allah. The terrorists are traitors to their own faith, trying, in effect, to hijack Islam itself" (Address to Joint Session of Congress, September 20, 2001).

26. It is *almost* not necessary to say that these challenges may come from inside *or* outside the borders of such a pluralistic regime.

27. Chesterton, *What I Saw in America*, 17.

28. Frost, "The Black Cottage," 57.

29. Tocqueville, *Democracy in America*, 1: 26, 299.

30. Ibid., 2: 122.

31. Ibid., 1: 393; 2: 121ff.

32. "Fortnight in the Wilderness," 395.

33. See Bellah, *Habits of the Heart*; Wolfe, *One Nation, After All*; Callahan, *The Cheating Culture*, 169.

34. Wolfe, *One Nation, After All*, 250ff.

35. Tocqueville's prediction that religious fanaticism of certain sorts would be prevalent in American society is borne out by a glance at recent census data, which demonstrate the increasing and astonishing variety of nontraditional religious beliefs among American citizens.

36. Winthrop, "A Model of Christian Charity." As Patrick Deneen observed in a speech in 2007, the essence of Winthrop's teaching *literally* has been concealed in contemporary American politics; President Ronald Reagan quoted the speech in a defense of the belief in human self-reliance ("The Alternative Tradition in America," speech at ISI Regional Leadership Conference, "Liberty, Place, and Community in the American Tradition," Charlottesville, Virginia, March 23, 2007).

37. Vonnegut, *A Man without a Country*, 66.

38. Plato, *Republic* (Bloom, trans.), 7.518d.

MULTICULTURALISM AND MORAL EDUCATION

The early and middle 1990s saw an outpouring of public and sometimes scholarly concern about the rise of multiculturalism in American colleges and universities.[1] The furor has died down somewhat since then. But many observers of higher education still do not view the rise of multiculturalism as a favorable development for moral education. They see an increasingly diverse range of ethnic, cultural, and racial groups populating our universities as challenging or threatening common values. It was easier to teach values, it is sometimes thought, when student populations were more homogeneous.

Part of what is going on here is what Thomas Scanlon has called "fear of relativism."[2] It is thought that these different cultural, ethnic, and racial groups have distinct sets of values, that no one of these groups has a privileged valuational stance, and that therefore we are faced with an inability of members of one cultural group to criticize or assess the beliefs and practices of one another.

In a larger sense, however, moral education and multiculturalism have developed without making much contact with one another. I want to remedy that disconnect by exploring ways that multiculturalism can be a *source* of common values rather than a threat to them. But first it must be noted that one source of the fear of relativism is quite misplaced. It is quite misleading to think of the groups composing contemporary pluralism in universities as all possessing a distinct set of comprehensive values, much less as actually *defined* by those values. The idea that they are is connected with the common practice of referring to all of these groups as "cultural" groups; of course, the common term "multicultural-ism" encourages this. But many of the groups in question are not helpfully thought of as cultural at all.

What defines, for example, African Americans, Asian Americans, Korean Americans, Haitian Americans, Latinos, Chicanos, whites, blacks, and Italian Americans is that each constitutes an important social identity shared with other members of the group in question. (Leave aside for the moment what makes these identities important, and how that is dependent on context.) These are the sorts of identities and affiliations students mean when they think of diversity or multiculturalism. They think of their campus as "diverse" to the extent that a broad range of such groups is present.

Some of these—"Latino," "Asian American"—are pan-ethnic identities. As Eric Liu points out so beautifully in his book *The Accidental Asian*, the ethnic groups that comprise these pan-ethnic identities (Korean, Vietnamese, and Chinese American for instance, among those composing Asian Americans) may have distinct cultures, but the pan-ethnic group itself does not. There is barely something usefully called "Asian American culture" or "Latino culture." Liu says there is more to the latter; at least all Latinos have some relation to the Spanish language (leaving Brazilians aside for the moment), whereas Asian Americans do not even have that. But this linguistic/cultural commonality is thin indeed; not only do many, probably most, "Latinos" not speak Spanish but many do not think they need to or should or that Spanish is important to their identity as Latinos, as that is roughly defined as persons whose ancestry lies in (Spanish-speaking) Latin America.

Though cultureless, these pan-ethnic identities can be very personally important to particular individuals. Indeed, in some cases, a "Latino" identity can be more important than a "Salvadoran" one, an "Asian American" identity than a "Korean American" one, even though the former are cultural and the latter not. The student of Salvadoran or Korean American ancestry may feel that she has received very little in the way of a distinct ethnoculture in her home, neighborhood, or other institutions of her upbringing. Perhaps she lived a fairly assimilated existence, in the sense of growing up in a cultural milieu of some group other than her ethnic group—among suburban whites or urban blacks, for example.[3] Or, in another direction, perhaps she grew up in such a culturally pluralistic milieu, surrounded by people from many different ethnocultures, that she has difficulty identifying with one of them exclusively. She might think of herself as a cultural cosmopolitan.

College is one of the prime settings in which pan-ethnic identities come to have a purchase on young people. It is a familiar phenomenon for students from assimilated backgrounds to find a strong community in fellow pan-ethnics. (This is, of course, not to deny that others, and sometimes even these same individuals, find community within an ethnic group on campus.) The differences between Chinese, Japanese, Vietnamese, Korean ancestry may seem less significant, largely because they are not strong cultural differences for these students, than the commonality as "Asian American." Such an identity has little to do with culture, and little to do with values. (In part because "culture" discourse is the lingua franca for talking about social identities and is often required for garnering a kind of official status and recognition in universities, these pan-ethnic identities are sometimes referred to by their members as "cultures" or cultural groups.)

Racial identities, such as black and white, should also not be conflated with culture, although, like pan-ethnic ones, they can be very important to students, and help to define what most people think of as "diversity." "Black," for example, is an identity that signifies a history of discrimination and stigmatization, a historical memory and identity arising from that history, and, often but by no means always, a sign of current disadvantage and sometimes prejudice and unequal treatment. No doubt there are also some cultural differences between American blacks and American whites. Ironically, however, because African Americans have had a cultural impact on mainstream American popular culture out of proportion to their numbers, the actual cultural differences between whites and blacks are much diminished, especially among younger people. Moreover, even where there is a cultural divide, it does not necessarily signify a substantial divide in *values*. Jennifer Hochschild and other survey researchers have found little in the way of differences in fundamental values between American whites and blacks; differences arise primarily in perceptions of the extent of racial discrimination and overall fairness in various social and institutional domains rather than about values.[4]

The *cultural* divide between blacks and whites is much smaller, one might say, than the *identity* divide. Increasingly, moreover, "black" is becoming an internally complex identity. As blacks from various parts of the world immigrate to the United States, the definitional link between "African American" and "black" weakens, and it becomes less clear which characteristics to associate with the broader category "black." The ways in which Dominicans, Puerto Ricans, Africans of various nations, Brazilians, and Caribbean blacks are (when they are, or are taken to be) "black" are multifarious.[5] The larger point is that race and racial identities are defined by experience, social position, and history, rather than culture or values. Even less cultural are other social identities important on college campuses often regarded as part of the "multicultural," such as those defined by gender and sexual orientation.

Thus the actual content of the identities that make up the increasing pluralism on our college campuses often has little to do with real cultural differences, and where it does, those differences do not necessarily have much to do with differences in the sorts of values that would raise worries about moral relativism. Yet such identity differences do raise moral challenges other than that of relativism. But these challenges can enrich the possibilities for moral education on college campuses, rather than detracting from them.

Moral Values in the University

Let me turn, then, to campus diversity as a source of common values and a resource for moral education. When we think of moral education, we most naturally think of individual students coming to understand, internalize, and commit themselves to certain basic values, which then become part of their character or sensibility—like respect, courage, justice, compassion, and thoughtfulness. But when the individuals are also part of a distinct institution, such as a university, and of the community and communities composing that institution, it would behoove us to look also at ways that values can be embodied in institutions as well as in individuals. Through policies, practices (official and unofficial), and explicit stances, institutions can also manifest certain values—as, for example, when the president of a university publicly condemns behavior on the part of some students that shows disrespect and disregard for the community at large, or for the community within which the university is located.

One more preliminary: For our purposes, we can distinguish three venues in which values in a college community can be taught, expressed, inculcated, and encouraged—the curriculum, classroom interaction, and extracurricular activity. A good deal of the opposition to multiculturalism in the early and middle 1990s focused on the curriculum (see note 1), where attempts to include non-Western cultures and the experiences of persons of color within Western societies, and especially the United States, were criticized. The moral dimension of this criticism was not always brought to the fore; often the criticism was that these newer curricular developments were not academically or intellectually worthy. Nevertheless, there were some important value underpinnings to the criticism. One was the fear of relativism mentioned above. A related one was the dislodging of "Western values" from the center of the curriculum. It was felt, at least implicitly and often explicitly, that Western values—for example liberty, democracy, equality—were superior to those of other civilizations, and that they should be taught to students as such. (I am not examining this view, only reporting it.)[6]

The response by defenders of multiculturalism to the criticism did not always foreground morality either, in part because the influential, postmodern version of multiculturalism did not readily admit of forthright moral commitments. But I will not pursue further the purely curricular dimensions of moral education in relation to multiculturalism, as this vast topic goes beyond the scope of this essay. Let me just make some brief comments. The appropriate basis for deciding the validity of curricular proposals must remain intellectual rather than moral. Whether an American history course should or should not contain more material than it currently does about Hispanics or African Americans, the basis for deciding this must lie in whether doing so gives a truer picture of the period or themes to be covered in the course. Although such decisions might have moral implications—giving more students an appreciation of a stigmatized or marginalized group, for example—those considerations should not drive the curricular decision. To foreground these moral implications would be to court a violation of the intellectual integrity for which the university must be committed as a condition of any other of its value commitments. Putting the moral before the intellectual might, for example, lead an instructor teaching about the transatlantic slave trade to withhold or downplay the role of Africans in selling (other) Africans to the European slave traders, on the grounds that white or other students might take from the unit the thought that since Africans were involved, white people should not be so concerned for their historical responsibility for slavery. It is not that the latter moral stance is not troubling; indeed, it is. The problem is that the moral should not trump the intellectual when it comes to curricular choices. If an instructor is concerned about a moral falsehood she is worried her students might take away from her class, she might give thought to how to discuss the issue in question so as to minimize that likelihood; after all, knowing the African role in the slave trade *should* not diminish the moral responsibility of Europeans, even if it sometimes has that effect in some students' minds. Discussing that issue explicitly would serve the end of moral education without detracting from the intellectual integrity of what is being taught. (Indeed, it can be argued that bringing such a moral discussion into the unit on the slave trade would deepen intellectual understanding.)

I would want to distinguish this purely curricular dimension of college courses from classroom interaction, an important source of learning as well. While classroom interaction usually revolves around the curriculum, it is nevertheless useful to look at classroom interaction as a distinct source or venue of moral education in its own right, distinct from the curriculum and also from various extracurricular activities and venues such as residential programming and interaction, student organizations, university events, and so on.[7]

The category of "moral values" is not necessarily a clearly defined one. In one direction, it shades into academic or intellectual values. For example, if a student learns to engage respectfully with other students in a classroom setting, in such a way that the student in question is able to learn from the other students, and they from her, this is on the one hand an academic value. But it is also a moral value—being respectful of others, especially of others with whom one is bound up in a common enterprise. In another direction, moral values shade into civic ones. The basis for distinguishing them is perhaps even less clear, but it might be helpful to think of civic values as those relating specifically to participation in and engagement with the polity, or, rather, various polities. For example, while respect for individual other persons might be more naturally thought of as a moral value, responsibility toward a community, such as the local community within which one's college is located, is a civic one. But I do not think anything of normative importance rides on this distinction, and it is also perfectly natural to think of civic values as a subset of moral ones, rather than as a different type of value.

Without attempting to be comprehensive, we can distinguish three distinct families of values that bear specifically on ethnic, cultural, racial, national (or national origin), and religious diversity on a college campus. (These are the kinds of groups I will have in mind when I refer generally to "identity groups.") These value families are *pluralism*, *equality*, and *community*. All are what I will call "diversity-related" values. They do not all involve valuing that diversity itself; only certain forms of "pluralism" do that. But they are values whose character involves a response to (these forms of) diversity. Each of these general categories of value contains several distinct values within it.

PLURALISM: TOLERANCE, ACKNOWLEDGMENT, AND APPRECIATION

Let us look first at pluralism—that is, values connected with the mere existence of diversity. One such value is *tolerance*. One wants members of different groups to tolerate or be tolerant of members of others. Intolerance would be a serious disvalue in a college community and is generally and rightly regarded as a character flaw in an individual. Examples might include Christians or Jews being intolerant of Muslims, whites of blacks, blacks of Latinos, or a religious group of homosexuals. As we can see, intolerance can operate within a category—members of one religion being intolerant of another—or across groups—members of a religion or a race being intolerant of a sexual-orientation group.

The virtue of tolerance is a complex one, because there are certain things which a moral person should not countenance and for which she is not regarded as "intolerant" for doing so (for example physical violence); because the virtue seems importantly context-dependent (it is appropriate to tolerate hate speech in certain contexts but not others); and because it has been thought that holding certain beliefs commits one to regarding those who lack such beliefs as wrong and not worthy of toleration (certain religious beliefs may seem to imply that holders of alternative beliefs must be wrong and not worthy of respect or toleration).[8] But for our purposes we can define toleration as treating in a civil manner persons of whom one disapproves for reasons related to race, ethnicity, culture, or religion.

While a college community characterized by widespread intolerance would be insupportable, at the same time, the good of tolerance seems morally limited in that particular context. If many students merely tolerated each other—disapproving of others' race, culture, or religion but treating each other in a civil manner—this would be a grim situation. One wants to set the bar concerning students' way of dealing with their diversity at a higher level than that. Tolerance is a necessary but far from sufficient pluralism virtue in a college community. And so we can arrive at a second pluralism-related virtue, which one might call "acknowledgment." Acknowledgment is a type of respect, but one directed toward the other in light of her specific identity that differs from one's own (that is, the identity that is tolerated in the virtue of tolerance). A Muslim does not merely want to be tolerated by a fellow student who is a Christian, but (also) acknowledged—respected in light of her being a Muslim. (If the Christian respected the Muslim as a fellow human being, this would not be the right kind of respect. I am using "acknowledgment" to mark the identity-focus of the kind of respect I have in mind.)[9]

Often (not always), students wish their identities to be acknowledged in the wider community, for example by fellow students, teachers, perhaps administrators. Black students generally wish their black identity to be acknowledged by others. They do not want to be treated in a manner that implies that their black identity is of no significance to them. To be treated in such a way may seem to them to constitute a lack of respect for who they are. The achieving of acknowledgment is far from automatic or simple. It involves recognizing what the identity in question means to that specific individual and then having a kind of regard for that individual in that light. So there is a cognitive element to the value, but the respect goes beyond merely recognizing that being a Muslim is important to Joan or that being black is important to Ahmad to a positive respect for Joan or Ahmad in light of those identities.

However, not all students of a given identity wish that identity to be acknowledged. This may be so for several reasons. The identity may not be important to the individual—"Sure I'm Italian American [Muslim, Jewish] but it doesn't really mean much [anything] to me." Or the identity might be important, but the individual does not need, or perhaps want, it acknowledged in the particular context in question. For example, someone at a college that has no specific religious identity might be quite religious but think of that identity as irrelevant to her relationship to the college community and to what she wants to get out of college. Then she will not particularly want it acknowledged by others. (This is not to say, of course, that such a person would want to be *dis*respected in light of the identity in question; and that might well hold as well for someone who was not very invested in the identity. Desiring a positive acknowledgment goes a good bit beyond desiring the absence of a negative one.)

I mention the religious case here, because there seems to have been a shift in recent years in the degree to which college students attending nonreligious colleges wish their religion to be acknowledged; or, to put it another way, to see their religion as an important part of their public identities within their colleges. There are probably several distinct reasons for this, but one of them is a more general sense that identities that are important to students personally should be publicly acknowledged identities. Racial and ethnic identities have held such a place for several decades now, indeed, as long as colleges have become open to racial groups who were formerly excluded. Sexual orientation, although somewhat outside the scope of this chapter, is nevertheless interesting in this connection, since some students very much want their sexual orientation to be acknowledged by others, while others very much do not.

It is worth recognizing that in this sense the desire for acknowledgment by others is subject to historical and situational change and variation and is not simply "natural" or a human given, as it is sometimes treated. Some students might come to desire such identity acknowledgment only because others do. They feel unacknowledged only because other students, or other groups, are garnering acknowledgment and they are not; otherwise, they might well not care, or not care very much. Also, there are asymmetries in acknowledgment. There is reason to acknowledge a black or Asian identity that is absent for whites. In general, there is a reason to acknowledge a "minority group" that there is not for a majority. Where whites are in the minority, acknowledgment applies to them in a different way than in the more frequent settings where they are a majority. In addition, as mentioned earlier, such a desire for acknowledgment of a particular component of one's identity is dependent as well on individual factors.

These contingencies, however, do not detract from acknowledgment's being a genuine value. When someone reasonably desires acknowledgment of an aspect of her identity in a particular public context, such as college, rendering that acknowledgment is a genuine value. It is so, in part, because respect is owed to every human individual, simply qua human being; and, as Charles Taylor has compellingly argued, when a certain (morally acceptable) social identity is central to an individual's personal identity, respect for that identity is required by the respect for the individual.[10] Its status as a general human value does not mean, however, that acknowledgment as I have defined it is not a distinctive diversity-related value. It is so because proffering respect across various social divides such as race and religion poses distinctive moral challenges that are not present in more homogeneous settings. To put the point simply, if I (who am neither black nor Muslim) am to respect Joan in light of her black or her Muslim identity, I must ensure that I have rid myself of the prejudices and stereotypes that, in my society, often stand in the way of that respect being granted.

Colleges have a role in fostering the value of acknowledgment in their students. It is not sufficient if members of a college community respect each other in spite of their differing identities. They must be aware of those identities as important to their fellow students (when they are important) and know enough about those identities to understand why they would be important and meaningful to their fellow students. Colleges can help attain that goal through the curriculum, classroom interaction, and extracurricular activities. When nonblack students learn more about blacks, their experiences, institutions, accomplishments, and histories, acknowledgment of black identity in the black students on campus is a natural result. It is not, of course, an *inevitable* result, since nonblack students may hold prejudices and stereotypes concerning blacks that survive learning more about blacks through academic study.

It is not necessary, or appropriate, for instructors to require, or even encourage, students to avow a certain identity, for example, as black, Muslim, or gay. However, classroom instructors can also foster acknowledgment through the way classroom discussions about identity-related (race, religion, or culture) matters are managed—fostering a climate of trust and respect that may allow students to reveal a component of their identity to the class in the course of a discussion when they feel that the identity is relevant. Instructors should also be aware of the ways that conversations on issues of race, religion, and culture manifest acknowledgment or its absence. A colleague related to me an exchange in which a student who identified as a Christian said that she disapproved of homosexuality but that she did not think ill of homosexual persons; she "hated the sin but loved the sinner." This student knew that there were gay students in the class and she genuinely wished to accord them acknowledgment; she thought that her stance toward homosexuals manifested such acknowledgment. However, at least one gay student in the class was very offended by the Christian student's remark and said so to the instructor (outside of class). The instructor found a way to bring the issue to the class as a whole; the Christian student was genuinely shocked that her stance was not experienced as respectful by the gay student, and she wanted to talk further about the issue. The instructor in this situation recognized her responsibility to the moral education of her students, of all of them, in finding ways of helping them show appropriate acknowledgment of one another in light of their identity differences and to discuss the complexities of doing so.

So far, I have described two distinct values related to pluralism in a college—that is, related to the coexistence of distinct identity groups of various kinds. Those values are tolerance and acknowledgment. There is a third, one that goes beyond acknowledgment. Acknowledgment requires that the student recognize the value and meaning that the identity in question has to the other student. But it does not require her to value that identity herself—to *appreciate* it.[11] That is, it does not require her to believe that it is a good thing for her as a member of that college community that black and Muslim persons are present in that community. Acknowledgment involves the thought "Identity X is meaningful to you and I acknowledge this in my respect for you." But this attitude is entirely consistent with indifference to whether persons of identity X are present in one's community or not. Yet, ideally I think we would want members of a college community to appreciate and welcome the presence of others of other identity groups. "I am pleased that persons of identity X are part of my community." This expresses appreciation.

Again, instructors have an important role in utilizing classroom interaction to foster appreciation, as they do acknowledgment and tolerance. They can be aware of the ways that members of different racial groups often have trouble "hearing" one another. White students are often defensive, taking observations by students of color as direct personal criticisms. Black and Latino students are sometimes too quick to render moral judgment on white students, not hearing a genuine desire to learn, or be informed. And the divide is not only between whites and nonwhites. There are barriers specific to each racial pairing. The more general point is that instructors can help their students to recognize these obstacles to their appreciating one another, can encourage sympathetic listening, can ask students simply to repeat what a student from another group has just said, can create an atmosphere of trust and openness in class that encourages students both to speak their minds and also to listen open-mindedly and appreciatively, can gently but pointedly help students identify prejudices and stereotypes and question them, and so on.

The Supreme Court's decision on affirmative action handed down in 2003 in the simultaneously heard cases *Grutter v. Bollinger* and *Gratz v. Bollinger* helps to illuminate the difference between acknowledgment and appreciation and why both are important values for a college community.[12] The majority opinion argues that having a diversity of ethnoracial groups on a campus is a legitimate goal for a college to seek and to use its admissions policies to foster. (Thus racial preferences are permissible.) The majority's argument for this view is not entirely consistent, but one part of it involves the idea that racial diversity is likely to provide a greater diversity of perspectives than its absence, and that this diversity of perspectives is of educational benefit to each member of the educational community.

There are some familiar problems with justifying racial diversity on the grounds of "perspectives" diversity (sometimes called "viewpoint" diversity, although these are not exactly the same thing).[13] I will return to these problems in a moment. What I want to focus on here is what the majority's argument implies about the stance that members of the college community should take toward members of the groups that benefit from the affirmative action program.[14] It implies that the student should recognize that her own education is being enhanced by the presence of members of these groups. It is a short step from there to an appreciation of individual persons from those groups. Of course, it is also possible to view these fellow students in a purely instrumental way, without any regard for them as individual persons; one might think "It is really interesting hearing Joan's Muslim point of view on U.S. foreign policy" and view Joan solely as an instrument to one's enhanced education. Nothing in the Supreme Court decision would argue against this; the decision does not prescribe moral attitudes. However, it is reasonable to see the "diversity rationale" given by the Court as suggesting a moral attitude of appreciation toward students in regard to social identities that contribute in some way to enhancing the shared life of the college and themselves individually.

Pluralism values flourish only in contexts of diversity. Where there is no diversity, it is impossible to have tolerance, acknowledgment, and appreciation. Of course there is still a large difference between the fact of pluralism—the mere existence of diverse identity groups—and the values related to pluralism. It is no virtue simply to have multiple groups at a college. They must be appropriately valued.

EQUALITY: INCLUSION AND SOCIAL JUSTICE

A second family of values concerns *equality*. Equality differs from pluralism. Pluralism (the value, not the fact) places a value on difference, or the particular differences in question; or (as in the case of tolerance) it derives value from an engagement with difference, even if the difference itself is not valued. Equality also recognizes difference. But the goal of equality is to ensure that all are treated equally, *independent* of those group differences. Equality values are about ensuring that group differences do not stand in the way of equal treatment.

There are several distinct kinds of equality values. One is "inclusion," a sense of belonging—a sense that one's group belongs, and feels that it belongs, at the college, and that the college "belongs to" them. Some groups and individuals take such inclusion for granted. Others, generally groups that have been historically underrepresented or absent from these institutions, do not. My own university, the University of Massachusetts at Boston, for example, is currently an all-commuter campus, with many older and returning students; it has about a 40 percent minority population, the highest of any four-year institution in New England. There is a fairly large contingent of working-class black and Latino students from the immediate area, who might not feel comfortable or included in many other institutions. A number of years ago the administration sought to build dormitories to attract a more traditional-age college student looking for a more traditional college experience; GPA and SAT admissions criteria have also been raised slightly. These initiatives led some black and Latino students to feel that they were no longer as welcomed at the university as they had formerly felt. They felt that the university "belonged to" them less than they formerly thought it did.[15]

As a value, inclusion operates most clearly at the institutional rather than individual level. That is, it is a responsibility of the institution to create a sense of inclusion for all, and specifically for groups who might be less prone to feel included, either for historical reasons or because they constitute a small minority on the campus. Some forms of such institutional inclusion are uncontroversial and obvious. Any university can recognize that in our current political climate, Muslim students might have reason to be concerned that they are not fully welcomed into their college communities. The college can address their concerns by having speakers and holding colloquia aimed at informing the larger community about Islam and its history, Muslim life and culture in various countries, and so on. (This is in addition to curriculum concerning these issues.) In addition to their educational benefits for the community as a whole, such events help the Muslim members of the community to feel that the larger community, or at least the official institution, is interested in them and welcomes them.

Helping members of a specific group to feel included raises familiar problems regarding whether to provide specific group-targeted attention or whether to ignore the differences and treat members of the group no differently from anyone else. If one is welcoming toward all groups equally, won't the minority groups experience this as welcoming of them? And if they see themselves singled out, even for a "positive" attention, mightn't this make them feel overconspicuous and not "really" part of things?[16]

One form that this inclusion dilemma takes is whether the college should provide separate spaces and programs for members of minority racial or religious groups. Such separate treatment can be seen as a necessary stepping stone on the way to full inclusion; a supportive and comfortable space for members of minority groups to better enable them to become full participants in the larger community. Some opponents of such programs dispute the empirical claims made on their behalf. They say that the separate programs have the effect of separating the minority students from the larger community, perhaps by making it too comfortable for them to remain in their separate spaces. But these two opposing views presumably have the same goal—inclusion of the group in the larger community.

Although inclusion is primarily an institutional value, it has an individual form as well. Individual students can be sensitive to the ways that particular persons, especially members of minority groups, may be indirectly excluded or discouraged from feeling fully part of the larger group. They may extend themselves to those members, bringing them into the larger group. (These "inclusive" individuals include not only members of the majority group but members of minority groups who themselves have already achieved inclusion, as it were.) This "inclusiveness" is, or involves, certain moral sensitivities—recognizing when others are, or are in danger of being, excluded; caring enough about these others' situation; having good judgment about how to negotiate the sensitive terrain of inclusion and exclusion, bringing people in in tactful ways. Sometimes the value of "inclusion" can involve a more public action. For example, if there is an expression of hatred or exclusion toward a group or member of a group qua member of a group, it might be good to demonstrate publicly against that expression and to show a public solidarity with the group targeted. This same value of inclusion can be expressed individually but more privately—for example, by showing appropriate, non-patronizing solicitousness toward members of the targeted groups who are known personally to oneself.

As I have understood inclusion, it is localized to one's own community; it is about being committed to the equal inclusion of all who warrant such inclusion in one's own community. In this respect, it is a "diversity"-related value that is analogous to academic integrity, civility, respect, and other such values regularly thought to be core values of an academic community. So inclusion is not the only equality value, since equality is also a more general value.

Indeed, one might think that equality as a general substantive value should be taught as part of a college education—in a category that might also include other political and personal values such as democracy, liberty, courage, justice, integrity, compassion, reflectiveness. (Some of these are individual virtues, some not. That distinction is not pertinent to this part of my argument.) On the one hand, equality has some claim to being a core American civic value; on the other, there is great divergence in conceptions of equality that lay claim to that status. For example, some see purely as a matter of equality in formal civic and political standing—a right to vote or to legal representation—others think some material conditions of equality are implied, such as health care or education up through certain grades. A slightly different formulation of the controversy is between those who see equality as equality of opportunity and others who think some equality of condition is required.

Given this indeterminacy, it would be logical to teach these very controversies as part of an understanding of equality as a core American value. But I want to look at equality as related to higher education in a different way, and that is in light of affirmative action. We have discussed the "pluralism" dimension of affirmative action, and its relation to pluralism values, especially acknowledgment. However, as has often been noted by critics of affirmative action, if colleges were looking for the kind of diversity of perspective and opinion that seems most pertinent to academic learning, their admissions policies would try to ensure a diversity of political and religious views and would not rely so centrally on race, an admittedly imperfect proxy for such diversity. They would seek to ensure a "critical mass" of libertarians, conservatives, liberals, socialists, republicans, and so on.[17]

Such considerations have led many to suggest that the true normative foundations for educational affirmative action do not lie in, or lie solely in, "diversity" but bear some relation to social justice. Specifically, affirmative action is meant both to compensate for past and present social discrimination against blacks and women and to aim to create greater equality in the future through education. This rationale for affirmative action was used by four of the Supreme Court justices in the 1978 *Bakke* case.[18] It is arguable that this rationale lives on in the way most universities that practice affirmative action understand it. But it would be understandable that the "official line" on affirmative action given to the public is "diversity" rather than "justice," since a majority in the *Bakke* case upheld the diversity rationale but rejected the justice rationale. Moreover, the University of Michigan affirmative action cases in 2003 reaffirmed the diversity rationale while continuing to reject the justice rationale, which in any case had been considerably weakened by intervening Supreme Court cases.[19]

Without pursuing the legal and political context of educational affirmative action further, let us assume that *both* pluralism (of many forms, including racial) *and* racial justice are sound normative underpinnings of affirmative action as currently practiced by many selective universities. Focusing on the latter, this could be taken to imply that racial justice, or racial equality, becomes more than a general social/political value: it becomes a core institutional one as well. From the point of view of the individual student, it thus becomes closer to academic integrity and inclusion than democracy and courage. What would this imply for moral education? It would mean that students should be instructed in the racial-justice rationale for affirmative action and encouraged to adopt racial justice as a value of their own. Presumably such instruction would take both curricular and noncurricular forms—discussions in residences, campus speakers, and so on. Of course, as with any politically charged value (that is, virtually any political value at all), there will be great differences of opinion, and it would be unrealistic to think that a college could produce 100 percent of its students signing on to affirmative action. Nevertheless, if many colleges are indeed committed to some degree to racial justice and see affirmative action as fostering that goal, making that fact and that argument a part of their moral education programs would be a reasonable and salutary endeavor.

To take one example of this, suppose one follows Elizabeth Anderson's argument that the main goal of affirmative action is integration. In her view, a white student may be personally enriched by a friendship with a black student; she may also benefit later in her enhanced ability to deal with a racially diverse group of coworkers. What the affirmative action rationale encourages is that students see these personal benefits as part of what it will take to create a racially integrated equal society. The white student is encouraged to recognize how blacks, or nonwhites in general, have been harmed by their exclusion from various domains of life, and that their ability to flourish as equals in society requires them to be able to interact comfortably with whites, and other nonwhite groups. So the white student is helped to recognize that for the sake of equality, her personal benefit from affirmative action has to be complemented by the reciprocal benefit of other students of color. Without that happening, the white student is not working within the spirit of the justice rationale of the affirmative action program.

COMMUNITY

Community is a third moral value. Community is a sense of bond among the members of an institution, involving trust, mutual concern, reciprocity, and cooperation in the shared educational enterprise. The idea of community requires and presupposes both inclusion and acknowledgment and appreciation. It requires inclusion, because the sense of community must embrace all its members. If any are left out, the community is deficient in that respect. Sense of community also requires acknowledgment and appreciation, because it requires a sense of respect among the members of the community; a recognition of those identity differences that are important to its individual members and a recognition of the value of those identity differences to the community as a whole.

The *general* value of community is like equality, and unlike pluralism, in not requiring identity differences for its value. What makes a sense of community a good thing is the trust and cooperation in the service of shared and worthy aims that raises the institution to a richer sort of human relationship among its members. This does not depend on identity diversity.

Indeed, some have argued that this sense of community is actually harmed by identity acknowledgment in the context of diversity and by the larger currents of multiculturalism. If students are concerned only about acknowledgment of their differences, how will they feel connected to students across those differences? I hope to have suggested ways that acknowledgment of difference can work in favor of rather than against community. Acknowledgment and appreciation are not the validating of retreat into comfort communities built around ethnicity and religion but are rather a reaching out beyond those communities to connect, through respect and empathy, with those in other groups. A case for such retreat can be made, as mentioned earlier, based on more distinctly educational goals. It can be argued that minority groups of various kinds will be likely to garner more support and feel more able to devote themselves to their studies, if they are provided with subcommunities of their own identity group and support from the larger institution for those subcommunities (in programmatic and residential forms). While this form would fall within an institutional "acknowledgment" of the identity in question, it would contravene the individual level of that value, which, as mentioned, requires reaching beyond, respecting, acknowledging, and appreciating those *not* in one's subcommunity. But even more strongly, such a form of institutional acknowledgment can be detrimental to the value of community that embraces the entire college community.[20] It does so by threatening to discourage identifying across differences with other students and recognizing that one is bound up with others in a common enterprise, while drawing on and valuing one's identity differences.

Although community presupposes acknowledgment and appreciation, and also the equality-based value of inclusion, the full value of community transcends them. The idea of community requires a more encompassing trust, concern, and sense of shared bond than appreciation provides. Appreciating involves seeing the student from a different race or religion as providing a benefit to oneself through her presence in the community. But it does not require what we want from a community, and a sense of community—a sense of being bound up together and together dedicated to the valued aims of the institution. Appreciation would not necessarily lead a student to join with someone from another identity group to plan a colloquium with differing voices on some issue of current importance to the campus or to the larger society—although it may well remove some obstacles to such projects. Only a sense of community provides this wider sense of connection among the members of the institutional community. Inclusion and appreciation provide a foundation for that sense of community, which then must be built.

Some have seen diversity or multiculturalism as a threat to common values and moral education in higher education. I have argued that diversity of ethnicity, race, and religion, at least, is an important source of values pertinent to moral education at that level—values that could not easily or even possibly be taught in their absence. Without claiming comprehensiveness, I have distinguished three such families of values—pluralism, equality, and community—each of which contains various distinguishable subvalues. All three of these families of values involve the development of empathy, moral sensitivity, and moral imagination, a moral awareness of social and cultural stereotypes and distancing mechanisms that are likely to distort a sympathetic perception of the other, and so on. Although in some sense each of these values is a general one that does not depend on a diversity context, their "diversity forms" present distinctive moral challenges and characteristics that render them not merely an application of general values such as respect and equality.

Notes

1. Many of the key documents in the public furor over multiculturalism are brought together in two collections—Aufderheide, ed., *Beyond PC*, and Berman, *Debating P.C.* Some of the influential books are: Schlesinger, *The Disuniting of America*; Atlas, *The Battle of the Books*; Bromwich, *Politics by Other*

Means; D'Souza, *Illiberal Education*; Kimball, *Tenured Radicals*; Gitlin, *The Twilight of Common Dreams*.

2. Scanlon, "Fear of Relativism."

3. The notion of "assimilation" has traditionally been understood as a conformity to the dominant culture of a nation, and an abandoning of an ethnoculture distinct from it (together with an acceptance by the dominant group of the group in question); but in recent sociological work on immigrant acculturation, it is recognized that an immigrant group can assimilate to a nondominant subculture, one distinct from either the original ethnoculture or the dominant culture. See essays in Foner and Frederickson, eds., *Historical and Contemporary Perspectives on Immigration, Race, and Ethnicity in the United States*, especially Jaynes, "Immigration and the Social Construction of Otherness."

4. Hochschild, *Facing Up to the American Dream*.

5. On cultural and other differences among American blacks, see Waters, *Black Identities*. On an attempt to articulate a distinct black identity in a trans-U.S. context, see Gilroy, *The Black Atlantic*.

6. A nuanced and balanced treatment of the "canon wars" in their curricular and political education dimensions is given by J. Peter Euben in *Corrupting Youth*.

7. Since curricular learning takes place largely through the medium of classroom interaction, it is striking that some defenders of curricular moral education pay very little attention to classroom interaction as a source of moral education. See, for example, Michael Walzer's defense of moral education in "Moral Education and Democratic Citizenship," as well as Calvert, "Political Education and the Modern University: A Prologue," in Calvert, *To Restore American Democracy*.

8. See Heyd, ed., *Toleration*, for a good collection exploring these and other complexities of toleration.

9. The distinction between virtues of treating others as human beings *independent* of their social identities, and treating them appropriately *in light of* these identities is explored, in the case of race, in my "Racial Virtues."

10. Taylor, "The Politics of Recognition." Taylor goes on to imply, misleadingly, that cultural identities are always important to individuals. More precisely, what he argues is that social identities are part of individuals' personal identities; but the only sustained example he gives of such social identities is a cultural one. His argument is thus reasonably taken as implying that he thinks cultural identities are important to all individuals, which they aren't.

11. I owe to Richard Weissbourd an emphasis on the idea, and terminology, of "appreciation."

12. *Gratz v. Bollinger* (02-516) 539 U.S. 244 (2003); *Grutter v. Bollinger*, 123 S.Ct. 2325 (2003).

13. The majority opinion is very clear that race is only a very imperfect proxy for perspective.

14. I am not examining what attitude "nonaffirmative action admits" should take toward "affirmative action admits," but only what attitude members of all groups (include members of those groups themselves) should take toward the blacks, Native Americans, and Latinos as a group on one's campus, without distinction as to whether some particular members would have been admitted in the absence of an affirmative action program. It is only their membership in that group, not whether they would have been so admitted, that is pertinent here.

15. I am reporting the feelings of the black and Latino students, to indicate what is involved in inclusion. I am not saying that complex policy decisions such as whether to build dormitories should be dictated solely by the feelings and views of one group of students.

16. The problem of equal vs. special treatment for marginalized groups is excellently treated in Minow, *Making All the Difference*. Minow calls this "the dilemma of difference."

17. Fullinwider and Lichtenberg, *Leveling the Playing Field*, provide an excellent account of this criticism of the diversity rationale (167–69).

18. *Regents of the University of California v. Bakke*, 438 U.S. 265 (1978). The process by which groups other than African Americans—Hispanics, Asians, blacks of other recent origins (Caribbean, African)—came to be included within the scope of affirmative action when they were not initially is a historically and morally complex matter. It is explored in Skrentny, *The Ironies of Affirmative Action* and *The Minority Rights Revolution*; and in Graham, *Collision Course*.

19. The only "racial justice" rationale that continued to be upheld in the University of Michigan cases was that an institution was permitted to use present affirmative action to remedy the effects of *its own* past discrimination. What it could *not* do—but what four justices had upheld in the *Bakke* case—was to remedy "societal" discrimination in general. (See Fullinwider and Lichtenberg, *Leveling the Playing Field*, chaps. 9 and 10.) In an important article on affirmative action, Elizabeth Anderson argues that the diversity rationale makes no sense within constitutional jurisprudence, and that the true purpose of affirmative action is what she calls "integration," that is, the integrating of blacks on a condition of equality with whites in all domains in society. She distinguishes such integration/equality from a purely compensatory argument, which she thinks does not justify affirmative action; but both are justice-based arguments (Anderson, "Integration, Affirmative Action, and Strict Scrutiny"). Anderson's or other justice rationales mean that religion, which seems to me particularly

central to pluralism concerns, is absent in affirmative action rationales, as it is indeed in most affirmative action programs.

20. This is not to deny that ethnicity-based communities can realize moral goods as well. For an argument to that effect, see Blum, "Ethnicity, Identity, and Community."

AGAINST CIVIC EDUCATION IN SCHOOLS

Mark Twain bragged that he never let school interfere with his education. Unfortunately, pedagogues today are rarely so clear about the crucial distinction between schooling and education. We need to be reminded that most of our teachers are not schoolteachers or professors, and most of what we learn we do not learn in school. Yet because of the widespread assumption that schools are the primary locus of education and that schoolteachers are the primary educators, whenever Americans are found to be ill-educated, we blame schoolteachers and let parents, coaches, employers, ministers, scout leaders, army officers, librarians, journalists, doctors, and museum docents off the hook. Thus, today, with widespread awareness of serious and measurable declines in various kinds of moral conduct, from responsible parenting to neighborliness, from basic honesty to voting, we rush to demand that schools and colleges provide moral and civic education.

While the focus of this volume is on colleges and universities and whether or not they ought to pursue some explicit form of moral and civic education, I want to suggest that a broader look at the debates over civic education in schools provides valuable lessons for higher education. What these debates, and the checkered history behind them, reveal is that academic institutions are ineffective agencies for general moral or civic education. Moreover, attempts to use schools for moral and civic education almost always corrupt the appropriate moral purpose of academic education: to inculcate the intellectual virtues.

The Aims of Education and the Aims of Schooling

Given the nearly universal consensus across the political spectrum that schools ought to promote civic virtue, arguing that they should not seems almost perverse. Public schooling in the United States is itself the product of passion for civic education. Universal, publicly funded schools for the purpose of republican civic education were first proposed by French philosophers and economists, such as J.-J. Rousseau and Baron Turgot, in the middle of the eighteenth century. Because J.-B. LaSalle (1651–1719), founder of the Society of Brothers of Christian Schools, had already established a widespread network of local Catholic schools in France, some French *philosophes* advocated publicly funded schools to counteract the moral and political influence of the Catholic Church. These French schemes for republican civic education in universal public schools were first realized, however, not in France but in the Netherlands in the first decade of the nineteenth century. But in the 1830s and 1840s, François Guizot and Victor Cousin, French liberals and successive ministers of public instruction, established a system of public schools for liberal and republican civic education in France. Just as the French *philosophes* had a decisive influence on Jefferson in the 1780s, so the French liberals deeply influenced Horace Mann, one of the founding fathers of American public education, in the 1830s.[1]

From its inception in America in the 1790s, "public education was to be republican civic education."[2] Although there is much to admire about this commitment to universal schooling, the dark side of civic education in public schools was evident from the beginning—not just in its strident anti Catholicism but also in its narrow conception of who deserved to be educated. Thomas Jefferson and his followers took the civic mission of public schools so seriously that they denied schooling to noncitizens, including women, blacks, and Native Americans.[3] And because the fundamental premise of civic education was that civic virtue was compatible only with Protestant religion, Horace Mann clothed his republican civic education accordingly.[4]

To understand the broad appeal of civic education in schools today, we must look at the fate of earlier forms of civic education in our public schools. Although an ecumenical and nondenominational Protestantism appeared to be an appropriate religious and moral basis for common schools in the America of the early nineteenth century, the arrival of large numbers of Catholics and Jews beginning in the 1840s called that assumption into question.[5] Most educators have long agreed that sectarian religious education, even of the ecumenical Protestant variety, violates the civic trust that underpins public support for common schools. How can Catholics and Jews, for example, be expected to financially support common schools that teach a nondenominational Protestantism? Today, debates about moral education in schools are following much the same pattern as did earlier debates about religious education. Liberal and conservative moralists argue that their brand of moral education is uniquely ecumenical and, hence, appropriate for common schools. Liberal moralists ask: Who can be opposed to students learning to become morally autonomous? Conservative moralists ask: Who can be opposed to students learning to become honest, courageous, temperate, and just?[6] But one person's moral ecumenism is another person's moral sectarianism: liberals are suspicious of conservative moralism just as conservatives are suspicious of liberal moralism. Proposals for moral education in public schools have thus become yet another front of the broader culture wars, and many educators are coming to the conclusion that both liberal and conservative moralism violate the civic trust that underpins common schools.

September 11 Strikes the Schools

Consider, for example, the fierce debates about civic education that erupted following the terrorist attacks of September 11, 2001. In response to demands from teachers about how to deal with the messy emotional, racial, religious, and political issues occasioned by the attacks and their aftermath, the National Education Association (NEA) offers a website titled "Remember September 11" full of materials about how to counsel distressed students, how to place 9/11 in some kind of historical, cultural, and international context, and what moral lessons might be drawn from the attack.[7] These moral lessons range from "Remembering the Uniformed Heroes at the World Trade Center" to "Tolerance in Times of Trial." Similarly, the National Council for Social Studies (NCSS) offers lesson plans for 9/11 on its website:[8] these materials range from "The Bill of Rights" to "My Name is Osama," the story of an Iraqi American boy taunted by his peers because of his name and Muslim customs. Although the materials offered by these organizations vary widely, their pervasive theme is well articulated by the president of the NCSS: "We need to reinforce the ideals of tolerance, equity, and social justice against a backlash of antidemocratic sentiments and hostile divisions."

The generally liberal civics lessons offered by the NEA and the NCSS were quickly attacked by conservatives for promoting an unprincipled tolerance, for focusing too much on America's flaws, and for failing to impart a proper knowledge and love of American institutions and ideals. A group of distinguished conservative educators and commentators published a set of their own civics lessons emphasizing the love of our nation and its ideals, the heroism of the rescuers of 9/11, and the need for better knowledge of our history and institutions.[9] These sharply divergent views of proper civics lessons led a *New York Times* news article to note that the anniversary of 9/11 threatened to bring the culture wars back into our classrooms.[10] Even leading political pundits could not resist entering the civic education fray. Thomas Friedman offered his mildly liberal "9/11 Lesson Plan" in which he championed our democratic government while admitting that the United States is not perfect and that our conduct abroad causes dismay even among our friends.[11] William J. Bennett offered a more conservative lesson by insisting that "American students should be taught what makes this nation great. . . . Even with its faults, America remains the best nation on earth."[12]

The strident polemics we frequently find in these civics lessons might well lead one to think that liberals and conservatives can find no common ground. Broadly, one might say that liberal responses to 9/11 emphasize the need to resist jingoism and to consider why hatred of America might be in some ways justified, while conservative responses emphasize our national virtues and the need for resolve to defend them in times of danger. According to conservatives, liberal civics lessons amount to little more than preaching unprincipled toleration even of the intolerable; according to liberals, conservative civics lessons amount to little more than preaching unprincipled patriotism and triumphalism. Still, despite these profound differences about the content of civic education, both liberal and conservative advocates insist that civic education in our schools must reach beyond mere civic knowledge and civic skills to shape our deepest civic values, attitudes, and motivations. In other words, they all agree that civic education must aim at imparting proper civic virtues, though they obviously disagree stridently about which virtues to impart.

Among contemporary political theorists, the debate over civic education closely parallels, albeit at a lower temperature, the polemics over the civics lessons of 9/11. Conservatives, such as Lorraine and Thomas Pangle, defend the views of those American founders who argued that the vast majority of Americans do not need to acquire the virtues of political participation, just the virtue of vigilant judgment of our elected officials.[13] By sharp contrast, the liberal Benjamin Barber insists that all citizens ought to be educated in the civic virtues necessary for competent political participation.[14] And where the Pangles emphasize the virtues of patriotism, zeal for public service, and vigilance, Amy Gutmann emphasizes toleration and mutual respect.[15] Even among liberals there is very little agreement about which civic virtues to teach in schools. Some liberal theorists insist that the political virtues of toleration, civility, and a respect for democratic procedure rest upon the acquisition of the moral virtues of individuality, respect for moral diversity, and autonomy.[16] In this view, liberal democratic politics depends upon morally liberal citizens. Other liberal theorists insist, by contrast, that liberal political virtues, such as political tolerance and respect for the rule of law and democratic procedures, do not depend upon liberal moral virtues such as respect for moral diversity or autonomy. One might be, for example, a very good citizen of a liberal democracy without being morally liberal.[17]

Analyzing the Components of Civic Education

What do these debates about civic education in schools teach us? In practice as well as in theory, we simply cannot agree about the appropriate civic virtues. In the face of such deep and seemingly intractable divisions, holding the education of our children hostage to culture wars over civic virtue seems imprudent at best. Yet despite their vociferous disagreements about the proper content of civic education, liberals and conservatives tend to agree that civic virtue is the proper aim of civic education,[18] although none of them defines what he or she means by virtue or how civic virtue differs from civic knowledge or civic skill.[19]

I will define civic knowledge as an understanding of true facts and concepts about civic affairs, such as the history, structure, and functions of government, the nature of democratic politics, and the ideals of citizenship. Civic skills are the trained capacities for deploying civic knowledge in the pursuit of civic goals, such as voting, protesting, petitioning, canvassing, and debating. Civic virtues integrate civic knowledge and civic skills with proper civic motivations, such as respect for the democratic process, love for the nation, and a conscientious concern for the common good. I follow Linda Zagzebski in defining virtues as success terms: in this view, a person does not have a civic virtue unless he or she has both the proper motivation and the knowledge and skills to be effective in civic engagements.[20] Being effective in civic engagements certainly does not mean that one is always or even often successful: political activity is unavoidably hostage to unpredictable contingency. But no one can claim to have civic virtue who lacks the knowledge and skills to cogently debate and take a stand on public affairs, to elicit the cooperation and support of fellow citizens, and to perform one's chosen or required public duties. In short, in my account, civic skills presuppose civic knowledge just as civic virtue presupposes civic skills.

Civic education ought to aim at civic virtue and not merely at civic knowledge and skills because without a virtuous motivation, knowledge and skills lack moral worth. After all, civic knowledge and skills are routinely put into the service of all manner of immoral political conduct, ranging from the deliberate subordination of the common good to self-interest, including the use of deception, manipulation, and coercion, all the way to a traitorous betrayal of the nation to its enemies. Voting, debating, petitioning, legislating, and administering can be instruments of evil and injustice if they are badly motivated. Proper civic motives need not be selfless or pure, but they cannot be wholly based upon greed or hatred. As it happens, there is good empirical evidence that civic knowledge tends to foster civic virtue—as citizens learn more about political institutions and principles, their political engagements become not only more rationally coherent but also more public-spirited.[21]

Most advocates therefore rightly assume that civic education must aim at civic virtue. Unfortunately, these advocates also assume that civic education aimed at civic virtue is a primary responsibility of public schools. Because of the nearly universal confusion of education with schooling, reflected in the pervasive use of the word "education" to mean only schooling, most advocates of civic education never even betray awareness that civic education need not mean civic schooling. Although most civic education has always taken place outside schools, advocates of civic education almost never consider the comparative advantages of schools and other agencies of civic education. Yet all the best empirical evidence tells us that schools are relatively weak instruments of civic education, especially of civic education aimed at civic virtues. Clear and sound thinking about civic education is impossible until we first learn to distinguish civic education from civic schooling and to theorize the relations between them.

How Schools Can—and Cannot—Contribute to Civic Education

Because our public schools have a long history of engaging in civic education, political scientists over the past five decades have attempted to answer basic questions such as: Where do citizens acquire their civic knowledge, skills, and virtues? What role do schools play in that acquisition? And, in particular, what role do high school civics courses play? While it is difficult to summarize the findings of the leading researchers since some focus on civic skills, some on civic knowledge, and some on civic attitudes, values, and motivations,[22] the best empirical studies show that schools can play a small though significant role in teaching civic knowledge. These same studies, however, also suggest that schools are wholly inept instruments at directly attempting to impart the proper motivations essential to genuine civic virtues. Those studies focusing on the acquisition of civic competence or civic skills find, not surprisingly, that these skills are mainly acquired not by children in schools but by adults in churches, unions, civic organizations, and workplaces.[23] According to these researchers, schools foster civic skills not by directly teaching civics but by encouraging students to volunteer in extracurricular organizations and to participate in student government.[24]

The claim that schooling contributes little to the acquisition of civic virtues may seem surprising. After all, there is a long-standing consensus among researchers that the civic knowledge and civic attitudes of an individual are best predicted by his or her years of schooling. For example, M. Kent Jennings and Richard Niemi survey a huge body of literature about the role of education in political socialization. They report a broad consensus that interest in politics, the possession of political skills, political participation, and support for the liberal democratic creed all increase with years of schooling.[25] Does this suggest that schools are effectively teaching civic virtue? Actually, there is no agreement about how to explain the simple correlation between educational attainment and civic virtue. Since years of schooling correlates strongly with parental intelligence, education, and socioeconomic status as well as with a student's own intelligence and subsequent socioeconomic status and occupation, it is very difficult to tease out the independent role of schooling. Perhaps some third factor, such as parental education or the student's own intelligence, causes both high educational attainment and civic virtue? Some researchers have found that schooling indirectly shapes political knowledge and attitudes by sorting students into various socioeconomic ranks, each with its own distinctive political culture.[26] Other researchers found that in addition to sorting students into socioeconomic ranks, schools also enhance the cognitive sophistication of students and that this greater cognitive sophistication fosters civic knowledge and more tolerant civic attitudes. The sheer cognitive and verbal sophistication fostered by schools seems to indirectly promote certain political attitudes: for example, a college education, especially in the liberal arts, seems to contribute to greater support for the liberal democratic creed. But this effect could not be traced to any particular curriculum or even pedagogical style.[27]

Thus schooling, by fostering greater verbal and cognitive sophistication, also seems to indirectly foster greater civic knowledge and greater political tolerance. But can schools directly impart civic knowledge and proper civic attitudes and motives through a curriculum in civic education? Most states in the United States require public schools to teach civics courses. Since advocates of civic education in public schools strongly support such courses, we must ask what role civics courses play in fostering desirable political knowledge, attitudes, and conduct. After a series of studies in the 1960s, Kenneth Langton and M. Kent Jennings published a very influential one focused on the effects of high school civics courses on a range of political knowledge, attitudes, values, and interests.[28] They found that the high school civics curriculum had very little effect on any aspect of political knowledge or values: "Our findings certainly do not support the thinking of those who look to the civics curriculum in American high schools as even a minor source of political socialization."[29] In 1974, Langton, Jennings, and Niemi revised and enlarged their original study. They now found that the educational level of parents and the amount of political discourse at home had a much greater impact on the measured knowledge and values than did high school courses; where high school civics courses had any effect, it was only on those students who were just finishing those courses.[30] A subsequent study by Paul Allen Beck and Jennings reconfirmed the impotence of civics courses but found that participation in extracurricular activities, both in high school and beyond, fosters later political participation in young adults.[31]

These and other studies created a lasting professional consensus that the scholastic curriculum in general has some effects on the knowledge but little or no effect on the values of students and that civics courses in particular have no effect on political knowledge or values.[32] Richard Niemi and Jane Junn challenge this consensus in their major study, *Civic Education: What Makes Students Learn.* They analyze data that enables them to study the effects of different kinds of civics courses on students' political knowledge and attitudes and hypothesize that certain kinds of teaching methods might significantly add or subtract from learning about politics.[33] They found that although the civics curriculum had much less effect on political knowledge and values than did the home environment, civics courses did matter. In particular, civics courses that were taken quite recently, included a large variety of topics for study, and incorporated discussion of current events fostered significantly greater political knowledge.[34] As with earlier studies, they found that although the curriculum had some effect on political knowledge, it had virtually no effect on political attitudes.[35] It is too soon to tell if this study will alter the existing consensus that civics courses do not matter; some early reviews suggest that that consensus is likely to prevail.[36] Indeed, since the Langton and Jennings study was focused on civic attitudes while the Niemi and Junn study was focused on civic knowledge, both studies converge on the qualified conclusion that civics courses have some small effect on civic knowledge but virtually none on civic attitudes. For those who look to schools as nurseries of civic virtue it is deeply puzzling to note that although we Americans have become vastly more schooled over the past half-century, we are also vastly less likely to vote or otherwise participate in politics or civic life. Our hugely increased scholastic attainments have accompanied broad declines in civic virtue and, perhaps even more surprising, no increases in civic knowledge.[37]

We should not be surprised by the evidence that civic virtue is not acquired by children in school. After all, our contemporary political scientists have merely ratified the wisdom of the greatest political philosophers, ancient and modern, who insisted that civic virtue is acquired only by adults from active participation in public affairs. Plato's guardians, for example, must wait until they are thirty-five years old to begin their fifteen years of civic education, which takes place not in school but in direct participation in governmental affairs.[38] Aristotle is also clear that "a youth is not a suitable student of political science" because, although the intellectual virtues can be taught, the moral virtues result from habit.[39] For Aristotle, civic education is the responsibility of the legislator, not the teacher: the legislator uses law to educate citizens by insuring that they acquire the right habits as they grow up.[40] Once citizens have grown up with the right civic virtues, then, as midcareer politicians, they might benefit from Aristotle's teaching about politics. Tocqueville beautifully captured the ancient view that schools foster academic knowledge just as politics fosters civic virtue: "The institutions of a township are to freedom what primary schools are to science; they put it within the reach of the people; they make them taste its peaceful employ and habituate them to making use of it."[41] What we find, then, in Plato, Aristotle, and Tocqueville are very sophisticated analyses of the various agencies of civic education and a conception of civic education that does not rely on the institution of the school or college.[42]

Both political philosophers and political scientists seem to agree, then, that deliberate instruction aimed at inculcating civic virtue is strikingly ineffective. Some knowledge of the structure and functions of government might well be taught in civics courses, but not proper civic attitudes, such as a desire to contribute to the common good, a respect for democratic values, a love of country, or toleration of opposed views. Yet advocates of civic education in schools insist that civic education must aim not just at knowledge but also at civic virtue. Naturally, advocates of civic education are free to insist that although existing methods of teaching civic virtue in schools are ineffective, some new and better kind of civics might work. Still, in the face of existing research, the demand that schools act as incubators of civic virtue is the perfect triumph of hope over experience.

Intellectual Virtues as the Moral Aim of Schooling

If schools cannot teach civic virtue, does this mean that academic education lacks any sort of moral dimension? The view that academic education involves the mere acquisition of amoral information and skills can be traced back to Immanuel Kant. According to Kant, no amount of academic learning can contribute to moral goodness. Arguing that it would be immoral to arm students with powerful intellectual weapons without any guidance about their use, Kant insisted upon the need for a supplemental moral education, so that information and skills are put to good moral ends.[43] Ever since Kant, most modern pedagogues describe academic education in amoral terms. Today, for example, Howard Gardner emphasizes the acquisition of disciplinary skills while E. D. Hirsch Jr. stresses the acquisition of a shared body of information, but both agree with Kant that academic education does not itself contribute to moral goodness.[44] Indeed, both those who decry efforts to pursue moral and civic education (from religious conservatives to Stanley Fish) as well as those who champion such efforts tend to take it for granted that academic education lacks a moral dimension.

By contrast, I will argue that academic education is itself a kind of moral education—the kind of moral education properly suited to the institution of the school. So I defend the primacy of academic education in schools, not on the grounds that it is fundamentally different from moral education but precisely on the grounds that it is a specific kind of moral education. As every good teacher knows, information and skills cannot be the sole aim of academic education because apart from a virtuous orientation toward truth, information and skills are mere resources and tools that can be put into the service of sophistry, manipulation, and domination. Only when the acquisition of information and skills is combined with a proper desire for true knowledge do we begin to acquire intellectual virtue, which may be defined as the conscientious pursuit of truth.[45]

A virtue is a disposition to do what is good and the skills to reliably achieve it. Virtues are not resources or tools that we use but aspects of who we are. By means of the acquisition of intellectual virtues we change from persons who are credulous and prone to systematic errors in judgment to persons who care about the truth and are reliably skilled in acquiring genuine knowledge. Since true beliefs about the world, in addition to being intrinsically valuable, are a necessary condition for moral conduct, intellectual virtues are essential to the acquisition of the other moral virtues. So an academic education in the intellectual virtues is as deeply transformative of persons as is any other kind of moral education.

Intellectual virtue stems from a desire for genuine knowledge, that is, cognitive contact with reality. The classical intellectual virtues were states of knowledge and truth already attained, such as science, wisdom, under-standing, and technique. But modern accounts of intellectual virtue are more modest and settle for the motivations and skills that reliably enable us to pursue truth. What is essential to all rational discourse is a shared commitment to search for what is true, not a presumption that we have already found it or ever will. Academic education should aim not just to equip us with information and skills but also to shape us into persons who care about genuine knowledge.

Human beings are essentially cognitively interdependent. Our primary source of, and vehicle for, knowledge is language, which we cannot learn by ourselves. Having acquired language, we cannot begin to reason and to learn without relying upon and trusting the discourse of our many teach-ers. Because of the inescapably social dimension of the pursuit of knowl-edge, truth seeking presupposes that our teachers are sincere in telling us what they believe to be true. Language itself presupposes a norm of sincerity of utterance; lying is inherently parasitic upon this norm of sincerity. To be sincere or honest means to report to others what you believe; sincerity is the harmony between what we believe and what we say. Being sincere is not to be confused with telling the truth, since one can be perfectly honest in reporting falsehoods just as one can easily lie by reporting the truth. But sincerity does have an indirect relation to the truth because to believe something is to believe that it is true; no one can believe what he is certain is false. Without the norm of sincerity, the relation of trust between speaker and listener would dissolve and, with it, the whole inescapably social project of seeking knowledge.

Nonetheless, because we are often mistaken about what we believe to be true, we often sincerely report what is false. So sincerity is not sufficient for truth telling, unless it is combined with the virtues of truth seeking. The first stage of my developmental hierarchy of the virtues of truth seeking consists of the virtues of carefulness, such as single-mindedness, thoroughness, accuracy, and perseverance. These seem, at first, to be skills rather than virtues; after all, can't a sophist or a crank be intellectually careful? The skills of intellectual carefulness become virtues only when students come to understand and to value these skills precisely because they promote genuine knowledge. At the second stage we find the higher-order virtues of intellectual courage, intellectual impartiality, and intellec-tual humility. Whereas teachers ought to focus on the virtues of intellectual carefulness in the primary grades, teachers in secondary school and in college ought to attempt to foster these higher-order virtues by requiring students to consider several points of view on a question, to stand up for their judgments, to be willing to consider new and unfamiliar ideas, and to admit the limits of their own knowledge. Teachers can powerfully reinforce these higher-order intellectual virtues pointing out the many temptations we all face to believe what is false because it is widely accepted or convenient or flattering. The goal is to encourage students to be conscientious in their beliefs, which means avoiding being either too credulous or too skeptical. The highest stage of intellectual virtue involves intellectual integrity and wisdom. At best, our teachers can attempt to be an example of these virtues. An intellectually integral person does not collect random facts but seeks coherence and relation in what he or she knows. A wise person seeks coherence not just in what he or she knows but in the whole of life; a wise person both enjoys knowledge and uses it to enrich and illuminate the moral and aesthetic dimensions of his or her life.

In what ways are these intellectual virtues moral virtues? If morality consists of norms governing our pursuits of various goods, then these virtues provide norms for how to pursue the good of knowledge. John Dewey thought that the aim of academic pedagogy was the inculcation of certain traits in students, among them open-mindedness, single-mindedness, sincerity, breadth of outlook, thoroughness, and responsibility. Dewey insisted that these academic or intellectual virtues "are moral traits."[46]

Like the other moral virtues, the intellectual virtues unite information, skill, and our deepest desires in that pursuit. In our practices of praise and blame we certainly treat the intellectual virtues as moral virtues. True, we often praise people for nonmoral qualities, such as strength, beauty, or intelligence, but we blame people only for moral failures, not for being weak, ugly, or stupid. Do we blame people for the quality of their beliefs? We surely do. We call them narrow-minded, careless, intellectually cowardly, rash, imperceptive, prejudiced, rigid, obtuse, superstitious, gullible, dogmatic, and fanatical. Finally, the quality of one's beliefs is inseparably connected to the quality of one's conduct. Virtues, both moral and intellectual, are success terms: they require not only a good motivation but also the information and skills to ensure reliable success. We cannot expect our moral conduct to be reliably virtuous except on the basis of sound knowledge of our world. Intellectual virtue is not sufficient for moral virtue, but it is necessary.

What evidence do we have that schools are the proper instrument for academic education? I noted above that empirical studies of civic education found that schools did have some small effect on civic knowledge even if virtually no effect on civic attitudes or virtues. There are no empirical studies, to my knowledge, of the effectiveness of schools in inculcating the intellectual virtues. But the most influential study of the effects of scholastic attainment on the knowledge of adults may be suggestive of the important role of schools not only in inculcating a body of information but also in fostering a disposition to the lifelong acquisition of knowledge. Herbert Hyman, Charles Wright, and John Reed, in their *The Enduring Effects of Education*, surveyed the knowledge of adults many decades after they had completed their schooling. They found not only that every year of schooling contributed positively to the knowledge base of adults but also that every year of schooling contributed positively to the propensity of adults to continue learning by reading newspapers, magazines, books, and seeking out opportunities for adult education. By including in their survey knowledge of current events, these researchers were able to establish that those adults who had the most schooling were also keeping abreast of current events most effectively. So we have some evidence that schools do effectively foster a lifelong love for learning.[47]

Once we see that the conscientious pursuit of knowledge is the inherent moral purpose of schooling, we will not be surprised by the absence of any agreement about which civic virtues we ought to teach in schools. Since none of the civic virtues is intrinsically related to the inherent moral purpose of schooling, there is no academically principled way to decide which civic virtues ought to be taught in schools. I quite strongly value a commitment to human rights, the rule of law, public service, and a love of our country, but I don't see what these noble virtues have to do with pursuing knowledge of physics, French, English, chemistry, history, and math. No catalogue of civic virtues can be shown to be a prerequisite of academic excellence, a part of academic excellence, or the product of academic excellence. Trying to decide which civic virtues to teach in schools is like trying to decide which sports or which crafts to teach: since none of these is intrinsically related to academic education, there are no academic grounds for deciding these matters.

Because civic education, like driver or consumer education, lacks an intrinsic relation to the academic curriculum, it quickly becomes regarded by teachers and students as ancillary and irrelevant. The purely ancillary nature of civics courses may help to explain why they prove to be so ineffective. To overcome this irrelevance, many advocates insist that civic education become incorporated into the core academic curriculum, so that English, history, and social studies courses impart lessons in civic virtue. But here we become impaled upon the fundamental dilemma of civic education: if we teach civic virtue in a way that respects the integrity of the academic curriculum, then civics becomes merely ancillary and irrelevant; but if, to overcome this irrelevance, we attempt to incorporate civic education into the academic subjects, then we inevitably subvert the inherent moral aim of those subjects by subordinating the pursuit of truth to civic uplift.

Why Civic Education Corrupts Schools

What happens to academic education when schools commit to the pursuit of civic education? Whether we look to the history of civic education or to the theories of civic educators, the answer is quite certain: the academic pursuit of knowledge is corrupted through a subordination of truth seeking to a civic agenda.

The history of civic education in the United States is a cautionary tale indeed. Many advocates of civic education invoke the prestige of Thomas Jefferson, who was a leading pioneer and prophet of using common schools for republican civic education.[48] What these advocates fail to notice, however, is how Jefferson's commitment to civic education corrupted his own intellectual integrity. Jefferson's initial vision of his proposed new University of Virginia reflected his lifelong commitment to the freedom of the human mind from every tyranny erected over it: "This institution," he wrote, "will be based on the illimitable freedom of the human mind. For here we are not afraid to follow the truth wherever it may lead, nor to tolerate any error so long as reason is left free to combat it."[49] But as a civic educator Jefferson could not bear the thought of future students at his university being exposed to and corrupted by politically incorrect ideas. Thus, in order to protect them from the seductive Toryism of David Hume, Jefferson spent two decades promoting the publication of a censored, plagiarized, and falsified edition of Hume's *History of En-*

gland.[50] When he could find no partners in this intellectual crime, he enlisted James Madison's support as a fellow member of the board of overseers of the nascent University of Virginia to draft regulations aimed at suppressing political heresy and promoting political orthodoxy. Jefferson and Madison succeeded in passing a resolution to "provide that none [of the principles of government] shall be inculcated which are incompatible with those on which the Constitutions of this state, and of the U.S. were genuinely based, in the common opinion." This resolution goes on to specify the texts that must be taught in the school of politics (Locke, Sidney, *The Federalist*, and U.S. and Virginia constitutional documents).[51] Moreover, Jefferson came to agree with Madison's argument that "the most effectual safeguard against heretical intrusions into the School of politics, will be an able & orthodox Professor."[52] To this end, Jefferson and later Madison worked to ensure that only those professors who espoused a strict construction of the U.S. constitution and the doctrine of states' rights would be appointed to the school of politics.[53] Because of his passion for civic education in republican virtue, Jefferson abandoned his commitment to intellectual freedom in favor of partisan indoctrination at his own beloved University of Virginia. That such a champion of intellectual freedom who swore undying enmity to every tyranny over the mind of man should himself attempt to whitewash, censor, and suppress what he called "heresy" powerfully illustrates the poisonous consequences of using schools as instruments of civic education.

Jefferson has truly been the poisoned wellspring of American civic education in schools ever since. American textbook writers in every epoch have systematically sanitized, distorted, and falsified history, literature, and social studies in order to inculcate racism, nationalism, every manner of religious, cultural and class bigotry, Anglo-Saxon superiority, American imperialism, Social Darwinism, anti-Catholicism, and anti-intellectualism.[54] An early text from 1796 warns of the danger posed by the importation of French ideas and persons: "Let America beware of infidelity, which is the most dangerous enemy that she has to contend with at present"; the author goes on to teach schoolchildren that Native Americans lack all science, culture, and religion, that they are averse to labor and foresight, and that "the beavers exceed the Indians, ten-fold, in the construction of their homes and public works."[55] Later, in the wake of large-scale Irish immigration, school texts began a massive campaign of slander and calumny against Roman Catholicism. Textbooks not only describe Catholicism as an anti-Christian form of paganism and idolatry; they even blame the Church for the fall of the Roman Empire. One speller asks: "Is papacy at variance with paganism?" One historian notes that no theme in school texts before 1870 is more universal than anti-Catholicism; according to these texts, Catholicism has no place in the American past or future.[56] In the period after 1870, religious bigotry gives way to racial bigotry and all non-Anglo-Saxon peoples are described as permanently and immutably inferior due to their intellectual, moral, and physical degeneracy. Beginning in 1917, many states began to pass laws forbidding any instruction in public schools that might be disloyal to the United States, including the teaching of the German language; at the same time, many states also passed laws requiring all public schoolteachers to be American citizens and to swear an oath that they will teach patriotism.[57]

Nor is this subordination of knowledge to civic uplift a relic of the past: in many states, creationism is taught in place of biology and geology because of the perceived moral dangers of Darwinism. And many states continue to require American history to be falsified in order to promote patriotism: the Texas Education Code provides that "textbooks should promote democracy, patriotism, and the free enterprise system"; this provision is still employed to sanitize the teaching of history in Texas.[58] The New York Board of Regents was found to have falsified, on moral grounds, most of the literary texts used in its exams; here classic literature was bowdlerized in the interests of political correctness.[59] Some systematic studies of current social studies and history textbooks find extensive evidence of how American history is now distorted, twisted, and falsified in order to emphasize the previously neglected contributions as well as the victimization of women and minorities.[60] Although Anglo-Saxon triumphalism now frequently gives way to multicultural victimization, nothing has changed in the American passion for subordinating truth seeking to moral and civic uplift.

No one should be surprised that American schoolbooks, like any fallible form of human knowledge, should often prove mistaken and misguided. But our textbooks do not go astray merely because their authors were fallible human beings sincerely seeking true knowledge; rather, these texts go astray because their authors deliberately subordinate the pursuit of knowledge to an agenda for civic education. Our textbooks are often explicitly anti-intellectual: they repeatedly emphasize that moral and civic virtue is far more important than mere knowledge.[61] What again and again proves fatal to the pursuit of knowledge is the conviction that civic virtue is more important than truth. Indeed, some leading contemporary advocates of civic education in schools frankly admit the need to sanitize and falsify history.[62]

In both practice and theory, there is compelling evidence that civic education poses a fundamental threat to academic education and to the acquisition of those traits of character, such as thoroughness, accuracy, perseverance, intellectual humility, and intellectual courage, which make us conscientious in the pursuit of true knowledge.

Conclusion: The Moral Purposes of School

What lessons should schoolteachers and college professors glean from the history of civic education in the schools? Instead of constantly subordinating knowledge to moral uplift, we ought to have more confidence in the sheer moral value of knowledge. As we have seen, the sheer cognitive sophistication cultivated in schools strongly contributes to political tolerance, that is, the willingness to extend civil liberties to those with whom we strongly disagree.[63] A leading team of political scientists offers this hypothesis: "If we are correct that the number of years of formal schooling acts to increase tolerance regardless of the manifest and subtle political content of that education, then educational attainment should act to increase tolerance even in regimes with contrary messages." They found strong evidence that years of schooling increased political tolerance even in communist Hungary. Ironically, intolerant regimes foster toleration simply by schooling their citizens—even when (or especially when?) that schooling is designed to foster political intolerance.[64] And efforts to teach political knowledge have been shown to promote political tolerance, active participation in politics, more coherent political opinions, and a more rational relation between participation and one's political goals.[65] So we ought to be confident that we are contributing significantly to civic virtue merely by attempting to impart genuine knowledge and, in particular, civic knowledge to our students. In light of the ineffective and often counterproductive nature of civic education aimed directly at civic virtue, we have many reasons to believe that schools are better advised simply to stick to their essential task of pursuing genuine knowledge. No doubt this scholastic kind of civic education is seriously deficient, but we must remember that most of what we learn in life is not learned in school and most of our teachers are not schoolteachers.

What is the relation of schooling to civic education more broadly? That is a very large question that would take us far beyond the scope of this essay. But I will briefly consider, by way of a partial answer, the relation of the intellectual virtues to the civic virtues. A good citizen ought to possess the intellectual virtues because they will help him or her to resist false beliefs; bad politicians frequently tempt us to believe things that are false by appealing to our national pride, our greed, our resentments, or our fears for the future. Intellectual virtue means precisely acquiring those dispositions that lead us to resist these temptations to false beliefs. A good citizen need not care only about the truth of his or her political beliefs; nor must a good citizen, as a partisan, advocate the whole truth. But a good citizen must care about whether the views he or she advocates are true. So intellectual virtue might be necessary for good citizens but hardly sufficient. An intellectual paragon might well be a lousy citizen: no amount of conscientiousness in the pursuit of truth constitutes or even reliably leads to a zeal for public service or the courage to defend one's nation. Indeed, as Plato famously observed, those who most sincerely love genuine knowledge are often the most repelled by the inevitable simplifications and distortions of political ideology and rhetoric. It is very difficult to reconcile a passion for knowledge with the political imperatives to advocate partial truths, to hide the truth at times, and to appeal to nonrational passions. None of this, I believe, amounts to a fundamental incompatibility between intellectual and civic virtue but it does suggest some real tensions and moral challenges. So a scholastic education is only a partial civic education and the intellectual virtues are only a part of the civic virtues.

What kind of moral and civic education is compatible with the academic integrity of schooling and the pursuit of knowledge? Schools can indirectly contribute to general moral and civic virtue by teaching, for example, civic knowledge and by encouraging participation in student government and in civic-minded extracurricular activities. Schools can teach about civic and moral virtue without attempting to inculcate them, just as they can teach about religion without preaching. Moreover, some moral virtues are necessary conditions for scholastic learning: respect for the right of all students, of whatever race or creed or gender, to learn and to express themselves; academic honesty; fairness in discipline, rewards, and grading; a willingness to learn from others; and much else. In short, the essential mission of schooling is to foster the acquisition of the intellectual virtues and of other moral virtues that may be necessary preconditions for that acquisition. But to attempt anything more is both unrealistic and dangerous.

Notes

This essay draws freely upon my article "Good Students and Good Citizens" in the *New York Times*, Sunday, September 15, 2002 (op-ed) and my article "Against Civic Schooling" in *Social Philosophy and Policy* 21 (winter 2004): 221–65.

1. For the origins of public schooling in Europe and America, see Glenn, *The Myth of the Common School*, 15–62; for France, see Nique, *Comment l'école devint une affaire d'état*.
2. Smith, *Civic Ideals*, 217.
3. Lawrence Cremin says of Jefferson: "Granted his abiding concern with the education of the people, he defined the people in political terms—as free white males." See *American Education*, 114. Rogers Smith says of the Jeffersonians: "Education came to be so identified with preparation for citizenship that noncitizens were often denied it." See his *Civic Ideals*, 189.
4. As Cremin says: "In essence, Mann accepted the propositions of the republican style of educational thought and recast them in the forms of nineteenth-century nondenominational Protestantism." *American Education*, 136–37.
5. As Diane Ravitch rightly observes: "Mann's nonsectarianism, we now recognize, was nondenominational Protestantism." See her "Education and Democracy," 18.
6. Liberal moral education is usually neo-Kantian and emphasizes critical reflection and autonomous choice; conservative moral education is usually neo-Aristotelian and emphasizes character formation and virtue.
7. http://neahin.org.
8. http://www.socialstudies.org.
9. See "September 11: What Our Children Need to Know" (Thomas B. Fordham Foundation, September 2002), http://www.edexcellence.net.
10. See Zernike, "Lesson Plans for Sept. 11 Offer a Study in Discord."
11. Friedman, "9/11 Lesson Plan."
12. Bennett, "A Time for Clarity."
13. See Pangle and Pangle, "What the American Founders Have to Teach Us about Schooling for Democratic Citizenship," 26–27.
14. Barber, *An Aristocracy of Everyone*, 5: "Citizens are women and men educated

for excellence—by which term I mean the knowledge and competence to govern in common their own lives. The democratic faith is rooted in the belief that all humans are capable of such excellence."

15. Gutmann, "Why Should Schools Care about Civic Education?," 81: "Should schools go beyond teaching the most basic virtue of toleration and also teach mutual respect?"

16. "It is probably impossible to teach children the skills and virtues of democratic citizenship in a diverse society without at the same time teaching them many of the virtues and skills of individuality or autonomy." Gutmann, "Civic Education and Social Diversity," 563.

17. For example, John Tomasi argues that politically liberal civic virtues ought to be compatible with liberal and nonliberal ways of life, not just with "some philosophical ideal of moral autonomy (such as that inspired by the work of Mill or Kant) but also those that come from more embedded, traditionalist ways of understanding reasons for action and attitude (the 'reasonable Romantics,' or citizens of faith)." See his "Civic Education and Ethical Subservience," 207–8.

18. According to the Pangles, however: "It is a mark of the grave difficulties into which our democracy has fallen that the very idea of civic virtue has passed out of currency." See "What the American Founders Have to Teach Us About Schooling for Democratic Citizenship," 21. In reality, as we have seen, the language of civic virtue is ubiquitous in debates about civic education.

19. In the report "The Role of Civic Education," as part of the National Standards for Civics and Government (Center for Civic Education, 1994), Margaret Stimman Branson distinguishes the three essential components of civic education as civic knowledge, civic skills, and civic dispositions, without attempting to theorize the relations among them. See www.civiced.org.

20. "A virtue, then, can be defined as a deep and enduring acquired excellence of a person, involving a characteristic motivation to produce a certain desired end and reliable success in bringing about that end." Zagzebski, *Virtues of the Mind*, 137.

21. See Galston, "Civic Knowledge, Civic Education and Civic Engagement." Galston's brief for civic knowledge fails, however, to consider the inadequacy of civic knowledge and the dangers of its misuse.

22. For a fuller analysis of the empirical literature on civic education, see my "Against Civic Schooling."

23. See Almond and Verba, *The Civic Culture*, 304, 355, 363–66, 381, 387; Almond and Verba, eds., *The Civic Culture Revisited*, 29.

24. See Verba, Schlozman, and Brady, *Voice and Equality*, 376 and 425. They find that American high schools provide civic education "not by teaching about

democracy but by providing hands-on training for future participation." Robert Putnam endorses these findings in his *Bowling Alone*, 339–40 and 405.

25. Jennings and Niemi, *Generations and Politics*, 230.

26. Ibid., 270.

27. On cognitive sophistication as the key link between schooling and civic knowledge and attitudes, see Nie, Junn, and Stehlik-Barry, *Education and Democratic Citizenship in America*, 39 and 161; Nie and Hillygus, "Education and Democratic Citizenship," 50. For college, see Jacob, *Changing Values in College*, 4 and 8.

28. Langton and Jennings, "Political Socialization and the High School Civics Curriculum in the United States." They examined the effects of these courses on political knowledge, political interest, spectator interest in politics, political discourse, political efficacy, political cynicism, civic tolerance, and participative orientation.

29. Black students were a partial exception to this rule: "The civics curriculum is an important source of political knowledge for Negroes" (865 and 860).

30. Langton, Jennings, and Niemi, "Effects of the High School Civics Curriculum," 191: "in the very short run the curriculum exerts what little effect it has on those under current exposure" (192).

31. Beck and Jennings "Pathways to Participation," 101–2: "those who engage in extracurricular activities are more likely to become politically active later on" (105).

32. See the discussion of the scholarly consensus in Niemi and Junn, *Civic Education*, 13–20. They comment: "The presumption that academic knowledge is gained entirely or even primarily in the classroom may be a truism for some subjects but not for civics" (61).

33. Ibid., 81.

34. Ibid., 123–24.

35. Ibid., 140.

36. See Greene, "Review of *Civic Education*." Greene performed a reanalysis of the Niemi and Junn data set and found that the variable of how recently the civics course was taken collapsed into whether a student is enrolled in a civics class at the time the civics test is taken: "If knowledge fades so rapidly that the only benefit of a civics class occurs while one is in it, then schools may not be able to do much to improve civics knowledge in the longer run." Greene found defects in other independent variables as well.

37. On this puzzle, see Nie, Junn, and Stehlik-Barry, *Education and Democratic Citizenship in America*, 99, and Michael X. Delli Carpini and Scott Keeter *What Americans Know about Politics and Why It Matters*, 199.

38. Plato, *Republic* (Bloom, trans.), 539e.

39. Aristotle, *Nicomachean Ethics* 1095a 3 and 1103a 15.

40. Ibid. 1103b 4, 1103b 21, 1180a 32.

41. Tocqueville, *Democracy in America*, 1: 1, 5 (p. 57).

42. True, Aristotle does recommend public or common schooling over private schooling (*Politics* 1337a 3; *Ethics* 1180a 14); but there is no evidence that he thinks these schools should aim at civic education; in fact, he prefers a liberal education for leisure over a civic education (*Politics* 1338a 21–32).

43. Kant, *Pädagogik*, 9: 449. Cf. *Grundlegung*, 4: 423; *Metaphysik der Sitten*, 6: 392, 444–45. All works in *Gesammelte Schriften*.

44. See Gardner, *The Disciplined Mind*; Hirsch, *The Schools We Need*.

45. See Zagzebski, *Virtues of the Mind*, 175–77.

46. Dewey, *Democracy and Education*, 356–57; cf. 173–79.

47. Hyman, Wright, and Reed. *The Enduring Effects of Education*, 80–93.

48. See, for one example, Pangle and Pangle, "What the American Founders Have to Teach Us about Schooling for Democratic Citizenship."

49. Jefferson, quoted in Levy, *Jefferson and Civil Liberties*, 157. Levy comments about this noble aspiration: "Six years later and only a few months before his death, he viewed the law school as the place from which the path of future generations would be lit by the vestal flame of political partisanship rather than by truth or unfettered inquiry."

50. On Jefferson's decades-long promotion of Baxter's plagiarized, falsified, and republicanized edition of Hume, see Malone, *Jefferson and His Time*, 6: 205–7; Bestor, "Thomas Jefferson and the Freedom of Books," 1–44: "It is embarrassing, to say the least, to find Jefferson recommending such a sorry combination of plagiarism, expurgation, and clandestine emendation" (18).

51. See the "Minutes of the Board of Visitors of the University of Virginia, March 4, 1825" in Bestor, "Thomas Jefferson and Freedom of Books," 43–44. Among the mandatory texts were the Virginia Resolutions of 1798–1800, which uphold the states'-rights, strict-constructionist interpretation of the Constitution, according to Bestor (27).

52. See Madison to Jefferson, February 8, 1825, in Bestor, "Thomas Jefferson and Freedom of Books," 41–42.

53. See the letters of Jefferson and of Madison in Bestor, "Thomas Jefferson and Freedom of Books," 39–44.

54. Among many histories of American civic education, see Smith, *Civic Ideals*; Pierce, *Civic Attitudes in American School Textbooks*; Elson, *Guardians of Tradition*.

55. Winchester, *A Plain Political Catechism Intended for the Use of Schools in the United States of America*, questions LX and LXV.

56. See Elson, *Guardians of Tradition*, 47–48, 53.

57. See Pierce, *Civic Attitudes in American School Textbooks*, 229–39.

58. See "Textbook Publishers Learn: Avoid Messing with Texas," *New York Times*, June 29, 2002, A1 and B9.

59. See "The Elderly Man and the Sea? Test Sanitizes Literary Texts," *New York Times*, June 2, 2002, A1.

60. See Sewall, "History Textbooks at the New Century"; Vitz, *Censorship*.

61. See Elson, *Guardians of Tradition*, 226.

62. William Galston rightly observes about the purpose of civic education: "It is unlikely, to say the least, that the truth will be fully consistent with this purpose." But he goes on to defend the imperative to falsify history in order to produce good citizens: "For example, rigorous historical research will almost certainly vindicate complex 'revisionist' accounts of key figures in American history. Civic education, however, requires a more noble, moralizing history: a pantheon of heroes, who confer legitimacy on central institutions and constitute worthy objects of emulation." See Galston, "Civic Education in the Liberal State," 90–91.

63. "It is the cognitive outcomes of education, rather than the positional outcomes, that are responsible for the connection between education and tolerance." Nie, Junn, and Stehlik-Barry, *Education and Democratic Citizenship in America*, 72.

64. "The communist regimes in Eastern Europe, with their emphasis for the last half-century on modernization through education, unintentionally created new generations of citizens who were prone to work for the toppling of the very regimes that saw to their education." Nie, Junn, and Stehlik-Barry, *Education and Democratic Citizenship in America*, 184.

65. See Carpini and Keeter, *What Americans Know about Politics and Why It Matters*, 219.

EDUCATION, INDEPENDENCE, AND ACKNOWLEDGMENT

It is not hard to be suspicious of the project of "moral education" in contemporary colleges and universities. To some ears, the very phrase will seem to hearken back to a different era in the history of American higher education: when college enrollment was largely the province of a small fraction of young Christian men; when moral philosophy was understood as a systematic and encompassing "capstone" subject, whose unity echoed the whole-ness of God; when a university president's address to the fresh-man class could include among its moral exhortations the admo-nition to "bathe daily" (along with the helpful reminder that "washing the parts conventionally exposed to the weather is not a bath"); and when the university's ethical mission was, some-times, expressed in terms of the cultivation of the manhood and virtue that qualified Anglo-Saxon Americans to rule their racial inferiors.[1] Some will find the idea of a specifically *moral* educa-tion troubling for different reasons: because the term "morality" (unlike, perhaps, "ethics") risks flattening a rich field of ques-tions about conduct into the single register of law, dutiful obe-dience, and righteous punishment;[2] or because that term (*like*, perhaps, "ethics") risks reducing politics and citizenship to mat-ters of individual virtue.[3] Some will find it hard to free the idea of moral education from the embrace of right-wing culture war-riors. Some will worry that making professors into moral ped-agogues threatens the university's central mission of rigorous intellectual inquiry.[4]

All these considerations leave me wary of the project of moral education. But that wariness itself also meets with resistance. Moral education is hardly reducible to its least-appealing historical or contemporary exemplars. Some defenders of moral education use the term inclusively, treating "morals" as synonymous with "ethics." Some show particular concern with the habits of mind and conduct that enable critical, active citizenship, pressing the ethical as far as it will go toward the political.[5] Especially for academics trained in political theory or philosophy, moral issues broadly construed are not so obviously alien to our intellectual specializations. Moreover, for scholars who do not produce expert knowledge of obvious instrumental value to states and corporations, the idea that our classrooms are sites of ethical and political education remains a tempting alternative defense of our institutional existence (although banking on that fund of cultural capital can easily foster preachiness, presumptive nationalism, or both).[6] And, finally, if "ethics" at bottom refers to the formation of character—that is, to the whole range of practices by which we give relatively stable shape to our conduct, against the background of some evaluative perspective—then college and university education would seem always to be implicated in ethics, even when it does not take up ethics as an explicit topic of reflection or make it an object of deliberate inculcation. Classrooms are, after all, scenes of instruction, in which, if only by example, we teach students the dispositions and habits that we take to be appropriate to various practices of inquiry and show them why these practices might be worth learning (even the ideal of value-free social science is itself an ethic, as Weber knew); and they are also scenes of often affectively intense and therefore formative interaction among students, instructors, and, in a somewhat different sense, their objects of study.

The point of what follows is not to overcome the ambivalence I have just charted. Instead, I want to try to inhabit that ambivalence and make it productive, asking *how* collegiate and university education might concern itself with ethics, and doing so while sustaining both my wariness about moral education and my sense of the inescapability of the ethical. My strategy is twofold. First, I focus on understanding the constitutive problems that characterize ethical education, without assuming either that those problems can be resolved tidily or that their irresolvability justifies the abandonment of attention to the ethical. What I hope to show here is that the *range* of problems constitutive of the project of ethical education is wider than we often notice; in particular, I will suggest that the familiar problem posed by the persistent presence of authority in educational practices—namely, that education seems liable to collapse into indoctrination—is, while genuine, nevertheless rooted in an excessively narrow view of what it means to be an ethical agent, and so of the aim of moral education. Second, in trying to spell out some of the dimensions of ethical education that a focus on the problem of indoctrination occludes, I will also focus less on moral education as a discrete project (pursued, for instance, through courses devoted explicitly to moral problems, in service-learning courses, or in ethically motivated extracurricular programs) than on the sort of ethical work that gets performed in the classroom even when ethics per se is not the topic at hand or the central point of the exercise. The classroom context to which I will refer, not because I take it to be paradigmatic of education as such but merely because I have some personal experience with it, is an introductory undergraduate course in Western political theory, organized around close readings of canonical texts; complicating matters a little, I will focus in particular on the reading and teaching of a text that is itself ethically fraught and so often brings ethical issues into the foreground: Karl Marx's "On the Jewish Question."

As Elizabeth Kiss's and Peter Euben's framing essay for this volume observes, one commonplace worry about moral or ethical education is that it will amount to little more than indoctrination.[7] This concern can be taken as an objection to moral education as such—that is how it seems to function for Stanley Fish, for instance; and it also echoes in some of the reasons for wariness about moral education with which I began[8]—but it can also and more usefully be understood as a concern internal to the field of the ethical; that is, as a problem that moral education seems to face on its own terms. The trouble is that, while education invariably seems to depend upon at least *some* relationships of authority (a point readily conceded, even emphasized, by critics of traditional models of education, from Dewey to Giroux),[9] the point of such education is not to reproduce students' subjection but to prepare them for and move them toward freedom and independence. As Amy Gutmann put it in an intervention into the debate about multiculturalism and the canon in the 1990s, "well-educated, open-minded people and liberal democratic citizens must *think for themselves*," and so must not be made to engage in the "idol worship" of the great books, or any others;[10] similarly, Kiss and Euben insist that a "political" as opposed to a "politicized" education will engage students in an "open-ended process of critical inquiry" that "seeks to cultivate the capacity for independent judgment."[11]

This way of setting the problem of moral education is so familiar as to seem second nature. Disciplinary political theorists, for instance, will recognize its long history in (what has now come to be called) "liberal" political thought. Concern with the relationship of authority to independence informed Locke's rejection of the notion that fathers possessed an "Absolute Arbitrary Dominion" over their children, along with his extensive reflections on the forms of parental and tutorial education that would enable young men to make the transition between being governed by others and governing themselves.[12] Kant represented enlightenment as an emergence from intellectual "immaturity" to self-reliance, while at the same time suggesting that the "hard shell" of obedience to civil authority might paradoxically be the external condition that "gives intellectual freedom enough room to expand to its fullest extent."[13] Similar terms structure John Stuart Mill's thought, from his passionate defense of individuality for a human being "arrived at the maturity of his faculties," to his qualified but firm defense of the paternalistic government of "uncivilized races" by Europeans, which "government of leading-strings," he insisted, could be justified only insofar as it prepared the subject populations "to walk alone."[14]

In each of these examples, education marks a point of discomfort, bringing into the foreground the paradoxical dependence of freedom and independence on something else: the discipline and constraint imposed by parents and guardians; obedience to the monarch; imperial rule. In political theory and philosophy, this has been liberalism's point of continued vulnerability to, and continuity with, its so-called communitarian critique.[15] I say "continuity" because this critique actually tends to share the basic thought that the point of moral or ethical education ought to be to facilitate the transformation of people into independent, self-governing agents: if for liberals this independence is paradigmatically experienced in an individual's act of unconstrained choice, for its critics—and especially for the neo-Hegelians among them—it is paradigmatically experienced in *knowing* who one is; that is, in coming to recognize oneself in the self-determining activity of a larger collectivity in which one is embedded.[16]

This way of framing the general aim and constitutive problem of moral education—indeed, of education in general—is, unsurprisingly, consonant with some familiar ways of approaching the study and teaching of subjects like political theory, including the sort of political theory that involves the reading of texts in the history of political thought. The first, liberal variant of this frame, for instance, might encourage us to conceive of such textual study as a kind of preparation for students' own critical reflection on, and judgment about, difficult questions of ethics and political life. In this view, the history of political thought would constitute a kind of bazaar of systems, arguments, and positions, which students ought to subject to rational scrutiny, accepting and adapting whatever is defensible and relevant, abandoning whatever isn't, and in the process honing their argumentative and analytic skills. The role of the instructor, in turn, would be to help students refine these skills by pressing them to intensify their skepticism at crucial points and also to enforce certain procedural conditions in the classroom, such as mutual respect and civility, that make rational discourse about these texts possible. The stated rationale of Harvard's core curriculum program, where I first taught the history of political theory as a teaching assistant in a course called "Moral Reasoning," exemplifies this approach: "The curriculum," it says, "should give students some practice in thinking critically about moral and ethical problems, examining their own moral assumptions, and judging with some objectivity the assumptions of various alternative traditions of ethical thought and practice."[17]

All on its own, of course, this highly formal and procedural rationale cannot explain why this sort of education in critical ethical reasoning should proceed through the teaching of historical texts, much less why it should proceed via some texts and not others—which is why this approach rarely, if ever, appears in an entirely pure form but is instead supplemented —and, often, challenged—by another view, in which the study of texts in the history of political thought is not (only) an analytic exercise but (also) a process in which "we" (that two-letter powder keg of the canon wars) can acquire a richer understanding of who we are by becoming acquainted with the traditions of thought that have helped to set our present horizons. Correspondingly, in this view, the instructor would serve more than a merely formal function; instead, his or her authority would be used to secure the generational continuity of these traditions (though not insulating them from transformation): for instance, by selecting the periods and texts to be examined; or by supplying students with the contextual information and material they need to make sense of the texts under study. The title of the undergraduate core curriculum sequence in which I now teach at Chicago, "*Classics* of Social and Political Thought," might be taken to signal this difference in pedagogical philosophy, although of course Chicago's official description of its core program also emphasizes the formal goal of facilitating critical thinking rather than "transfer[ring] information."[18]

These two characterizations, while highly stylized, do seem to me to reflect two fairly common ways of describing the ethical aims and pedagogical methods of undergraduate education in the history of political theory, which are often invoked in more or less uneasy combination. The relationship of tense interdependence between these approaches also echoes an older and wider tension in the history of American higher education between an emphasis on the acquisition of the formal skills of investigation and reasoning, reflected, for instance, in the post–Civil War rise of the elective system at institutions like Harvard; and an emphasis on the transmission of a particular body of knowledge or intellectual heritage, exemplified by the rise of general education programs in the twentieth century, which were at least in part reactions against the incoherence and decline thought to have been brought on by earlier reformers' excessive indulgence of student choice.[19] Still, I want to suggest that these ways of thinking about the aims and problems of ethical education, and about instruction in the history of political theory, influential though they are, hardly exhaust the possibilities—and the best way to make this point is to return to the guiding assumption that informs both of these approaches, namely, that the central aim of ethical education is to prepare students for one sort or another of *independence.*

In many respects, of course, the picture of education as a preparation for independence is compelling, partly because social, legal, and political institutions *do* afford more room for self-guided action to adults than to children; and partly because the phenomenon of the newborn infant's profound dependence upon adults for its physical survival is easily converted into a general parable about the significance of childhood and adulthood. Yet the problem is that even "mature" human agents are not fully independent, partly because whatever independence people possess bears the traces of the rewards and punishments through which it was brought into being, and also because people act in an intersubjective field that is constitutively unpredictable, capable of surprising us in fulfilling and also in shattering ways, and never susceptible to a final, reassuring comprehension, at least as long as we are still acting. This way of thinking about human action has a long and distinguished history, ranging from the Greek tragedians' humbling portrayals of the consequences of hyperbolic claims to self-sufficiency, to Hannah Arendt's insistence upon the difference between freedom and "sovereignty," to the psychoanalytic exploration of the haunting of the self by the slag of its own ongoing formation. From this point of view, to plot human life on a trajectory from infantile dependence to mature independence is less to describe than to fantasize, and efforts to shape the world in ways that sustain these fantasies have exacted a tremendous ethical and political toll.[20]

Elsewhere, drawing on some of these ideas, I have argued that many forms of ethical and political injustice, especially those that now tend to be understood in terms of failures to see and respect the identities of others, might better be understood as failures of "acknowledgment"—that is, as forms of blindness to our own condition of practical finitude, expressed in and sustained by social and political practices and institutions that secure a semblance of independence for some through the subordination of others.[21] Understood in these terms, "acknowledgment" is an interestingly para-ethical concept. On the one hand, it is not obviously the object of concrete obligations to particular others in the way that respect or recognition might be. Nor does it fit easily into the sort of approach to ethics and politics that sees justice as the reliable result of the cultivation of a stably virtuous individual character, since part of what acknowledgment acknowledges is the exposure of *êthos* (and thus of ethics) to a field of action it cannot completely master.[22] On the other hand, it also seems possible that acknowledgment is the sort of thing that might be taught or learned, though not through direct exhortation: insofar as a wide range of particular practices and forms of conduct depend for their successful performance upon an acceptance of finitude on the part of their participants—having a conversation is one obvious example—then coming to know how to do the thing in question must include learning the acknowledgment that partly constitutes it; teaching acknowledgment, in turn, might involve redescribing such activities and practices in ways that highlight their dependence upon acknowledgment; showing what would count as acknowledgment in this or that particular case; motivating acknowledgment by making vivid the value or appeal of the activity in question; and cultivating acknowledgment by presenting contexts and occasions for its practice.

I have already mentioned that a theoretical appreciation of acknowledgment can be found in some of the works of the Athenian tragedians; but it is also possible to understand the *institution* of tragic performance as, in part, educational in just this way. As Peter Euben, among others, has suggested, tragedy stood in a complicated relationship to the official ideologies and dominant self-understandings of Athens: on the one hand, its incorporation into an important civic festival made it into a device for the expression and validation of those ideologies and understandings; on the other hand, the confinement of the festival to a discrete moment on the civic calendar and to the contained physical space of the theater *also* made it possible for tragic performance to call into question the certitudes that, at another level, it reproduced.[23] Understood as a political institution, then, tragedy exemplifies the turning back upon itself and the self-exposure that, I have suggested, is a mark of acknowledgment, giving dramatic representation to the fact that, as Euben puts it, human beings wish to but "cannot establish some impermeable place or identity without denying their capacity for action and freedom."[24] And, crucially for my purposes here, tragedy did all of this not through abstraction and rational argument but through the absorbing representation of the concrete doings of particular characters, which played off and manipulated the identifications and investments of its audience; its "characteristic method of instruction" was thus "analogical, allusive, and indirect."[25]

In this respect, at least, it may be useful to think of the practice of teaching and reading the history of political theory by analogy to tragic drama: not because works of political theory belong to the specific literary genre of tragedy (though some might well be read that way) but in the sense that the work of teaching, like dramatic performance, proceeds in part through the cultivation and exploitation of various sorts of identification with and investment in its "characters" precisely in order to expose its audience to the effect of the twists and turns, including reversals and catastrophes, these characters encounter. For teachers of literature this will sound platitudinous, but it cuts against some dominant understandings of what works of political theory are and why we teach them. For instance, it resists the notion that such texts are reducible to *positions* that one could either accept or reject, drawing our attention instead to the ways in which texts are the records of the kinetic activity of thought and writing, and not just results. It also encourages us to attend at least as much to the ways in which such texts fail to achieve (what we take to be) their intended or desired effects—that is, to the moments of inconsistency and incoherence at which, under the pressure of phenomena, a work's terms get away from it—as to the ways in which they succeed.[26]

The aim of teaching political theory, understood in these terms, is not (merely) to endow students with the capacity to make rational decisions among a stock of available philosophical positions; nor does it simply enable them to find themselves in or through the texts that make up "our" tradition. Instead, the potential ethical effect of this sort of reading is threefold. It can demonstrate what Arendt might have called the "non-sovereign" character of the practice of political theory, offering us memorable examples of the ways in which theoretical insight emerges—sometimes unnoticed by an author—out of an ongoing and never entirely satisfactory effort to make sense of the world by finite human beings.[27] It can show how the will to systematicity, taken to an extreme, can turn against the cause of understanding. And it can also show how theory at its strongest often *depends* upon the theorist's self-exposure to contingency—not just to the possibility of failure but to (for example) serious and sometimes transformative engagements with lines of inquiry, or fields of phenomena, that seem at best obliquely related to one's current questions. To learn all of this, and to learn it by coming to feel it in relation to some text or texts that you have been brought to identify with or care about, is one form of acknowledgment. It is less a preparation for the independence we promise our students (and ourselves) than a way of dealing productively, rather than resentfully and destructively, with the partial but real failure of that promise.

To provide an example of this sort of reading, let me turn briefly to a text I have taught regularly for several years and which poses some acute ethical questions of its own: Karl Marx's early essay "On the Jewish Question."[28] This essay is a staple of undergraduate surveys in modern political theory as well as of more advanced courses in political philosophy, social theory, and other subjects, though it is surely not as widely taught as, say, the *Communist Manifesto*. The twenty-five-year-old Marx wrote the essay in 1843, when he was just finding his own voice and beginning to distinguish himself from other members of the loose circle of philosophical, religious, and political radicals commonly known as the Young Hegelians—which makes it, importantly, a liminal document of Marx's transition to "maturity."[29] For political theorists in particular it is widely read and taught today because it contains one of Marx's most vivid critiques of a certain kind of political liberalism, exemplified by the achievements of the eighteenth-century revolutions, which responds to differences and inequalities in social power by seeking to confine their operation to the private sphere and thereby to insulate the supposedly neutral and universal state from their influence, rather than by undertaking a more thorough and radical transformation of social life. The result, Marx famously charged, was not genuine "human" emancipation but mere "political" emancipation, in which people's lives are split between the nominal freedom they enjoy as citizens and the real unfreedom to which they continue to be subject as members of civil society.[30]

Two related features of this text make it especially challenging to teach. The first is that it was written as a critical review of two essays on the "Jewish question" in *Vormärz* Prussia by Marx's friend and fellow radical Bruno Bauer; these essays, largely forgotten except by specialists in the period, were themselves critical responses to an even more obscure series of articles published by a conservative writer in defense of a government proposal to roll back many of the terms of the 1812 Edict of Emancipation governing the civil status of Prussian Jews.[31] Marx's essay is thus a highly localized intervention, and it shows; teaching it as part of a wide-ranging survey course—or even as part of a more specialized course on Marx—requires both filling in a great deal of context and glossing over or ignoring even more. Second, "On the Jewish Question"—or, more specifically, the brief second part of the essay, corresponding to the second of the two articles by Bauer that Marx reviewed—is thick with anti-Semitic language, including especially associations of Judaism with the cult of money and "huckstering."[32] Although the text no longer quite provokes the degree of scandal it aroused when, in 1959, Dagobert Runes published the first complete (though tendentious) English translation under the title "A World without Jews," claiming to reveal the hidden continuity between Marx's ideas and the eliminationist anti-Semitism of the twentieth century,[33] it is still a source of palpable discomfort in the classroom, and it is not always obvious how to make the discomfort productive. Indeed, a quick and unscientific survey of syllabi available on the Web suggests that instructors remain divided about whether to assign the second part of the essay at all.

What I want to suggest here, however, is that "On the Jewish Question" troubles us as instructors not, or not only, because it is a "hard case" for familiar approaches to ethical education but because those approaches do not seem to capture the stakes and challenges of teaching this text. For instance, if we take the problem of ethical education to be how to use classroom authority to develop rather than suppress or displace the capacities of students to reason independently and think critically, then a "hard case" might be one that seemed likely to produce such violent disagreement in the classroom that it would interfere with rational discourse. In my experience, however, the trouble with "On the Jewish Question" is *not* that its arguments press students beyond the bounds of civility; instead, it is that its use of anti-Semitic language is not clearly part of what they recognize as an argument, much less one they are inclined to defend, and so they are unsure *how* to engage the second part of the essay except by declaring it distasteful. Likewise, if we take the problem of ethical education to be how to use classroom authority to ensure the continuity of important and formative traditions of thought, then a "hard case" might be one in which a single work seemed both vital and pernicious; but even for the censoriously inclined, "On the Jewish Question" makes things relatively easy precisely because of the division between its two parts: you do not *need* to read the second half of the essay to understand Marx's distinction between human and political emancipation. But then again, you do not *need* to read Marx's essay at all in order to understand that distinction: it can be summarized in a lecture or in a textbook without much trouble (and without all that distracting historical context!). What is troubling about "On the Jewish Question," in other words, is tied to whatever it is in that text—in any text—that can be reduced neither to a rational argument nor to an ideational content separable from its form and occasion of appearance.

What if, by contrast, we approached "On the Jewish Question" as an occasion for teaching acknowledgment in the sense I have described? Doing so would allow us to focus attention precisely on the junction between the two parts of the essay that otherwise seem to occupy incommensurable discursive spaces, asking what work the anti-Semitic language in the second half of the essay does for Marx and how it serves (for good or ill) the work of critique that dominates the essay's first half, and which is usually taken to represent its "argument" or "real point."[34] Students might, for instance, be brought into a sort of preliminary receptivity to, or investment in, Marx's project as they discover that the critique of "political emancipation" he sketches in the first part of the essay echoes some of their own uncertainties about the works of liberal political thought that have preceded Marx on the syllabus.[35] They might also find themselves puzzled by aspects of Marx's own critique: for example, by his hesitation between two different accounts of what is involved in the insulation of state from civil society that he calls "political emancipation," one of which portrays the very distinction *between* state and civil society as political emancipation's *effect*, and the other of which—anticipating the dogmatic and reductionist economism of some of Marx's own later work, and of some powerful versions of Marxism—sees political emancipation merely as the "consummation" of an economic logic that had been present in civil society all along.[36] These developments might, in turn, set the scene for a treatment of Marx's rhetoric in this essay, including not only his associations of Jews and Judaism with money and commerce in the essay's second half but also the series of metaphorical substitutions through which Marx turns a debate over the legal status of Prussian Jews into an occasion to discuss not only Jews but also Christians and indeed "*religious* man in general"; and not only religion but also a wide range of other "distinctions" including those of "birth, social rank, education, [and] occupation"; and not only these social distinctions but also the institution of private property.[37]

Indeed, it is this practice of metaphorical substitution that has come to seem to me like the ethical crux of Marx's essay, though not only because (as some ethical critics have suggested) the mere experience of encountering and engaging a metaphor has a peculiar power to implicate the reader or hearer in its work of figuration and so to shape or even "colonize" the mind.[38] Reading generously, we might bracket the question of Marx's own *attitudes* toward Jews, and toward his own Jewish heritage,[39] and understand Marx's chains of metaphorical substitution in both halves of the essay as rhetorical strategies meant to change the subject of a public discussion from religion to capitalism. Such a reading would fit well with Marx's substitution of "real" or "everyday" Jews for the "sabbath" Jew; with his suggestion that the former category includes Christians; and with his claim—a trace of his emerging economism—that "an organization of society which would abolish the preconditions and thus the very possibility of huckstering" would simultaneously cause Jewish "religious consciousness" to evaporate.[40] The problem, however, is that at this stage Marx's writing lacks any serious or extended engagement with the subject of political economy on its own terms, much less any effort to *defend* the suggestion that the dynamics of capitalism are fundamental while cultural and spiritual phenomena are ephemeral: in "On the Jewish Question," that claim rests upon nothing other than Marx's own rhetorical substitutions and gestures of unmasking, which play off of his audience's predisposition to see commerce as the "secret of the Jew."[41] The trouble, then, is not simply that Marx repeats, and so involves his readers in the repetition of, pernicious imagery; it is that, precisely in his effort to leave questions of culture and religion behind, Marx exploits and renews the rhetorical power of a widespread cultural association, itself tied to a structure of social and political inequality that was irreducible to, even as it intersected with, inequalities of class.

Marx's substitutions, in other words, are never quite as complete, his equivalences never quite as unidirectional, as his own confidence in the fundamental character of political economy might have led him to believe, and it is Marx's self-imposed blindness to the cultural logic of his own rhetorical practice that is, for me anyway, the most troublesome aspect of "On the Jewish Question."[42] And this blindness, importantly, is closely associated with the *second* of the two possible versions of the critique of political emancipation between which (as I suggested earlier) Marx hesitates in the first part of the essay—the one that reifies "civil society" as an entity that lies behind the fictions of the state and operates according to its own, preexisting logic. By tracking the workings of Marx's metaphors in this way, then, students might also discover something about the limits and costs of a certain kind of theoretical ambition: while Marx's second version of the critique of political emancipation promises a greater degree of conceptually informed practical mastery over the social world, his pursuit of that more ambitious critique, at this stage anyway, implicates Marx in ways he does not acknowledge or intend in an ongoing practice of social and political subordination. That is Marx's tragedy, or one of them. If there is an ethical effect of reading Marx in this way, it is less that it enables students (or teachers) to pass righteous judgment over him than that, in sustaining a stance of simultaneous sympathetic identification with and spectatorial distance from Marx and his work, it may help us feel those limits and costs in relation to our own theoretical practice too.

On that reflexive note, and recalling my promise to sustain my ambivalence toward moral and ethical education, I will conclude skeptically, returning to the theme of ethical education as the site of certain constitutive problems. The first of these should be suggested immediately by the reading of Marx I have just offered. That reading is one that has emerged for me in bits and pieces over the course of several years, not only out of my own work on the text but also out of my experience of teaching it in small seminars as well as lectures. There is no guarantee that *any* student in a future course, much less all of them, will have the experience I have described; and the risk that they will not is, I want to say, built into the description of the experience, which depends heavily upon students' involvement, both in the sense of their engagement and investment in the "story" of Marx's thought, and in the sense of their active participation in the work of reading his text. Notice that this is *not* the problem of indoctrination, which sees a potential conflict between authoritative instruction and students' independent use of their critical faculties: the danger here is not so much that students will have a reading *imposed* upon them that they might otherwise be inclined to challenge or resist as that they will be left unaffected by an elaborate, precise, and well-defended reading that is performed for rather than by or with them.[43] (In this respect at least, the aesthetics of traditional theater and the aesthetics of instruction are importantly different.) It is for this reason that I continue to think that ethical education may work best when it is allowed to work on its own time and without being pursued too insistently or explicitly as a project.

Second, notice that the sort of reading I have described requires a peculiar combination of postures toward a theoretical text. On the one hand, it requires, among other things, a prolonged suspension of judgment; an effort to understand an author's aims as far as possible on his or her own terms; and an imaginative attempt to feel the force of the problems or puzzles the author took himself or herself to be confronting, as well as the promise (and difficulties) of his or her strategies for confronting them. All of this, in practice, can translate to something that looks like a certain kind of reverence for the text and/or its context, and it can demand a studied resistance, in the name of anti-anachronism, to hasty efforts to establish the contemporary relevance of a historical document. On the other hand, this sort of reading also depends for its ethical effect on the capacity to perceive and elaborate analogies between the situation and work of a historical text and contemporary practical contexts, and such analogical work can be stifled by an overzealous insistence upon insulating the reading of a work from the extracurricular interests, concerns, and investments of its readers. Of course, put in those terms, the problem—call it the problem of insulation—may not seem especially severe. All it requires is a balance between those two postures of insulation and exposure, or, perhaps, a division of labor between the contexts in which each posture is appropriate: the insulated study undertaken in the college or university classroom could, for instance, be seen as *preparation* for students' engagement with the "real" world outside the classroom, much as, on some accounts of the educational power of drama, the disciplined witnessing undertaken in the discrete space of the theater prepares citizens for (but does not substitute for) participation in the larger social and political life of the polis.

Yet this whole way of talking about the relationship of the classroom to the world is, though not exactly wrong, problematically incomplete; and this is, to my mind, the more severe version of the problem of insulation. Colleges and universities *are* institutionally and culturally discrete and insulated places; classrooms do follow their own norms of inquiry and behavior (which are not quite like those that prevail in workplaces, homes, and other social spaces); and these forms of separation help make possible much of what is of value in higher education. But colleges and universities are, of course, also workplaces (mine is the largest single employer on the South Side of Chicago); they own the properties in which many of their students and employees (and, often, people with no other connection to the institution) make their homes; they have often extensive power over the physical shape and social conditions of the cities they occupy; they are often highly capitalized investors; they are intricately connected both to private industry and to the state, including especially its military face; they are provisioners of credentialed labor. Their insulation is only relative, just as the independence of any agent is only relative, and just as—as Marx at least intermittently saw—the separation of the putatively universal state as well as of the domain of "civil society" out of a larger field of social relations is only relative. The most serious challenge for a practice of ethical education is to make productive use of that insulation and the conditions it provides while also helping students to see the ways in which their university education is not merely preparation for action that will happen later, elsewhere, in the real world, but already itself a form of worldly activity with ethical and political stakes. Of course, many of us who have built careers and selves in higher education may be more in need of learning that lesson than our students; and if history is any guide, they may be more likely to teach it to us than the other way around.[44]

Notes

Thanks to Elizabeth Kiss, Peter Euben, and anonymous readers for Duke University Press for their comments on earlier versions of this essay, and to the other participants in the Kenan Institute for Ethics conference "Debating Moral Education" (March 2004) for stimulating and educational conversation on this subject.

1. As late as the first decade of the twentieth century, only 5 percent of Americans aged eighteen to twenty-two enrolled in college; see Thelin, *A History of American Higher Education*, 169. On the history of moral education in the nineteenth century, see Sloan, "The Teaching of Ethics in the American Undergraduate Curriculum, 1876–1976," and Reuben, *The Making of the Modern University*, which is especially useful on the changing relationships among ethics, science, and religion. On bathing, see Benjamin Ide Wheeler's "An Address to Freshmen" (1904), 84. On racialized conceptions of the university's ethical mission, especially in the period of the Spanish-American-Philippine war, see, e.g., Townsend, *Manhood at Harvard*, chap. 4; Brechin, *Imperial San Francisco*, chap. 7.

2. See, e.g., William Connolly's account of the irreducibility of ethics to code-based morality in *The Ethos of Pluralization*; Bernard Williams's critique of morality in the name of ethics in *Ethics and the Limits of Philosophy*; and the critiques of "moralism" in Bennett and Shapiro, eds., *The Politics of Moralizing*, and Brown, *Politics Out of History*. Liberal moral and political philosophy often specifies the relation between ethics and morality differently, nesting "local" or "particular" ethical obligations within, and allowing them to be trumped by, "universal" moral commitments, rather than understanding mo-

rality as itself an ethical formation; for a recent version, see Appiah, *The Ethics of Identity*, 230ff.

3. See, in addition to the sources in the previous note, Lauren Berlant's critique of the personalization of the political in *The Queen of America Goes to Washington City* and Bonnie Honig's critique of ethical theory's focus on extraordinary dilemmas in "Difference, Dilemmas, and the Politics of Home."

4. See Fish, "Aim Low," and the critical discussion in Kiss and Euben, "Aim High: A Response to Stanley Fish," in this volume.

5. In "Aim High," for example, Kiss and Euben use "moral" and "ethical" interchangeably; they systematically pair these terms with "political" and especially "civic"; and they draw on Euben's extended defense of democratic political education in *Corrupting Youth*. On the persistent difficulty of insulating ethics from its various "others," see Harpham, *Getting It Right*, chap. 1.

6. On the complicated relationship between the production of expert knowledge and moral education in the self-understandings of the emergent social science disciplines in America, see Reuben, *Making of the Modern University*; Bryson, "The Emergence of the Social Sciences from Moral Philosophy."

7. See also Macklin, "Problems in the Teaching of Ethics."

8. Fish, "Aim Low."

9. Dewey, "My Pedagogic Creed," 88; Giroux, *Schooling and the Struggle for Public Life*, chap. 3.

10. Gutmann, introduction to *Multiculturalism*, 16–17; emphasis added.

11. Kiss and Euben, "Aim High."

12. Locke, *Two Treatises of Government*, II, sec. 64; *Some Thoughts Concerning Education*, e.g., secs. 94, 212.

13. Kant, "An Answer to the Question: What Is Enlightenment?," 54, 59.

14. Mill, *On Liberty*, 64; *Considerations on Representative Government*, 232ff.

15. See, e.g., Taylor, "Cross-Purposes."

16. On this fundamental affinity, see my *Bound by Recognition*, e.g., 11–13.

17. "Introduction to the Core Curriculum," http://www.courses.fas.harvard.edu/core/redbook_2002.html (visited August 30, 2005). Although the same document acknowledges that "Moral Reasoning" courses may "enlarge the students' awareness of how people have understood the nature of the virtuous life," its emphasis is consistently procedural: it explains, for instance, that "the courses [in Moral Reasoning] are offered in the expectation that they will help students realize that it is possible to reflect reasonably about such matters as justice, obligation, citizenship, loyalty, courage, and personal responsibility"; it pointedly notes that the aim of the Core Curriculum is *not* to ensure that the students have acquired "mastery of a set of Great Books"; and it insists that "the courses within each area of the program are equivalent in

the sense that, while their subject matter may vary, their emphasis on a particular way of thinking is the same."

18. "Liberal Education at Chicago," http://collegecatalog.uchicago.edu/liberal/index.shtml (visited August 30, 2005).

19. See Reuben, *Making of the American University*; Rudolph, *Curriculum*. For a detailed account of the "dynamic and contested" history of general education at Chicago since the 1920s that complicates this story, see Boyer, *Three Views of Continuity and Change at the University of Chicago*, 35–84.

20. For a psychoanalytic work of political theory that focuses on the specific place of images of childhood, maturation, and parental authority in the American political imagination, see Rogin, *Fathers and Children*.

21. Markell, *Bound by Recognition*, esp. 32–38 (discussing the difference between the terms *recognition* and *acknowledgment*, and the use of the latter term in the work of James Tully and Stanley Cavell).

22. Ibid., esp. chap. 3.

23. See Euben, *Corrupting Youth*, e.g., 73; Euben, introduction to *Greek Tragedy and Political Theory*; Cartledge, " 'Deep Plays' "; Hall, "The Sociology of Athenian Tragedy"; Goldhill, "The Great Dionysia and Civic Ideology"; and Zeitlin, "Thebes."

24. Euben, *Corrupting Youth*, 176.

25. Cartledge, " 'Deep Plays,' " 19. In using the term "identification" here I do not mean to suggest that the efficacy of tragedy depended upon its audience experiencing the action of the play just as though it were happening to them, but only that the self-understandings and identifications of the audience will help to shape (though they will not determine) the intensity and quality of the responses they have toward characters they see as like and unlike (but not necessarily indistinguishable from) them in various respects. For a rich discussion of the psychology of audience response, especially as addressed in the poetics of Plato and Aristotle, see Halliwell, *The Aesthetics of Mimesis*.

26. These are by no means novel propositions on my part: they inform a number of otherwise quite different varieties of academic political theory, mostly those touched by one or another version of the "linguistic turn." My point is simply that these practices of political theory, which fit uneasily at best into official divisions of the field into "normative political philosophy" and "history of political ideas," are also at cross-purposes with some dominant ways of talking about the ethical and educative functions of undergraduate instruction in political theory.

27. On freedom as "non-sovereignty," see Arendt, *The Human Condition*, 234.

28. Marx, "On the Jewish Question."

29. For the general context, see Toews, *Hegelianism*; McLellan, *The Young Hegelians and Karl Marx*.

30. Marx, "On the Jewish Question," 32–34.

31. On this context, see Carlebach, *Karl Marx and the Radical Critique of Judaism*, chap. 4; for discussion and sources on the broader context of Jewish emancipation in the first half of the nineteenth century, see Markell, *Bound by Recognition*, chap. 5.

32. Marx, "On the Jewish Question," 48.

33. Marx, *A World without Jews*, ed. Dagobert Runes, v–xi; Runes's translation crucially rendered Marx's German term *Judentum* into English as "Jewry" rather than "Judaism," which made it sound as though Marx were calling for the "emancipation of society from Jewry" (45). At the same time, the response of one of Marx's most notable defenders—that the meaning of *Judentum* that was "uppermost in Marx's mind throughout the article" was not "Judaism" but rather "commerce" (which was one colloquial sense of the term in German at the time)—is, as I will explain, question begging (McLellan, *Marx before Marxism*, 141–42).

34. For a similar account of how best to approach the issue of anti-Semitism in Marx, see Brown, *States of Injury*, 101–2 n. 10.

35. Or, in a more specialized course, their uncertainties about Hegel's political philosophy: in this respect Marx's "Critique of Hegel's Doctrine of the State" works admirably as scene setting for "On the Jewish Question."

36. Marx, "On the Jewish Question," 45. For a more detailed account of this tension, see Markell, *Bound by Recognition*, 129–30.

37. Marx, "On the Jewish Question," 32, 33.

38. Booth, *The Company We Keep*. On the peculiar force of metaphor as tied to its status as *energeia* in Aristotle's *Rhetoric*, see Halliwell, *Aesthetics of Mimesis*, 189–91.

39. For a psychobiographical approach to Marx that deals with these questions, see Seigel, *Marx's Fate*.

40. Marx, "On the Jewish Question," 48–49. This is, in effect, the reading advanced by such defenders of Marx as David McLellan (see n. 33 above).

41. Ibid., 48.

42. On the directionality of metaphor, see Markell, *Bound by Recognition*, afterword.

43. In another context ("The Insufficiency of Non-Domination") I have suggested that we think of this as the difference between being dominated (that is, subject to the arbitrary control of another) and being usurped (that is, having one's active involvement in events displaced).

44. The ongoing student campaign for university divestment from Sudan is a powerful case in point. At the University of Chicago, the campaign has been, at this writing, unsuccessful; much of the resistance to divestment has cen-

tered around the Kalven Report (1967), a document on "the university's role in social and political action," which concluded that the university could not take *collective* action on social and political issues without endangering the individual freedom of inquiry, action, and protest of its students and faculty, and thereby threatening its own core mission (http://adminet.uchicago.edu/adminpols/pols-provost/kalverpt.pdf [visited July 5, 2007]). Still, though the Kalven Report downplayed the university's imbrications on a broader field of social power ("the sources of power of a great university should not be misconceived. Its prestige and influence are based on integrity and intellectual competence; they are not based on the circumstance that it may be wealthy, may have political contacts, and may have influential friends"), the report also acknowledged that at times the university could not help but act in its corporate capacity—for example, in situations involving its "ownership of property"—and allowed that "in the exceptional instance these corporate activities of the university may appear so incompatible with paramount social values as to require careful assessment of the consequences." Much of the student campaign has aimed to persuade administrators that the genocide in Darfur constitutes such an "exceptional instance." For a fascinating account of the formulation of the Kalven Report which touches on these issues, see Kalven, "The Unfinished Business of the Kalven Report," *Chicago Maroon* (November 28, 2006; http://maroon.uchicago.edu/online_edition/view points/2006/11/28/ [visited July 5, 2007]).

THE POWER OF MORALITY

This essay explores two related questions. The broader one asks: How are we to relate notions of morality to politics? For a focus on morality often entails a troubling avoidance of the dilemmas posed by power and plurality in politics, but moral claims do, and arguably must, play a significant role in political discourse and mobilization. There is, therefore, great controversy over the value or danger of that role. Accordingly, this essay also asks a second question: What is (or must be) distinctive about "moral education" in a community that seeks to foster a *democratic* politics? To pursue these two questions, the essay begins by introducing the general idea of tension between morality and politics, and it proceeds by comparing the different ways that Tocqueville, William Blake, and James Baldwin conceive both morality and moral education in democratic life.

Why these three, who are rarely if ever included in academic conversations about morality, moral education, and politics? Just as their exclusion suggests what is problematic about that conversation, so including them can complicate and thereby enrich it. For while Tocqueville embeds morality in culture, arguing (against Kant) that culture is anterior to rationality and (moral) reasoning, Blake exposes the problem of hegemony in culture, and so in what is *called* moral, and Baldwin, by focusing on race, exposes how hegemony is a moral and not only political problem. In the Euro-American world, indeed, ruling conceptions of the moral always betray the constitutive injustice of the capitalism, colonialism, and slavery that Blake calls "empire" and Baldwin calls "white supremacy." At the same time, Blake and Baldwin advance an oppositional politics that transforms how we might understand both the moral dimension in politics and the ways that a true moral education must be worldly and political—or it will be a sham.

The Tension between Morality and Politics

We can best introduce and contextualize these arguments and voices by tracing two different ways of conceiving the danger in moral talk. By one view, theorists who focus on morality and moral education evade, devalue, or supplant politics. That focus can take universalist or particularist forms. In some readings of Plato, and in liberal versions of democratic theory, politics is imagined as a rational practice of moral argument and becomes an exercise in deliberation about moral rules or justice, and about how to apply those rules to particular cases. In communitarian forms of democratic theory, theorists imagine a moral understanding so thick and deep that citizens embody a familial harmony prior to any moral reasoning, and politics becomes an exercise in sharing a world. Whether conceived in philosophically universalist or culturally particularist terms, however, these ways of focusing on morality tend to evade the very conditions that make politics inescapable and valuable. How so?

Politics arises, this argument goes, because of constitutive conditions that include unequal power over resources and rules, conflicting perspectives and interests, and the partiality of human actors, conditions that preclude universal agreement about what is common, or good, or to be done. Theorists (and reformers) who focus on morality, or on an ideal of justice as a form of morality, are dreaming that unequal power and deep conflict can be resolved by the stable (moral) framework they would produce by moral reasoning or invoke as thick cultural attachment. As if to overcome conditions of conflict and partiality by imagining (the possibility of) deep and abiding moral consensus, deliberative and communitarian thinkers—despite other obvious differences—supplant politics.[1]

To summarize this first critical view, talk about morality among democratic theorists avoids the realities of unequal power and deep cultural difference. By a second critical argument, though, the worldly practice of morality is a dangerous form of power. For the language of morality—by categories of good and evil as well as innocence and guilt—seems tightly bound to policing and punishing bodies. Moral language seems to engender and justify literal violence, while the rich complexity and messy ambiguity of life are subjected to the sword of dichotomous categories. The emergence of fundamentalism in the last thirty years only confirms how morality is not only a resource to hold power accountable but a language inseparably linked to or instantiated in practices of power. Critics of enlightenment rationality and moral universalism have long argued that those who conceive of politics as the application of moral rules will exercise power in ways that devalue or even destroy plurality, while maintaining their illusion of innocence. In metropolitan and colonial forms of social control, moral talk authorizes power in the language of redemption.[2]

To oppose the reduction of politics to morality as a dream of consensus, and to resist the practice of "morality" as a form of power, however, is not to say that morality and politics are simply antithetical. After all, Machiavelli says human beings must "fight like men" and not only like "beasts," by law and not only by the fraud and force he links to the fox and lion. Arendt and Nietzsche also depict a vexed tension—not dichotomy— between morality and politics, because they show the value, not only the cost and danger, of morality as we understand it. For them, the absence of aspiration or inability to project values, and failure to critically judge conduct and engage in self-reflection, are grave political (also cultural or spiritual) dangers.

So what view of morality (and moral education) is needed for a democratic politics? To pursue this question, let us briefly explore the differing but related ways that Tocqueville, Blake, and Baldwin conceive morality and politics. To do so will suggest ways to reimagine what "democracy" is or might mean.

Morality and Politics I: Tocqueville

Tocqueville is not ambivalent about morality, which he considers essential to a vibrant democratic politics. As democracy "relaxes political bonds," he says, "moral bonds must be strengthened." Why? Because "liberty cannot be established without morality, nor morality without faith." Why? Because a people must be "moral, religious and temperate in proportion as it is free," that is, because political liberty depends on self-limitation. By "morality" he means a passionate frame of reference, located beneath willful agreement and rational argument, which links human agency and responsibility to law-like standards of conduct construed as nonconventional constructs. He thus quotes John Winthrop:

> There is a two-fold liberty. . . . [Natural liberty] is common to man with beasts and other creatures. By this, man . . . hath the liberty to do what he lists; it is a liberty to evil as well as to good. This liberty . . . cannot endure the least restraint of the most just authority. . . . This is the . . . wild beast which all the ordinances of god are bent against, to restrain and subdue it. The other kind of liberty I call civil or federal; it may also be termed moral, in reference to the covenant between god and man in the moral law, and the politic covenants and constitutions among men themselves. This liberty is the proper end and object of authority, and cannot subsist without it; and it is a liberty to that which is good, just, and honest. This liberty . . . is maintained and exercised by way of subjection to authority; it is of the same kind of liberty wherewith Christ hath made us free.[3]

A distinction between liberty and license, Tocqueville argues, must be internalized as morality to ensure that citizens are capable of self-determination, yet self-limiting in their exercise of power. When publicly endorsed and individually inscribed, ideas of moral law create a stable frame that stands apart from, to enable and contain, democratic energies. "In the moral world everything is classified, systematized, foreseen, and decided beforehand; in the political world everything is agitated, disputed, uncertain. In the one is a passive though voluntary obedience; in the other, an independence scornful of experience and jealous of authority." He thus says, "[Liberty] considers religion as the safeguard of morality, and morality as the best security of law and the surest pledge of the duration of freedom." Individual independence and political liberty depend on the self-regulating capacities of citizens; self-regulation in personal and political senses—but also agitation, dispute, and experiment among citizens—depends on a moral and religious authority at once beneath and beyond politics.[4]

To sustain the distinction between liberty and license, and to justify the self-regulation on which liberty depends, he defends not the "truth" but the political "utility" of theistic religious faith. Yet Tocqueville's view of its pragmatic and political value changes in crucial and instructive ways. For in volume 1 of *Democracy in America*, theist faith engenders a salutary (moral) self-limitation of the revolutionary energy released by equality; here "morality" is a container to limit the rebellious agency that Tocqueville fears will destroy the enduring constitutional forms that enable political liberty. In volume 2, though, the danger he fears is not revolution but a democratic despotism that engenders political withdrawal and absorption in private life.

Theism now serves to "mitigate" acquisitive individualism, by teaching the claims of others and of a soul whose needs are not material; in addition, faith in god, and thereby in the sanctity of conscience, enable assertion against the worldly authority of public opinion and a powerful state. In volume 2 morality remains a necessary condition of democratic life, but less as a salutary limit on (majoritarian) power, on the willful agency of the demos, and more as an essential antidote to atomization, materialism, and political docility.

In differing ways, then, Tocqueville argues for a necessary relation between "the spirit of religion" and "the spirit of liberty" and depicts the authority of religion and morality as the only defense against nihilism. As a result, paradoxically, in both volumes he places morality beneath human convention, and beyond political contest and choice. For this reason, too, he endorses confining women in a domestic sphere, to implant the (moral) self-regulation that entitles (male) children to citizenship. Moral education thus names not political encounter with worldly evil but a catechism in the home to sustain a prepolitical cultural "consensus" about the distinction between good and evil as well as liberty and license.

Still, as this domestic regime serves moral order, so both are meant to serve the worldly agency and political liberty that he calls "the art of association." He depicts townships and voluntary associations as "schools of liberty," forms of moral and political education that teach self-limitation, connectedness to others, adjudication of difference, judgment of (in)justice, and collaborative action. While he makes "morality" a condition of political liberty, then, he also construes citizenship in prosaic forms, not through voting but in embodied acts of association, as a condition of moral adulthood.

Tocqueville's project too readily collapses moral education and cultural indoctrination; its gendered division of labor makes female exclusion the enabling condition of political liberty; and, likewise, it removes from political contest the authority of what is called morality. Despite his overt politics, however, his assemblage of religious faith, morality and voluntary association has repeatedly animated social movements that have contested the constitutive exclusions that enfranchise only some people as citizens and shape in grossly invidious ways how they understand and practice morality. After all, the black church and the civil rights movement signal how "the spirit of religion" can enable people to form associations and act in concert: as they protest exclusion, they at once invoke and recast prevailing moral norms and political concepts, take moral education into the streets, and democratize politics.[5]

Morality and Politics II: William Blake

Before we turn to race and civil rights, however, we should consider a mediating and intermediary figure, William Blake. Why Blake? By carrying the Protestant Reformation to its libidinous and democratic conclusions, he turns Tocqueville inside-out in ways that prefigure more recent social movements and cultural politics. Partly, Blake is noteworthy for invoking the Christian gospel to equate morality with love and not with law. Partly, therefore, he is an inaugural voice in the recurring argument that what an emerging middle class *calls morality* is an ideology serving the hegemonic power of a class.

"The gospel is forgiveness of sins and has no moral precepts," he says, and so he stands against what he calls "the moral law." "When Satan first the black bow bent / And the Moral Law from the Gospel rent / He forged the Law into a Sword / And spilled the blood of mercy's law." Moral law, originating in Moses' Thou Shalt Not, means prohibition, guilt, punishment, and fear. That is partly because morality enshrines abstract and purifying dichotomies, whereas Blake sees "contraries," which credit the evil in good and the good in evil. But also, moral law serves the worldly hegemony of some over others: moral law is *their* law, the law of the state and priests, the powerful and respectable, not the common and stigmatized. What Tocqueville calls a moral "consensus," even a "consensus universalis," is thus depicted by Blake as a limited horizon of norms defining the blasphemous, seditious, insane.[6]

Because morality as law empowers one class of people to rule others through the internalization of prohibition, Blake's gospel is an antinomian defense of love: suspicion of reason and justification by faith is a powerful (and recurring) way to question authority and hegemony, to defend the soul-competence and carnal life of the disenfranchised. Blake thus opposes discourses that soon govern personal and political life: against utilitarian philosophy and behavioral psychology, he depicts impulses he calls pride and love; against Newtonian mechanics of action and reaction, he forges a language of transformation; against a morality of prohibition, he imagines cultivating care and creativity in human beings. He rejects *what is called* morality, then, to transform what morality means.

For Blake believes in the golden rule, in treating people as ends not means, and on this ground he opposes a world organized by force and exploitation, by state power—and by fidelity to morality as a law of prohibition. Reciprocal relations of acknowledgment cannot be generated by law, let alone by force, but only by transforming hearts and minds. As Paul and Milton argued before him, only grace empowers people to fulfill (and to supersede) the law. Because "god becomes as we are so that we may be as he is," Blake argues, the very idea of original sin is a blasphemous denial of our latent divinity, and we are called not to self-regulation in Tocqueville's Puritan terms but to what Blake calls "exuberance." While one who seeks goodness in conventional moral terms will try to obey an external god, then, Blake argues that the task is to draw out the divinity—the love and "poetic genius"—within each human being.

As Jesus thus talked not of good and evil but of life and death, of fruitfulness and barrenness, so Blake's idea of incarnation transforms what we mean by morality. Organized morality surely has some good in it—harming let alone killing others is wicked—but it seeks (and fails) to hinder sinful desire rather than foster the god within. For Blake, "honest indignation is the voice of god" and his ethos of forgiveness presumes "severity of judgment" as a first step, but for the sake of "bringing out" the god within, not punishing sin. Still, by relating morality to love rather than law, does Blake evade the institutional structures to which Tocqueville relates "the spirit of religion" as a necessary supplement?

Surely, a language of the god or grace within is Blake's way to address the profound limitations of a politics that uses a language of self-interest to conceive motivation and action. Political action may begin with self-interest and enlarge it, as Tocqueville argues, but Blake seeks a deeper transformation in the character of subjects, their desire, and their projects. For Blake, self-interest is a self-defeating basis of *democratic* relations, which require people whose perception and action is not trapped in "the mind-forged manacles" of subject-object duality. A vibrantly embodied rather than formal democracy requires citizens who acknowledge the implication of each in the lives of others, the role of vision in shaping the world they see and remake, and the efficacy of eliciting desire rather than enforcing norms.[7]

By linking moral ideas to the worldly power of a class and yet also to questions of internal motivation, Blake turns Tocqueville inside-out and inaugurates countercultural politics: only by erotic energy can people enact rather than betray the moral aspiration toward reciprocity that underwrites democratic relations. Advocates of this shift from will to desire, and from law to action, Blake says ironically, belong to "the devil's party," because their challenge to moral law is perceived as "license" and called "evil." While Tocqueville's view of morality produces a politics that ranges from Christian evangelism to militant abolitionism, therefore, Blake prefigures the heretical Protestantism whose logic of incarnation dispenses with theism and recasts morality in libidinal and aesthetic terms. In this countertradition, morality is learned not by catechism in homes and churches but by personal experiments and worldly struggles with inherited norms and reified institutions. Morality comes not transcendentally from outside to inside but emerges immanently, in the experience of engagement, not as law or doctrine but as a way of living.[8]

Morality and Politics III: James Baldwin

Rather than directly trace the tradition of heretical Protestantism that carries Blake to American ground, I would consider the issue of race and use the voice of James Baldwin to recast Blake's view of hegemony, his account of love as a moral practice, and his irony about morality. On the one hand, how should we view arguments about morality and moral education that ignore race (and therefore, power) in American life? On the other hand, how does attending to American racial history—both to white supremacy and the struggle against it—change our view of morality, and of moral education?

To begin, we need to credit how morality has been racialized in American history because, as blackness has signified license, what Toni Morrison calls "insanity, illicit sexuality, and chaos," so moral self-control and moral worth have been coded white in the political imaginary governing American life. It is for this reason that Tocqueville, though horrified by slavery, fears the emancipation of African Americans. But figures from William Lloyd Garrison and Frederick Douglass to Martin Luther King also bespeak how moral appeals to god and conscience enabled (in Tocquevillean ways) American abolitionism, even as they also "blackened" the morality and rights supposedly signaling whiteness. Meanwhile, a Dionysian Christianity, as Norman O. Brown calls it, has erupted in recurring episodes of countercultural creativity that reorient agency from moral law to love. How, then, does Baldwin relate race, morality, and politics?[9]

In his essays, Baldwin depicts slavery and racial inequality as something like the original sin of American politics: democratically authorized racial domination is the constitutive element shaping "American" identity. Likewise, American politics has never been democratic, he therefore claims, because equality always has been understood and practiced in a limited, exclusionary way. By insisting that racial domination is not an unfortunate anomaly but central to American liberalism, he denies that liberalism here produces an exemplary civic nationalism. Rather, American freedom, the liberal freedoms of those who call themselves white, is to this day premised on American slavery, the material exploitation and cultural domination of people marked racially other. What is the moral significance of this paradox?

In *The Fire Next Time* Baldwin declares:

> The crime of which I accuse my countrymen, and for which neither I nor time nor history will ever forgive them, is that they have destroyed and are destroying hundreds of thousands of lives and do not know it and do not want to know it. One can be, and indeed must strive to become, tough and philosophical concerning destruction and death. . . . But it is not permissible that the authors of this destruction should also be innocent. It is the innocence which constitutes the crime.[10]

Baldwin initiates the moral and political education of his nephew by saying, "This innocent country set you down in a ghetto in which, in fact, it intended that you should perish. You were born where you were born and faced the future you faced because you were black and for no other reason." Baldwin thus urges his nephew: "Try to remember that what they do and cause you to endure does not testify to your inferiority but to their inhumanity and fear." Accordingly, there is no basis for their impertinent assumption that they must accept you. The really terrible thing . . . is that you must accept them . . . with love. For these innocent people have no other hope. They are still trapped in a history they do not understand and until they understand it they cannot be released from it.

Indeed, "we, with love, shall force our brothers to see themselves as they are, to cease fleeing from reality and begin to change," for we cannot be free until they are free.[11]

What constitutes the innocence he calls the crime? Baldwin uses the moral category "innocence" ironically, to denote not excusable ignorance but a blindness that is culpable because it is willful. To render others invisible, to deny their reality and dominate them, is a crime, and about it Baldwin says "whoever debases another debases himself." But to disavow the fact or reality of this denial, and to disclaim its consequences, is the innocence he denounces. It is a refusal, not to acknowledge others but to acknowledge that we enact this denial. It is refusing to admit the exercise of power, or credit its benefits. This innocence is a moral catastrophe, and it characterizes American culture, as well as prevailing forms of democratic theory.

Baldwin depicts whites as crucified by the contradiction between their "moral beliefs" in equality and human dignity and their conduct toward those they exploit and dominate. White Americans profess to value equality, the golden rule, individual dignity and self-determination, and so are haunted by a bad conscience about betraying these "moral beliefs."[12] But they cannot be faithful to these beliefs and subjugate every sixth person. White supremacy is to some degree a solution to the contradiction between egalitarian principles and grossly unequal practices. Fictions of black inferiority attribute inequality to the subordinated rather than to the conduct of their oppressors.

By the very idea of blackness as "inhuman excess," and by the inhuman excess of rape, terror, and minstrel representation to impose this fiction, those oppressors build an identity as a superior—civilized and moral— "white race," justifying the privilege and violence that otherwise violate their professed moral norms. White supremacy thus names a state of exception that constitutes and betrays an exclusionary republic. But to sustain the enabling fiction of blackness they must "deny" the "human reality, the human weight and complexity [of the black man], and the strain of denying the overwhelmingly undeniable has forced Americans into rationalizations so fantastic that they approach the pathological."[13]

We refuse to acknowledge that we live by domination not equality, partly because we assume that we deserve our history, as if our privileged social position signals our moral virtue. But for Baldwin, the meaning of our history is that "white people, who had robbed black people of their liberty, and profited by this theft every hour that they lived, had no moral ground to stand on." We deny unequal power and a history of domination to sustain what Baldwin calls our "myths" about ourselves, especially concerning our moral virtue and our exceptional liberalism. To maintain our innocence in these regards, we also endlessly revise melodramas of black pathology and fictions of race, locating in others the moral issues (of irresponsibility, especially) we do not face in ourselves.[14]

But the moral issue cuts more deeply. For if we "put you in the ghetto where [we] *intended* that you should perish," then our innocence requires dissociating from our own destructiveness by projecting it onto those we destroy. We project onto them the "license" and violence we deny in ourselves, and in the name of moral law we exorcize these specters of darkness, as if we could triumph over ourselves by controlling the sym- bolically charged bodies of others. For Baldwin, we disavow our own worldly violence because, at bottom, we deny the darkness that is within us, and within every human being. As a result, our conception of life, and so of morality, is abstract and sterile:

> The American vision of the world—which allows so little reality, gener- ally speaking, for any of the darker forces in human life, which tends to paint moral issues in glaring black and white—owes a great deal to the battle waged by Americans to maintain between themselves and black men a human separation which could not be bridged. . . . It is now beginning to be borne in on us—very faintly . . . and very much against our will—that this vision of the world . . . protects our moral high- mindedness at the terrible expense of weakening our grasp of reality. People who shut their eyes to reality simply invite their own destruc- tion, and anyone who insists on remaining in a state of innocence long after that innocence is dead turns himself into a monster.[15]

Partly, whites use racism to disclaim responsibility for racial domina- tion; partly, their fear of blackness creates a moral(istic) worldview hostile to a life that seems unforgivably stained by sex and willful particularity, by messiness and obscurity, by tragic reversals and by death. American liberalism and its fundamentalist alter-ego are vulnerable to this critique of innocence, since they evade both racial domination and the tragic. But Baldwin also fears that critics of white supremacy repeat the moralism that dichotomizes good and evil like white and black. "The protest novel" from Harriet Beecher Stowe to Richard Wright, he argues, "reinforces the principles which activate the oppression" it decries, because it weds racial categorization to moral dichotomy by narratives of damnation and redemption.

In Stowe's novel, that principle "might be called a theological terror, the terror of damnation," for "the spirit which breathes in this book is not different from the spirit of medieval times which sought to exorcize evil by burning witches, and is not different from the terror which activates a lynch mob." Even though "the avowed aim of the protest novel is to bring greater freedom to the oppressed," it is animated by a "fear of the dark" that "makes it impossible" for our life to be "other than superficial" and that may "put to death our freedom." Stowe emasculates Tom and embraces sentimentality because she is terrified of blackness, but Baldwin argues that Wright becomes her inverted alter-ego. The real tragedy in his story of Bigger is that

> he has accepted a theology that denies him life, that he admits the possibility of his being sub-human and feels constrained, therefore, to battle for his humanity according to those brutal criteria bequeathed to him at his birth. But our humanity is our burden, our life; we need not battle for it, we need only to do what is infinitely more difficult—that is, accept it. The failure of the protest novel lies in its rejection of life, the human being, the denial of his beauty, dread, power, in its insistence that it is his categorization alone which is real and which cannot be transcended.[16]

Baldwin thus identifies a moral and not only political problem in theologies of redemption that moralize the world into a dichotomized black and white, and in the moralization of social position that occurs when privileged or subaltern groups use categories of innocence and guilt. Either way, people evade the human complexity and political responsibility he associates with tragedy. An alternative to such moralization, he says, seems to be available in the liberal humanism of Max's final speech in Wright's *Native Son*. It says, as Baldwin puts it: "though there are whites and blacks among us who hate each other, we will not; there are those who are betrayed by greed, by guilt, by blood lust, but not we; we will set our faces against them and join hands and walk together into that dazzling future when there will be no white or black." For Baldwin, "this is the dream of all liberal men, a dream not at all dishonorable but nevertheless, a dream," for it would rise above "the real battle," which "proceeds far from us in the heat and horror and pain of life itself where all men are betrayed by greed and guilt and blood lust and where no one's hands are clean." "Our" faith in "good will," in what some democratic theorists now call the civil and reasonable, is here revealed as another form of innocence.[17]

Morality, Tragedy, and (Democratic) Politics

How then does Baldwin's account of power and self-denial recast prevailing views of morality and moral education? Like Tocqueville he embeds morality in culture: both see the forming power of moral beliefs as they are lived as customs, "habits of heart and mind." But like Blake, Baldwin sees hegemony and not only culture. Accordingly, he does not set the authority of morality apart from or beneath politics, and as important, he sees how ideals that seem common at an abstract level are practiced in deeply antithetical ways. Isn't that the lesson of conflict about Christianity, or about slavery, abortion, and same-sex desire in a society supposedly committed to equality and self-determination? He thus focuses not on articulating ideals or validating claims, that is, a political theory of justification, but rather on the political realities of power and practice.

Since he therefore links morality to racial (and heterosexual) hegemony, he idealizes neither the abstracted universalism of an American "creed" nor the moral *gemeinschaft* of local community. Attending to race and power, indeed, reveals how universalist and communitarian conceptions of moral education are profoundly damaged by racial innocence, whether by devaluing the reality of difference in ways that equate whiteness and moral universality or by ignoring power to imagine a local "we" and its thick moral norms. For this reason alone, his voice rejects prevailing forms of democratic theory in the United States.[18]

If the way people unreflectively view and practice morality is structured by unequal power and cultural hegemony, then moral education tends toward indoctrination unless it is refracted by a wider political optic. Moreover, if what people call moral allows or even mandates exclusionary violence, they are not simply making a cognitive mistake to correct by good teachers or curricula imparting new information. Baldwin witnesses no mere contradiction between "moral beliefs" about equality and white supremacy: he is naming a profound derangement in our perception of others, a fundamental misrecognition of ourselves, and a refusal of acknowledgment that (mis)shapes every dimension of life. The problem is not only violating the ideal of equality in practice but willfully denying our power and responsibility, as well as the meaning of our conduct in the lives of others. Among themselves the enfranchised of course talk of moral virtue, but from the perspective of those they do not count as real, such talk is not only hollow but absurd—and immoral—because it disavows the exclusions and self-denial on which it rests. If this innocence constitutes the crime, but neither enunciation of moral rules nor evocation of *gemeinschaft* addresses it, what does?

For Baldwin, only political struggle can shift how people define and practice what they call morality. If hegemony turns love into law by making morality a noun rather than a verb, a democratic politics must translate law back into an agonal energy. As speaking and protesting bodies reject invisibility, they provoke our self-reflection about our willful innocence and expose our authority for how we judge conduct and exercise power. Political action not only bespeaks moral aspiration in terms of how people want to be treated but produces the moral education of both those who undergo it and those who witness it. While innocence is criminal for Baldwin, then, the alternative is not guilt in its personal sense. In his political narrative, rather, people move from innocence or bad faith to what Stanley Cavell calls acknowledgment, that is, toward taking political (and not only personal) responsibility—both for the conduct they disavow and for the commitments they profess—in ways that reconstitute political community.[19]

For Baldwin, the premise of political action and moral education is that we human beings are capable of "accepting ourselves as we are," which is the paradoxical condition of changing who we are. A democratic project requires faith in such capacities for acknowledgment and self-overcoming, which are as much moral as political. So for Baldwin, black protestors address enfranchised whites by words and deeds, by ideals enacted, in ways meant to provoke whites to accept the truth about their history but also their power to change it. Exposure to previously unheard voices enacts a moral and not only political lesson, about their capacities to exclude but also to listen and engage. Dialogue, in his own textual practice, or in worldly politics, can provoke people to "accept," that is, to name and take responsibility for, their capacities for violence or evil, but also for acting otherwise.

The opposite of "innocence" for Baldwin, then, is not guilt but a "maturity" that he considers essential to democratic life. In ways that echo back to Machiavelli, indeed, he links moral maturity and democratic practices to the loss of innocence. For democratic politics risks everyone's moral purity in actions whose outcome no one can guarantee but must take responsibility for. As Baldwin shows repeatedly, addressing not only whites but any who equate oppression with moral superiority, we inescapably "betray" the willful, carnal particularity that marks us as human beings, not saints. To "accept ourselves as we are," he insists, is to accept "the dark stranger" in each and all, which means accepting human capacities for willful self-regard let alone violence, the waywardness of our desire, the impossibility of fully knowing our intentions or guaranteeing their outcomes. In these ways Baldwin advances a tragic view of life—which is not moral—and thus a tragic view of the value, limits, and danger in morality. He takes up Blake's antinomian critique of the moral hegemony by which Tocqueville contains democratic life, and like Blake, too, he advances a contrary practice he calls love and depicts as an engagement across difference. But Baldwin does not idealize the human capacity for love, anchor it in the deep order of creation, or imagine it enabling the harmony of beloved community. His idea of love signals human capacities to acknowledge those we have not counted as real and to "accept ourselves as we are" rather than live in bad faith, but love's redemptive power in such regards can only illuminate momentarily, never banish, the darkness within and surrounding us.

For Baldwin, therefore, moral life is unimaginable without what he calls love, but political engagement with others is the crucial medium of moral education, the essential provocation to moral maturity. For exposure to plural voices, engagement in dialogue, and experience with the dilemmas of power transform how we grasp universality, practice ideals, apprehend motives, and credit human limitation—in ways otherwise difficult, perhaps impossible, to learn. Political life teaches the value and meaning of moral ideals but complicates our sense of their relationship to embodied practice and the exercise of power, while chastening any inclination to view life in exclusively moral (and thus in moralistic) terms. By putting our souls in each other's keeping, but also at risk, democratic politics reveals the place—limited and not only necessary, problematic and not only valuable—for what we call morality.

Notes

I am indebted to Peter Euben for helping me to clarify the views I express in this essay.

1. Call this a Machiavellian view of the tension between moral norms and political life.
2. If Machiavelli sees morality as an evasion of the dilemmas entailed by power and plurality, Nietzsche signifies the chorus of critics who see morality as a form of power.
3. Tocqueville, *Democracy in America*, 1: 12, 42–44.
4. Ibid., 43–44.
5. On the ways that Tocqueville unnecessarily limits conflict in volume 1, see Reinhardt, *The Art of Being Free*, and Connolly, *The Ethos of Pluralization*. While Tocqueville in volume 2 foresees the "soft" despotism that Foucault calls normalization, his "antidote" is to sustain traditional forms of moral law and conscience, whereas Foucault seeks an "aesthetics of existence" that moves beyond both the moral and the normal.
6. Blake quoted in Thompson, *Witness against the Beast*, 9. The best account of Blake and his view of morality, and the one to which my own is most indebted, is Frye, *Fearful Symmetry*. The best account of Blake's counterhegemonic politics is Erdman, *Prophet against Empire*. For Blake's own words, see "There Is No Natural Religion" and "the Marriage of Heaven and Hell" in *Blake: Complete Writings*.
7. What Blake calls love denotes the capacity to act (rather than will) that Arendt calls the "I can," the miraculous power she distinguishes from will, finds in Jesus, and identifies with political freedom. What he calls "poetic genius" is not only the creative imagination central to every form of romanticism but the "vision" by which theorists and actors at once represent, call into being, and reconstitute political community.
8. There is an ambiguity in the lineage of heretical Protestantism, which runs from Blake to Walt Whitman, Allen Ginsberg, and Norman O. Brown. One voice in it says: life is a "moral" phenomenon. For partly, the universe displays

a moral law Emerson calls compensation: every act has its costs, and as Baldwin argues, you always "pay" for what you do. And partly, natural existence in every aspect is seen as symbolically charged and meaningful. But another voice says: life is *not* moral, we are led to resentment by the moral demands that we impose on life and each other, and to *chasten* this "moral" sense, we must "love" unredeemed life in its amorality.

9. Morrison, "Introduction: Friday on the Potomac," xv; Brown, *Love's Body*.

10. Baldwin, *The Fire Next Time*, 15–16.

11. Ibid., 17–21.

12. Here is Baldwin, in the only passage where he cites "moral beliefs": "The moral beliefs of a person or a people are never really as tenuous as life—which is not moral—very often causes them to appear; these [moral beliefs] create a frame of reference and a necessary hope, the hope being that when life has done its worst they will be enabled to rise above themselves and triumph over life. Life would scarcely be bearable if this hope did not exist. Again, even when the worst has been said, to betray a belief is not by any means to have put oneself beyond its power; the betrayal of a belief is not the same thing as ceasing to believe. If this were not so there would be no moral standards in the world at all. Yet one must also recognize . . . that confronted with the impossibility of remaining faithful to one's beliefs, and the equal impossibility of becoming free of them, one can be driven to the most inhuman excess."

13. Ibid., 88.

14. Ibid., 36.

15. Ibid., 89.

16. Baldwin, "Everybody's Protest Novel," *The Price of the Ticket*, 33. His concern about moralized categories linked to narratives of innocent virtue anticipates by fifty years the vicissitudes of identity politics and those who criticize its "moralism." Yet he also insists that subalterns cannot escape but must instead rework what Wendy Brown calls a "wounded attachment." For Brown's concept presumes that there is some other kind of attachment, whereas Baldwin assumes every attachment is wounded and thus needs to be reworked, in the Nietzschean sense of *amor fati*, into a condition of possibility.

17. Baldwin, "Many Thousands Gone," *The Price of the Ticket*, 78.

18. See Balfour, *Evidence of Things Not Said*, for a compelling analysis of Baldwin's relationship to prevailing forms of democratic theory.

19. Cavell, "Knowing and Acknowledging," and *The Claim of Reason*.

HUNGER, ETHICS, AND THE UNIVERSITY
A Radical Democratic Goad in Ten Pieces

This is an immoderate essay, forged at once in the flames of a radical democratic ethos and a deep suspicion regarding a substantial portion of what is called "moral education." Hunger, that aching in the gut, is at once a prism, a call bell, and potentially a blinder. Hunger is among the most urgent of situations. This urgency at once demands an ethical-political response and critically illuminates many contemporary efforts at moral education. Yet the urgency of hunger can also harbor its own blindness if it is construed only as a call to satiation. If universities are to adopt ethical-political stances toward the world that serve as more than ideologies, or new modes of disciplinary power, or feel-good exercises which leave most of what is unjust in place, or knee-jerk radicalism—I suspect that we will have to invent arts of negotiating between and entwining responsibilities for the hunger of the belly and the hunger of the mind. This is a small gesture toward that end.

Each year at the beginning of the twenty-first century, over 11 percent of the people—about thirty-four million—in the richest country in the world were "food insecure," which means that they found themselves skipping meals, facing hunger, taking drastic steps to avoid it, because they couldn't afford to eat. (Additionally, tens of millions live with the knowledge that they are never more than a couple of pay checks or a job dismissal notice away from this situation in which they see some of their friends, relatives, and neighbors.) Even at the end of the extended economic boom during the 1990s the number stood at thirty-one million people—lots of them kids—living with the proximate specter of hunger. Food insecurity and hunger are not merely problems that we haven't yet successfully tackled. They are *systematically produced* by the political economy in which we live. Most earning minimum wages and supporting households are food insecure, as are vast numbers of those at the official federal "poverty" level. And this urgent metonym of class power and poverty intersects with other modes of power such that the rates increase about three-fold for households headed by women, blacks, and Hispanics (all statistics from USDA).

What might it mean to talk about moral education in the context of such systemically engendered *corruption?* I emphasize this word to evoke both the bodily suffering and the systemic core of the problem. The corruption to which I refer isn't addressed by fine-tuning mechanisms of oversight and accountability to make the system work as it should. My point is that even when the system—not only its mechanisms of exchange and administration but also its patterns of knowledge production and pedagogy—is working "well," so too is the production of hunger and widespread oblivion to it. Corruption speaks not only of the moral debasement of a situation in which, as Rabbi Abraham Heschel framed the message of the Jewish prophets, "few are guilty, but all are responsible," but also of the literal bodily degeneration of those millions who are born hungry and who die young because of hunger and related ills, and the degeneration of a collective body that produces this situation.[1] What does teaching "values" mean, when many of these values are often articulated in ways that are complicit with this system of power/suffering, or relatively silent about it, or incapable of disturbing the production of deafening indifference, or lead only to the occasional charitable trip to the soup kitchen on the way to the oblivious high-paying job in the corporate firm?

Time was when hunger-talk was honest, blunt, and a central focus of many intellectuals. And it is clear that it was closely linked to the emergence of a new political economic morality—a new moral education. According to Karl Polanyi, these themes received their earliest articulation in 1786, in

Joseph Townsend's *Dissertation on the Poor Laws by a Well-Wisher to Mankind,* which proclaimed:

> Hunger will tame the fiercest animals, it will teach decency and civility, obedience and subjection, to the most perverse. In general it is only hunger which can spur and goad them [the poor] on to labor. . . . Legal constraint [to work] is attended with much trouble . . . whereas hunger is not only peaceable, silent, unremitting pressure, but, as the most natural motive to industry and labor, it calls forth the most powerful exertions; and, when satisfied by the free bounty of another, lays lasting and sure foundations for good will and gratitude.[2]

In a world where some and not others are confined to dirty and servile work, the specter of an aching in the gut is to spur and mold people into the norms of labor and constitute a morality of docility, acceptance, deference, and thankful allegiance to the powerful. In the first decade of the nineteenth century Townsend's discourse was taken up across a wide ideological spectrum. This includes not only Malthusians but traditionalists such as Burke, who affirmed economic liberalism and its constitutive relation to hunger in part as a persistent and detailed mode of governing the poor (without "government") for purposes of public security, and utilitarians like Bentham, who argued that hunger would be both a vital and sufficient force to drive the poor into his panoptic "industry houses"— nightmare utopias of moral betterment and productivity where they could be subjected to minute and continuous "inspectability" and administration—a "mill to grind rogues honest and idle men industrious."[3] As Polanyi and Foucault have argued quite convincingly, the panopticon exemplifies a type of moral administrative power and pedagogy that begins to circulate widely in the nineteenth century.

Hence, at the same time that Kant theorizes a kingdom of persons as "ends in themselves," Townsend inaugurates a political economic morality that has at its heart the need for working-class people to feel in their gut the *specter of their own end itself*—the prospect of their death—in order to be taught the life of hard work at miserable pay, civility, and obedience; in order to be taught their true value in market society. Michel Foucault provides a more penetrating account of panoptic power than Polanyi, for he details the ways in which it isolates people (architecturally separating them in more rigid ways from broader social and historical contexts, and also separating them from each other within the new disciplinary cellular spaces) and reconstructs their relations wholly in terms of the objectives of narrowly construed productivity. These separations and disciplined connections then become the new imaginary which simultaneously produces material goods, class power, and hunger, while minimizing the solidarities, modes of witness, and questioning that might resist these in the name of other alternatives. Yet what Foucault omits is the extent to which the urgency of feeling one's end in hunger was central to the beginning of the "new man" made into commodified socially and temporally detached (from places, communities, traditions, unwonted solidarities, etc.) labor, well-constituted to conform to the needs of an increasingly mobile political economy of productivity—and incapacitated when it comes to initiating anything beyond these requirements. The way this feeling of death abstracts and reconstitutes selves resonates (albeit very paradoxically and only partly) with those aspects of Kant's moral thought which constitute us as the most abstracted ends and thereby also inhibit our capacity for beginning historically specific ethical and political action that might challenge the limits of the given modes of "rationality."[4] What I mean is that our ethical capacities to see, feel, and actively respond to suffering and generate social and political alternatives are profoundly rooted in multifarious and textured human *relationships* that exceed the dominant scripts in manifold ways. Insofar as our economic, political, and moral experiences and vocabularies reflect and reinforce abstract isolation, on the one hand, and interactions that are increasingly disciplined on the micro level in homogenizing ways, on the other, our ethical capacities degenerate. I think Polanyi shows how facing the prospect of one's end in hunger played a role in abstracting selves from multiplicitous relationships and driving people into new disciplinary modes of power. Unwittingly, Kant's morality correlates with—and provides too little to effectively resist—the damages associated with selves thus abstracted in the everyday functioning of new systems of productivity. Kant's philosophy of personhood inscribes (in its radical abstraction from particularity) an abstraction that is fomented by a political economy that systematized the prospect of hunger. Thus, the moral freedom that characterizes persons as ends in themselves is a form of unfreedom insofar as it conceals the particularities of selves and relationships that are an integral condition for the possibility of a freedom which might initiate action that challenges political economies that commodify people. In this way there is a profoundly haunting double entendre in the phrase "ends in themselves"—a resonance between ends and the prospect of death by starvation.

The widespread experience of hunger played a vital role in both detaching commodified people from their various local contexts and traditions and articulating a new metaphysics with profound implications for ethical inquiry and political agency. Polanyi's history captures this tenor repeatedly, as he writes of a new "evangelical fervor" for the self-regulating market, a "fanaticism of sectarians" with a "blind faith in spontaneous progress," "an emotional faith in spontaneity . . . a mystical readiness," and "uncritical reliance on the alleged self-healing virtues of unconscious growth."[5] Connected to a political economic process enabled by a visceral fear of one's early *end* was the birth of a new temporality in which the present was understood to be already animated by a future which, as "self-healing," permitted no interruption, no regulation. Pure futurity is the "end of history." A future which might feature a necessary and radical transformation of the present is precluded by the very way that the present defines itself as eternally self-correcting in an unlimited way: as the present is always already the future, which always already contains the principle of its own still further future "self-healing" correction, every ethical political initiation toward another world is declared, in advance, impossible. History as the movement of time in which human formations come and go is replaced by a notion of time governed forever by the present formation. And all this is linked to the widespread specter of an aching in the gut, which our society has proved quite skilled at producing for all its capacity to generate wealth.

This brief sketch is, I think, extremely pertinent to any discussion of ethics and higher education. Hunger is among the most urgent of situations. Yet it is integrally connected to modes of power that—from the micro production of selves to macro production of theodicies of history and political economy—simultaneously produce this urgency and sever it from ethical and political reflection and action that might transform the world in response. Indeed, as time goes by in the end of history, we no longer hear the Townsends, Malthuses, Burkes, and Benthams of the world openly articulating the links between hunger, the moral education of the masses, and our political economy. They still dominate the conversation, but they have mastered the arts of esoteric speech—rarely mentioning hunger and speaking instead simply of necessary unemployment, keeping the minimum wage very low if at all, disciplinary reconstitutions of the moral fiber of the poor, inflationary dangers, and so forth. The theodicy of capitalist political economy has learned to disclose its wounds primarily in softer light that largely renders publicly invisible and unthought hunger and its urgency, while it absorbs within itself and in advance the domain of legitimate responses to a "situation that is improving though we have more to do." We have become mostly indifferent to the urgency of hunger. That its widespread presence should pose no challenge to our basic frameworks in fundament, is a *doxa* that "goes without saying, because it comes without saying."[6]

Two things in this context strike me about so many well-meaning liberal academics who are concerned about the unethical character of the contemporary world and higher education: First, they rarely mention hunger, and I wonder if this is not one important factor contributing to a certain lack of urgency that pervades too many of such discourses (while the right wing has mastered the rhetoric of urgency for disciplinary schemes to secure the order). Second, the discussions tend to focus on renderings of honesty, courage, character, respect, fairness, generosity, and so forth that are framed as if they could be achieved without doing much at all to question and change the basic parameters of our political economic relationships, practices, and the associated theodicy of history that has bound our ethical-political imaginations. It is as though, if we just walk our paths with moral rectitude and perhaps a little bit of tinkering at the edges of things—that might be enough. But what if many of these sanctioned paths are directly corrupt for the evil they do, or indirectly corrupt for the responsibilities they deny? What if we would have to *walk very different paths in very different ways* for ethics and ethical education to have much sense at all? What if a *world* of different paths and modes were necessary, and what if they were necessary *now*—because our situation is as urgent as an aching in the gut? What if ethical education in absence of the pressure of these questions might share much more than it would like to with the "Well-Wisher to Mankind" who formulated a pedagogy of "decency and civility, obedience and subjection, gratitude and good will" and thus laid the foundations for a political economy of hunger?

The pain of hunger indissociably gives rise to a most visceral questioning: how then will I feed my self—my child, this friend, this stranger—in a context which denies us? This same pain can also demand answers that are, on both personal and macro-political scales, dead ends—potentially engendering an egoism that is oblivious to others, or merely selfish pursuit within the current framework of alternatives. So the ethical-political issue, it seems, is how to receive the urgency and the system-questioning pressure it brings, without killing the space of this opening by knowing "too well" what justice entails. How might we avoid the trap of teaching ethics to undergraduates in ways that presume that we professors know what and how they must learn? How might we avoid the traps of forms of service-learning that assume students know what and how the communities into which they are sent must learn and do? How might we avoid the traps of ethics education that uncritically accepts conceptions of the self and the order in our efforts to engender ethical sensibilities? It is precisely here that the hunger of universities concerned with ethical-political education *might* play an important role beyond the confines they often reinforce.

The hunger for knowledge has taken many different forms—not all of them desirable by any means. Yet the forms that seem to me most promising are those concerned with questions that probe the possibilities for transcending in desirable ways the limits of present orders of knowing and doing. They have a hunger for that which is beyond present "truths" and "necessities" that upon close examination are implicated in unfreedom and suffering. I think universities, at their best moments, can be places where this hunger is cultivated, nurtured, and engaged with the world beyond its walls. Kant, who contributed significantly to theorizing the modern university, theorized enlightenment precisely as "an exit," a "way out," an "escape" (*Ausgang*) from humans' "inability to use [their] own understanding without guidance from another." By this latter turn of phrase, at his most insightful, he meant not that we should ignore others' thoughts in our thinking but that we should work to release the "ball and chain" of a lazy reason that accepts the dogmas of the current order as necessary and universal.[7] Radicalizing this formulation with and against

Kant, Foucault wrote of an enlightenment ethos as a "limit attitude," "at the frontiers," questioning "in what is given to us as universal, necessary, obligatory, what place is occupied by whatever is singular, contingent, and the product of arbitrary constraints . . . a critique that takes the form of a possible transgression."[8] This hunger for other ways of thinking and being —which Foucault described not as a devouring curiosity but as a curiosity consumed by the "question of knowing if one can think differently than one thinks, and perceive differently than one sees"—is an absolutely vital aspect of the university and vital as well to imagining and pursuing ways of eliminating hunger and the system of commodified labor, disciplinary power, and theodicies of history with which it is entwined. These systems are nearly two hundred years old and they live on in most efforts to critique and transcend them. Animated by the urgency of hunger, we will have to work hard at the limits of our knowing if we are to move beyond "solutions" that reproduce the very hunger, power, and theodicy they were meant to escape. In other words, the ethical and political hunger of the university is *empty* if divorced from the aching in the gut of millions, but efforts to abolish the hunger will likely be *blind* if divorced from the hunger of the university at the frontiers of knowledge.

Yet there are many ways to be blind. Drawing upon Aristotle's discussion in *De anima*, Derrida notes that bees lack eyelids and thus *always* see. They know a lot but can't learn. They lack the ability not only to hear but also to close off sight—that shutting of the eye at regular intervals—which Derrida links to being able to listen better; whereas "man can lower the sheath, adjust the diaphragm, narrow his sight, the better to listen, remember, and learn."[9] Playfully deflecting an imaginary suggestion that he seeks "to cultivate an art of blinking," he nevertheless proclaims that the university "must not be a sclerophthalmic [dry eyed and unblinking] animal." Derrida argues that we must relax our teleological energies periodically, rhythmically, like blinking our eyes, so we might practice an enlightenment more infused with "listening." He evocatively seeks this possibility " 'in the twilight of an eye,' for it is in the most crepuscular . . . situations of the Western university that the chances for this 'twinkling' of thought are multiplied."[10]

One way of remaining sclerophthalmic and blind is linked to the way we often conceive of "frontiers of knowledge," which today many so often interpret as a cutting edge in time: according to the temporal matrix of the neoliberal theodicy which sees—as we have already noted in relation to Polanyi—the present as the cutting edge of history animated by a self-healing future. Within this frame, traditions of "the past" are to be discarded from contemporary ethical-political dialogues and struggles, as are insurgent efforts that would lean into the future against the grain of "history." (Or, where "tradition" is not to be discarded, it is to be *deployed* for the functional requirements of the present order, but not as a set of sources and ghosts that might radically contest the imperatives of this order.) If the university seeks a chance to make a contribution to transforming a world that produces hunger, it will have to nurture much better than it has spaces for different and not infrequently *rival* modes of inquiry. This is especially the case as it seems that our political economy is relatively unique—according to economic anthropologists—in its systematic deployment of the threat of hunger. The time is ripe for listening to traditions and emerging groups that have done or are doing better in this regard.

I think this means that the notion of "frontiers of knowledge" will have to shift from being the edge inhabited by the most advanced "moderns," to being the spaces of scholarly and practical engagement at the edges *between* different groups. With MacIntyre and Mignolo, I think this calls for *universities that create more space to cultivate ethical-political modes of enquiry and pedagogy*, between, for example, neo-Thomists, Jews, indigenous peoples, liberals, Islamic traditions, radical democratic genealogists, and so on.[11] It will take multiple efforts to think differently, each with some organizational autonomy and a will to engage at the intersections of myriad efforts.

Yet I suspect that this blinking and pluralized hunger for knowledge, the university's hunger, will amount to very little ethically if it does not simultaneously pursue myriad forms of engagement at another frontier, namely, that between itself and those who live beyond its walls—or slave within its walls—in or more proximate to hunger and poverty. If, as I've briefly suggested, the hunger of the belly and the hunger of the mind must be entwined in new ways that interweave urgency and reflection concerning the suffering of the present order, a crucial aspect of this project must involve political modes of engagement with communities struggling with poverty. These cannot be limited only to charity, or "service," but must involve receptive efforts to learn from and with those who are struggling politically in the neighborhoods and regions of the world that "always get dumped on and never get plowed."[12] We need to move our inquiring and collaborative work to those places. I think we need to do this not only as a central part of exploring and inventing radical democratic possibilities for transforming the present order but also because of a sense that our imaginations are as starved and constrained as are the bellies of millions of people. As Adorno liked to quote Benjamin: "While there is a beggar, there is a myth."[13] It may well be that one vital condition of possibility for *thinking* differently hinges very much upon *seeing, being, and doing* differently—receptively engaging other lives, dwelling in the forbidden zones of our cities, inventing other modes of ethical-political relationships and power across the lines that confine both the belly and our imaginations. The urgency of ethics and politics springs from both places. Undoubtedly such efforts will take many agonistic and contested forms. This is both necessary and good. But where such efforts are entirely absent, I worry that much ethics talk in the university will be little but a sham.

Blasphemy! Is not the above suggestion diametrically opposed to one of the most sacred foundations of the life of the mind (and institutions devoted to it), namely, the presumption that the task of thinking requires disinterest, distance, spaces walled off from the immediacies of everyday life—and most especially the urgency of hunger—in order to thrive? Wouldn't crossing the lines and confusing the distinct purposes that delineate these spaces lead to the destruction of precisely what is most precious about higher education? This danger is not to be taken lightly. It is real and requires constant renegotiation. Yet not crossing these lines is a real danger as well (not to mention the powerful corporate imperatives that ceaselessly colonize the spaces of higher education today with such ease, I think, in part because of the political and economic blindness engendered by naive "liberal humanist" assumptions about sharp lines between knowledge and power). Our assessments of and responses to relative dangers always hinge on the terms with which we construe and measure them.

Here I want to suggest that rethinking hunger in relation to human be-coming, thinking, and imagining can help us reconsider the dangers and possibilities at hand. And no one has done so more profoundly than the German thinker Ernst Bloch.

Bloch is an extremely complicated and difficult thinker. At times perhaps he exaggerates his claims, offers insufficient support for them, and mini-mizes other elements of the human situation that put pressure on the central themes he pursues. In the present context I am interested in him as an *evocative* thinker, one who opens windows for us to begin seeing ways beyond some of the impasses sketched above—and doors through which we might move in tentative exploration. Reading Bloch as an evocative thinker here (which is generally how I think he should be read), I am less concerned to defend or elaborate his claims in detail than I am to show how they might spur reflection on the thematic of our twin hungers of belly and mind. Bloch suggests ways beyond reified understandings of humans, the present order, and "the end of history," and he helps advance paths for understanding the politics and production of knowledge that might shift our sense of ethics and higher education in more promising ways. As an evocation, this reading of Bloch is intended as an invitation to urgent conversation rather than as a foundation or conclusion. The ques-tion I bring to my reading of Bloch (which I think is similar to the one he brings to the world) is not so much "Is this true?" as it is "What might it be possible to see, become, and do better than we currently see, are, and do?" How might Bloch challenge our turning away from the hungry, our aver-sions to hunger, our abstraction from the body, and our sense of a present beyond which there are no alternatives?

Many thinkers follow Hobbes's rendering of hunger as egoistic appetite which, unchecked, tends toward a war of all against all that is "nasty, brutish, and short." Another major path of modern thinking follows Locke in locating the most profound aspect of the self *beyond hunger* in rational self-possession. In contrast to Locke, for Bloch, human life is most deeply that which "does not have what belongs to it, but rather searches for it and intends it outside, i.e., . . . is hungry."[14] Yet far from ensconcing us in egoism, this fact is what *might* draw us into relations of differential soli-darity with others, as well as a longing, hope, and action for more adequate thinking and a better world. Hannah Arendt suggests in many places that hunger, and more generally the urgency of need, tends to close down the space for distinctively political freedom by welding into one mass a mob unyieldingly driven to satiate immediate needs. My reading of Bloch does not seek to lose sight of this ever-present and dangerous possibility. Rather it seeks to locate other potentials that *also* imbue experiences of and responses to hunger. We cannot suppress the closures of urgent need by banning them from the political realm, for their very necessity makes such a ban futile in absence of the most odious modes of subjugation. A better strategy may be to reinterpret and respond more generously to the neediness within human beings in order to cultivate resources for caring for plurality. Bloch suggests that our hunger harbors calls and connections that can animate and inform such efforts. It is not that our hunger can be reduced to such care—no more than it can be reduced to closure. It is rather that hunger harbors possibilities that are vital not only for a world that is more receptive and generous to unfolding human plurality and flourishing but also to resisting the pressures of closure that hunger also harbors. For me, Bloch and Arendt should not be read so much as alternatives to each other but rather as forming a vital tension we ought to maintain as we are animated by and negotiate our responses to hunger. Here I write with an ear more attuned to the much overlooked Blochian side of this tension.

In a manner that profoundly illuminates the issues at hand, Bloch *reads* hungering as pivotal to ethical-political life, the life of the mind, and the relation between the two. Bloch's claim, as I read him, is not that our hungering tends inexorably to give birth to his rendering of it, but, nevertheless, that it solicits and lends itself to such an interpretation, and that this interpretation suggests a vision of and mode of participating in the human condition that is compelling precisely insofar as it transcends many of the problems engendered by alternative understandings. If Hobbes sometimes writes of himself as an eye doctor whose task is to improve our ethical-political vision, Bloch might be read as one who accepts this as central to the theorist's task and then offers a radically different reading. Reading, or interpreting the human condition, becomes for Bloch something that is *engendered by the very hunger it seeks to interpret*—in a manner that propels a circle that is essentially never transparent and cannot be finished. The status of Bloch's claims can only be assessed in relation to alternative interpretations in light of what they illuminate, the responsiveness they nurture, and the modes of life they thus facilitate or impede. Of course, I am interested in them in relation to the failures I have identified through the lens of Polanyi's critical reading of market society.

For Bloch, hunger, like all of the human condition, is not a fact that is simply present. Rather it is infused with what he calls "forward dawning" or "not yet"—hope for a fullness that is not yet present. Hunger *shares* this character of opening to the future, but it is also *exemplary* of human being as hopeful, insofar as its relation toward the not yet has a particular poignancy and intensity, even if there are many other possible ways of living and interpreting it. How hopeful our hunger may be, and how hopeful we humans may become, depends, however, not simply on the presence of hunger but on how well we acknowledge and interpret its futurity (one could say: how well we hunger for our hunger); how well we respond to and act in light of it.[15]

Bloch suggests that we are beings who hunger for situations less degrading and more conducive to thriving; we thirst for well-being, knowledge, and a better world; we feel ourselves searching from an empty place toward a world beyond ourselves and beyond its present configuration. Hence, he writes, "'Longing' [is] the only honest state in all men" (45). This longing comes from an empty place—first and most literally the gut, but it is simultaneously entwined with and generative of an unfolding abundance of wishing, imagining, and experimentation that is distinctively human. For Bloch, to acknowledge hungering as elemental, is to situate theory and ethics—including his own—within this ongoing movement that none can "possess," yet all can sense and evoke in ways that inform politics with hope.

Our hunger emerges from deep within our bellies as a drive to stay alive. Yet far from locking us in a state of solipsism, the universality of hungering can open us to others and the world beyond. Bloch argues that "the unemployed person on the verge of collapse, who has not eaten for days, has really been led to the oldest needy place of our existence and makes it visible. In any case, sympathy with the starving is the only widespread sympathy there is, in fact the only one that is widely possible. ... [T]he cry of the hungry is probably the strongest single cry that can be directly presented" (65). Though the exaggerated form of this statement seems to marginalize other deep streams of compassion, his overall point seems important: The sight of others in hunger opens lines of elemental responsiveness—corporeal communication beyond the limits of our individual flesh. We can and do, of course, resist this radically discomforting sense of flesh-crossing vulnerability and suffering, but Bloch contends that face to face with another hungry person we have great difficulty doing so for long. Interestingly, this would partly explain the proliferation of ordinances, geographical constructions and practices, highly policed relational taboos, and energetic mobilizations of ideological discourses that impede such witness. Thus, this most basic drive both engenders and illuminates our own vulnerable neediness and harbors a compassionate call. It *both* harbors an urge that calls our unjust order deeply into question, *and* it can fuel a security-seeking fear of such questioning which can engender the reactive policing that perpetuates and intensifies unjust orders. This suggests (in a way that perhaps exceeds Bloch's own understanding) that hunger lends itself to radically opposed possibilities. Bloch's project is to seize the more promising *potentia* that is "not yet conscious" and render some of its possibilities more explicit in order to participate in their realization.

Hunger, Bloch argues, is not a static human drive but rather is always *becoming* in historically variable relations with the perceived world, other needs, and others. And sometimes our hunger transforms in ways that seek not simply different objects but more radical renewals in which our vulnerability and longing tend beyond extant horizons: "Hunger cannot help continually renewing itself. But if it increases uninterrupted, satisfied by no certain bread, then it suddenly changes . . . becomes rebellious, does not go out in search of food merely within the old framework. It seeks to change the situation which caused its empty stomach, its hanging head" (75). As nagging and persistent, our longing sometimes solicits critical reflexivity concerning our self, structural situation, and the relations with others that generate and sustain our experiences of deprivation. In this process, our hungering can stimulate our imaginations of and efforts to experiment (with a "revolutionary interest") toward alternative situations that would transcend unjust ills of the present. Vital to such transformations is the emergence of solidarities and collaborations nourished in part by sympathetic communications among hungering and hunger-prone bodies.

On Bloch's account (contra Hannah Arendt), this hunger-related solidarity with others need not develop toward a community that would devour human difference in the indistinction of our basic neediness. Rather, such compassion and communication *can* (but doesn't necessarily) provide a dynamic opening toward others through which we might come to acknowledge them as *distinct relational centers* of hunger, dynamic longing, and imagining. Indeed, it is an indispensable condition of such acknowledgment, if there is to be any. The self as a *reflective* hungering being (reflective significantly *because* it hungers), then, comes to understand itself as a being beyond self and other possession—a being *essentially drawn outside itself*. Such reflective hunger hungers to be responsive to a world of others it comes to know and desire *as others* whom it cannot and should not seek to consume—lest it proliferate the contradictions and deprivations of all efforts to do so and simultaneously deny the abundant richness of human plurality. As we reflect deeply upon our becoming as hungering beings *as such*, Bloch suggests, the character of our hunger shifts from a consumptive focus toward efforts to valorize and create conditions conducive to the generative dimension of our coexistence as plural hungering creatures. We then increasingly hunger to participate with others in the articulation of and struggle toward a community that better enables diverse hungering and hoping selves to flourish together. We become, quite literally, *eccentric,* drawn into "external orbits" in relation to other beings (91).

Nowhere is this clearer than in Bloch's rendering of *utopia* through the lens of hunger where, I think, Bloch is profoundly suggestive for considerations of ethics, politics, and ultimately higher education. Hungering, Bloch suggests, is paradoxically an emblematic root of *both* the desire to satiate human neediness *and* the infinite fecundity of our insatiable hopeful longing. Utopia must be wrought in response to tensions between *both* of these dimensions of our becoming at once.

On the one hand, the struggle to address our hunger appears to harbor a telos of urgent and radical *satiation*. Hunger stimulates wishes, visions, and fantasies of a world of *fulfillment* beyond all deprivation (including, of course, beyond situations constitutive of self-defeating longings that perpetuate experiences of deprivation). Our daydreams beyond deprivation "journey to the end," as Bloch puts it. Beyond "world-improving roaming," or endless striving—which can be a hellish vertigo always threatened with Nothing—hunger endlessly stimulates humans toward fantasies of "arrival"; the imagination of unimaginable conditions beyond want where all our needs and all the potentials of our own, others,' and the world's being would be fully realized (95). We imagine and strive toward a world where all potentials for flourishing that are not yet conscious and have not yet become would be fully manifest. The teleology that surges forth here—animating and orienting our striving—aims in a profound sense toward an absolute, an *"anticipated keeping still"* (289; Bloch's emphasis) in an astonished state beyond need, an insipient *summum bonum*. Human experimentation thus driven manifests hunger as a "force of production" in history. Bloch, as we see below, finds this yearning problematic and simultaneously irresistible. In the midst of an endless proliferation of ideologies justifying various modes of suffering and deprivation, these images of "All" energize a radical demythologizing resistance and imaginative struggle toward alternatives in the face of powers that seek to abort the fecundity of human yearning and possibility. Would not an ethics education deprived of this energetic urgent hope for a perfect flourishing sell short our critical and generative capacities?

Nevertheless, the image of and demand for fulfilled utopic hope can be as detrimental to our flourishing as it may be conducive to it. While our hungering strives beyond hunger toward satiated fullness, simultaneously, as we reflect upon ourselves as hungering beings, we discover the presence of an equally grand and *inexhaustible potential in us which yearns critically and imaginatively beyond every present that claims to encompass satiation and fullness.* As we examine this *insatiable longing* retrospectively, we discover that time after time it discloses detrimental aspects of given orders as well as alternative possibilities. A close look at our hungering discloses that we harbor a tremendous latency that is "not yet conscious" (or "has not yet become") and is precisely a crucial wellspring of our vitality and ethical-political engagement. We thus come to valorize this latent unquenchability within and between us such that we project it onto our hopeful imaginings of utopian futures. In so doing, we help free the future from our possessive grasp. Beyond a hope for the future as a satiated fully realized "all," we come to appreciate that "it cannot be so because the future dimension . . . itself contains *unmastered* Now, i.e. darkness, just as the Now itself still contains *unopened* future, i.e. newness, and surges forward to meet it" (297).[16] In other words, even as our hungering suggests that we must strive politically toward conditions conducive to the satiated fulfillment of human potential, it *also* calls us to recognize, respond to, and nurture humans as essentially hungering, striving, imagining beings harboring dynamic, abundant, and unpredictable aspects "opening out on to the as yet unarrived" (139). This latter is paradoxically a constitutive aspect of hope. Any ethical pedagogy or politics that seeks simply to free us of *this* poverty and its related abundance would be a travesty.

Let me elaborate a few of the interrelated ethical, political, and pedagogical stakes of this brief (and thus sketchy) excursus on Bloch's evocation of hunger-born hope. First, I hope to have gestured toward some of the ways in which the hunger of the belly and the hunger of our imagination might be—contra some prevalent assumptions—not only compatible but also intrinsically and informatively connected with one another. Bloch's interpretation of our hunger(ing) can shed light on both some of the *purposes* of human inquiry and political life (i.e., ideal satiation and pregnant latency) as well as the centrality of *modes* (i.e., urgency and tensional complexity) of opening onto unexpected newness, through which these purposes might at once be sought and unsettled. Far from engendering a simple-minded dogmatism (though the drive for satiation always risks this), careful reflection upon our hungering being calls us beyond our complacency with the present *as well as* our complacency with alternative static ideals and arrangements in light of which we would transform it. These lessons strike me as utterly crucial to a dialogical ethics of higher education *and* of politics, albeit in ways that are not identical.[17]

Second, and related to the first point, Bloch sharply illuminates ways in which the highest pursuits of philosophical, theological, and political inquiry are deeply connected with our relation to the hunger of the "least of these" among us. The absence of the pressures of hunger and the voices of the hungry in our practices of knowledge production at once enables and requires a broad array of ideological concealments (such as those Polanyi discusses) that have repercussions which undermine many of the more rarified pursuits of ethical and theoretical inquiry. For, if Bloch is right, the denial of transformative witness to the hungry (and the conditions that make them so) requires an intense mobilization of mystifying energy that tends to instigate other sorts of denials and misrepresentations of hunger(ing) as an elemental aspect of human becoming.

In contemporary political and economic discourses, this myopia frequently takes the form of pronouncements concerning the "end of history," as well as ethical visions of the human self as essentially autonomous, independent, and in possession of relatively static forms of ethical reason. Hunger, vulnerability, dependence, and tragic finitude—even in many humane discourses such as political liberalism—primarily appear as deviations from this basic condition, rather than constitutive aspects of humans that are profoundly generative as well as a poverty (or, in a sense, generative *in relation to* our poverty).[18] The ideological insistence upon the sharp lines separating academic inquiry from the pressures of everyday life like hunger manifests itself, in turn, even in many efforts to cross these lines. This can be seen in relatively deaf (albeit well-intentioned) versions of service-learning and relatively deaf projects such as the UN Millennium Development project. Though these latter bring academic knowledge into contact with real-world people and problems, they do so in manners that greatly marginalize the importance of *receptive* engagements and relationships with those who will, otherwise, be reduced to targets of presupposed ideals. Hence the hungry and impoverished become more objects than subjects of knowledge—in ways that secure the very knowledge brought to bear upon them from dynamics that might transform it from "below." Bloch's work illuminates this vicious circle and incites us to decommission it in the name of more hopeful practice and ethical-political theory.

Third, these points suggest that ways beyond these modes of misconstrual and political containment will have to begin, in no small part, by engaging the question of hunger *with the hungry and those more proximate to hunger than most of us in ivory towers.* This is both an intellectual and a political task, and each will likely fall short if it seeks to proceed very far in absence of the other. Bloch's work suggests that wall-crossing and purpose-confusing relationships and pedagogical practices *with* the poor are essential to *invigorating* a sense of ethical urgency—an *energetic hungering*—that seems to disappear wherever such relationships and engagements are lacking. In other words, the problem is not only (as suggested above) that the *thematics* of hunger are actively "disappeared" when such relationships are absent but that the *energy and urgency of hungering*—for ethical and political change, and for knowledge that would provoke and enable it—itself disappears from discourses born in and carried along by constructed distances from those on the undersides of history. I think this is true of discourses produced in academically remote locations *across the political spectrum.* Perhaps the *most* unethical and antipolitical effect of these constructed distances lies precisely in the dissipation of urgency—above and beyond the content mystification that such distances also produce.[19] While I am deeply sympathetic with critiques of moralism, they take a wrong turn if they are construed to condone the lack of urgency that is already all too pervasive.

Inquiries and pedagogies that move in the suggested alternative directions will by no means be easy or without great dangers. The hungry and the poor are—in different ways—as damaged and indifferent as most academics and we know little about how to form relationships across the walls and power-lines of indifference that saturate our lived geographies. Nearly everything remains to be invented. In closing, I gesture toward a couple of forums that seem promising in this regard.

In scores of cities across the United States, the Industrial Areas Foundation (IAF) and other groups are organizing grassroots democracy coalitions across lines of race, ethnicity, religion, nationality, class, and ideology to address myriad forms of suffering in our society and to build radical democratic countercultures and powers. Associated with some such efforts are organized gatherings for intellectual engagement that mix things up by drawing students and faculty in universities along with those outside the academy involved in grassroots leadership together in ways that are beginning to inform ethical-political understanding and generate some of the urgency to which I have alluded above. Ernesto Cortez and others in the IAF Southwest region regularly host such meetings in the Interfaith Educational Network (IEN), and Southeast regional IAF organizer Gerald Taylor, along with several organizers and academics (including myself), has organized a similar forum called the Third Reconstruction Institute (TRI). The IEN developed in an effort to gather organizers and leaders together every couple of months to benefit from seminar discussions with leading scholars on themes such as race, political economy, religion, civil society, democracy, and so forth. Such seminars provide an opportunity for those engaged in the urgencies of everyday political organizing to *step back* from these immediacies and reflect more broadly. Yet many of the academics who have participated in these events attest to the power of these gatherings in a different way. For many academics, the experience of having our work seriously and critically addressed by people engaged in related daily specific struggles is a powerful and transformative experience. Not only do many academics learn a great deal from everyday knowledges and approaches but they also find themselves infected by a sense of urgency in relation to their work that is often lacking in strictly academic settings. At the intersection between grassroots activists and academics, new modes of knowledge, new types of energy and urgency, and new senses of possibility are generated that many are coming to believe are crucial for reconfiguring practices of higher education in ways that are at once critical and energized toward public questions and purposes.

The TRI emerged recently, more than a decade after the IEN, and the academics who participated in its founding seek to provide a forum where the meaning and practices of scholarship and pedagogy can undergo transformations through dialogue with nonacademic grassroots leaders. We academics have a distinct interest in this conversation that exceeds the interests of the organizers—even as our diverse interests overlap in ways that facilitate common work. Typically about a dozen academics in the TRI engage in discussion with about three dozen people active in grassroots democracy across the Southeast.[20] These discussions have been by no means easy, but at some point during each two-day seminar there have been epiphanies that are significant and that endure for many of us. In each seminar conversation we have had to negotiate fruitful connections between the more theoretical propensities of most academics involved and the more specific, narrative, and immediately pragmatic orientations of many of the grassroots activists. As there are no set genres for such engagements, those in each meeting are drawn to *invent* modes of interaction in ways that are far less necessary when, say, academics meet in typical established settings. This creates a certain edginess in the room that is often energizing and theoretically rich in unsuspected ways, as numerous specific stories of experiences of racism, for example, mingle with theoretical efforts to theorize race. Though we are still very much in a formative stage, most involved are encouraged by the possibilities that appear to be powerful even if they are still rather inchoate.

Yet these gatherings that cross the lines and confuse the purposes of mainstream academia are frustrating in lots of ways too, and I suspect that this is significantly a good thing. Sometimes academics are frustrated by what they take to be the lack of sufficient theoretical concern and subtlety on the part of some of the nonacademics as we discuss theories of race, democracy, or labor law. This seems to leave certain frameworks insufficiently interrogated. Analogously, some grassroots participants find more theoretical emphases in the conversations too abstract, irrelevant, "pie in the sky." The nagging question "What the hell are we trying to do here?" is never too far away from many of us. Moreover, those who are most literally hungry and very poor are not yet present—and the least educated people in the room sometimes express difficulty and frustration following conversations that many academics thought were pitched at a widely accessible level.

Why do I think this frustration is "significantly a good thing"? First, because it tends to keep us on our toes and spurs our creative efforts within the seminars to reinvent our modes of engagement, our focus, our senses of purpose—our relationships. Perhaps it helps open us to each other and to aspects of truth that would otherwise be harder to come by. Second, because I think it has effects that one could call *pluralizing* and *permeating*. By *pluralizing*, I mean that the frustrations *also* generate a sense of the need for other kinds of conversations and engagements that exceed this grouping. I leave these seminars grateful for what has happened in them and also with a renewed gratitude for other contexts for ethical and political inquiry and practice—undergraduate classes, graduate seminars, interdisciplinary faculty seminars, intimate conversations with other political theorists, and conversations as an activist with other activists. I leave with a renewed sense of the scholarly and political value of the coexistence of *different spaces* and the value of *moving to and fro* among them. I also leave knowing that many of the least-well-off were not present and this animates my appreciation for and involvement toward efforts to organize in ways that extend the range of those involved in the conversation—in churches, soup kitchens, neighborhood organizations, and so forth.

By *permeating*, I mean that the frustrations and the epiphanies in the TRI move into and inform my creative efforts in other spaces, into which I bring new stories, insights, questions, modes of participation, urgent energies, possibilities, and a sense that, say, an advanced graduate seminar on philosophies of "self and other" allows us to do valuable and specific kinds of work, but that it must be transformed in ways that respond to what has been gained and what has not yet been gained in TRI. It is a question of *translating* the questions, insights, and energies from one space to another —and back. Each space of learning overflows its bounds, and energizes and inflects the transformative work in the others—even as it highlights the value of their distinction. Hopefully, in some modest ways, the discrepant sections of the present essay are partially emblematic of the plurality and permeation of modes of engagement, energy, and thematic work that I am suggesting here.

I suspect that this plurality of related spaces for inquiry, pedagogy, and struggle might provide some initial intimations of possible shapes and flows for more intelligent, ethical, and democratic relationships between those at work in universities and those who are focused elsewhere and in other ways—including those who are currently hungry. The point of criticizing the prevalent fabrications of structural, geographical, and ideological oblivion in dominant practices of higher education is not to suggest alternatively that we should collapse distinct spaces into a universalized proximity. This would neither satiate nor be conducive to the ongoing articulation of our hunger-driven hopes. The idea, rather, is to urge that we inhabit a variety of reciprocally informed, inspired, and inflected spaces that draw us into multiple reflective and political relationships—directly and indirectly—with the "least of these" among us in order to discern and struggle toward a radically better world.[21] Further, the idea is to encourage our receptivity toward those in our reflective spaces who have regular engagements with those who are not (e.g., receptivity to pastors who regularly engage with the very poor in their churches or soup kitchens).

Lacking this affirmation of plurality and permeation, I suspect that the complacency of most academics toward the hungering and suffering of the least-well-off will remain profoundly ideological, apathetic, and self-serving. No amount of discourse on moral education will change that. Everything hinges on our efforts to constitute creative spaces of inquiry and pedagogy that are ethical and political insofar as they flee not from witnessing and transformative engagement with the hunger in the depths of human bellies that is inextricably entwined with the hunger driving our aspirations to ever-new heights.

Yet for all the pluralism, tension, difficult translating, patience, and obliqueness that is so crucial for our struggles toward justice, truth, and democracy —and for all our legitimate concerns about the dangers of moralism, still, as the bumper sticker says: if you're not outraged, you're not paying attention.

The point, as I see it, is not to fashion a politics or moral education beyond outrage but to invent ways of mobilizing, chilling, and refracting it toward thoughtful revolutionary change.

Notes

1. Heschel, *The Prophets*, 1: 16.
2. Quoted in Polanyi, *The Great Transformation*, 113.
3. Sir Leslie Stephen, quoted in ibid., 121.
4. For a detailed analysis of Kant on this score, see my *Rethinking Generosity*.
5. Ibid., 135, 76, 33.
6. Here I am thinking of Pierre Bourdieu's understanding of deeply inscribed meanings through which we fundamentally perceive the world and in relation to which we have great trouble becoming conscious. See *Outline of a Theory of Practice*, 167.
7. Kant, "An Answer to the Question: 'What Is Enlightenment?,' " 54–55.
8. Foucault, "What Is Enlightenment?," 45. I develop the dialogical ethic in Foucault's conception of enlightenment in *Self/Power/Other*.
9. See Derrida, "The Principle of Reason," 5.
10. Ibid., 20.
11. See MacIntyre's proposal in *Three Rival Modes of Moral Enquiry* and Mignolo's work on the recent genesis of indigenous universities in Central and South America, for example, *The Idea of Latin America*. I discuss the question of inquiry and political practice across different traditions in relation to liberalism, MacIntyre, Derrida, education, and urban grassroots political organizing in *Beyond Gated Politics*.
12. This line is from the Ani DiFranco song "Not So Soft," *Like I Said* (Righteous Babe Records, 1993).
13. Adorno, *Negative Dialectics*, 203.
14. Bloch, *The Principle of Hope*, 1: 287–88. Hereafter cited in text with page number in this section.
15. As I read things, hunger is a certain pregnancy in human being and Bloch is a midwife. There are other ways to read Bloch, and Bloch is not entirely consistent.
16. In this sense Bloch writes of a "crack" in every utopic imagining—a "blind spot," the "unrealized." Hence, Bloch writes (in a very difficult but important passage) of a *"melancholy of fulfillment: no earthly paradise remains on entry without the shadow which the entry still casts over it. . . . A trace in Realizing itself is even still felt and is present where appropriate goals have been Realized or where monumental dream-images appear to have entered reality with skin and hair, with body and soul. There is a realizing which disregards the

deed of the realizers themselves and does not contain it; there are ideals which pretend to be elevated, remote from tendency, abstractly fixed, and thus also suppress the unfinished, unrealized aspect of their realizers. Precisely in the melancholy of fulfillment this most profoundly not yet fulfilled aspect in the subject announces itself in exactly the same way as the insufficient aspect in the fixed material of the ideal criticizes itself within it. *It is therefore also necessary increasingly to set free the element of realizing simultaneously with the element of the future society"* (299; Bloch's emphasis).

17. Relatedly, negotiating the tensions of hunger-born hope might illuminate central questions of ethical pedagogy: relations between vision and receptive listening; between idealism and relentless critique; between form and openness; between authority and insurgency; between expert knowledge and wider publics; between the hunger of the mind and the hunger of the belly.

18. For a fuller critique of political liberalism on this score, see Coles, *Beyond Gated Politics*; and MacIntyre, *Dependent Rational Animals*. Bloch saw similar manifestations of such power-laden cognitive cramping throughout the history of philosophies that privileged static being over becoming. Relatedly, he argued that the complex ideological energies of class power constrained the optics of transformation in the psychoanalytic discourses of his day in relation to the fact that "no matter how loud hunger bellows, it is seldom mentioned by the doctors here" (65).

19. My point here is not to condemn distances as such, for myriad types of periodic distance may be conducive to thinking and practice. Rather, I seek to critique the construction of particular distancing practices that are too uniform, unmodulating, impervious, and totalizing insofar as they resist juxtaposition with and learning from knowledges and practices born of counterproximities.

20. We academics are mostly from Duke at present, though our plan is to build a consortium of universities that will host this institute.

21. Elsewhere I have written at length about receptive modes of democratic engagement. I think encouraging students to learn through involvement in such practices provides an important alternative to some more traditional forms of service-learning. See my chapter "Moving Democracy" in *Beyond Gated Politics*.

WHICH VIRTUES? WHOSE CHARACTER? IV

IS THERE AN ETHICIST IN THE HOUSE? HOW CAN WE TELL?

The hallway outside my college's library was lined with tables where staff members were busily looking up names, handing out papers, and taking measurements. It was early in the spring semester, and students who hoped to graduate in May were moving down the tables checking off items on a long list of preparatory tasks. They were being measured for caps and gowns, solicited by salespeople for class rings and engraved invitations, and invited to participate in a class gift to the college. Earlier they had received a printout showing whether all of their core and major requirements would be completed by the end of the spring term, and some had received polite but firm reminders about their outstanding fines or fees.

There is one requirement, though, that we will not find on any such list, at my college or anywhere, even though it was required of most college seniors a century ago. This was a mandatory senior seminar on moral philosophy, taught by the president or the dean. I wonder what the prospective graduates might have said if the dean had been sitting by the last table in the line with a sheet informing them that they must complete such a seminar before they can "walk." But it is just as well that the students would resist such a requirement, since the dean would have little chance of persuading the president to teach such a class to all the seniors each spring term.

For better or worse, over the course of a century, mandatory instruction in moral philosophy has disappeared from the liberal arts curriculum. True, there is still a course requirement in philosophy or religious studies at many colleges that represents a distant descendant in the same genetic line, but the characteristics of the ancestor are hardly recognizable. In such courses today ethics is usually addressed historically or in a comparative context. Instructors take care to avoid saying anything that might be construed as indoctrination in order to encourage the voicing of diverse views. Such courses differ very little among large universities and small colleges, whether they fall into the public, nonsectarian private, or church-related category. The study of what is right was once at the core of liberal arts curriculum in the United States, but today it is not to be found in campus classrooms.

The goals of liberal education today include a broad awareness of Western (and sometimes non-Western) systems of thought and hierarchies of value, together with the ability to employ a range of conceptual tools to analyze and clarify opposing claims concerning religion and morality. But you could scan a hundred syllabi for introductory courses in philosophy and religion without finding one whose stated goals include the teaching of ethics and the improvement of students' moral character. Universities today teach about morality, but they do not presume to teach morality.

Why Morality Has Left Center Stage

The retreat from morality as a subject of instruction in higher education in North America has been motivated by many factors. One of the most important has been the gradual transformation of an institution that served as an exclusive means of access to a young nation's social elite into a broad and widely accessible gateway to effective citizenship. Growing religious diversity and the diminishing role of mainline Protestantism, in higher education and in society, have also played an important role. The presidents who addressed the seniors of an earlier epoch could usually assume that the young men before them came from respected Protestant families and that they would soon join their parents in the pews and in the professions. No such assumptions can be made today.

We must also be wary of assuming that moral philosophy classes ever served their announced purposes very effectively. College graduates of the nineteenth century may have had a better sense than today's graduates of how to comport themselves as gentlemen in polite society, but the prevailing moral standards of their day condoned what we would judge to be outrageous and unapologetic racism, sexism, and elitism. At the highest levels of American society, robber barons despoiled the environment and exploited their workers with a rapacity exceeding that of the Enron executives and Ponzi scheme salesmen of the twenty-first century. "Unionbusting" today involves publishing negative ads and undermining union leadership, where a century ago it involved the crack of billy clubs on skulls. The golden age of moral philosophy in the liberal arts curriculum was by no means, then, a silver age of ethical conduct.

Plato wonders in the *Meno* whether it is possible to teach virtue. If it is indeed teachable, he observes, then we should have no difficulty in identifying its most qualified and effective teachers. All of the leading candidates for that role prove to be unqualified, however, and Plato appears to draw the conclusion that virtue must not be something we can acquire by learning, after all.[1]

This flies in the face of the experience of every parent and teacher who has observed, and helped to advance, the halting steps toward moral maturity and responsibility that mark the passage from childhood into adulthood. Plato's conclusion is surely offered in an ironic spirit. He has exposed the inadequacies of those who claim to teach morality only in order to remind every seeker after truth that it is not enough to follow blindly after purported experts on moral matters. Rather, we must test their teachings against the challenges that arise from argument and experience. The self-proclaimed experts may prove to have no knowledge at all to offer, but only arrogance masquerading as wisdom.

The contemporary academic scene reproduces a dilemma strikingly similar to that which troubled Plato. College catalogs abound in lofty rhetoric concerning the profound effects of four years' study in this particular institution's implementation of the liberal arts curriculum in nurturing future leaders of the nation and the world. Alumni magazines highlight numerous examples of men and women whose deep sense of calling, nurtured during their years of study, has led them to fight tirelessly against oppression and injustice. But when we look closely at the content of the curriculum, we find very little that directly addresses the question of how to discern right and wrong. There are ethics courses, to be sure, in which students learn to define moral terms and use them precisely, to trace the fortunes of aretaic and deontological and consequentialist theories of the good, and to contrast Confucian and Thomistic conceptions of the virtuous man. But if we interrogate the instructors about whether the goals of these courses include the cultivation of virtue, we will receive a quick and emphatic denial. And there will probably be a quick warning call as soon as our back is turned, alerting the public relations office that there's another of those irritating visitors on campus, probably from a right-wing magazine or a caucus of disgruntled alumni or taxpayers.

Catalogs and presidential speeches assure us repeatedly that study of the liberal arts strengthens morality and instills virtue, but they do not tell us how. If virtue can indeed be taught, where can we find its teachers? There is no longer a mandatory seminar in moral reasoning, and there is scarcely a trace of moral instruction remaining anywhere in the curriculum, and yet college study is widely assumed to foster a deeper sense of moral conviction. Is this assumption warranted? Or has some other social institution stepped into the gap and undertaken to teach morality, occupying a role from which the academy has retreated?

Where Ethics Lives Now, Part A: The Professions and Their Rules

As a matter of fact, there are still ethicists in the house, in substantial numbers—outside the campus as well as inside ivied walls. But they are not where we expect to find them, and their job descriptions might surprise us. A large cadre of professionals is carrying on the task of moral education, day in and day out, in American society. But when we discover who they are, we may wonder how well they are serving the rest of us.

We will take note of two groups whose moral pronouncements have a profound but seldom acknowledged influence on contemporary American morality. The first is found in the realms of business, industry, and law, and its principal role is to enforce rules that distill the distinct duties and responsibilities of these professions.

In her fictional youth, Joanie Caucus of "Doonesbury" enrolled in a course in legal ethics (at a thinly disguised Boalt Hall, UC Berkeley). A distinguished professor stood before a huge amphitheater full of law students and intoned something along these lines: "This law school trains responsible, ethical practitioners of the law who seek not self-aggrandizement but a more just and more equitable society. Our new required first-year course, 'Right and Wrong 101,' is devoted to that end." A student hand was raised: "Will this stuff about right and wrong be on the exam?" Came the instant response: "No, no, of course not."

Today ethics is "on the exam" in most graduate programs in the professions, in the form of required courses in the ethics of business, engineering, or law. The scope and intent of such courses, however, are often closely tailored to the expectations of the graduates' future employers. Well-prepared executives, engineers, and lawyers will be expected to know and observe a highly specific set of standards for professional conduct. Such courses focus less on ethical integrity in a broad sense than on conformity to rules protecting future employers and partners from litigation and criminal prosecution.

Ethics as it is taught in engineering colleges and law schools, in other words, is not so much a matter of relentless moral and spiritual self-examination and moral inquiry, as Socrates demanded, as of avoiding civil and criminal liability. Rather than encourage students to reflect on the qualities that constitute a virtuous character, professional-school ethics courses tend to focus on how many months an engineer or lawyer must wait after resigning from a firm or partnership before going to work for a competitor or a government regulatory agency. Engineering ethics classes do not tarry over Socrates's questions such as whether the virtues are many or one, but they offer guidance on when you can be prosecuted for helping your golf partner circumvent a sealed bidding process. These are not trivial matters, and explicit guidelines governing such relationships help maintain trust between professionals and their clients. But focusing on such specific issues often means neglecting larger questions of moral character and responsibility.

This emphasis is strikingly evident if one scans the employment listings for executive positions online or in major newspapers for those that relate to ethics. A major insurance company, for example, advertises for an "Ethics and Compliance Officer," whose principal duty is "research and identification of legislative and regulatory requirements and trends and the collaborative development and implementation of risk mitigation activities with key operational partners." A biotech firm uses a more generic job title, "Director of Legal and Regulatory Compliance," for a position that involves "developing and directing organization's ethics, business conduct and compliance function for worldwide operations."[2] Scientific and engineering societies have adopted codes of ethics, and they regularly sponsor informational sessions at their meetings that emphasize the rules that practitioners must follow in order to avoid conflicts of interest and prevent lawsuits.

Here, then, is one of the places where we find practicing ethicists at work today: in the realm of professional codes of conduct. The ethical experts in this realm are the teachers of narrowly focused courses on professional ethics in graduate schools of law, business, and engineering. Compliance officers charged with the task of overseeing the implementation of specific guidelines for professional practice, keeping their employers out of legal trouble, also have considerable expertise in ethics in this narrow sense.

In this account I may have exaggerated the narrowness of vision with which these ethicists undertake their work. It is true that many corporations have adopted codes of ethics that go well beyond "lawyer-proofing" and emphasize a broad range of contributions to the community. The credo promulgated by one major pharmaceutical corporation, for example, recognizes the responsibility of the corporation and its employees to doctors, nurses, and patients; to local and global communities; and, finally, to stockholders.[3] The code of ethics of the American Institute of Electrical Engineers begins with this uplifting prologue:

> Honesty, justice, and courtesy form a moral philosophy which, associated with mutual interest among men, constitutes the foundation of ethics. The engineer should recognize such a standard, not in passive observance, but as a set of dynamic principles guiding his conduct and way of life. It is his duty to practice his profession according to these Canons of Ethics.[4]

From this height, however, we descend rather quickly to matters such as holding a financial interest in a client firm and honoring "the principle of appropriate and adequate compensation for those engaged in engineering work."

Where Ethics Lives Now, Part B: The Advice Columnists

There is a second community of ethics professionals, and they can also be found in the daily newspaper—not in the employment ads but in the social and cultural pages. These are the syndicated advice columnists. Their daily dispatches offer advice on dealing with parents and children and in-laws, resolving financial or emotional difficulties in marriage, coping with job stress, climbing out of debt, and all the other crises of modern life. There are advice columns for the single and the married, columns directed primarily to African Americans or Asian Americans, columns for those who uphold traditional manners, and hipper-than-thou columns for Generation X.

Most such columns resemble informal therapy more than ethical inquiry. Questions and their answers gravitate around questions concerning difficulties with parents or partners, emotional adjustment, and coping with depression or anger. An unusual column that takes ethics as its primary subject, however, appeared for the first time in 1999 in the pages of the "gray lady" of daily journalism, a newspaper too dignified to publish comic strips or conventional advice columns. Randy Cohen's "Ask the Ethicist" question-and-answer column appears weekly in the *New York Times Magazine,* and National Public Radio includes a live question-and-answer segment with Cohen in its weekend news programs. The format is precisely the advice column formula: readers' queries about difficult choices elicit a paragraph or two of practical advice, usually witty, sometimes tongue in cheek. Cohen's style owes more to the alternative weekly press ("The Straight Dope" by Cecil Adams, "Savage Love" by Dan Savage) than to Ann Landers and Dear Abby, but—as in these models—there is usually a serious intent discernible beneath the surface flippancy.

Cohen claims no academic qualifications for his role. In an interview in an online journal, he describes his undistinguished record at two colleges and claims never to have taken a course in ethics or philosophy, citing instead as relevant preparation for his current role his experiences writing for television. "Writing for David Letterman is not such unlikely training for writing about ethics as it might first appear," he observes in the introduction to his book *The Good, the Bad, and the Difference.*

Cohen adds, in the magazine interview, that he has been learning on the job. He does not categorically reject the relevance of traditional modes of ethical theory, but he disputes the possibility of any ethical universals. "There are many ethical precepts that I find useful and am not bound by. Like the categorical imperative—there are times when I will invoke it, but other times, it doesn't seem to be a helpful tool for the situation."[5] Immanuel Kant would not be amused to learn that what he regarded as reason's unalterable command to every free and moral being, the essence of "the moral law within," is just another pair of pliers in this modern ethicist's toolbox.

Cohen's usual practice is to dispense very specific advice to his inquirers, but it seldom follows a predictable pattern. You should confront your teenage son about his possible drug use, he advises a worried mom. It's OK to enjoy the show when your neighbor showers each day with the curtains open, he tells a nosy neighbor who wonders whether voyeurism is wrong. To a teenager whose parents have given him their permission to see an R-rated movie but who can't get in unless he lies to the manager about his age, Cohen responds: What's a little lie? Stop worrying.[6]

If there is an implicit theory of morality behind Cohen's advice, it runs along these lines: act with integrity and principle, when it's practical and not overly burdensome, but don't go overboard. Life is too short to be a hero. Many other personal advice columnists tread the same path, offering practical advice that is relatively unencumbered by principles and rules. "Ethical instruction" may be too grand a label for the down-to-earth advice that is the daily fare of these columns' readers, but behind the specific advice lies a vision of the good human life: a life that is devoted not to searching self-examination or heroic self-denial but to getting along, receiving one's due, and enjoying life's pleasures.

The contrast between the two sources of ethics that I have identified here is sharp, and it is instructive. For contemporary American society, ethics connotes one of two quite disparate kinds of discourse: on the one hand, applying rules for professional conduct and the avoidance of litigation, under the authority of professional societies and the threat of disciplinary action by regulatory bodies; on the other, informal dispensing of advice grounded in nothing more systematic than a friendly stranger's intuitions. Ethics is either a matter of assiduous compliance with rules whose violation can land you in court, or it is an intuitive and open-ended process of figuring out what makes sense, isn't too much trouble, and feels right.

We have only a limited need for expert advice in the realm of morality, on this bifurcated picture. Ethics includes some rigid rules that attach to particular professional positions, and after we have learned the basics in a required graduate course it is a good idea to sign up now and then for a weekend review workshop. For the rest of our lives, morality is a matter of getting along and getting by, and neighbors and friends can probably help us more than a Ph.D. ever would. In professional settings we should take care to play by the rules, but our own conscience, stirred up now and then by a newspaper column that catches our eye, will tell us what we ought to do in ordinary situations.

What is the doctrine that is implicitly taught by these two schools of ethics? We might sum it up in this way: The fulfillment of Socrates's quest for the best human life does not lie in a transcendent realm of metaphysical reality, as he supposed, but is already within everyone's grasp. The best life is one in which you follow the rules that will keep you out of trouble in your professional activities and, in every other situation, follow your heart and do what makes sense to you.

Where Ethics Lives Now, Part C: The University

But what about the university campus? Does this bifurcated model of morality reign there too? Not to the same degree as in the broader culture—the direct impact of the two models sketched above, for example, is small. To be sure, the conception of morality that they exemplify is pervasive in contemporary culture, and it enters every campus by means of television and popular entertainment. But one of the distinctive—and incalculably precious—features of the university environment is the openness of students to new ideas and challenges, fostered by the social function of higher education as a rite of passage to adulthood and by the restless energy that accompanies the processes of identity formation in adolescence.

What, then, are the dominant influences on students' thinking concerning moral choices? Who, and where, are the ethics experts on campus? And is it possible for them to instill a more rigorous and more demanding vision of the moral life than that of the surrounding culture? The answer to this question can be found primarily in the presence and influence of three distinct groups. Let me describe each of them in turn and describe the contribution that each makes to students' moral formation.

First, figuring most prominently in most academics' conception of campus life, there are the instructors standing in front of their classrooms. Whether consciously or unconsciously, whether systematically or haphazardly, they serve as moral guides to students. Many would deny if asked that this has anything to do with their responsibilities or their function as members of the faculty, but it is a role that all faculty do in fact occupy and that contributes one of the most important elements of the moral atmosphere on any campus. It is not just professors in humanities disciplines such as religion, philosophy, history, and literature who play this role but faculty in social sciences and sciences as well. Even if only a few courses explicitly address ethical questions, every class is to some degree a class in ethical conduct.

For it is not so much the content but the conduct of classroom discourse that shapes students' conceptions of how to conduct their lives. There they learn what it means to disagree forcefully but respectfully, and they observe how much or how little concern their instructors show when a few students are unable to grasp critical concepts. Instructors teach their students about morality by the way in which they write and grade tests, structure assignments, and respond to student complaints. Only a small minority of university students envision their future selves following the same vocation as their professors, but all students are influenced by what they see in their instructors' understanding of their own vocation. They can know the difference between a truly dedicated teacher and one who is merely earning a paycheck, between one who is insincere and one who has a genuine commitment to students' intellectual and personal welfare. They can distinguish readily between a scholar engaged in passionate pursuit of deeper understanding and a status-seeker always trying to climb the ladder to a more prestigious institution. These differences inform students' reflections on their vocational plans and preparations, and they shape students' sense of what it means to do one's life work with integrity and commitment.

Second, a smaller but equally influential army of ethics teachers can be found in the student life staff. Student deans, resident directors, and dorm advisors interact with students in many ways, many of them directly related to concrete moral choices. It is not just when students do something foolish and short-sighted, and then face disciplinary sanctions that student life staff become involved in students' personal and moral lives. In residence life programs, student organizations, intramural games, and volunteer service, college staff members work in close cooperation with students, not as authorities but as facilitators. From the first days of orientation through "senior week" activities, student life employees help students learn who they are and decide what they value. Their interactions are usually less structured and more informal than those of faculty members with students, and for that among other reasons students in stress or difficulty often turn to them for a listening ear and a word of advice.

And what sort of guidance does this segment of the campus community typically offer? They may dispense gruel as thin as that of the newspaper advice columnists: Try to be fair and to act with integrity, but if you get along with others and stay out of their hair it's OK to do pretty much anything you want. Toe the line and avoid really heinous misbehavior that will get you into serious trouble, but don't worry too much about alcohol abuse, hazing, or immature sexual behavior—peccadilloes that will probably draw only an indulgent wink, not a disciplinary sanction, if you play your cards right.

I am exaggerating again, I hasten to admit. Although this sort of non-direction is certainly found on many campuses, it is probably not typical. At best, through conversations and programmed activities and through disciplinary interactions, student life staff members continually challenge students to advance to a deeper level of critical awareness of their own choices. They emphasize that compliance with campus rules is only a small part of the more important task of developing a stronger sense of moral direction and personal integrity. Discipline for misbehavior becomes the occasion for serious reflection on why a student has fallen short not just of college expectations but also of the expectations other students have of her—and indeed that she has of herself.

Whether student life staff members see themselves as having the authority to offer any specific moral guidance to students varies widely, not just from campus to campus but from individual to individual, and in any case their influence is often implicit and indirect. Institutional setting makes a significant difference. At a small church college, students and staff alike expect to spend time exploring issues of ethics and personal responsibility, but their counterparts at a large state university might find this turn of conversation surprising and perhaps unwelcome.

And yet on every campus, of whatever affiliation and size, we will find some student life staff who are deeply engaged in the most serious and searching moral inquiry with the students. Even when topics of morality are seldom brought to the surface in conversation, they are addressed in practical terms through personal relationships with resident directors, floor advisors, and counselors that form part of the context of a student's life on campus. No other group exercises so profound an influence over students' moral growth as does the student life staff.

Before moving on to the third group of ethics teachers, let me mention in passing a group whose role varies enormously from one campus to another, which I will consider here to be a subset of the student life community: those who coordinate religious life on campus. These include college-appointed chaplains, youth pastors attached to off-campus student centers, priests and pastors and rabbis at nearby congregations, and lay volunteers. In various ways that reflect differences of institutional history, size, character and context, a religious presence can be found on nearly every North American university campus regardless of its past or present affiliation or lack thereof.

For some students, religious leaders serve as the most important and influential moral guides and teachers of all. The relationship between a campus pastor and a student involved in worship leadership may be as close as any relationship between adults and students on campus. It is misleading, however, to point to campus chaplaincy as the principal mode of ethical teaching in the university today. Its visibility and influence differ dramatically from one campus to another, and even where it has a prominent public role its scope is limited to a subset of the student population. For our purposes, I will simply note that this is one example, highly potent in some instances, of the influence of student life staff.

Let me turn to the third major group of ethics experts that we find on every campus: the student leaders of major campus organizations. Adolescents, we know, are profoundly influenced by the examples and opinions of their peers. But not all have comparable influence. Students are particularly likely to observe, admire, and emulate those who have risen to high levels of visibility and responsibility in the student culture of the campus. Which individuals and organizations play the most important role depends on the specifics of campus history and culture. Captains and star players on sports teams, student government leaders, organizers of political rallies, and student journalists are usually among them. Rank-and-file students see these peers as representing something they may aspire to.

The relationship of student leaders to the members of their organizations is likely to involve relatively little explicit discussion of matters of morality and personal responsibility. But beneath the surface, there is a great deal of ethical instruction taking place. Students pattern their choices, and even their lives, on other students whom they admire. This is to say that the most influential teachers of ethics on our campuses, in the long run, are probably other students—individuals whom we as faculty and staff members tend to see as recipients rather than sources of instruction.

There are three different groups, then, that offer ethical guidance to students today. None bears a very close resemblance to the college president holding forth on moral philosophy to the assembled seniors, to be sure. But each plays a vital and influential role in shaping students' sense of what is expected of them as responsible adults.

Ethics on Campus: Two Modern Fallacies

With all these teachers on hand, should we not expect that ethics will be taught effectively to all who venture onto our campuses as students? Alas, no. It is beyond the scope of this essay to assess the moral climate on today's campuses, but it is clear that serious and sustained problems of student conduct, particularly in upholding academic integrity and taking responsibility for destructive and self-destructive behaviors, are present at every college and university. Alcohol abuse is a serious concern not just at the traditional "party schools" but at the most conservative and close-knit college communities as well. The prevalence of cheating on assignments and tests is notoriously difficult to measure accurately, but anyone who asserts that it is absent from her campus is engaging in self-deception.

This moral deficit, however, does not arise from a dearth of teachers of ethics. It results instead from uncritical acceptance of two false dogmas that, for the sake of our colleges and our students, we need to challenge.

The first fallacy could be labeled the *Doctrine of the Separation of Student Body and Student Mind*. Hardly anyone today defends classical Cartesian dualism, and yet our campuses are organized as if it were unquestioned truth. For the cultivation of students' minds, the faculty takes responsibility. Instructors hold themselves responsible for preparing engaging lectures, setting challenging assignments, and keeping their own intellects continually sharpened by research and scholarship.

How students conduct their lives outside of class, however—what they do on weekends, how they begin to build friendships and romantic relationships, what they eat and drink—is considered to lie wholly outside the faculty's concerns. For that half of the divided student, we have sports, intramurals, parties, and student life staff. This bifurcation implies that learning is separate from living, and it suggests that the intellectual quest of the classroom has nothing particular to do with the social dimensions of life. In class, you should study and try to earn good grades and acquire knowledge that will serve you well in your future life and work; outside of class, however, you should do whatever makes you happy. Thinking too much about the choices you make in your personal life will only distract and confuse you, and the best life is one in which you fit in with peers and enjoy yourself. That is the message subtly conveyed by our campuses' hermetic division between the academic and the social.

The second false dogma has to do with whether ethical questions, in the end, have answers. They do, of course. After all, no one seriously questions whether there are things parents ought not to do to their children, or owners to their pets. Yet many of our contemporaries have convinced themselves that these are no more than personal preferences and that the demands of morality have no validity unless you personally endorse them. This attitude infects the campus deeply.

What began as an attitude of respect for the independence and growing maturity of students has mutated into a dogma that we might call the *Law of Moral Demurral*: no one's moral standards are valid for anyone else. This amounts to an eleventh commandment: "Thou shalt not tell thy neighbor what to do." Faculty members are no less prone to embrace this fallacy than are student life staff. Reluctant to challenge students who take advantage of others, ignore the rules, victimize their friends and lead impressionable fellow students into destructive behaviors, the believers in this dogma stand back and hesitantly ask whether all the students' values have been carefully weighed in this situation. Not wanting to appear moralistic and judgmental, they scrupulously avoid applying moral categories but ask whether students have considered carefully how their current actions fit with their overall systems of value. Motivated by an implicit belief in this law, resident directors and professors alike dispense a tentative query even when what is needed is the verbal equivalent of a swift kick in the pants.

Both dogmas have been overstated here to make them more clearly recognizable. But behind the exaggeration lies a troubling truth about our campuses, which reflects in turn a troubling situation in our society. We really don't believe what the college catalogs say about college fostering ethical and social as well as intellectual growth. As a society, we can't even agree that moral questions have answers.

Can We Make Room for the Ethicists in the House?

The tradition of a mandatory seminar on moral philosophy for seniors is long dead, and no dean or president who wants to keep his or her job until the end of the year would dream of trying to bring it back to life. But the space that it once occupied in the moral formation of students has not been filled with equivalent sources of ethical guidance. Hardly any academic or co-curricular programs set it as a goal to enhance students' moral maturity and foster a stronger sense of personal integrity. Societal attitudes that identify the demands of ethics largely with codes of specific professional responsibility, relying on the easygoing hedonistic pragmatism of advice columnists for all the rest of life, are seldom effectively challenged on college campuses.

Still, there are teachers of ethics—many of them, in diverse settings. On our campuses, there are the professoriate, the student life staff, and the leaders of student organizations and activities. What students learn about morality on campus they learn primarily from these three groups.

But do the members of any of these groups really believe that they have something of substance to teach? Many do not. Instructors believe they have the duty, and the authority, to convey to students a deeper understanding of history or biology or accounting, but not of morality. Student life staff see their role as settling conflicts, enforcing a few of the more serious campus rules, and helping everyone get along better. Student leaders are themselves in need of guidance as they learn to shoulder adult responsibilities.

If none of our teachers of virtue have anything that they believe they can teach, from whom will students learn? In the end, they will learn from each other, without any systematic assistance in learning what it means to grow morally, namely, to critique, challenge, and refine a vision of what makes a life worthwhile. Offered no coherent or articulate ethical framework beyond the encouragement to fit in and enjoy their lives, students will model themselves on peers and adults whom they admire. In good times they will make themselves comfortable and get along. But in times of crisis and conflict, when hard choices arise and it takes a keen eye for moral nuance and a courageous heart to move forward, they will be woefully unprepared.

And what will be the outcome? This is a question that should trouble the sleep of anyone involved in higher education today. The absence of any effective ethical content in the university curriculum may produce a future generation of parents and corporate leaders who are no better prepared or qualified to solve the urgent problems of the day than physicians would be to perform surgery if they had learned medicine from their friends and conferred their own diplomas.

But the picture I have painted is far too bleak in at least one respect. Few of those who act as if they affirm the two fallacies identified above really believe that intellectual and social life should be kept altogether separate, or that moral questions cannot be answered. They act as if these absurdities were true because of expectations that have been built up in the academy, but they actually know better. Having recognized the damage done by these false dogmas, most participants in the academic enterprise—faculty members, student life staff, and students alike—are ready to engage in serious moral discourse concerning the problems that face contemporary society. They have little practice at this, because they have come to believe it is not their job.

We need, in the academy, to make room for a deeper engagement with ethical issues. We have ethicists in the house, many of them both highly skilled in moral analysis and deeply committed to living lives of integrity. Most of them see little connection between these traits and their work as professors, deans, and resident directors. We need to adjust our expectations of both students and faculty in ways that will enhance, not impede, more effective relationships of moral guidance and effective ethical modeling.

How likely is it that the nation's campuses will shift in this direction? Change will doubtless come in response to local developments, good and bad. Growing awareness of environmental degradation and the hidden costs of industrial agriculture, for example, is already motivating many students to think more deeply about issues of justice that span continents and generations. Highly publicized misbehavior, particularly when it involves high-profile athletes, can be the catalyst for a serious reexamination of the moral atmosphere on a campus. To varying degrees, in locally directed ways, many campuses will direct more focused attention to issues of moral as well as intellectual growth. Even if others do not immediately follow suit, the example of the leaders in this shift is likely to be widely noted and eventually emulated.

The resources needed for a renewed sense of the ethical core of liberal education are already in place on every campus. Neglect of moral issues in the past generation has arisen not from ignorance of what morality is, nor from a serious belief in the two "laws" I describe above. It has resulted, rather, from the conviction that morality is no longer the business of the university and from faculty reluctance to acknowledge the way that their influence on students reaches far beyond the academic. But there remain some faculty members, and many campus life staff and campus chaplains, who hold to a more integrated vision of students' lives. They are ready to assist faculty members when they are ready to engage more thoughtfully and intensively in the moral formation of their students.

Sometimes this will not work out well at all: some faculty members will forsake detachment only to embrace an intrusive sort of moralism, strong on conviction and weak on mutual respect. Others will find their new role as moral guide so uncomfortable that they will retreat back into the supposedly value-free realm they have long inhabited. But there will be others who find that, when they are ready to engage students in dialogue about ethical as well as academic matters, both their own sense of satisfaction in their work and students' sense of accomplishment in their studies are greatly enhanced. Rightly rejecting the hegemonic assumptions of nineteenth-century university training in Christian ethics, which in many cases would have been more accurately labeled "morality and propriety for a white male Protestant elite," they will find new ways to combine respect for pluralism and openness to diverse viewpoints with a firm grasp on the attitudes, habits, and relationships that mark a man or woman as a person of moral integrity.

The moral climate on campus today is not healthy. Students face more complex and perplexing ethical challenges than ever, but they receive scarcely any guidance from the adults with whom they interact each day on how to cope with them. The traditional remedy for moral rootlessness that our grandparents swore by—liberal doses of moralism dispensed by the college president—is no longer available, and by clinical standards it never worked very well anyway.

The new treatments offered by our culture are no more effective. Student needs for direction are not well served by a narrow construal of ethics as following the rules of a profession or by seat-of-the-pants newspaper advice columns. We need stronger medicine than this.

And more effective treatments will become available, initiated by those who are already fellow participants in the academic enterprise, when we make room in our academic institutions for all to relate to one another as thoughtful and responsible moral agents. We will find that we actually know a lot and can teach each other a great deal, about what this means.

There are lots of ethicists in the house. We only need to build institutional structures and expectations that will permit them to get to work.

Notes

I am indebted to both Peter Euben and Elizabeth Kiss, and to fellow participants in the colloquium that they organized at Duke University in 2005, for insightful comments on an oral version of this essay. My colleagues in the Philosophy Department at Calvin College and an anonymous reader for Duke University Press offered constructive critiques of earlier written versions.

1. *Meno* (Hamilton and Cairns, trans.), 380.
2. Both examples are from the job search site Monster.com, from a long list of job listings shown when a search is conducted with "ethics" as a keyword.
3. "Our Credo," Johnson & Johnson, found at http://www.jnj.com.
4. "Principles of Professional Conduct of the American Institute of Electrical Engineers," which can be found at http://ethics.iit.edu/codes under the organization's name. This is a useful collection of ethics codes compiled by the Center for the Study of Ethics in the Professions at the Illinois Institute of Technology. The code was adopted in 1950.
5. *Media Bistro*, April 29, 2002: http://www.mediabistro.com.
6. The first example is from the NPR broadcast of February 15, 2004; the others from an "ethics quiz" on a publicity site for *The Good, the Bad, and the Difference*.

THE POSSIBILITY OF MORAL EDUCATION IN THE UNIVERSITY TODAY

Both students and faculty today tend to be skeptical about the possibility of moral education. Indeed, one sometimes suspects that there is little consensus about the objectives of liberal education generally. In part because of the growth and specialization of knowledge, and perhaps in greater part because of the passing of a (relatively) homogeneous cultural elite, we no longer have an image of what an educated person must know, and therefore how the curriculum should be structured. Nonetheless, judging from the actual practices of most colleges and universities, there appears to be a fair amount of agreement on at least three broad goals: the mastery of a specific subject, breadth of learning, and the integration of different areas of knowledge. In this essay I will draw on these accepted goals to argue for a fourth, the cultivation of practical judgment as a form of moral education.

The strongest consensus appears to be on the goal of mastery: even a casual Web search of university and college curricula reveals that most schools require a formal major of some sort, often specifying that students demonstrate their command of a subject through a "capstone" project or performance, or a structured set of seminars or courses. The goals of breadth and integration are also widely accepted, although they have been approached in different ways at different times and in different institutions. Among the most common means are "core" curricula or "generalization" requirements, which obligate students to take courses outside of their areas of concentration.

There are many reasons for the commitment to these goals, and to liberal learning generally. The claims of specialization are perhaps the most obvious: as Weber argued, knowledge "has entered a phase of specialization previously unknown and . . . this will forever remain the case." Thus, any "really definitive and good accomplishment is today always a specialized accomplishment."[1] In short, because of the increasing specialization and division of academic work, the (relative) mastery of some area of learning is not a goal we can reasonably reject.

The goals of breadth and integration of knowledge can be justified from a variety of perspectives. Many would invoke some ideal of human excellence, viewing the narrow specialist as impoverished as a human being. But one might also support liberal learning on more prosaic grounds, arguing that even specialists must be able to locate their discipline in relation to other areas of study in order to understand or advance their own areas of learning, and to communicate their results effectively. Thus, specialization or mastery must be complemented by a commitment to breadth and integration, and so the liberal arts curriculum is designed to enable students to develop a critical awareness of the modes of inquiry characteristic of different disciplines, and to provide students with an exposure to their central ideas and methods. Ideally, our curricula call for students to develop the skills necessary to understand complex arguments from different domains, to critically assess them, and to restate these arguments in other terms. By creating bridges among discourses based on different assumptions or motivated by different concerns, liberal arts institutions can help to sustain what might be called a common communicative culture; unlike the traditional ideal of a common intellectual culture, in which liberal arts graduates are exposed to a common *content* in their education, the common culture to which we can aim today is rather more formal, including ways of knowing, inquiring, arguing, disagreeing, representing, and expressing. It is a culture that facilitates or even makes possible communication among specialists, and—as I will argue below—it can provide an opening for citizens to participate in public life.

If we think of liberal learning as contributing to a common communicative culture, we can see why the cultivation of practical judgment is also a critical goal. Most would probably agree that liberal education is not merely an intellectual achievement but also involves reflection on the ways our knowledge can and should be used. In fact, that is one of the reasons we aim to create a common communicative culture. In order to address the problems we face, we generally have to use knowledge drawn from different areas of learning, and so must find ways to communicate across those divides. Consider, for example, the range of specialists we as citizens must draw on to understand and respond effectively to global warming. In the first place, we have to turn to natural scientists from a variety of fields to understand, at least at a basic level, why increasing concentrations of greenhouse gases (e.g., carbon dioxide, methane) cause the earth's temperature to go up, why it is reasonable to suppose that this warming results from human activity, the countervailing factors and their likely effects (e.g., changes in cloud cover, effects of changing atmospheric conditions and temperature on the oceans), and the possible physical and biological consequences of global warming (e.g., melting of icecaps and glaciers, decreasing salinity of the oceans, changing weather patterns, impact on different types of ecosystems). Second, we need to consult economists, historians, geographers, sociologists and others to understand the social processes through which greenhouse gases are produced; these social processes include human activities and technologies (industrial production, deforestation, generation of energy from fossil fuels, etc.) *and* the institutions through which these activities and technologies are produced, organized, and sustained (e.g., capitalist and market institutions, subsistence agriculture). Third, political scientists and other specialists in the policy process, as well as the social scientists mentioned above, can help us grasp both the policies that could address the problem (and their relative costs and benefits) and the capacities of different political (and other) institutions to adopt these kinds of policies. Obviously, even well-informed citizens could not possibly master all of these fields of study, nor can specialists in any one of those fields do so. At best, one can aim at having enough understanding to have confidence in one's views and to decide where one should direct one's own energy and activity in order to address these issues, and that is only possible if the culture provides the means through which specialists can communicate with other specialists, and with nonspecialists. Specialized knowledge is not adequate by itself. Needless to say, synthesizing what one can learn from experts in order to reach a practical judgment about what *we* ought to do, and about what *I* ought to do to affect the collective outcome, requires practical wisdom.

Even if we can agree on the need for practical judgment, that doesn't mean we can agree that cultivating it should be a goal of a liberal education, since we may doubt the legitimacy or even the possibility of doing so. One reason for this doubt is skepticism regarding the cognitive status of moral and political judgments. This skepticism is widely shared among our students, who are quick to dismiss or relativize "value" judgments as "matters of opinion," or even taste. As they become more sophisticated, their reasons for their skepticism may deepen, but their skepticism is seldom challenged. Indeed, the better the education, the more likely it is to be reenforced, as more and more of their deepest assumptions are identified and held up to critical scrutiny. To the extent that liberal education undermines the "naturalness" of traditions, it casts into doubt the very possibility of finding a standpoint from which considered judgments can be made, and so encourages a retreat into subjectivism.

Our students often think that democracy itself requires moral skepticism. For isn't it easier to practice the democratic virtues of tolerance, compromise, and respect for others (including their opinions) if we abandon the view that there are right or wrong answers to the questions we face? Don't these virtues themselves rest on skepticism, for why should we tolerate error? And how can we respect it? Sometimes students will even argue that efforts to criticize or challenge a value position are "undemocratic." Many would argue the reason we should count everyone's opinions equally is that moral and political judgments *are* simply matters of "opinion." If it were possible to provide rational grounds for practical knowledge, then it would be one more subject of "expertise," and moral experts, not common citizens, would be the proper rulers. Thus, the very effort to provide rational arguments for practical judgments seems to threaten what they view as an essential presupposition of democracy.

There is an obvious irony here: this line of thought, leading to skepticism about moral knowledge, presupposes the judgment that democracy and equality are fundamental moral values, to which everyone should subscribe. The same may be said about our students' ready espousal of relativism in various forms. They insist upon toleration or even celebration of difference, precisely on the grounds that each cultural grouping (or even each individual) can somehow find a unique "truth"—that's "true for you," they often say—yet they are often outraged if someone bucks the consensus and refuses to accept the legitimacy of someone else's values or way of life (unless that someone else is or can be depicted as a [member of] a dominant class or group). But there are deeper concerns that cannot be so readily dismissed. I will address three: the charge that universalist conceptions of morality are implicitly (or even explicitly) imperialist, the fear of relativism, and the idea that even such basic notions as human agency involves some form of imposition. I don't pretend to fully answer each of these large claims, but I will try to sketch the direction an answer may take. My objective is not to settle large questions about the foundations of morality but to suggest a conception of moral education that is rooted in the moral and political concerns with which our students—and all citizens—wrestle.

Imperialism

Not so long ago a common story about the nature of morality (and so moral education) was often told. In this story the development of morality was depicted as an ever expanding circle of moral concern, as people came to realize that obligations were owed not only to members of their own tribe, or ethnos, or religion, but that all humans were entitled to equal concern and respect. And this move from particularism to universalism in the broad sweep of history was thought to be paralleled by a similar growth in individual moral development, as epitomized, for example, in Kohlberg's account of moral development, according to which each individual (at least ideally) develops from a childish submission to the external authority of one's parents and their commands to adult autonomy in which one's judgments are based on universal moral principles. This story of moral development from "tribal" or group-oriented selfishness to the recognition of the human dignity of all was particularly appealing to people on the left or "progressives," who were committed to unmasking the myths that sustained unjust hierarchies by subjecting them to rational critique: emancipation was to follow enlightenment. In many quarters today this view is seen to be insidious—disguising a politics of imposition in the name of liberation. And there is some truth in that charge, as many critics have pointed out. Universalist ideologies can and have been used to "justify" hideous policies. But that truth isn't very interesting—is there any idea that can't be twisted to cloak policies aimed at other objectives? The deeper claim is that the idea of universal moral principles, which are grounded in considerations that are rooted in permanent aspects of the human condition and in the principles of reason, cannot be what they purport to be. It is said that human life is too protean to fit into any set of categories without remainder, and the effort to do so will necessarily be imperialistic, forcing different cultures and ways of life into a mold that does violence to them. Many of our best students thus come to view universalist moral and political theories suspiciously, as parochial, Western views, rather than as genuinely universal.

Far from undermining the possibility of moral education in the university today, this suspicion offers the occasion for such education. The point is not to contest but to engage this critique. Indeed, there is much to be said for it, as can be seen by recent critical scholarship on the history of European imperialism and political theory. Thus, critics charge that Locke's vision of fundamental human equality and natural rights actually serves to provide an ideological rationalization for the dispossession of the native peoples of America, since their "failure" to make "productive" use of the land licensed Europeans to claim the land for agriculture, and to kill or enslave those who "unjustly" resisted them.[2] To take another example, critics now paint Mill not (or not so much) as the champion of liberty but as an apologist for colonial rule, justifying it on the grounds that immature peoples can only be ruled despotically until they have acquired the capacity for self-rule—that is, until they have acquired an education that makes "them" like "us."[3] To be sure, that view may be less despicable than the common racist accounts that deny that "natives" can ever be like us, and so must forever be subjugated and exploited, but that is to damn with faint praise.

Acknowledging the cogency of these critiques does not mean that we have to generalize them to an indictment of moral univeralism. Engaging them historically, we can, as Muthu shows in his careful examination of the writings of Diderot, Kant, and Herder, argue that commitment to universalism in morality is consistent with the rejection of imperialism. Indeed, as Muthu suggests, when the universality in question involves a recognition of what Muthu calls "cultural agency," that is, the (universal) human capacity to shape a way of life, moral universalism is incompatible with imperialism. For Kant, in particular, what is essential to our humanity is the capacity for setting our own ends on the basis of cultural traditions and ideas that we can appropriate and use innovatively, and so this capacity necessarily leads to the creation of difference. Thus, respect for humanity—the core of Kantian universality—requires respect for difference and leads to the condemnation of imperialism. As Muthu argues, "The more the universal category of the human was particularized, the more meaningful and robust it became in moral practice."[4] In pursuing these inquiries, I should emphasize, our aim must not be to persuade our students to endorse universalist moral principles but to engage them seriously in political and ethical reasoning, so that the views they come to adopt emerge from sustained intellectual encounters in which they learn to articulate their own thinking and to respond to others.

Relativism

If one of the major reasons for doubts about the possibility of moral education is the loss of authority of universalism, its twin is the bogey of relativism, which hangs over all ethical discourse today. The fear that relativism arouses is that it threatens the authority ethical claims could have over us. Since each "we" invents (however unselfconsciously) its own morality, the only authority that moral principles could have is the authority that (any particular) "we" invests in them. So morality becomes something like New Year's resolutions—something we make, but can (and do) unmake. So understood, morality cannot bind us, and so moral principles cannot do what we want of them—to give us binding reasons for doing one thing rather than another. If morality is only what "we" decide it is, then why should we conform to a moral principle, when doing so is inconvenient? And once we come to see moral beliefs as conventional in this way, it is an easy step to subjectivism—to narrowing the "we" to smaller and smaller circles until it becomes "I." And as I recognize that different groups pursue different values, and worship different gods, adherence to any of those competing views ceases to be unselfconscious. I come to realize that

> so long as life remains immanent and is interpreted in its own terms, it knows only of an unceasing struggle of these gods with one another. Or speaking directly, the ultimately possible attitudes toward life are irreconcilable, and hence their struggle can never be brought to a final conclusion. Thus, it is necessary to make a decisive choice. (Weber, "Science as a Vocation," 152)

But, as MacIntyre asks, "How can that which we adopt for no reason have any authority over us?"[5]

Both MacIntyre's worry and Weber's drama seem overblown. Both presuppose a view of knowledge generally, and moral knowledge in particular, according to which truth has authority over us precisely because it reflects or captures the inherent structure of (ethical) reality itself, that is, as it really is in and of itself—or something along those lines. But since we can never know that the concepts we employ in describing the world or in making moral judgments "really" correspond to the "inherent structure" of the world (let alone an independently existing order of moral facts, whatever that would be), such a view is untenable. Behind MacIntyre's and Weber's position is a false dichotomy: either we have genuine knowledge, which imposes itself on us in some rationally acceptable way, or we have pure subjectivity, mere commitment. This is great drama, but it ignores what Williams calls "common sense" or "plain" truths, such as "today is Tuesday" or "Mummy has just gone out of the room,"[6] which can be used to test, criticize, and refine theories and the larger narratives we use to orient our lives. Granted, the existence of ordinary truths does not mean that we can confidently proclaim that some overarching theory or historical narrative is true, but it is enough to defeat the radical skepticism our students often put forward. For they provide a basis on which we build broader theories and interpretations, while acknowledging that any claims we put forward are fallible, subject to criticism, revision, or even refutation. Nonetheless, reliance upon broad and action-guiding (but fallible) theories can be reasonable to the extent that they are grounded in evidence and survive criticism.[7]

With regard to moral knowledge more specifically, there is no difficulty in distinguishing between merely personal or subjective claims, and moral claims, for the latter are put forward from what Hume called the "common point of view":

> When a man denominates another his *enemy* . . . he is understood to speak the language of self-love and to express sentiments peculiar to himself. . . . But when he bestows on any man the epithets of *vicious* or *odious* or *depraved*, he then speaks another language and expresses sentiments in which he expects all his audience are to concur with him. He must here, therefore, depart from his private and particular situation and must choose a point of view common to him with others.[8]

In a similar vein, Scanlon speaks of a requirement "to justify one's actions to others on grounds they could not reasonably reject," and Barry talks about the "agreement motive."[9]

This is not to say that people will always be able to reach moral agreement when they are willing to adopt a common point of view and to put forward reasons for their positions that they believe the other party should be willing to accept. There is obviously substantial moral diversity, with different people putting forward different views about the proper ends and purposes of human life, and how our lives fit into a larger, cosmic whole if, indeed, they do in any significant or meaningful way. People may put forward opposed visions of how we should live because they subscribe to different religions or philosophical frameworks, and even when they hold common values, they may weigh them differently. One person might take moral duties to others to be overriding, while another would be willing to violate those duties if doing so would enhance an important life-project, such as artistic or scientific accomplishment.

On the other hand, it is easy to exaggerate that diversity, to neglect shared human interests. There may be deep disagreement among people regarding the ends which they pursue, the goods they believe are necessary to a fully realized human life, but they nonetheless share certain "common bads," so to speak. As Walzer has argued, although conceptions of the good may be plural, "it is not the case that every version of the good life has an opposite that is a version of the bad life. Rather, one of the standard forms of badness is an opposition to or denial of the principles and rules that make all the versions possible."[10] We are all vulnerable in important ways: we can be killed or enslaved, our bodies can be maimed, we can be denied the information we need to make choices, we can be denigrated and humiliated, and so lose confidence in our own value or in the value of our choices. This list can be lengthened almost indefinitely, and every item on that list provides a point of at least potential agreement among people who differ in other important ways.

I put these considerations forward not as *obiter dicta* regarding the nature of truth (or more specifically moral truth) or as an outline of a core set of basic values but simply to show how we can move from a common formulation of the idea of relativism to a critical encounter with the assumptions underlying that formulation, and to sketch how normative discourses can be tractable. The point of moral education, like liberal learning generally, is not to instill a set of dogmas or convey "information" but to enhance the critical capacities of our students and to enable them to join a variety of cultural conversations, including ethical and political discourses, as full participants, by providing them the knowledge of how those conversations have gone in the past and enhancing their imaginative capacities.

Agency

One of the principal "forms of badness"—perhaps *the* principal form—is the denial of the agency of others, for protecting one's agency, one's ability to live one's life according to one's own beliefs and choices, is necessary to realize virtually any version of a good life one might hold. But this view, so commonsensical, has come to be contested and may well be the deepest source of skepticism about the possibility of moral education today. The assumption that agency is in some sense essential to us as persons or human beings, and the (associated) view that morality involves justification to others, are implicit in my discussion of relativism above. And the assumption of human agency, as we all know, has been subjected to withering criticism:

> Popular morality . . . separates strength from expression of strength, as if there were a neutral substratum behind the strong man, which was *free* to express strength or not to do so. But there is no such substratum; here is no "being" behind doing, effecting becoming; the "doer" is merely a fiction added to the deed—the deed is everything.[11]

And Foucault adds, "The 'Enlightenment,' which discovered the liberties, also invented the disciplines."[12] These critics point out that capacity for choice, for governing (I use the term advisedly) one's life in accordance with one's beliefs and values, and the qualities (or virtues) necessary to this capacity such as self-control and the ability to defer gratification, are not "natural" but must be developed through a process of conditioning and control, through which a person comes to acquire the necessary self-discipline to be capable of exercising agency. And this process of conditioning and control is obviously in tension with the value of free, self-direction.

Unlike suspicions about universalism or the easy acceptance of relativism, our students don't come to us with doubts about the moral value of agency. These doubts are sown in the university itself, and while we can't teach freshmen or sophomores without hearing our students invoke some form of relativism, we are more likely to encounter skepticism about agency among our juniors and seniors. Still, there are echoes of this concern in all quarters. Often, for example, our students—rightly—express reservations about strong models of moral responsibility, especially when they bear upon issues of blame and punishment. At least in politically liberal schools, many are quick to voice suspicions about policies they see as "blaming the victims" and justifications for inequality that invoke the superior virtues (hard work, effort, intelligence, etc.) of the privileged. And these obvious limits on agency prepare them for the more radical critiques of agency put forward by Nietzsche, Foucault, or Connolly.

But it is important not to mistake the significance of these critiques. Nietzsche's point is not to deny that we—today—have the capacity for agency, and certainly not to deny that agency is of moral significance, but only to insist that our agency is not given or "natural," that it is a product of a certain history, and reflects particular struggles and the impositions of certain forms of discipline. But that does not alter the fact that we have come to be agents—perhaps the deed once was everything, but we are now doers or, as Nietzsche puts it, we have become creatures who have "the right to make promises" (57). Moreover, our agency must carry normative weight for us, since no one could accept a norm or practice that systematically undercuts his or her capacity for agency. As O'Neill has argued, if people with different moral visions are "to share principles, action on the principles must leave the agency of each member of the plurality intact";[13] for no

> plurality can choose to live by principles that aim to destroy, undercut or erode the agency (of whatever determinate shape) of some of its members. Those who become victims of action on such principles not merely *do not* act on their oppressor's principles; they *cannot* do so. Victims cannot share the principles on which others destroy or limit their very capacities to act on principles.[14]

This is not to deny at least the possibility that conditions of subordination and oppression could be so pervasive that the oppressed come to hold the identity which the society imposes on them, though one may doubt that such "happy slaves" have ever existed.[15] Rather, the point is conceptual: it is contradictory to say that I can affirm principles that deny me the capability of affirming principles.

In embracing the moral importance of agency, it does not follow that one must be committed to the value of autonomy, in a strong sense involving critical reflection on one's goals and principles, or a commitment to some ideal of self-legislation. These notions are often tied together, with the value of autonomy being grounded on our capacities, as Mill put it, "of perception, judgment, discriminative feeling, mental activity, and . . . moral preference."[16] But one can affirm agency—which is necessary if one can be said to be living one's own life—without affirming autonomy. One might, for example, reasonably believe that one should defer to religious or moral authorities in making decisions about how to live, or one may wish to live a spontaneous, nonreflective life. But if it is to be one's own life, one must not be subject to certain forms of coercion and deception, nor prevented from objecting to the purported justifications offered by others for actions that affect one in significant ways.

Affirming the value of agency does not mean that we have to exaggerate it, to make conceptions of blame and responsibility bear more weight than they can or should. We can affirm the importance of agency without believing that everyone is capable of fully rational self-control and then demonizing those who fail to live up to this standard. We can recognize that "philosophies that elevate self-control and duty imperceptibly bring it about that violence against the self, which they celebrate as the central jewel of ethics, becomes violence against others."[17] To the extent that Nietzsche's and Foucault's warnings help us remember that, their teachings are essential to any program of moral education today.

Democracy

At the beginning of this essay I noted the common view that skepticism is necessary to democracy, because only skepticism is consistent with political equality.[18] But I would argue that overcoming fashionable skepticism about moral education is important to the realization of democracy. The retreat to subjectivism and relativism which underlies that skepticism is ultimately corrosive of democracy itself, because it undermines the possibility of public discourse. It deprives discourse of seriousness by denying the expectation that discourse can lead to agreement reflecting a rational consensus on issues of public life, or even to provide participants with reasons to modify their positions. Absent the possibility of reasoned agreement, discourse is reduced to the display of opposed positions, rather than the consideration of reasons that are intended to convince, not merely sway, an audience. Moreover, this view breeds a certain cynicism, encouraging the development of manipulative attitudes toward others. For it supports a view of public life as inherently governed by the play of power and the calculation of interest—of politics reduced to, in Lasswell's phrase, "who gets what, when, and how."[19]

I do not wish to put forward a naive view of democracy as a process of public deliberation that reliably produces the general will, and certainly not to rest the case for moral education on such a fantasy. There is a tendency to juxtapose "communicative" interactions to "strategic" interactions, interactions aimed at a cooperative search for "truth" or its surrogates versus those aimed at control and manipulation of the other in order to attain one's own goals. Though a useful heuristic, this is obviously not a real dichotomy. We cannot imagine democracy without conflict that cannot be resolved, at least in real time, and it is hard to believe that there are in some sense "correct" answers to many political conflicts on which sincere and well disposed contestants would eventually converge.[20]

But even more important, in many cases the problem is not to resolve conflicting views through discourse or, failing that, fair compromise, but to get an issue on the agenda in the first place. Consider, for example, a perennial of American politics—universal access to health care. In some form this issue has been on the agenda for a long time, but how is it to be defined and engaged? For many, this is not a technical question about the effective delivery of health care but a moral question about what is required in order for us to be a decent society. But how do we shift the terms of debate to reflect that concern? We can't simply stand up and say it—we need to face Lasswell's questions:

Who
Says What
In Which Channel
To Whom
With What Effect?[21]

To get a message across, we need to find a medium, identify an audience, and gain their attention, and often that can only be done by noncommunicative tactics—by some form of strategic action such as taking control of a dominant medium to spread one's message. Disadvantaged groups who lack such power may have to adopt other forms of strategic action ranging from mounting propaganda campaigns to street theater and civil disobedience. Michael Moore's recent film *Sicko* is an example of the kind of propaganda that may be necessary to get an issue on the agenda; it may well be effective in shifting the terms of discourse, but no one could deny its manipulative dimension.

Even if we can get something on the agenda, there is no guarantee that deliberation will determine the political outcome, even if the polity provides ample settings for deliberation. The sheer complexity of modern political life virtually guarantees that many issues that are deliberatively engaged will be resolved in ways that are at best only partially responsive to deliberative processes, because the political system displays what we might call "systemic" properties. We like to think of political decision making as involving a three-step process: gathering inputs or demands, deliberation on the different inputs or demands, and reaching a resolution that more or less reflects the range, intensity, and popular support for different demands and some degree of social learning from the debate or deliberation among advocates of different views. But this image is a heroic idealization; the actual formation of social policy is both highly dispersed and occurs over time, involving numerous feedback loops, and outcomes are only weakly related to participants' objectives.[22]

Acknowledging the centrality of nondiscursive processes in democracy does not, however, require that we abandon the ideal of deliberation and the possibility of the political as a sphere of freedom, in which citizens can take stock of their situation, and seek deliberately to shape the collective conditions of their lives. No doubt it is essential to recognize the limits of this ideal, but the recognition of limits does not require that we abandon it, nor that we surrender to any given account of those limits—for surely they are not fixed but are themselves responsive to political activity. But this ideal can be realized only if citizens share what I called above a common communicative culture and come to understand the possibility of discursively testing and revising their moral and political claims in response to the arguments and evidence presented by others. Ultimately, then, the promise of moral education of the sort defended in this essay is to provide them with the practice and the experience of moral and political argument —including arguments questioning the possibility of moral education itself—necessary for a rich form of democratic activity and citizenship.

Notes

1. Weber, "Science as a Vocation," 135; hereafter cited parenthetically in the text.
2. See David Armitage, "John Locke, Carolina, and the Two Treatises of Government," and the works cited therein for a discussion of some of these issues.
3. See, e.g., Parekh, "Superior People"; for a thoughtful and balanced discussion, see Pitts, *A Turn to Empire*.
4. Muthu, *Enlightenment*, 123; hereafter cited parenthetically in the text.
5. MacIntyre, *After Virtue*, 41; hereafter cited parenthetically in the text.
6. Williams, *Truth and Truthfulness*, 45, 46; hereafter cited parenthetically in the text.
7. For a very readable and succinct account of how we can meaningfully think about truth, including ethical or moral truth, without falling into Weber's or MacIntyre's traps, see Putnam, *Bowling Alone*. See also Williams, *Truth and Truthfulness*.
8. Hume, *An Inquiry Concerning the Principles of Morals*, 93.
9. Scanlon, "Constitutionalism and Utilitarianism," 116; Barry, *Justice as Impartiality*, 164–68.
10. Walzer, "Nation and Universe," 535.
11. Nietzsche, *On the Genealogy of Morals*, 45; hereafter cited parenthetically in the text.
12. Foucault, *The Foucault Reader*, 211.
13. O'Neill, "Ethical Reasoning," 718.
14. O'Neill, *Constructions of Reason*, 213.
15. See Scott, *Domination and the Arts of Resistance*, for a powerful critique of the idea that subordinate groups internalize the images projected onto them as well as the value/belief system of dominant groups.
16. Mill, *On Liberty*, 59.
17. Blackburn, *Ruling Passions*, 269.
18. See, e.g., Dahl's discussion of "guardianship," in *Democracy and Its Critics*, 66–67; although Dahl does not explicitly endorse skepticism, much of the argument flirts with that idea in the way it rejects the possibility of "objective moral truths" or even "intersubjective validity."
19. The title of one of Lasswell's best-known works, though he uses the same phrase to define politics in *World Politics and Personal Insecurity*, 3. I would emphasize, though, that this phrase by no means captures his account of politics or democracy, and the contrast that I draw in the text should not be taken as a criticism of his views, which are considerably more complex. For a sampling of that complexity, see Greenstein, "Harold J. Lasswell's Concept of Democratic Character." For an insightful discussion of how his views evolved after 1935, see Katznelson, *Desolation and Enlightenment*, 134–45.

20. Habermas may be the theorist most deeply committed to the opposition between communicative action and strategic action, but he acknowledges that there are many issues which cannot be communicatively or consensually decided but represent conflict that can only be resolved through compromise. In those cases, he insists, the parties must be sufficiently equal to insure that the compromise is fair. See, e.g., *Between Facts and Norms*.

21. Lasswell, "The Structure and Function of Communication in Society," 37.

22. See Zolo, *Democracy and Complexity*, which offers a powerful statement of a systemic view of the political process, one that excludes any conception of politics as capable of providing an overall rational ordering of social relations. See also Barry, *Justice as Impartiality*.

IS HUMANISTIC EDUCATION HUMANIZING?

In Roman Polanski's film *The Pianist* there is a scene in which an ss officer discovers the Jewish protagonist of the story hiding in a bombed out building in Warsaw. After discovering that the Jew is a pianist and hearing him play a Chopin nocturne, the officer is moved to feed and protect the Jew. The audience is led to the thought that an appreciation of classical music has morally redemptive power. The officer appears to recognize the Jew's humanity in this moment of cultural resonance between them: only human beings create cultures; art in all its forms testifies to our humanity. In fact, the character of the ss officer is based on Wilm Hosenfeld, an ardent Catholic who risked his life repeatedly to save Jews and Poles, regardless of their artistic gifts.[1] This suggests that faith might be a more reliable ground for moral goodness than cultural sophistication. To go one step further, intellectual or cultural sophistication, to the extent that it tends to undermine faith, might be morally dangerous. The fact that the Holocaust began in the land of Bach, Mozart, and Beethoven certainly ought to give us pause. We might well wonder: "Is humanistic education humanizing?" Or, conversely, "Is it just as likely to corrupt ordinary goodness?"

If ever there was a perennial question in the Western tradition, this question certainly qualifies. It is the question at issue between Aristophanes and Socrates, where it takes the form of the possibility of distinguishing philosophy from sophistry.[2] It is the question asked by the French Academy and answered by Jean-Jacques Rousseau in the *First Discourse*. Rousseau makes the case that intellectual sophistication corrupts:[3] it is fueled by vanity, and it fuels vanity in turn. Moreover, the development of reason can detach a man from the sentiments of his heart so that he becomes dehumanized and desensitized. Only the philosopher is able to thoroughly silence the natural voice of pity. Peasant women in the marketplace have more moral fiber.[4] Here is a question upon which Rousseau and Edmund Burke are in substantial agreement. According to Burke, the development of abstract reasoning in morals and politics undermines the "just prejudices" that are the foundation of civilization and our only protection against barbarism. Philosophical moral principles most often serve as rationalizations for political projects that are actually fueled by dangerous passions of vanity, greed, and ambition.[5]

One can find equally eminent testimony in the Western tradition on the other side of this question. In Plato's *Republic*, it is the education in music that tempers the ferocity of the guardian warriors and prepares them to serve a just political order.[6] Shakespeare wrote:

The man that hath not music in himself,
Nor is not moved with concord of sweet sounds,
Is fit for treasons, stratagems, and spoils . . .
Let no such man be trusted.[7]

Hume quoted Ovid: "A faithful study of the liberal arts humanizes character and permits it not to be cruel."[8] His claim could not contrast more starkly with Rousseau's depiction of the philosopher in his study closing his ears to the cries of those in the street below.

Many professors who teach introductory courses in the history of Western philosophy (courses that often begin with Plato and end with Nietzsche) confront this controversy directly. What are we doing? Do we leave students baffled by the variety of moral positions to which we have exposed them? Perhaps they exit our courses believing that moral reflection is an intellectual game that cannot provide substantial grounding for action or guidance with respect to purposes but can serve well to rationalize whatever purposes one adopts. They may walk away from our courses having honed their skills in defending their prejudices and with the feeling that a smug and self-satisfied attitude toward one's prejudices is perfectly appropriate in the absence of any real intellectual authority. Of course, we prefer to think that the effects of our activity are quite different. We hope that the exposure to a rich variety of philosophic alternatives will produce a little humility in our students, perspective on their own particularity, and the capacity for judgment in the light of a universe of possibilities that they had never before imagined. We hope that these, in turn, will produce a sense of common fate with all who share the human condition. In other words, we like to think that, if we are Socrates, our students are Plato and not Alcibiades.

But the truth is that they are probably both. If we ask ourselves why the question of the ethical effects of a humanistic education is a perennial one, the answer has to be that both responses to the question are true. A humanistic education can make people better or worse. It has the potential to improve people but also the risk that, in some of its forms, it tends to corrupt them. Moreover, the same education can make some people better and others worse. The character of the student often determines the outcome. For these reasons our question is not primarily a question of the content of the curriculum, though it has implications for curriculum. It is a question of the relation between intellectual development and character development. So we must ask ourselves how what happens intellectually through humanistic studies can have a positive effect on the character of our students, or at least one that is benign. Can college professors at least conduct themselves so as to avoid the risks involved in this enterprise and "first, do no harm"?

Before addressing these issues, some clarification is in order. What do I mean by a "humanistic education" when I seek to understand its ethical effects? I do not mean specific courses whose subject matter is "ethics." I do not mean a course of study devoted to the Great Books or focused on the humanities disciplines. I mean an education in the liberal arts, which includes the humanities, the social sciences and the physical and biological sciences, along with mathematics and languages. Nothing that belongs to human civilizations is foreign to the liberal arts. A student of the liberal arts becomes acquainted with a wide range of modes of inquiry and with the products of human thought in every area. It is a humanistic education and not a theological one; it is a general education and not a technical training. And finally, it is an education conducted in the spirit of free inquiry, whatever the subject. Questioning governing orthodoxies is a hallmark of what a liberal arts education is meant to be.

So what is the ethical impact of a liberal arts education? In recent years, as scandals in politics and business have drawn attention to the moral caliber of America's elites, concern with moral education at the college level has burgeoned. Reformers look to the college experience as a promising arena for efforts to inculcate values and habits of character that will support professional integrity in the next generation. Many of these efforts involve targeted programs (to prevent plagiarism or to promote public service, for example), or curricular reform (introducing required ethics courses). I am suggesting that the question be approached much more broadly to look at the ethical consequences of a liberal arts education *itself*. The question can be restated: what is the relationship between intellectual development of a certain kind and character development at a certain age? To answer this question, we need to know something, first, about our students and, then, about ourselves.

Our Students

Discussions of moral education at the university level often make two important, tacit, but fallacious assumptions: that students arrive at universities and colleges as yet unformed and that professors are the determining influence that shapes them. Efforts at reform often begin as if the question were "How can *we* make *them* more ethical?" I would like to suggest that this is not quite the right question. First of all, students arrive on campus with the most important tasks of character formation already completed. They are not blank slates or balls of putty. In fact, many of them are already better people than many of us will ever be—a point that deserves emphasis. They come from families that are the primary forces in their moral lives. Anyone who deals with plagiarism cases and sees the different responses of parents to their children's transgressions will recognize clearly the dominance of parental attitudes in the moral development of their children. Professors, as compared to parents, have relatively little influence. My psychotherapist friends who work with college students tell me that their clients speak constantly about their parents and their peers, and almost never about their professors. We should not be surprised at this.

Students also arrive on campus with a highly developed sense of their own values and commitments; they are not blank slates in this respect either. It would be wrong to assume that they are so impressionable that they simply will accept without question whatever is on offer. Moreover, they tend to resist what they see as overt efforts to refashion their character or values, particularly when such efforts appear to them to be tinged with sanctimoniousness.

Nonetheless, our students are likely to change quite a bit during their college years, if only because they are young adults. The years from seventeen through twenty-two involve considerable growth and development. One of the chief developmental tasks our students face is the consolidation of identity,[9] which involves separating from their parents and experimenting with new identifications. Here, professors play a role in exposing students to adults who are different from their parents and allowing them to imagine, and perhaps to adopt, alternative self-images. Everyone knows someone for whom a college professor was an important influence, often in discovering a heretofore unimagined vocation. Professors play a similar role in exposing students to ideas, values, and beliefs that differ significantly from those familiar to the student from his or her previous milieu. It is not uncommon, for example, for people to experiment with new belief systems in college, adopting radically different commitments for a time, only to return "home" in later years.[10] Whether such changes are temporary or permanent, knowing that experimentation with beliefs and ideals is "age appropriate" for college students suggests that it is important for colleges to provide students with the opportunity to confront and explore genuinely diverse intellectual and ethical alternatives. At their age, they are uniquely open to the power of such experiences.

These brief observations are meant to emphasize that any discussion of the ethical impact of a liberal arts education should begin by recognizing that students arrive at college at a particular stage of their development, with certain characterological dispositions and beliefs already in place, but responsive to new experiences and ideas. As for us—what we do certainly makes a difference, but we are not as powerful as we sometimes like to think.

Intellectual Development and Character Development

How, then, should we think about the role of professors as educators in the moral development of students? My first point is that we need to think in a realistic way about who our students are and where they stand in the developmental process. My second thought is that we need to know more about the process of moral development itself; in particular we need to know the relation between its intellectual components and the development of character.[11] Of course, these might be considered as entirely independent of one another so that we could imagine two extremes of disjunction between them: an individual capable of highly sophisticated reasoning and an acutely perceptive judge of character who nonetheless indulges his perverse will, on the one hand, and an individual with integrity, fortitude, and the best intentions but very poor judgment, on the other. While these are genuine possibilities, it seems to me that intellect and character are not strictly separable in every respect.

Let me suggest several possibilities for conceiving of their connection with one another, each with different implications for our question. According to George Eliot, writing in *Middlemarch*, "We are all of us born in moral stupidity, taking the world as an udder to feed our supreme selves."[12] The default position, so to speak, is narcissism or egotism.[13] These can be overcome only through a process of moral education which is largely a matter of direct experience but also can be affected by the vicarious experience of reading. From this perspective, we might think of moral development as a process of cultivating a certain set of capacities that draw us out of our "supreme selves," some characterological and some intellectual: empathy, judgment, and responsibility among them. Empathy and judgment in particular might be improved by broadened experience, direct or vicarious, as well as by practice in seeing the world from multiple viewpoints, learning to be a discerning judge of character, and so forth.[14] These are capacities that can be nurtured particularly through literary and historical studies. A liberal arts education is often said to contribute to a moral education precisely by cultivating empathy and judgment in just this way. This approach to the issue supports the claim that a humanistic education is humanizing.

An alternative view which is also compatible with this claim is to think of the process of moral education not as a process of cultivating moral capacities but as a process of removing impediments to good judgment. From this point of view, people are assumed to have basically decent instincts, and the default position is a kind of robust common sense. The problem arises when prejudices, neuroses, and other sorts of characteristic dispositions lead to failures of moral judgment and sensibility. People who are either too trusting of authority or compulsively contrarian; people who are inveterate optimists or characteristically cynical; people whose identity is bound up with political or religious allegiances that require loyalty to certain principles which they find it threatening to question—all of these types will be blind in certain characteristic respects in their ability to see moral issues clearly. And if these fixed blindnesses are not removed, no amount of exposure to the greatest products of the human mind will lead to moral improvement. From this point of view, it is not exposure to historical or literary examples or to any particular material that matters. The crucial thing is the approach of a liberal arts education: learning to think critically, to subject prejudices to examination, to submit one's opinions to the discipline of yielding to the better argument or the preponderance of the evidence, and so forth.[15] Having developed these intellectual virtues, we will be less likely to be led astray by characterological deficiencies.

Taking this view one step further leads to the claim that intellectual development itself entails certain values and disciplines that impact character. Intellectual integrity involves such factors as honesty, openness to doubt and to competing evidence and arguments, the discipline to submit one's judgment to those conclusions that are best supported by the evidence, and the willingness to accept disagreement, rather than treat it as disloyalty.[16] The goal of a liberal arts education is not only intellectual sophistication but also intellectual integrity. And with respect to integrity, intellectual integrity and integrity altogether are not so far apart. To the extent that institutions of higher education are communities that uphold and foster the norms of intellectual life, they can make a positive difference in the ethical life of their students. To internalize the norms that govern intellectual inquiry involves habits and emotional dispositions that can only be called characterological. For example, we would expect to find students developing the habit of self-scrutiny with respect to their own motivations when making moral judgments. We can hope that they would inwardly condemn themselves as cowards if they found themselves resisting a conclusion because it was uncomfortable for them in some way. Students ought to feel guilty or ashamed if they suppress unpopular doubts; if they act against their better judgment; or if they "made the weaker argument the stronger" for the sake of personal advantage or the satisfaction of their vanity. A humanistic education should teach students to hate "the lie in the soul."[17]

If this were the whole story, our question would be easy to answer. We would conclude that a humanistic education humanizes by cultivating capacities for empathy and judgment, by valorizing impartiality as the antidote to bias and prejudice, and by inculcating personal integrity. But we know that there is another side to this argument, and that a humanistic education is not always humanizing. We need to consider the ethical risks it entails along with its positive potentialities. At the outset of this essay, I invoked Aristophanes, Burke, and Rousseau as voices warning of these risks. And while they agree that the cultivation of the intellect can be a risky business, they differ in their understanding of what those risks are.

Aristophanes and Burke bring to our attention the dangers of undermining commitments to social conventions and social authority which are necessary to sustain political life on the basis of consensus, rather than force. Relying on individual judgment as the supreme authority in matters of ethics can be corrosive of the norms that bind a community. Subjecting all received opinions to questioning may weaken the foundation of every public consensus—after all, are there any opinions that can claim the status of unassailable truths? Every society functions on the basis of incomplete and uncertain opinions, which must often be taken for truths. These are Burke's "just prejudices." To the extent that a humanistic education emphasizes individual judgment, the power of reason, and the questioning of "received wisdom," it can induce intellectual habits that run counter to important characterological dispositions of loyalty, respect for authority, and deference to tradition.

While it may well be the case that every particular community requires allegiance to shared norms that are not entirely defensible on rational grounds, it is not clear to me that a humanistic education is a threat to that allegiance, for two reasons. First, the process of examining conventional wisdom, of "putting it to the test," is just as likely to strengthen commitment as to undermine it. "Received wisdom" becomes "considered opinion."[18] Second, one might well conclude, after examining the issue thoroughly like Aristophanes and Burke, that they are correct about the status of opinion in society and the necessity for respect for traditional norms. Rational inquiry and humanistic learning do not necessarily lead to excessive claims for individual reason or for rationality per se. Overestimating individual rationality is the real problem that concerns Burke, but it is not a problem that necessarily arises from a humanistic education. Such an education might just as readily produce a humbling sense of the limits of individual rationality.

Rousseau emphasizes a different sort of danger, one that Burke and Aristophanes also recognize, and one that I think is more threatening. This is the danger that the knowledge and skills acquired through a humanistic education will be employed to construct sophisticated rationalizations of self-serving actions and beliefs. Intellectual development can proceed apace without producing corresponding progress in character development. Instead, new intellectual acquisitions can fuel competitive vanity, feed arrogance, and support a kind of laziness or complacency. While, for many people, new intellectual experiences can be challenging and uncomfortable, spurring personal growth, other people simply absorb such experiences into their preexisting sense of self and use them to buttress their settled commitments. In this way, a humanistic education could be said to make people worse. Without it, they have their selfish impulses or even malicious will. With it, they have these and the wherewithal to justify their selfishness or maliciousness to themselves and to others in plausible ways. Humanistic education can corrupt by producing, in some people, sophisticated self-righteousness.

And here, it seems to me, is a problem that is particularly acute in young adults. The problem is rationalization, not lack of self-control. Of course, young adults often do lack self-control. There are times when they know that what they are doing is wrong, but they have no impulse control.[19] This is the sort of problem that has to be confronted by student affairs departments on college campuses, but it is not particularly closely related to the process of humanistic education. More often, I think, and more importantly for our question, young adults convince themselves that what they want to do is the right thing to do, or that the position that is psychologically comfortable for them is the right position. In other words, they rationalize.[20] They are not particularly self-aware or self-critical when it comes to their own motivations in making these judgments. Professors should not play therapist and attempt to uncover the personal motivations that are often the real driving force behind such rationalizations. And professors should not see themselves as primarily in the business of forming character. But professors can contribute to the development of the personal discipline of honesty that undermines rationalization. The cultivation of intellectual integrity is an antidote to the vice of rationalization. Fortunately, to provide an education that is more likely to make people more ethical and less likely to corrupt them, we need only conscientiously adhere to the norms of integrity inherent in the academic enterprise, whether we teach moral philosophy, chemistry, economics, or any other subject. But this is not as simple as it sounds. It requires a considerable degree of critical self-awareness on our part.

Ourselves

It is undeniable that higher education sometimes produces sophistry, and professors are also the products of higher education. Intellectual sophistication without good character can do more harm than good. For instance, arrogant and vain people find it difficult to accept simple, common truths if only because they are simple and common, preferring to shine by providing elaborate rationales for shocking and daring propositions, if not worse. Academics are well known for turning common sense on its head in self-serving displays of righteous superiority. Rousseau, Burke, and Aristophanes were right to warn of these dangers. Socrates responds to Aristophanes in his *Apology*, offering the principles that distinguish his activity as a philosopher from the corrupting sophistry that intellectual sophistication can produce. Very loosely, they are (1) avoid doing injustice; (2) "know thyself"; and (3) care about the right things. Taking each of these in turn in relation to this discussion, we might consider whether these principles could serve as the basis for a professional ethics for college professors. Can the Socratic response help us to distinguish contemporary sophistic intellectualism from the sort of humanistic education that is humanizing? What might these Socratic principles mean in our context?

"Avoid doing injustice." This suggests a fair consideration of the evidence, responsible treatment of alternative points of view, commitment to the truth, a critical stance toward the framing of the question, and so forth—"doing justice" to the subject at hand. Moreover, we can teach whatever we teach with a sense of wonder and a sense of limits: these breed humility. They are an antidote to the arrogance, vanity, and self-certainty that lead to certain forms of moral failure.

"Know thyself." It is important to tell students when our knowledge falls short, when a problem appears perplexing, when we struggle with doubt. We need to cultivate skills of reflective self-awareness in ourselves, as well as in our students, and to maintain vigilant scrutiny of our own tendencies to rationalize. Without diminishing our authority in the classroom, it is important to recognize when we use that authority in self-serving ways, particularly in seeking converts to our own causes. Once we have recognized it, we need to figure out why we do this and how to control ourselves.

"Care about the right things." For Socrates, this meant to care for the state of your soul. It meant to care about what was enduring, rather than the ephemeral goods associated with the life of the community such as wealth, honor, victory, or position. It is actually quite surprising how much emphasis is placed in the *Apology* on this question of care. Socrates claims that he is ignorant, but he does know what is worth caring about, and this is the crucial thing that sets him apart. Professors should care about the integrity of the intellectual enterprise and the enduring values that support it.

I think that this is essentially what we mean when we talk about a campus atmosphere that is "intellectually serious." It entails an openness to the possibility that intellectual experiences can be transformative; that intellectual development can reach "under the skin" to the level of character. This is why it is so important for us to understand better the relation between intellectual development and character development in young adults. Every one of the arguments supporting the claim that a humanistic education is humanizing shares the premise that intellectual development can have profound effects on character. In contrast, the claim that a humanistic education is corrupting assumes that getting an education is like getting a set of tools that a person can use for whatever projects he or she already has.

For professors to "care about the right things" involves being intellectually serious themselves, continuing to learn, in the classroom and out, in ways that might be transformative and sharing that openness to education with their students.

Conclusions

It is important to retain a modest estimate of the impact of a humanistic education. Such an education can make people more ethical, but it doesn't always have that effect. Some people, by the time they get to college, are not open to its potential for positive transformation. Instead of being shaped by their education, they appropriate it and mold it to fit their characteristic dispositions. Some are surely made worse in the process. For many, the result is probably ethically indifferent: they emerge from their college experience with new knowledge and skills but otherwise relatively unchanged. But at its best, a humanistic education, because of the values entailed in the enterprise, can promote resistance to the temptations of rationalization and strengthen the grounds of integrity. The better we understand the relation of intellectual development and character development, the better we will be able to maximize the positive and minimize the negative potential of the educational enterprise. At the same time, this analysis suggests that we might do well to think less about how *we* can improve *them* and more about overcoming the obstacles, personal and institutional, to conducting *ourselves* with integrity.[21]

Notes

1. Oren, "Schindler's Liszt."
2. See particularly Aristophanes, *The Clouds*, and Socrates, *Apology*.
3. In Rousseau's day, "to sophisticate" meant "to corrupt." A "sophisticated" wine was an adulterated wine, not a Chateauneuf-du-Pape (*Grand Larousse*, 6:5598). For examples of usage from Voltaire, Montesquieu, and others, see Littré, *Dictionnaire de la langue française*, 7: 281–82.
4. Rousseau, "Discourse on the Origin of Inequality," 55.
5. Burke, *Reflections on the Revolution in France*, e.g., 7–8. See also Aristophanes, *The Clouds*, and Oakeshott, "Rationalism in Politics," 9–11. For Burke and Oakeshott, it is practical reason not philosophy that is the antidote to sophistry in moral reasoning.
6. *Republic* (Bloom, trans.), 376e, 401e, and 410d. "Music" here means any activity done under the guidance of the Muses and includes speeches, tales, and poetry. Today, we would say "humanities."
7. *Merchant of Venice*, 5.1.82–87.
8. Hume, "Of the Delicacy of Taste and Passion," 12.
9. The other is the development of the capacity for intimacy. See Erikson, *Childhood and Society*. See also Kroger, "Identity Development during Adolescence"; Marcia, "Identity in Adolescence." I am indebted to Dr. Rosalind Abram and Dr. Lida Jeck for their insights about the psychology of young adults.
10. This observation also would suggest that evaluating the ethical impact of educational reforms might require longitudinal studies. "An achieved identity is typically the result of a period of high exploration and experimentation." Nakkulaand Toshalis, *Understanding Youth*, 38.
11. Lawrence Kohlberg is known for the view that intellectual development is foundational for moral development. His position has been challenged by Robert Coles and Jerome Kagan, among others.
12. *Middlemarch*, 193.
13. Represented in Eliot's novel by Rosamunde and Bulstrode respectively.

14. Hume, "Of the Delicacy of Taste and Passion." See also Grant, "Political Theory, Political Science, and Politics," 582–86.
15. For an example, see Locke, *Of the Conduct of Human Understanding*.
16. Grant, "The Ethics of Talk."
17. Plato, *Republic*, 382b.
18. Mill, *On Liberty*.
19. See Kotulak, "Teens Driven to Distraction."
20. We all rationalize, of course. But I think the tendency to righteousness without nuance is characteristic of youth and linked to its equally characteristic idealism. See Keniston, *Youth and Dissent*.
21. My approach to this subject has been guided throughout by Richard Weissbourd in "Moral Teachers, Moral Students." I would also like to thank him for very helpful comments on an earlier draft of this essay.

PLAYERS AND SPECTATORS   *Sports and Ethical Training*
in the American University

When we think of ethical training at colleges and universities, we most likely think of one of four things: the study of ethics in the classroom, the modeling of ethical behavior by faculty and staff in their personal lives or in their research, the insistence that students act in ethical ways in their personal interactions or in their academic activities, or the participation of students in service-learning. However, while these activities may be good in their own right, I do not believe that they are forms of ethical training. These activities may make students more aware of what adults believe to be ethical; they may make them more reflective about their own ethical views; and they may give them a greater awareness of human diversity; but they will not make them act or even want to act ethically. To be ethical action must be good and voluntary, and it must spring from character and not merely from momentary self-interest. Ethical training thus entails not merely the transmission of the norms of ethical action but also the inculcation of the motivation to observe them. This means forming a character that wants the right things at the right times in the right amounts.

In reflecting on ethical training at colleges and universities, we immediately confront the problem that their families and communities have already formed most young people. It thus seems that there is little we can do to reshape them. However, this may not be the case. Erik Erikson argued many years ago that young people are particularly susceptible to reorienting their lives during late adolescence. When they come to college, they come into a new environment, they are largely free from parental influence, they typically live among their peers, and they are confronted with a critique of their belief structure at precisely the time they are establishing their own independent identities. Their college years would thus seem to be a time when they are particularly susceptible to retraining. While there is some truth in this view, it is not clear that faculty and staff can have a decisive impact on this process. We academics want to believe that our students are deeply influenced ethically by what they learn in our classes and from our inspiring examples. However, this conclusion tells us more about our own wishes than about our actual effect on our students. Three issues dominate the lives of most college students—alcohol, sex, and a concern about their future lives and careers. With respect to the first two, we can do little more than set general boundaries that we know will be transgressed, and while we may have some influence on students' career and life choices, our voices murmur softly in comparison to the insistent voices of their peers, the demands of their parents, and the din of the larger society that envelops them. Moreover, ethical training is not just teaching; it is the habituation of desires, and it requires not just a few inspirational lectures per week but a closer, long-term relationship.[1] For this reason, Plato's Athenian stranger recommends in the *Laws* that older men attend drinking parties with the young to help them learn how to drink responsibly. Perhaps our campus alcohol policies would be more effective if we required fraternities to have an appropriate number of faculty or staff members present for their bacchanalia. Similarly with sexual mores, students would undoubtedly benefit from mandatory discussions of their romantic lives with their advisors. While that would combat the apathy that generally surrounds advising, I assume, for the purposes of this essay, that such reforms are unlikely to be implemented anytime soon.

I want to suggest in what follows that if we want to have an impact on our students' ethical lives, we must close our books, put away our lectures, and begin by asking what kinds of activities actually do shape student opinions and habits, and what pursuits train them ethically for life beyond the college. While there are a number of different subjects we could and indeed should consider, here I will examine the ways in which students are shaped ethically by their experience of sports at college.[2] This question has two aspects. First, how and in what ways does the participation in sports at all levels help students become ethical beings? Second, how does the spectacle that sport provides shape their notions of what is and is not ethical? In order to give us some perspective on these questions, I will first discuss the role that sports played in inculcating ethical values in ancient Greece, classical Rome, and nineteenth-century Britain. I will then try to show how sports in the American context combine elements of all three of these cultures. Finally, I will suggest that while this combination is a potent form of ethical training, maintaining a balance among these three elements is difficult and requires our constant attention, especially today in the face of demands of the larger public for continually more exciting entertainments.

Albert Camus once remarked that the only place he had ever learned ethics was in sports.[3] While this may be something of an exaggeration, it does point to the important role that sports play as a form of ethical training. We come to embody norms by living and acting them out. Organized play in general is one of the first and most important ways in which we do this. This fact will be obvious to anyone who has played or watched children play tag, hide and seek, or pickup basketball. They compete with one another but always according to rules, and rules that they enforce themselves without recourse to an impartial judge. The penalty for not playing by the rules is not playing, that is, social exclusion and the end of the game itself.

Clifford Geertz has argued that sports are a form of deep play in which the innermost values of a culture are expressed.[4] Learning the rules of competitive games is one of the principal ways in which children begin to embody values. Sports are playful forms of regulated competition that present fundamental human struggle in symbolic form. The games that we watch and play are variations on a primordial story that we enact over and over again. They teach us the value of skill and cunning but also hardness, stamina, courage, loyalty, and rule-abidingness, virtues that sustain us throughout our lives.[5] Sports in this sense teach us a great deal of what we need to succeed ethically in life and present us with heroic models for our emulation. Sports also foster in us a sense of human community. Playing on a team, we learn to subordinate our individual goals to those of the group as a whole, and in watching our teams play we come to identify with others in our community over and against those of our competitors. Chants of "USA, USA," or "Go to hell Carolina" are vivid examples of the powerful community-forming effect that sports have. Sports in this sense train us and provide us with ethical standards that engage our passions like little else does.[6]

The role of sports as a vehicle for ethical training is deeply rooted in human experience. The first section of the Sumerian epic of Gilgamesh describes the ethical education of the king, a young, unrestrained ruler whose desires are not so dissimilar from those of our undergraduates. He wants to party, drink, and have sex. These desires impose a considerable burden on his subjects. Since they cannot order him to act differently, they must find some way to bring him to control himself. Such self-discipline, however, presupposes the recognition that there is something higher and more desirable than sensual pleasure. To make this apparent to him they arrange a wrestling match between him and a powerful wild man, Enkidu. Gilgamesh wins, but he does not then return to his old lifestyle. He is transformed by the experience, learning that there is something higher than bodily pleasure, and that is victory. Moreover, he comes to see that victory depends upon self-discipline and friendship. These characteristics, according to the story, make him not merely a king but the first memorable king and grant him a kind of immortality. We thus find at the very beginning of human history the recognition of the importance of athletic competition as an essential element in ethical training.

The ethical importance of sports in most early societies is evident from the fact that sporting events are almost always associated with religious festivals. From the beginning there is a sense that athletic competition brings out the best in human beings, or indeed that it lifts human beings above themselves to a quasi-divine status. The sacred character of sports was particularly evident among the ancient Greeks. The funerary games that Achilles stages in honor of Patrokles in the *Iliad* are only the first of many examples. The Olympic games themselves were originally a festival to Gaia and later honored Zeus. These festivals reenacted the fundamental struggle that characterized the order of the gods and the cosmos. The world, as the Greeks understood it, was an *agon*, a struggle or competition, and no part of Greek life was excepted from such struggle.[7]

All participation in athletics for the Greeks was a reenactment of this *agon* at the heart of things. Indeed, the term *athlêsis* meant "a contesting," "a struggle." Athletic participation, however, was not just a religious ritual; it was the part of the basic ethical training of the Greek citizen. Gymnastic, as Plato and Aristotle among others argued, is a necessary component in the training and habituation of the desires that is essential to the development of virtue.[8] In practice, Greek sports played a crucial role in *paideia*, and particularly in the production of moderation, courage, and endurance. While all adult citizens above a certain age were expected to spend some part of each day in the *agora*, from an even earlier age they were expected to exercise in the *gymnasium*. The immediate goal of such training was the inculcation of virtue, which had as one of its by-products developing the skills necessary for the citizen warrior.

What perhaps most distinguished Greek sports in the classical period was the radically individualistic character of the competitions. This individualism reflected the aristocratic values of the heroic age that were embodied in different ways in classical Greek society but that were at odds with the faceless character of the Greek phalanx. Sports thus did not teach citizens to be team players—indeed outside Sparta there were almost no team competitions. Rather sports provided citizens, and particularly the nobility, with an outlet for self-assertion that constantly threatened to undermine the social fabric of the polis.[9] The Greek citizen believed that winning was everything, but he learned in the context of sports that competition had to be structured by rules.[10] Individual winners were accorded a heroic and at times almost divine status. Pindar immortalized a number of these athletes in his poetry, and hero cults formed around others.[11]

The Greeks were not merely participants; they were also avid spectators of the games and flocked in great numbers to the various athletic festivals. These athletic festivals were similar in many ways to their dramatic festivals. Both had a deep religious foundation. For the spectator the festival was the occasion to catch a glimpse of the divine as it shone forth from the best of the competitors. Nietzsche says in the *Birth of Tragedy* that until Sophocles, the only real character in Greek drama was Dionysus, who appeared always masked as one or another human being. In the Greek athletic competition, one might say that it was not Dionysus but Heracles who emerged from concealment. Indeed, those who won competitions in the four chief festivals were actually given the name Heracles.[12]

The Roman view of sports was quite different from that of the Greeks. In fact the Romans saw the Greek dedication to athletic training as the source of their slavery because it led them to neglect military exercises.[13]

For the Roman citizen the only appropriate physical training was military, and sports were left to slaves. Indeed, free men were not allowed to fight in the arena. The gladiatorial contests originally were an Etruscan funeral custom, but in contrast to the funeral games of the Greeks that were meant to honor the spirit of the departed warrior, their gladiatorial games were supposed to provide him with companions. They thus resembled sacrifices more than competitions. Indeed the gladiatorial games were always a drama depicting the domination of the state. Hence, the oath given to the emperor by the competitors, "We who are about to die salute you." It is true that many of the gladiators had public followings and that in later years the most popular of them were generally spared death, but that does not change the basic purpose of the games. What was presented in the arena was not a contest intended to reveal the divine element in man as a measure of human excellence but a slaughter, a spectacle or entertainment that allowed the citizens to experience the death-dealing power of the state that both protected and sustained them without having to run the risk of death in actual battle.[14]

Sports in nineteenth-century Britain also had an explicitly ethical purpose, but this purpose was quite different than that of the Greeks and Romans. It aimed rather at the formation of a ruling class to govern not merely Britain but also its far-flung empire. While the British elite of the eighteenth century cultivated leisure, in the nineteenth century they turned to energetic outdoor activity.[15] In keeping with this transformation, British public schools introduced sports into their curriculum as a way of sublimating sexuality, counteracting Romantic *Weltschmerz*, and producing what Thomas Hughes in *Tom Brown's School Days* called muscular Christian gentlemen.[16] Such play was at first voluntary but in practice soon became obligatory.[17] Sport in fact came to occupy a position of greater importance than academics. Nor did it remain confined to the public schools. It was soon introduced at Oxford and Cambridge and quickly came to play a similarly important role in college life. After leaving college, many former students formed what they called "old boys clubs" in order to continue to play the sports they had come to love in their earlier years.[18] These clubs were the basis for the development of sports as they exist in Britain and in much of the rest of the world today.[19]

In contrast to Greek athletics, the games of the British were predominately team-oriented. The goal of the games was also not so much victory as team play and sportsmanship (a concept unknown to the Greeks).[20] Strict adherence to the rules was a matter of honor. If a team committed a foul, for example, they would often voluntarily withdraw their goalkeeper, allowing the other team to score. The ethical goal was the creation of group loyalty and a notion of honor and rule-abidingness that would sustain students not merely in the rough and tumble of domestic politics and economics but in the management of lonely imperial outposts where they were surrounded by natives whose customs were radically different from their own.[21] The success of this system of ethical training was widely recognized. Baron de Coubertin, founder of the Olympic Games, called British sport "the corner-stone of the British Empire," and after their loss in the Franco-Prussian war the French sought to establish a similar system, recognizing that while they had produced excellent scholars they had not produced men who could lead in worldly affairs.[22]

In early-nineteenth-century Britain these sports did not attract a large number of spectators, who preferred horse racing and horse race betting. The rise in the number of spectators was in fact proportional to the increase in the number of former players. The community-building force of sports was probably nowhere else so strong. This was further increased by the adoption of these sports by middle-class and lower-working-class men. For the most part, these crowds did not give their loyalty to the relatively aristocratic college teams but to their local club teams. In the context of the dislocations of industrialization, this attachment to a team helped give some sense of rootedness to workers who no longer lived in their rural communities but in larger and more impersonal industrial towns and cities.[23]

In America, sports have also served as a powerful force in ethical training, but the purpose or goal is less distinct than in Greece, Rome, or Britain. In large measure this is the result of the fact that we are an aggregate people and our ethical views are not as clearly defined or directed. Like the Greeks we lay tremendous emphasis on victory. "It's not whether you win or lose that matters, but whether you win." "Show me a good loser and I'll show you a loser." Statements like these are indicative of a general attitude that requires no further explanation. Like the British, however, we also place great emphasis on the importance of teamwork and sportsmanship. Indeed, we take this so seriously and believe it so necessary to success in life that we guarantee equal access and support for girls and women as well as boys and men.

The individualism and team character of American sports are often in conflict with one another. This fact led Bartlett Giamatti to remark that while we behave like the English, we think like the Greeks.[24] In his view, winning for us is not everything, but it is important, powerful, and beautiful in itself—something as essential to a strong spirit as striving for a healthy character. Sportsmanship and team play, however, are also highly regarded. We praise the effort not merely of the star but of the role player who learns how to help his team succeed. What Giamatti overlooks and what we need to add is that we are also as addicted as the Romans were to watching sports. Sports in this sense are a vivid dramatization of American social and political life. To be sure, there is no oath to the emperor, but there is always at almost every athletic competition from high school on the playing and singing of the national anthem. For the American spectator as for his Roman counterpart, sports thus present a particularly compelling vision of our national life.[25]

At the heart of this vision is competition, and it is competition that is intrinsic to the American way of life. America in this sense, however, is only the culmination of the modern project by which man seeks to win mastery over nature, and thereby prominence among men.[26] Contemporary sports are thus a reenactment of the foundational truth of the modern age, articulated first by Bacon, that knowledge and effort produce power, and that power produces victory and preeminence.[27] Contemporary sports, however, are therefore also and necessarily a portrayal of the tensions in the modern project. There is a strong emphasis on the individual, that is, the star player, but also on the team as a unit. The tensions between these two are obvious and reflect in many ways the tension between our commitment to individualism and our proclivity for voluntary and economic association.[28] Sports help us learn how to negotiate this fundamental conflict. Players learn to subordinate their individual desires and skills to the good of the group. The team, however, also learns that it cannot simply suborn its stars if it is to succeed. Sports in our colleges and universities reflect these general tendencies and tensions and play an important role as the center of the college community. To be a Dukie, for example, is not to study with Fred Jameson or perform heart transplants in

Duke Medical Center but to play or root for the Blue Devils. To be a Buckeye is to live and die by Ohio State football. This may seem an exaggeration to some, but it is one of the factors that make American universities real communities in contrast to their European counterparts. The extension of this community beyond the campus to include alumni and other aficionados is also in large measure a product of the popularity of college sports.

The role of sports in the contemporary university has been criticized by James Shulman and William Bowen in their book *The Game of Life*. They argue that intercollegiate sports are incompatible with the fundamental academic values of the university. What lies behind their argument is the view that the university is or at least ought to be the place of the mind, and that it is the mind (and not the body) that should there be cultivated and ennobled. This view rests on a distinction of mind and body that is itself problematic, but it is also at odds with the manifest needs of our students. It is certainly true that undergraduates are concerned with their academic work, but they struggle more with the insistent demands of their bodies and with the pressures of their peers. For them the university is not principally a place of learning and research but a transient community in which they come of age, largely without parental or adult supervision. It is the place where they struggle to master their desires, to learn how to fit into a society of peers, and to figure out what they are going to do in life.[29]

Sports play an important role in helping many of them come to terms with these issues. Aristotle remarks in the *Nichomachean Ethics* that there are five things that are generally considered to be good in life: pleasure, money, honor, wisdom, and friends. He suggests further that human beings are moved by their passions for one or some combination of these. The ethical life of virtue is attained by the habituation of these passions, that is, the formation of a character that wants the right amount of each of these. Immersed in their studies and research, faculty often assume that the university is a place only for science and the cultivation of wisdom, or what Aristotle called the intellectual virtues. From this perspective, the problem of ethics at the university is principally the problem of ethics in study and research. Here questions of plagiarism and academic dishonesty loom large. In some cases faculty members see their task as having an added moral dimension in convincing students to promote political, social, or moral causes that they (the faculty members) believe to be just.

While this may at times take on the appearance of indoctrination, it can never be out of place to raise the question of justice or promote what one believes to be a reasonable answer to it. Faculty, however, seldom see it as their responsibility to help students learn how to deal with pleasure and pain, or the desire for fame, glory, or preeminence. They also do not concern themselves a great deal with the communal lives of their students. What guidance the university offers in this respect is left almost entirely to the bureau of residential life. Sports by contrast help students learn to deal with pleasure and even more with pain, give them an opportunity to strive for preeminence in a regulated environment, provide them not with an abstract intellectual image but a concrete experience of justice, and help them learn to both assert their individuality and coordinate their actions with their fellow human beings under conditions of stress and uncertainty.

While sports involve physical training and exercise, their ultimate goal is competition. In fact, training for sports is called athletic training because it is a preparation for competition. Competition is a means by which we measure ourselves against others. The ultimate measure of success is victory. The desire for victory is at its core a desire to be recognized and acclaimed. It is this desire for acclaim or approbation that promotes the development of what Aristotle called the moral virtues. Exercise for its own sake is mere drudgery or work. Even when health is its end, exercise and the restraint of our desires merely put long-term satisfaction ahead of immediate satisfaction. Sports, by contrast, offer a qualitatively different reward and that is the recognition of preeminence or what the Greeks called glory.[30] The character of this reward, however, varies with the different levels of competition.

The broadest participation in sports in college takes the form of ad hoc play, pickup games in the gym or on the field or the quad. Frisbees fly, balls are shot or kicked or struck, legs run and jump, arms push and throw, sweat drips from brows, and chests swell or fall in victory or defeat. These games are policed and disputes adjudicated not by an impartial judge but by the players themselves. All this voluntary activity has no other end than joy in the game and hope of victory. The happiness of the victors may be greater than that of the losers, but even the vanquished are happy to have played and hope that on another day they will come out on top. At this level, sports are a source of exercise and health, but this is not all. They are also a means by which we learn to live in competitive and cooperative association with others. Each game is a momentary community consisting of students, and in some instances faculty and staff, all interacting in a nonhierarchical and often interracial setting.[31] Success depends not merely on individual athletic skills but on democratic "political" skills for the mutual coordination of individual behaviors in a collective environment. It is hard to overestimate the importance of this kind of play for the development of the virtues and skills necessary for democratic citizenship. Of particular importance in this respect is the acceptance and obedience to the rules of the game. Ad hoc competition also gives individuals a chance to obtain recognition. The results of the games are not publicized or recorded, but the players know who played well or poorly and are able thus to look with satisfaction or dissatisfaction on the way they measure up.

At a more organized level there is intramural and club competition, generally organized and overseen by the university athletic departments. These games involve not random individuals but established teams (often corresponding to a residence unit, school, or department) that practice and work together to a common end. Their games are more serious and are arbitrated by impartial judges or referees. Competition in this case is more formal, and records of the result are kept and posted. There are no monetary returns to the players, but there are rewards beyond the play itself. These rewards are lesser forms of honor or glory called "bragging rights" won in fair competition. The participation in such teams also requires the voluntary organization of team activities by team members and at least some rudimentary training or practice. They are thus activities that require not merely democratic interactions but the exercise and development of leadership skills, skills that are easily as useful to students in later life as anything they learn in the classroom. They also serve to enhance the community spirit of the unit with which the teams are associated.[32]

At a still higher level come interscholastic sports that may or may not involve scholarship players but that are professionally coached, financially supported, and officially sanctioned by the university. These players and teams represent the university, are indeed its public face to much of the world. The individual players subordinate themselves to yearlong training regimens under strict adult supervision. Compared to those of their classmates, their daily lives are highly structured, and they are habituated to levels of exertion and pain that are radically different from those of most other students. This experience is what the Greeks had in mind when they spoke of the development of courage and endurance. This experience clearly prepares them in many quite important ways for the more regimented working life of their postcollege years.[33]

At the same time it is fairly clear that it also exacts a toll on their academic performance. Shulman and Bowen assume that the academic underperformance of athletes is a bad thing, but this conclusion is not as unequivocal as they imagine. After all, none of the students is forced to participate in sports. Why then do relatively large numbers of them choose to do so? First, many if not most of them enjoy the pursuit of excellence in their particular sport and desire to put themselves in the care of a master or expert in the field. Second, they enjoy the thrill of the game and the pursuit of victory. Third, they enjoy being on a team with the intense forms of friendship that this entails. Fourth, they have pecuniary interests either in maintaining their scholarship or in preparing for a professional career in their sport. Fifth, they seek honor or glory and all the benefits thereof. Their experience of sports and the effect that their participation in sports has on them thus is in a sense a combination of Greek and British experience.

The pursuit of glory, however, requires an audience. The size and character of this audience varies by sport and place. Football and basketball and to a lesser extent soccer and hockey have become spectator sports at most colleges and universities, whereas cross country, wrestling, and other "minor" sports are largely neglected by the wider public. The members of the audience for college sports include family members, friends, and other members of the student body. Within the larger university community the audience may also include faculty, staff, alumni, and those who choose for one reason or another to identify as fans of a particular team. The glory or fame available to any player is thus in large measure proportional to the popularity of his or her sport. Football and basketball teams often have huge followings and come in many ways to embody the spirit of the college or university, but this is seldom the case for tennis, golf, or water polo, to take only three examples. The community-building character of sports on campus, however, should not be underrated. As in nineteenth-century Britain, sports become gathering points for dislocated individuals, binding together students who are separated from their families and communities. Sports in this way give a kind of communal spirit and corporate identity to the university.

Sports not only help to foster what Aristotle called the moral virtues; they also present a powerful and persuasive image of justice. This notion of justice is bound up with the notion of the game. Games are structured according to rules, and participation is voluntary. To choose to participate in the game is to agree to abide by the rules and to accept the result of the contest, which is to say, that someone will win and someone will lose.[34] This image of justice is clearly associated with the notion of the equality of opportunity and is diametrically opposed to equality of results. Sports begin with the assumption that everyone plays according to the same rules. The outcome of the competition is held to be fair when all parties obey the rules. No one complains that a winner ought to share his victory with the loser. The fundamental axiom of American sports from the inter-city playground to the Super Bowl is that "Winners play on."

Sports in this sense teach a hard lesson about justice. Some players and teams are simply better by natural endowment, others by practice and coaching, but the fact that they win does not lead to a demand to change the rules to hobble them in some way. There is no maxim in principle in sports, no demand for redistributive justice. Rather defeat spurs losers to work harder in order to become winners. The competitive nature of sports in this sense intensifies the physical and moral training of all of the participants. The notion of justice that we learn and see displayed in college sports has a powerful effect, far outweighing what we say in the classroom, providing students with concrete habits and persuasive images that serve them well in the world beyond the university.[35]

The audience for college sports, however, is not confined to members of the college or university. Particularly since the advent of televised sports, college football and basketball have garnered a national audience. And it is this anonymous audience and its demand for ever grander and more exciting entertainments that pose the great danger not merely to the academic purposes of the university but to its ethical purposes as well. While the Greek and British heritage of sports promotes an ethical life, our Roman lust for spectacles endangers it. Insofar as the American spectator becomes Romanized, that is, becomes an anonymous spectator with little connection to the actual human beings who participate in sports, he or she becomes a mere consumer, passive, happy to watch others display their skill and courage, but never seeking to emulate them. For this audience sports are a catharsis, an occasion when they can let their passions run without constraint. Such audiences are all too ready to turn thumbs down to coaches and teams who don't please them, or who don't please them well enough or soon enough.

This anonymous audience beyond the university has an impact upon college sports because colleges and universities have chosen to accept the monetary rewards they have to offer. They pay to be entertained, not merely for their seats in the stadium or their contributions to the school's general fund but by their willingness to watch commercial advertising on television. Sports in this way become a big business with profit to be made in many different ways and by many different people both inside and outside the university. The dangers that these profiteers pose for college sports are too well known and documented to require explanation.[36] I want to focus only on the effect this has on the ethical training that sports provide.

Even before many of the athletes come to the university they feel the impact of this demand. This occurs in a number of ways but principally through their club teams with year-round national schedules and camps supported by athletic shoe companies. Instead of coaches concerned with the moral and physical education of the young people, they are brought into contact with many whose motives are purely mercenary, those who see the players not as objects for moral improvement but as dupes for exploitation. The recruitment of athletes also gives them an undue sense of their own worth, turning their justifiable pride into what is often an ugly arrogance. It also leads the university not merely to bend its admission standards to admit less-qualified students but to accept athletes it knows do not want to be students and will never graduate. Such recruits benefit the team and give the university a higher sports profile, but they do not participate in or add to the intellectual life of the university. For them the university is just a pathway to the pros.[37]

This said, scholarship sports do make education possible for many students who would otherwise be unable to afford college. While many college recruits dream of playing professional sports, the vast majority are sufficiently rooted in reality to recognize how unlikely that is. They and their parents are happy that they simply get to go to college. The unreasonable expectations of the abstract public for success and the university for a return on its investment, however, often make such an education very difficult because of the immense demands in terms of both time and effort put on these athletes. First, they are asked to exercise and practice for many hours per week and to play an excessive number of games. They are also often discouraged from taking difficult courses that would demand too much of their time and attention. All of this produces a higher-quality athletic product but it also leads to something other than virtue. Indeed, the training of the body that is essential to ethical life and virtue often gives way to the brutalization of the body that both Plato and Aristotle feared, and that later Greek athletics also experienced. Virtue in this way is replaced by animality. Under such circumstances and with a pecuniary return in mind, the desire for glory, for the praise due superior talent and performance, gives way to a desire for celebrity. The adulation of the anonymous public thus turns virtuous athletes into gladiators fit only for the arena.

The coach's role as a source of physical and ethical training is also undermined by the demands of this anonymous public. The pressure put on them to win at all costs gives them incentives to cheat and to sacrifice the best long-term interests of their players for their own immediate need of a winning season. It also creates perverse incentives to tolerate and indeed conceal the morally reprehensible actions and indeed even the illegal activity of players in order to retain their services.

As bad as the effects are on the individual players and the coaches, the overall effect on ethical life at the university may be worse. The problem arises because of the transformation of the community into a mass public. This has at least two consequences. The first is the loss of a sense of responsibility for one's actions. Submerged in the partisan mass, the spectators' ordinary notions of morality and justice are suspended. They scream profanities, throw soda bottles at opposing players and their families, and riot after games. This in part certainly has to do with the conjunction of rabid partisanship and alcohol, but it is also simply an expression of mob behavior. The second and related consequence is the demonization of the opponent. Players and fans of the opposing team cease to be human beings and are transformed into a scarcely human enemy.[38] This effect is both magnified and exploited by media and commercial interests, imbuing the game with a quasi-moral or even quasi-religious meaning for many of the fans.

Within the context of the university the enormous importance this anonymous public gives to sports distorts the educational enterprise. Limited resources are shifted from the general support of athletic competition at the ad hoc level (i.e., student athletic facilities) and at the intramural level to the support of scholarships, coaching, and so on for interscholastic sports. Coaching salaries vastly outstrip those of faculty members and administrators. The university even begins to market itself not as an academic institution but as a sport experience. In extreme cases the very success of the university comes to be measured by the success of its football or basketball team, as if an all-American halfback were more important to the actual business of the university than a Nobel Prize winner. The Romanization of college sports in this way engenders the view that the whole academic enterprise is a sideshow.[39] It also associates the university with the marketing of products such as alcohol that the universities struggle to control on campus.

The problems that arise as a result of this massification of college sports have led many academics to conclude that we should simply eliminate interscholastic sports in the American university. It would be a mistake to believe that this should or even could be done. Sports have a positive effect on ethical life in the university in helping to inculcate the moral virtues. They tie us in this way to the lived experience of the humanist tradition.[40] They also balance the searching critique exercised elsewhere in the university, and this is a balance that is dangerous to disturb.[41] Alumni and the general public are willing to overlook or tolerate much of what we do because their gaze is focused elsewhere, and particularly on sports. Sports programs also have a profound effect on attracting students to the university, and the market clearly rejects purely academic institutions. The example of the University of Chicago's attempt to eliminate football is unequivocal. Indeed, one commentator has argued that despite the outcry over big time college sports, "grassroots support for serious competition as a valuable component of a young person's education has only grown."[42] Athletic success brings in revenue, pleases alumni, attracts potential students, and gives the university a reputation in the world. It neither should nor can be eliminated.

To admit the necessity for the continued existence of sports in the university, however, is not to admit the necessity for the continued existence of sports in their current form. The university is not just an academic institution and is not just concerned with the mind and the intellectual virtues, but these are its foremost objects. It is thus necessary to find a balance between the university as place of mind and body. Here faculty and alumni often pull in opposite directions. The question that we have to face then is how to find such a balance. This requires not ideology, or enthusiasm, or a cost/benefit analysis, but practical reason or what the Greeks called *phronêsis*. A good beginning would be the emphasis on sports for all students, perhaps even making participation in sports mandatory for all students. Second, the university must step back from the rabid commercialization of its intercollegiate sports. This would require cutbacks in the funds for intercollegiate athletics including a reduction in the total number of scholarship athletes and an expansion of spending on facilities, coaches, and trainers for intramural and ad hoc sports. This would also entail the limitation of the length of intercollegiate seasons, and a real respite for athletes from mandatory training. It would also require student athletes to be students in more than name, relegating top athletes who were not interested in study to minor professional leagues.

Sports in American universities are a powerful source of ethical training both for participants and spectators. Contemporary collegiate sports, however, also pose a real challenge to the ethical mission of the university. There is great promise in sports and great danger. We need to encourage students to play productively on teams rather than giving up their freedom to become performers in the arena. We need, in other words, to produce citizens with virtues suitable to a democracy rather than performers who dance only for despots.

Notes

1. In this respect we do a much more consistent job in training graduate and professional students.
2. Similar arguments could be made for other realms of student life including theater and musical performance, both of which require teamwork and offer students the opportunity to perfect their skills under adult leadership. They also provide an opportunity for the pursuit of fame or recognition, and thus the possibility to learn moderation in such a pursuit. However, in contrast to sports they do not involve the confrontation with bodily pain and are thus less concerned with the development of courage in its traditional sense.
3. Camus, "The Wager of Our Generation," 12.
4. Geertz, "Deep Play," 26.
5. Holt, *Sport and the British*, 173.
6. Shulman and Bowen, *The Game of Life*, 11.
7. Giamatti, *The University and the Public Interest*, 78. The combat sports—

wrestling, boxing, and the pankration—were also quite brutal. Injury was common and death not unknown, and the ability to suffer in silence was praised above all else. Poliakoff, *Combat Sports in the Ancient World*, 9.

8. Plato and Aristotle, who both included gymnastic training as part of the education of citizens, recognized that it was necessary to curb the appetites, but they also saw that if it was not under the guidance of reason, it could lead to the brutalization of human beings. The end of physical training in this sense was nobility but not animalism. Giamatti, *The University*, 79.

9. Poliakoff, *Combat Sports*, 105.

10. Perhaps even greater than the desire of winning was the immense Greek fear of losing. Poliakoff, *Combat Sports*, 107.

11. The fact that he was paid to do so does not vitiate the general point.

12. Decline of Greek sports was largely a consequence of their popularity that led to a professionalization of athletic life, replete with training regimens, specific high protein diets, etc. This led to the development of a human physique at odds with the Greek ideal of the beautiful.

13. Poliakoff, *Combat Sports*, 96.

14. This is further substantiated by the fact that the arena was also the site of public executions, which typically preceded the games.

15. Holt, *Sport and the British*, 88; Giamatti, *The University*, 80.

16. Holt, *Sport and the British*, 91, 98.

17. "A Punch cartoon of 1889 shows a headmaster in full academic garb addressing a new boy with the words 'Of course you needn't *work* Fitzmilksoppe: but *play* you must and shall.'" Holt, *Sport and the British*, 97.

18. Even the British business elite often seemed more interested in play than work. Holt, *Sport and the British*, 74.

19. Ibid., 135.

20. Giamatti, *The University*, 79.

21. Holt, *Sport and the British*, 96.

22. Ibid., 1, 94.

23. Ibid., 167–68.

24. Giamatti, *The University*, 82.

25. This has led some commentators to claim that sports spectacles belong to the realm of the sacred and not the profane. See Mathisen, "From Civil Religion to Folk Religion," 23.

26. Sports are not simply recreation or mindless play. They shape habits of thought and action and enact a specific model for the larger workings of American society, a model that celebrates competition and those who emerge victorious. Pamela Grundy, "*The Game of Life*: A Historical Perspective," http://www.trincoll.edu/.

27. Allen Guttmann identifies seven intertwined features that work together to make modern sport—secularism, equality of opportunity to compete, bureaucratization, specialization, rationalization, quantification, and the quest for records—and asserts that modern sport arises from the scientific worldview. *From Ritual to Record*, 45.

28. Grundy sees the competitive drama on football fields as a dramatization of business enterprise. See "The Game of Life," in *Learning to Win*, 3.

29. These considerations led Robert L. Simon to remark, "Surely their [universities'] primary role should not be to simply produce more professors. . . . If one additional major function is to train people to function as intelligent citizens in a democracy, many of the skills learned in sport and developed through competition (and expressed to spectators through scheduled contests) can contribute to such a goal." "Does 'The Game of Life' Really Score?" http://www.trincoll.edu.

30. Giamatti remarks, "We know the sharp, keen, irreplaceable taste of victory—how the pride surges, how loyalty to one another and to the larger institution is forged in such moments, how cohesion and joy and connection of each to each galvanize all of us, participant and spectator, when we win. The moment may be fleeting, but the emotion never finally fades." Giamatti, *A Free and Ordered Space*, 189.

31. The ease with which high school athletic teams are integrated is highlighted by the great difficulty in integrating high school cheerleading squads. Grundy, "The Game of Life," 9.

32. Teams in this sense stand midway between a family and a corporation and thus train young people in the kinds of skills they need to make the transition from childhood to adulthood. Teams are also of limited size and, unlike the military, for example, do not require the complete submersion of the individual. Individual preeminence thus remains a possibility within the context of group effort.

33. Grundy suggests that there is a connection between the rise of intercollegiate athletics and the need for teamwork in rising industrial civilization, especially with the end of slavery and large-scale immigration both of which heightened competition ("The Game of Life," 2). Experiences in sports and particularly team sports as they are practiced in the American university are especially valuable for women. They provide an opportunity for women to compete physically in a public space before spectators in pursuit of glory. They also provide an important training in teamwork under conditions of physical competition and stress that serve women well in their postcollege years, especially as they move into traditionally male-dominated fields that put a

premium on teamwork. The scholarships made available for female athletes not only make a college education possible for some who otherwise might not be able to afford it; they also add greater diversity to the student body. All this notwithstanding, there are still important differences between men's and women's sports. The most obvious is the continuing absence of women's teams in the most extreme contact sports, football and wrestling. Moreover, rules in other contact sports such as lacrosse are modified to eliminate most contact. Soccer and basketball are then the principal contact sports for women. The absence of extreme contact sports for women clearly brings an element of inequality into sports in the colleges and universities, especially since football is clearly the most popular of college sports. Women in this sense seem to be deprived of the equal opportunity to pursue glory. Unequal in this case, however, may not mean unjust. As many cross-cultural studies have shown, the tendency to combative violence is overwhelmingly male and confined largely to the fifteen-to-thirty-five age group. Women are much less likely to commit violent acts. If there are no combat sports for women, this may be because there is less demand for them among women themselves. Moreover, if the goal of sports is essentially ethical, as I have tried to suggest, women may have less need for sports that help to habituate and temper the tendency to excessive violence. The differences in the availability of various sports for men and women thus need not be a reflection of sexist institutional arrangements. These differences may also make it possible for women to participate in sports on their own terms and without being required to assimilate to male models.

34. Competition sustains the contest but it also threatens extinction if not checked by adherence to the rules. Hoffman, *Sport and Religion*, 215.

35. Alumni often note that football mirrored their values and worldviews more than the classroom. Grundy, "The Game of Life," 4.

36. It would be a mistake to believe that these abuses are peculiarly American or modern. As Stephen G. Miller remarks, "Nobility and valor, greed and avarice, glory and glorification, unions and contract negotiations, heroics and heroization, corruption and vilification, the evolution of physical competitions (including women's competitions) into an entertainment industry, and the development of noncompetitive physical exercises were all present in the athletic world two millennia ago." *Arete*, 201. It is of some importance that the demands of the audience have a lesser impact on women's sports and are thus less likely to distort their ethical purposes.

37. We see from the example of baseball that this problem could be eliminated or at least ameliorated by the development of minor leagues for football and basketball.

38. Among players this demonization seldom occurs.
39. Giamatti, *A Free and Ordered Space*, 191.
40. Novak, "The Natural Religion," 38.
41. Grundy, "The Game of Life," 10.
42. Ibid., 8.

BIBLIOGRAPHY

Adams, Henry. *The Education of Henry Adams*. New York: Penguin, 1995.

Adorno, Theodor. *Negative Dialectics*. Translated by E. B. Ashton. New York: Continuum International Publishing Group, 2004.

Almond, Gabriel, and Sidney Verba. *The Civic Culture*. Princeton, N.J.: Princeton University Press, 1963.

——. *The Civic Culture Revisited*. Boston: Little, Brown, 1980.

American Anthropological Association. *Statement on Ethnography and Institutional Review Boards*. Arlington, Va.: American Anthropological Association, 2004.

Anderson, Elizabeth. "Integration, Affirmative Action, and Strict Scrutiny." *NYU Law Review* 77 (2002): 1195–271.

Appiah, Kwame Anthony. *The Ethics of Identity*. Princeton, N.J.: Princeton University Press, 2005.

Arendt, Hannah. *Between Past and Future*. New York: Penguin, 1993.

——. *Eichmann in Jerusalem: A Report on the Banality of Evil*. New York: Penguin, 1994.

——. *The Human Condition*. Chicago: University of Chicago Press, 1958.

——. *The Life of the Mind*. New York: Harcourt, 1971.

——. "What Is Freedom?" *Between Past and Future*. New York: Penguin, 1993.

Aristophanes. *The Clouds. The Complete Plays of Aristophanes*. New York: Bantam Books, 1988.

Aristotle. *Nicomachean Ethics*. Translated by Richard McKeon. New York: Random House, 1941.

Armitage, David. "John Locke, Carolina, and the Two Treatises of Government." *Political Theory* 32, no. 4 (2004): 602–27.

Arthur, J., and A. Shapiro. *Campus Wars: Multiculturalism and the Politics of Difference*: Boulder: Westview Press, 1995.

Ashmore, Robert B., and William C. Starr. *Ethics across the Curriculum: The Marquette Experience.* Milwaukee: Marquette University Press, 1991.

Astin, A., et al. *The American Freshman: Thirty-Five Year Trends.* Los Angeles: Higher Education Research Institute, Graduate School of Education and Information Studies, University of California, Los Angeles, 2002.

Atlas, James. *The Battle of the Books.* New York: Norton, 1992.

Aufderheide, Patricia, ed. *Beyond PC: Toward a Politics of Understanding.* St. Paul, Minn.: Graywolf Press, 1992.

Baldwin, James. *The Fire Next Time.* New York: Dell, 1977.

——. *The Price of the Ticket: Collected Nonfiction, 1948–1985.* New York: St. Martin's Press, 1985.

Balfour, Lawrie. *Evidence of Things Unsaid.* Ithaca, N.Y.: Cornell University Press, 2001.

Barber, Benjamin. *An Aristocracy of Everyone.* New York: Oxford University Press, 1992.

Barry, Brian. *Justice as Impartiality.* Oxford: Oxford University Press, 1995.

Battistoni, Richard. *Civic Engagement across the Curriculum: A Resource Book for Service-Learning Faculty.* Providence, R.I.: Campus Compact Press, 2001.

Beck, Paul Allen, and M. Kent Jennings. "Pathways to Participation." *American Political Science Review* 76 (1982): 94–108.

Bellah, Robert. *Habits of the Heart: Individualism and Commitment in American Life.* Berkeley: University of California Press, 1996.

Bennett, Jane, and Michael Shapiro. *The Politics of Moralizing.* New York: Routledge, 2002.

Bennett, William J. "A Time for Clarity." *Wall Street Journal,* September 10, 2002.

Berlant, Lauren. *The Queen of America Goes to Washington City.* Durham, N.C.: Duke University Press, 1997.

Berman, Paul, ed. *Debating P.C.: The Controversy over Political Correctness on College Campuses.* New York: Dell Publishing, 2002.

Bestor, Arthur. "Thomas Jefferson and the Freedom of Books." *Three Presidents and Their Books,* edited by Arthur Bestor, 1–44. Urbana: University of Illinois Press, 1955.

Blackburn, Simon. *Ruling Passions.* Oxford: Oxford University Press, 1998.

Blake, William. *Blake: Complete Writings.* Edited by Geoffrey Keyne. London: Oxford University Press, 1969.

——. *Marriage of Heaven and Hell.* New York: Dover, 1994.

Bloch, Ernst. *The Principle of Hope.* Translated by Neville Plaice, Stephen Plaice, and Paul Knight. Vol. 1. Cambridge: MIT Press, 1995.

Blum, Lawrence. "Against Civic Schooling." *Social Philosophy and Policy* 21 (winter 2004).

——. "Antiracism, Multiculturalism, and Interracial Community: Three
Educational Values for a Multicultural Society." *University of Massachusetts
Office of Graduate Studies and Research Distinguished Lecture Series 1991–1992.*
Boston: University of Massachusetts Press, 1992.

——. "Ethnicity, Identity, and Community." *Justice and Caring,* edited by K. A.
Strike, M. S. Katz, and N. Noddings. New York: Teachers College Press, 1999.

——. "Racial Virtues." *Working Virtue,* edited by Rebecca Walker and P. J.
Ivanhoe. Oxford: Oxford University Press, 2007.

Bok, Derek. *Our Underachieving Colleges.* Princeton, N.J.: Princeton University
Press, 2006.

——. *Universities and the Future of America.* Durham, N.C.: Duke University
Press, 1990.

——. *Universities in the Marketplace: The Commercialization of Higher Education.*
Princeton, N.J.: Princeton University Press, 2003.

Booth, Wayne C. *The Company We Keep: An Ethics of Fiction.* Berkeley: University
of California Press, 1988.

Bourdieu, Pierre. *Distinction: A Social Critique of the Judgement of Taste.*
Translated by Richard Nice. Cambridge: Harvard University Press, 1984.

——. *Homo Academicus.* Translated by Peter Collier. Stanford, Calif.: Stanford
University Press, 1988.

——. *Outline of a Theory of Practice.* Cambridge: Cambridge University Press, 1990.

Boyer, John W. *Three Views of Continuity and Change at the University of Chicago.*
Chicago: University of Chicago Press, 1999.

Brechin, Gray. *Imperial San Francisco: Urban Power, Earthly Ruin.* Berkeley:
University of California Press, 1999.

Bromwich, David. *Politics by Other Means: Higher Education and Group Thinking.*
New Haven, Conn.: Yale University Press, 1992.

Brooks, David. "The Organization Kid." *Atlantic Monthly,* April 2001.

Brown, Norman O. *Love's Body.* Berkeley: University of California Press, 1990.

Brown, Wendy. *Politics Out of History.* Princeton, N.J.: Princeton University Press,
2001.

——. *States of Injury.* Princeton, N.J.: Princeton University Press, 1995.

Browning, Christopher R. *Ordinary Men: Reserve Police Battalion 101 and the Final
Solution in Poland.* New York: Harper Perennial, 1998.

Bryson, Gladys. "The Emergence of the Social Sciences from Moral Philosophy."
International Journal of Ethics 42, no. 3 (1932): 304–23.

Burtchaell, James Tunstead. *The Dying of the Light: The Disengagement of Colleges
and Universities from Their Christian Churches.* Grand Rapids, Mich.: W. B.
Eerdmans, 1998.

Callahan, Daniel, and Sissela Bok. *Ethics Teaching in Higher Education.* New York:
Plenum Press, 1980.

Callahan, David. *The Cheating Culture: Why More Americans Are Doing Wrong to Get Ahead*. New York: Harcourt, 2004.

Calvert, Robert, ed. *To Restore American Democracy: Political Education in the Modern University*. Lanham, Md.: Rowman and Littlefield, 2006.

Camus, Albert. "The Wager of Our Generation." *Resistance, Rebellion, and Death*. New York: Vintage, 1960.

Caputo, John. *Against Ethics: Contribution to a Poetics of Obligation with Constant Reference to Deconstruction*. Bloomington: Indiana University Press, 1993.

Carlebach, Julius. *Karl Marx and the Radical Critique of Judaism*. London: Routledge, 1978.

Carnochan, W. B. *The Battleground of the Curriculum: Liberal Education and the American Experience*: Stanford, Calif.: Stanford University Press, 1993.

Carpini, M. X. D., and S. Keeter. *What Americans Know about Politics and Why It Matters*. New Haven, Conn.: Yale University Press, 1997.

Carter, Stephen. *Civility*. New York: Harper Perennial, 1998.

Cartledge, Paul. "Deep Plays: Theatre as Process in Greek Civic Life." *The Cambridge Companion to Greek Tragedy*, edited by P. E. Easterling. Cambridge: Cambridge University Press, 1997.

Cavell, Stanley. *The Claim of Reason*. New York: Oxford University Press, 1999.

——. "Knowing and Acknowledging." *Must We Mean What We Say?*, 238–66. London: Cambridge University Press, 1976.

Center for Academic Integrity. *The Fundamental Values of Academic Integrity*. Clemson, S.C., 1999.

Chesterton, G. K. *What I Saw in America*. London: Dodd, Mead, 1922.

Cohen, Randy. *The Good, the Bad, and the Difference*. New York: Random House, 2003.

Colby, Anne, Elizabeth Beaumont, Thomas Ehrlich, and John Corngold. *Educating for Democracy: Preparing Undergraduates for Responsible Political Engagement*. San Francisco: Jossey-Bass, 2007.

Colby, Anne, et al., eds. *Educating Citizens: Preparing America's Undergraduates for Lives of Moral and Civic Responsibility*. San Francisco: Templeton Foundation, 2003.

Coles, Robert. "The Disparity between Intellect and Character." *Chronicle of Higher Education*, September 22, 1995, A68.

Coles, Romand. *Beyond Gated Politics: Reflections for the Possibility of Democracy*. Minneapolis: University of Minnesota Press, 2005.

——. *Rethinking Generosity: Critical Theory and the Politics of Caritas*. Ithaca, N.Y.: Cornell University Press, 1997.

——. *Self/Power/Other: Political Theory and Dialogical Ethics*. Ithaca, N.Y.: Cornell University Press, 1992.

Colleges That Encourage Character Development: A Resource for Parents, Students, and Educators. Philadelphia: John Templeton Foundation, 1999.

Connolly, William. *The Ethos of Pluralization*. Minneapolis: University of Minnesota Press, 1995.

Connor, W. Robert. "Moral Knowledge in the Modern University." *Ideas* 6, no. 1 (1999): 56–69.

Cremin, Lawrence. *American Education: The National Experience, 1783–1876*. New York: Harper and Row, 1980.

D'Souza, Dinesh. *Illiberal Education: The Politics of Race and Sex on Campus*. New York: Free Press, 1991.

Dahl, Robert. *Democracy and Its Critics*. New Haven, Conn.: Yale University Press, 1989.

Derrida, Jacques. "The Principle of Reason: The University in the Eyes of Its Pupil." *Diacritics* 13, no. 3 (fall 1983).

Dewey, John. *Democracy and Education*. New York: Macmillan, 1916.

——. "My Pedagogic Creed." *The Early Works, 1882–1898*. Carbondale: Southern Illinois University Press, 1972.

Dietz, Mary. "Working in Half-Truth: Habermas, Machiavelli and the Milieu Proper to Politics." *Turning Operations: Feminism, Arendt, and Politics*. New York: Routledge, 2002.

Duffy, F. A , and I. Goldberg. *Crafting a Class: College Admissions and Financial Aid, 1955–1994*. Princeton, N.J.: Princeton University Press, 1998.

Eagleton, Terry. "The Death of Self-Criticism." *Times Literary Supplement*, November 25, 1995, 6.

Ehrenberg, R. G. *Tuition Rising: Why College Costs So Much*. Cambridge: Harvard University Press, 2000.

Ehrlich, Thomas, ed. *Civic Responsibility and Higher Education*. Phoenix: Oryx Press, 2000.

Elias, J. L. *A History of Christian Education: Protestant, Catholic, and Orthodox Perspectives*. Malabar, Fla.: Krieger Publishing, 2002.

Eliot, George. *Middlemarch*. New York: Bantam Books, 1985.

Elson, R. M. *Guardians of Tradition: American Schoolbooks of the Nineteenth Century*. Lincoln: University of Nebraska Press, 1964.

Emerson, Ralph Waldo. *Selected Essays, Lectures and Poems*. New York: Bantam Books, 1990.

Engell, James, and Anthony Dangerfield. *Saving Higher Education in the Age of Money*. Charlottesville: University of Virginia Press, 2005.

Erdman, David V. *Prophet against Empire*. New York: Dover, 1977.

Erikson, Erik H. *Childhood and Society*. New York: Norton, 1963.

Euben, J. Peter. *Corrupting Youth: Political Education, Democratic Culture, and Political Theory*. Princeton, N.J.: Princeton University Press, 1997.

——. Introduction. *Greek Tragedy and Political Theory*. Berkeley: University of California Press, 1986.

——. *Platonic Noise*. Princeton, N.J.: Princeton University Press, 2003.

Fine, Benjamin. *Democratic Education*. New York: Crowell, 1945.

Fisch, Linc. *Ethical Dimensions of College and University Teaching: Understanding and Honoring the Special Relationship between Teachers and Students*. Vol. 66, *New Directions for Teaching and Learning*. San Francisco: Jossey-Bass, 1996.

Fish, Stanley. "Aim Low." *Chronicle of Higher Education*, May 16, 2003. http://chronicle.com.

——. "Consequences." *Doing What Comes Naturally: Change, Rhetoric, and the Practice of Theory in Literary and Legal Studies*. Durham, N.C.: Duke University Press, 1989.

——. *How Milton Works*. Cambridge: Belknap Press of Harvard University Press, 2001.

——. "Intellectual Diversity: The Trojan Horse of a Dark Design." *Chronicle of Higher Education*, February 13, 2004, B23. http://chronicle.com.

——. "Is Everything Political?" *Chronicle of Higher Education*, March 29, 2002. http://chronicle.com.

——. "Liberalism Doesn't Exist." *There's No Such Thing as Free Speech . . . And It's a Good Thing Too*. New York: Oxford University Press, 1994.

——. "Make 'Em Cry." *Chronicle of Higher Education*, March 5, 2004. http://chronicle.com.

——. *Professional Correctness: Literary Studies and Political Change*. Oxford: Clarendon Press, 1995.

——. "The Same Old Song." *Chronicle of Higher Education*, July 11, 2003. http://chronicle.com.

——. "Save the World on Your Own Time." *Chronicle of Higher Education*, January 23, 2003. http://chronicle.com.

——. "Why We Built the Ivory Tower." *New York Times*, May 21, 2004, A23.

Fitzgerald, F. Scott. *This Side of Paradise*. New York: Scribner's, 1920.

Flathman, Richard. "Liberal versus Civic, Republican, Democratic, and Other Vocational Education: Liberalism and Institutional Education." *Political Theory* 14, no. 1 (1996): 4–32.

Foner, N., and G. Frederickson, eds. *Historical and Contemporary Perspectives on Immigration, Race, and Ethnicity in the United States*. New York: Russell Sage, 2004.

Foucault, Michel. *Discipline and Punish: The Birth of the Prison*. New York: Pantheon Books, 1977.

——. *The Foucault Reader*. Edited by Paul Rabinow. New York: Pantheon Books, 1984.

———. *Power/Knowledge*. New York: Pantheon Books, 1980.

———. "What Is Enlightenment?" In *The Foucault Reader*, edited by Paul Rabinow. New York: Random House, 1984.

Franklin, Benjamin. *The Autobiography of Benjamin Franklin*. New York: Touchstone, 2004.

Fraser, Nancy. *Justice Interruptus: Critical Reflections on the "Postsocialist" Condition*. New York: Routledge, 1997.

French, Peter, and Jason A. Short, eds. *War and Border Crossings: Ethics When Cultures Clash*. New York: Rowman and Littlefield, 2005.

Friedman, Marilyn. "Beyond Caring: The Demoralization of Gender." *Science, Morality, and Feminist Theory*, edited by M. Hanen and K. Nielsen. Calgary: University of Calgary Press, 1987.

———. *Feminism and Community*. Philadelphia: Temple University Press, 1995.

Friedman, Thomas L. "9/11 Lesson Plan." *New York Times*, September 4, 2002.

Frost, Robert. "The Black Cottage." *The Poetry of Robert Frost*. New York: Henry Holt, 1979.

Frye, Northop. *Fearful Symmetry*. Princeton, N.J.: Princeton University Press, 1947.

Fullinwider, R. K., and J. Lichtenberg. *Leveling the Playing Field: Justice, Politics, and College Admissions*. New York: Rowman and Littlefield, 2004.

Gallin, A., ed. *Ex Corde Ecclesiae: Documents Concerning Reception and Implementation*. Notre Dame.: University of Notre Dame Press, 2006.

———. *Negotiating Identity: Catholic Higher Education since 1960*. Notre Dame: University of Notre Dame Press, 2000.

Galston, William. "Civic Education in the Liberal State." *Liberalism and the Moral Life*, edited by Nancy Rosenblum, 90–91. Cambridge: Harvard University Press, 1989.

———. "Civic Knowledge, Civic Education and Civic Engagement: A Summary of Recent Research." Paper presented at the Civic Virtue Symposium, Campbell Public Affairs Institute, 2002.

Garber, Marjorie, Beatrice Hanssen, and Rebecca L. Walkowitz, eds. *The Turn to Ethics*. New York: Routledge, 2000.

Gardner, Howard. *The Disciplined Mind*. New York: Penguin, 1996.

Geertz, Clifford. "Deep Play." *Daedalus* 101, no. 1 (1972).

General Education in a Free Society. Introduction by J. B. Conant. Cambridge: Harvard University Press, 1945.

Geuss, R. *The Idea of a Critical Theory: Habermas and the Frankfurt School*. New York: Cambridge University Press, 1981.

Giamatti, A. Bartlett. *A Free and Ordered Space: The Real World of the University*. New York: Norton, 1988.

———. *The University and the Public Interest.* New York: Atheneum, 1981.

Gilligan, Carol. *In a Different Voice.* Cambridge: Harvard University Press, 1983.

Gilroy, Paul. *The Black Atlantic: Modernity and Double Consciousness.* Cambridge: Harvard University Press, 1993.

Giroux, Henry. *Schooling and the Struggle for Public Life.* Minneapolis: University of Minnesota Press, 1988.

Gitlin, Todd. *The Twilight of Common Dreams.* New York: Metropolitan Books, 1995.

Glazov, Jamie. "The University Is Not a Political Party, or Is It?" Frontpagemagazine.com, March 28, 2003.

Gleason, P. *Contending with Modernity: Catholic Higher Education in the Twentieth Century.* New York: Oxford University Press, 1995.

Glenn, Charles Leslie. *The Myth of the Common School.* Amherst: University of Massachusetts Press, 1988.

Glover, Jonathan. *Humanity: A Moral History of the Twentieth Century.* New Haven, Conn.: Yale University Press, 2000.

Goldhill, Simon. "The Great Dionysia and Civic Ideology." *Nothing to Do with Dionysus? Athenian Drama in Its Social Context,* edited by John J. Winkler and Froma I. Zeitlin. Princeton, N.J.: Princeton University Press, 1990.

Gould, E. *The University in a Corporate Culture.* New Haven, Conn.: Yale University Press, 2003.

Graham, Hugh Davis. *Collision Course: The Strange Convergence of Affirmative Action and Immigration Policy in America.* Oxford: Oxford University Press, 2002.

Grant, Ruth. "The Ethics of Talk: Classroom Conversation and Democratic Politics." *Teachers College Record* 97, no. 3 (1996): 470–82.

———. "Political Theory, Political Science, and Politics." *Political Theory* 30, no. 4 (2002): 577–95.

Greene, Jay P. "Review of *Civic Education.*" *Social Science Quarterly* 81 (June 2000): 696–97.

Greenstein, Fred I. "Harold J. Lasswell's Concept of Democratic Character." *Journal of Politics* 30, no. 3 (1968): 696–709.

Gross, Jane. "A Long-Distance Tether to Home: New Technology Binds College Students and Parents." *New York Times,* November 5, 1999, B1.

Grube, G. M. A. *Plato: Five Dialogues.* Indianapolis: Hackett, 1981.

Grundy, Pamela. *Learning to Win: Sports, Education, and Social Change in Twentieth-Century North Carolina.* Chapel Hill: University of North Carolina Press, 2001.

Gutmann, Amy. "Civic Education and Social Diversity." *Ethics* 105 (April 1995): 557–79.

——, ed. *Multiculturalism: Examining the Politics of Recognition*. Princeton, N.J.: Princeton University Press, 1994.

——. "Why Should Schools Care about Civic Education." *Rediscovering the Democratic Purposes of Education*, edited by Lorraine Smith Pangle and Thomas L. Pangle, 73–90. Lawrence: University of Kansas Press, 2000.

Guttmann, Allen. *From Ritual to Record: The Nature of Modern Sports*. New York: Columbia University Press, 1978.

Habermas, Jürgen. *Between Facts and Norms*. Cambridge: MIT Press, 1996.

Hall, Edith. "The Sociology of Athenian Tragedy." *The Cambridge Companion to Greek Tragedy*, edited by P. E. Easterling. Cambridge: Cambridge University Press, 1997.

Halliwell, Stephen. *The Aesthetics of Mimesis: Ancient Texts and Modern Problems*. Princeton, N.J.: Princeton University Press, 2002.

Harpham, Geoffrey. *Shadow of Ethics: Criticism and the Just Society*. Durham, N.C.: Duke University Press, 1999.

Harpham, Geoffrey Galt. *Getting It Right: Language, Literature, and Ethics*. Chicago: University of Chicago Press, 1992.

Hart, D. G. *The University Gets Religion: Religious Studies in American Higher Education*. Baltimore: Johns Hopkins University Press, 1999.

Hartley, Matthew, and Elizabeth L. Hollander. "The Elusive Ideal: Civic Learning and Higher Education." *The Public Schools*, edited by Susan Fuhrman and Marvin Lazerson. New York: Oxford University Press, 2005.

Hellenbrand, H. *The Unfinished Revolution: Education and Politics in the Thought of Thomas Jefferson*. Newark: University of Delaware Press, 1989.

Herschel, Abraham. *The Prophets*. Vol. 1. New York: Harper and Row, 1962.

Heyd, David. *Toleration: An Elusive Virtue*. Princeton, N.J.: Princeton University Press, 1996.

Hill, Christopher. *The World Turned Upside Down: Radical Ideas during the English Revolution*. New York: Penguin, 1978.

Hinman, Lawrence. *Ethics: A Pluralistic Approach to Moral Theory*. Fort Worth, Texas: Harcourt Brace, 2004.

Hobbes, Thomas. *Leviathan*. Edited by Edwin Curley. Indianapolis: Hackett, 1994.

Hochschild, Jennifer. *Facing up to the American Dream: Race, Class, and the Soul of the Nation*. Princeton, N.J.: Princeton University Press, 1996.

Hockstader, Lee. "Surprise Front-Runner in La. Governor's Race: Son of Indian Immigrants Seeks 'Bubba' Vote." *Washington Post*, October 4, 2003, A6.

Hoekema, David A. *Campus Rules and Moral Community*. Lanham, Md.: Rowman and Littlefield, 1994.

Hoeveler, J. D. *Creating the American Mind: Intellect and Politics in the Colonial Colleges*. Lanham, Md.: Rowman and Littlefield, 2002.

Hoffman, Shirl J., ed. *Sport and Religion*. Champaign, Ill.: Human Kinetics Publishers, 1992.

Hofstadter, R., and W. P. Metzger. *The Development of Academic Freedom in the United States*. New York: Columbia University Press, 1955.

Hogan, D. "Moral Authority and the Antinomies of Moral Theory: Francis Wayland and Nineteenth-Century Moral Education." *Educational Theory*, winter 1990.

Holmes, Alexander B. *Ethics in Higher Education: Case Studies for Regents*. Norman: University of Oklahoma Press, 1996.

Holt, Richard. *Sport and the British: A Modern History*. Oxford: Clarendon Press, 1989.

Honig, Bonnie. "Difference, Dilemmas, and the Politics of Home." *Democracy and Difference: Contesting the Boundaries of the Political*, edited by Seyla Benhabib. Princeton, N.J.: Princeton University Press, 1995.

Horowitz, H. L. *Campus Life: Undergraduate Cultures from the End of the Eighteenth Century to the Present*. New York: Knopf, 1987.

Hume, David. *An Inquiry Concerning the Principles of Morals*. Indianapolis: Bobbs-Merrill, 1957.

———. "Of the Delicacy of Taste and Passion." *Selected Essays*. Oxford: Oxford University Press, 1994.

Hunter, James Davison. *The Death of Character: Moral Education in an Age without Good or Evil*. New York: Basic Books, 2000.

Hutchins, R. M. *Education for Freedom*: Baton Rouge: Louisiana State University Press, 1943.

Hutton, James G. *The Feel-Good Society: How the "Customer" Metaphor Is Undermining American Education, Religion, Media and Healthcare*. West Paterson, N.J.: Pentagram Publishing, 2005.

Hyman, H. H., C. R. Wright, and J. S. Reed. *The Enduring Effects of Education*. Chicago: University of Chicago Press, 1975.

Jacob, Philip E. *Changing Values in College*. New York: Harper and Row, 1957.

Jay, Martin. *The Dialectical Imagination*. Boston: Little, Brown, 1973.

Jaynes, Gerald. "Immigration and the Social Construction of Otherness." *Historical and Contemporary Perspectives on Immigration, Race, and Ethnicity in the United States*, edited by G. Frederickson and N. Foner. New York: Russell Sage, 2004.

Jennings, Bruce, James Lindemann Nelson, and Erik Parens. *Values on Campus: Ethics and Values Programs in the Undergraduate Curriculum*. New York: Hastings Center, 1994.

Jennings, M. Kent, and Richard G. Miemi. *Generations and Politics*. Princeton, N.J.: Princeton University Press, 1918.

Joseph, James. "Public Values in a Divided World: A Mandate for Higher Education." *Liberal Education* 88, no. 2 (2002): 6–16.

Kant, Immanuel. "An Answer to the Question: What Is Enlightenment?" *Political Writings*, edited by Hans Reiss. Cambridge: Cambridge University Press, 1991.

———. *Gesammelte Schriften.* Edited by Königlich-Preussischen Akademie der Wissenschaften zu Berlin. Berlin: de Gruyter, 1902–.

———. *Groundwork of the Metaphysics of Morals.* Translated by H. J. Paton. New York: Harper Torchbooks, 1964.

Katznelson, Ira. *Desolation and Enlightenment.* New York: Columbia University Press, 2003.

Keniston, Kenneth. *Youth and Dissent.* New York: Harcourt Brace Jovanovich, 1967.

Keohane, Nannerl O. "Moral Education in the Modern University." *Proceedings of the American Philosophical Society* 142, no. 2 (1998): 244–57.

Kettering Foundation. *Higher Education Exchange*, edited by David W. Brown and Deborah Witte. Dayton, Ohio: Kettering Foundation, 2003.

Kimball, Roger. *Tenured Radicals.* New York: Harper Collins, 1991.

King, Patricia. "Why Are College Administrators Reluctant to Teach Ethics?" *Synthesis* 10, no. 4 (1999).

Kiss, Elizabeth. "The Courage to Teach, Practice, and Learn: Student Affairs Professionals as Moral Educators." *Exercising Power with Wisdom: Beyond in Loco Parentis*, edited by James Lancaster. Asheville, N.C.: College Administration Publications, 2006.

Kohlberg, Lawrence. *The Philosophy of Moral Development.* Vol. 1. San Francisco: Harper and Row, 1981.

Kotulak, Ronald. "Teens Driven to Distraction." *Chicago Tribune*, March 24, 2006.

Kroger, Jane. "Identity Development during Adolescence." *Blackwell Handbook of Adolescence*, edited by G. Adams and M. Berzonsky, 205–26. Cambridge: Blackwell, 2003.

Kupperman, Joel. *Character.* New York: Oxford University Press, 1991.

Lagemann, E. C. *Private Power for the Public Good: A History of the Carnegie Foundation for the Advancement of Teaching.* Middletown, Conn.: Wesleyan University Press, 1983.

Lane, J. C. "The Yale Report of 1828 and Liberal Education: A Neorepublican Manifesto." *History of Education Quarterly* 27, no. 3 (1987): 325–38.

Langton, Kenneth, and M. Kent Jennings. "Political Socialization and the High School Civics Curriculum in the United States." *American Political Science Review* 62 (1968): 852–67.

Langton, Kenneth, M. Kent Jennings, and R. Niemi. "Effects of the High School Curriculum." *The Political Character of Adolescence: The Influence of Families and Schools,* edited by P. A. Beck, M. K. Jennings, E. Andersen, B. G. Farah, R. Jansen, K. P. Langton, T. E. Mann, and G. B. Markus. Princeton, N.J.: Princeton University Press, 1974.

Lasswell, Harold D. *Politics: Who Gets What, When, How.* Glencoe, Ill.: Free Press, 1936.

———. "The Structure and Function of Communication in Society." *The Communication of Ideas,* edited by Lyman Bryson. New York: Harper and Brothers, 1948.

———. *World Politics and Personal Insecurity.* New York: McGraw-Hill, 1935.

Latour, Bruno, and Steven Woolgar. *Laboratory Life: The Social Construction of Scientific Facts.* Beverly Hills: Sage Publications, 1979.

Lauter, P., and F. Howe. *The Conspiracy of the Young.* New York: World, 1970.

Lebow, Richard Ned. *The Tragic Vision of Politics.* Cambridge: Cambridge University Press, 2003.

Lentricchia, Frank. *Modernist Quartet.* Cambridge: Cambridge University Press, 1994.

Leslie, W. B. *Gentlemen and Scholars: College and Community in the "Age of the University," 1865–1917.* University Park: Pennsylvania State University Press, 1992.

Levy, Leonard W. *Jefferson and Civil Liberties: The Darker Side.* Cambridge: Harvard University Press, 1963.

Light, Andrew. "Public Environmental Philosophy." *Higher Education Exchange,* edited by David White Brown and Deborah Witte. Dayton, Ohio: Kettering Foundation, 2003.

Littré, Émile. *Dictionnaire de la langue française,* vol. 7. Paris: Gallimard et Hachette, 1958.

Liu, Eric. *The Accidental Asian: Notes of a Native Speaker.* New York: Vintage Books, 1998.

Locke, John. *Of the Conduct of Human Understanding.* Edited by Ruth Grant and Nathan Tarcov. Indianapolis: Hackett, 1996.

———. *Some Thoughts Concerning Education. The Educational Writings of John Locke,* edited by James L. Axtell. Cambridge: Cambridge University Press, 1968.

———. *Two Treatises of Government.* Edited by Peter Laslett. Cambridge: Cambridge University Press, 1988.

Longino, Helen. *Science as Social Knowledge: Values and Objectivity in Scientific Inquiry.* Princeton, N.J.: Princeton University Press, 1990.

MacIntyre, Alasdair. *After Virtue.* Notre Dame: Notre Dame University Press, 1981.

———. *Dependent Rational Animals: Why Human Beings Need the Virtues.* Peru, Ill.: Open Court Publishing, 1999.

———. "The Idea of an Educated Public." *Education and Values: The Richard Peters Lectures*, edited by Graham Haydon, 15–36. London: University of London Press, 1987.

———. *Three Rival Modes of Moral Enquiry: Encyclopedia, Genealogy and Tradition*. Notre Dame: University of Notre Dame Press, 1998.

Macklin, Ruth. "Problems in the Teaching of Ethics: Pluralism and Indoctrination." *Ethics Teaching in Higher Education*, edited by Daniel Callahan and Sissela Bok. New York: Plenum Press, 1980.

Mahoney, K. A. *Catholic Higher Education in Protestant America: The Jesuits and Harvard in the Age of the University*. Baltimore: Johns Hopkins University Press, 2003.

Malone, Dumas. *Jefferson and His Time*. Vol. 6, *The Sage of Monticello*. Boston: Little, Brown, 1981.

Marcia, James E. "Identity in Adolescence." *Handbook of Adolescent Psychology*, edited by J. Adelson. New York: John Wiley, 1980.

Markell, Patchen. *Bound by Recognition*. Princeton, N.J.: Princeton University Press, 2003.

———. "The Insufficiency of Non-Domination." Political Theory 30, no. 1 (February 2008): 9–30.

Marsden, G. M. *The Soul of the American University: From Protestant Establishment to Established Nonbelief*. New York: Oxford University Press, 1994.

Marx, Karl. "Critique of Hegel's Doctrine of the State." *Early Writings*, edited by Rodney Livingstone and Gregor Benton. New York: Penguin, 1992.

———. "On the Jewish Question." *The Marx Engels Reader*, edited by Robert C. Tucker, 26–52. New York: Norton, 1978.

———. *A World without Jews*. Edited by Dagobert D. Runes. New York: Philosophical Library, 1959.

Mathisen, James A. "From Civil Religion to Folk Religion: The Case of American Sport." *Sport and Religion*, edited by Shirl J. Hoffman. Champaign, Ill.: Human Kinetics Publishers, 1992.

McClellan, B. Edward. *Moral Education in America*. New York: Teachers College Press, 1999.

McCumber, John. *Time in the Ditch: American Philosophy and the McCarthy Era*. Evanston, Ill.: Northwestern University Press, 2001.

McLellan, David. *Marx before Marxism*. New York: Harper and Row, 1970.

———. *The Young Hegelians and Karl Marx*. London: Macmillan, 1969.

McMurtrie, Beth. "Silence, Not Confrontation, Over 'Mandatum.'" *Chronicle of Higher Education*, June 14, 2002.

Mearsheimer, John J. "The Aims of Education." *Philosophy and Literature* 22, no. 1 (1998): 137–55.

Mellow, James R. *Invented Lives: F. Scott and Zelda Fitzgerald.* New York: Ballantine, 1986.

Merelman, R. M. *Making Something of Ourselves: On Culture and Politics in the United States.* Berkeley: University of California Press, 1984.

Meyer, D. H. *The Instructed Conscience: The Shaping of the American National Ethic.* Philadelphia: University of Pennsylvania Press, 1972.

Mignolo, Walter. *The Idea of Latin America.* New York: Blackwell, 2005.

Milgram, Stanley. *Obedience to Authority: An Experimental View.* New York: Harper and Row, 1974.

Mill, John Stuart. *On Liberty* and *Considerations on Representative Government. On Liberty and Other Essays,* edited by John Gray. Oxford: Oxford University Press, 1998.

Miller, Stephen G. *Arete: Greek Sports from Ancient Sources.* 2nd ed. Berkeley: University of California Press, 1991.

Minow, Martha. *Making All the Difference: Inclusion, Exclusion, and American Law.* Ithaca, N.Y.: Cornell University Press, 1990.

Morison, S. E. *The Founding of Harvard College.* Cambridge: Harvard University Press, 1935.

Morrison, Toni. "Introduction: Friday on the Potomac." *Race-ing Justice, Engendering Power,* edited by Toni Morrison. New York: Pantheon, 1992.

Moulds, George Henry. "The Decline and Fall of Philosophy." *Liberal Education* 50 (1964).

Murphy, James Bernard. "Against Civic Schooling." *Social Philosophy and Policy* 21 (winter 2004): 221–65.

——. "Good Students and Good Citizens." *New York Times,* September 15, 2002.

Muthu, Sankar. *Enlightenment against Imperialism.* Princeton, N.J.: Princeton University Press, 2003.

Nakkula, Michael J., and Eric Toshalis. *Understanding Youth: Adolescent Development for Educators.* Cambridge, Mass.: Harvard Education Press, 2006.

National Academy of Sciences. *On Being a Scientist: Responsible Conduct in Research.* Washington: National Academy Press, 1995.

"New England's First Fruits (1643)." *The Founding of Harvard College,* edited by Samuel Morison. 1935. Cambridge: Harvard University Press, 1995.

Nie, Norman. *Education and Democratic Citizenship in America.* Chicago: University of Chicago Press, 1996.

Nie, Norman, and D. Sunshine Hillygus. "Education and Democratic Citizenship." *Making Good Citizens: Education and Civil Society,* edited by Diane Ravitch and Joseph P. Viterri, 30–57. New Haven, Conn.: Yale University Press, 2001.

Nie, Norman, Jane Junn, and Kenneth Stehlik-Barry. *Education and Democratic Citizenship in America.* Chicago: University of Chicago Press, 1996.

Niebuhr, Gustav. "Salem Journal: Witches Appeal to a Political Spirit." *New York Times*, October 31, 1998, A8.

Niemi, Richard G., and Jane Junn. *Civic Education*. New Haven, Conn.: Yale University Press, 1998.

Nietzsche, Friedrich. *On the Genealogy of Morals*. Translated by W. Kaufmann and R. J. Hollingdale. New York: Vintage, 1969.

Nique, C. *Comment l'école devint une affaire d'état (1815–1840)*. Paris: Nathan, 1990.

Novak, Michael. "The Natural Religion." *Sport and Religion*, edited by Shirl J. Hoffman. Champaign, Ill.: Human Kinetics Publishers, 1992.

Novak, S. J. *The Rights of Youth: American Colleges and Student Revolt, 1798–1815*. Cambridge: Harvard University Press, 1977.

Nussbaum, Martha. *Cultivating Humanity: A Classical Defense of Reform in Liberal Education*. Cambridge: Harvard University Press, 1998.

Oakeshott, Michael. "Rationalism in Politics." *Rationalism in Politics and Other Essays*, 5–42. Indianapolis: Liberty Fund, 1991.

O'Neill, Onara. *Construction of Reason*. Cambridge: Cambridge University Press, 1989.

——. "Ethical Reasoning and Ideological Pluralism." *Ethics* 98 (1988).

Oren, Michael B. "Schindler's Liszt." *New Republic*, March 17, 2003, 25–28.

Ozar, David. "Learning Outcomes for Ethics across the Curriculum Programs." *Teaching Ethics* 2, no. 1 (2001): 1–29.

Pangle, Lorraine Smith, and Thomas L. Pangle. "What the American Founders Have to Teach Us about Schooling for Democratic Citizenship." *Rediscovering the Democratic Purposes of Education*, edited by Lorraine M. McDonnell, P. Michael Timpane, and Roger Benjamin, 21–46. Lawrence: University of Kansas Press, 2000.

Parekh, Bhikhu. "Superior People: The Narrowness of Liberalism from Mill to Rawls." *Times Literary Supplement*, February 25, 1994, 1.

Pavela, Gary. "Fifteen Principles for the Design of College Ethical Development Programs." *Synthesis* 10, no. 2 (1999).

——. "A Renewed Focus on Student Ethical Development." *Synthesis* 10, no. 2 (1999).

Perry, Michael. *The Idea of Human Rights: Four Inquiries*. New York: Oxford University Press, 1998.

Perry, William G. Jr. *Forms of Ethical and Intellectual Development in the College Years*. San Francisco: Jossey-Bass, 1999.

Pierce, Bessie Louise. *Civic Attitudes in American School Textbooks*. Chicago: University of Chicago Press, 1930.

Pitts, Jennifer. *A Turn to Empire*. Princeton, N.J.: Princeton University Press, 2005.

Plato. *The Collected Dialogues of Plato, Including the Letters*. Translated by E. Hamilton and H. Cairns. Princeton, N.J.: Princeton University Press, 1982.

———. *Crito. Five Dialogues*. Translated by G. M. A. Grube. Indianapolis: Hackett, 1981.

———. *Euthyphro, Apology, Crito, Phaedo, Phaedrus*. Translated by H. N. Fowler: Cambridge: Harvard University Press, 1999.

———. *Protagoras*. Translated by C. C. W. Taylor. Oxford: Oxford University Press, 2002.

———. *The Republic*. Translated by Allan Bloom. New York: Basic Books, 1991.

Polanyi, Karl. *The Great Transformation: The Political and Economic Origins of Our Time*. Boston: Beacon Press, 1957.

Poliakoff, Michael B. *Combat Sports in the Ancient World: Competition, Violence, and Culture*. New Haven, Conn.: Yale University Press, 1987.

Putnam, Hilary. *Ethics without Ontology*. Cambridge: Harvard University Press, 2004.

Putnam, Robert. *Bowling Alone: The Collapse and Revival of American Community*. New York: Simon and Schuster, 2000.

Ramsey, P., J. F. Wilson, and G. F. Thomas. *The Study of Religion in Colleges and Universities*. Princeton, N.J.: Princeton University Press, 1970.

Ravitch, Diane. "Education and Democracy." *Making Good Citizens: Education and Civil Society*, edited by Diane Ravitch and Joseph P. Viterri, 15–29. New Haven, Conn.: Yale University Press, 2001.

Rawls, John. *Political Liberalism*. New York: Columbia University Press, 2005.

———. *A Theory of Justice*. Cambridge: Harvard University Press, 1971.

Reinhardt, Mark. *The Art of Being Free*. Ithaca, N.Y.: Cornell University Press, 1997.

Reisman, D., and G. Grant. *The Perpetual Dream*. Chicago: University of Chicago Press, 1978.

Reuben, Julie A. *The Making of the Modern University: Intellectual Transformation and the Marginalization of Morality*. Chicago: University of Chicago Press, 1996.

———. "Reforming the University: Student Protests and the Demand for a 'Relevant' Curriculum." *Student Protest since 1960*, edited by Gerard J. DeGroot, 153–68. New York: Addison Wesley Longman, 1998.

Rich, Adrienne. "Toward a Woman-Centered University." *On Lies, Secrets, and Silence: Selected Prose, 1966–1978*, 125–55. New York: Norton, 1979.

Rogin, Michael Paul. *Fathers and Children: Andrew Jackson and the Subjugation of the American Indian*. New Brunswick, N.J.: Transaction Publishers, 1991.

Rorty, Richard. *Contingency, Irony, and Solidarity*. Cambridge: Cambridge University Press, 1989.

Ross, Dorothy. *The Origins of American Social Science*. New York: Cambridge University Press, 1991.

Rousseau, Jean-Jacques. "Discourse on the Origin of Inequality." *The Basic Political Writings*. Indianapolis: Hackett, 1987.

Royce, J. *Race Questions, Provincialism, and Other American Problems*. New York: Macmillan, 1908.

Rudolph, Frederick. *The American College and University: A History*. New York: Knopf, 1962.

———. *Curriculum: A History of the American Undergraduate Course of Study since 1636*. San Francisco: Jossey-Bass, 1977.

———. *Essays on Education in the Early Republic*. Cambridge: Belknap Press of Harvard University Press, 1965.

Sanford, N., and J. Adelson. *The American College: A Psychological and Social Interpretation of the Higher Learning*. New York: John Wiley, 1962.

Scanlon, Thomas. "Contractualism and Utilitarianism." *Utilitarianism and Beyond*, edited by Amartya Sen and Bernard Williams. Cambridge: Cambridge University Press, 1982.

———. "Fear of Relativism." *The Difficulty of Tolerance*. Cambridge: Cambridge University Press, 2003.

Schlesinger, Arthur Jr. *The Disuniting of America*. New York: Norton, 1992.

Schrecker, E. W. *No Ivory Tower: McCarthyism and the Universities*. New York: Oxford University Press, 1986.

Schwartz, Arthur J. "It's Not Too Late to Teach College Students about Values." *Chronicle of Higher Education*, June 9, 2000, A68.

Scott, James C. *Domination and the Arts of Resistance*. New Haven, Conn.: Yale University Press, 1990.

Seigel, Jerrold. *Marx's Fate*. Princeton, N.J.: Princeton University Press, 1978.

Sewall, Gilbert T. "History Textbooks at the New Century." *A Report of the American Textbook Council*. New York: American Textbook Council, 2000.

Shapiro, H. "Liberal Education, Moral Education." *Princeton Alumni Weekly*, January 27, 1999.

Shulman, James L., and William G. Bowen. *The Game of Life: College Sports and Educational Values*. Princeton, N.J.: Princeton University Press, 2001.

Skrentny, David. *The Ironies of Affirmative Action: Politics, Culture, and Justice in America*. Chicago: University of Chicago Press, 1996.

———. *The Minority Rights Revolution*. Chicago: University of Chicago Press, 2002.

Slaughter, S., and L. L. Leslie. *Academic Capitalism: Politics, Policies, and the Entrepreneurial University*. Baltimore: Johns Hopkins University Press, 1997.

Sloan, Douglas. *Faith and Knowledge: Mainline Protestantism and American Higher Education*. Louisville, Ky.: Westminster John Knox Press, 1994.

———. "The Teaching of Ethics in the American Undergraduate Curriculum, 1876–1976." *Ethics Teaching in Higher Education,* edited by David Callahan and Sissela Bok. New York: Plenum Press, 1980.

Smith, Barbara Herrnstein. *Belief and Resistance: Dynamics of Contemporary Intellectual Controversy.* Cambridge: Harvard University Press, 1997.

Smith, Rogers. *Civic Ideals.* New Haven, Conn.: Yale University Press, 1997.

Smith, Wilson. *Professors and Public Ethics.* Ithaca, N.Y.: Cornell University Press, 1956.

Stites, F. N. *Private Interest and Public Gain: The Dartmouth College Case, 1819.* Amherst: University of Massachusetts Press, 1972.

Sugrue, M. "We Desired Our Future Rulers to Be Educated Men: South Carolina College, the Defense of Slavery, and the Development of Secessionist Politics." *History of Higher Education Annual* 14 (1994): 39–72.

Sumner, W. G. *What Social Classes Owe to Each Other.* Caldwell, Id.: Caxton Printers, 1986.

Taylor, Bill. "Integrity: A Letter to My Students." http://www.academicintegrity.org.

Taylor, Charles. "Cross-Purposes: The Liberal-Communitarian Debate." *Philosophical Arguments.* Cambridge: Harvard University Press, 1995.

———. "Neutrality in Political Science." *Philosophy, Politics, and Society,* edited by Peter Laslett and W. G. Runeiman. Oxford: Blackwell, 1967.

———. "The Politics of Recognition." *Multiculturalism: Examining the Politics of Recognition,* edited by Amy Gutmann. Princeton, N.J.: Princeton University Press, 1994.

Thelin, John R. *A History of American Higher Education.* Baltimore: Johns Hopkins University Press, 2004.

Thompson, E. P. *Witness against the Beast.* New York: New Press, 1993.

Tocqueville, Alexis de. *Democracy in America.* 2 vols. Translated by Phillips Bradley. New York: Vintage, 1990.

———. "Fortnight in the Wilderness." *Journey to America,* edited by J. P. Mayer. New York: Doubleday, 1971.

Tomasi, John. "Civic Education and Ethical Subservience." *Moral and Political Education,* edited by Stephen Macedo and Yael Tamir, 193–220. New York: New York University Press, 2002.

Topper, Keith. *The Disorder of Political Inquiry.* Cambridge: Harvard University Press, 2005.

Towes, John Edward. *Hegelianism: The Path toward Dialectical Humanism.* Cambridge: Cambridge University Press, 1985.

Townsend, Kim. *Manhood at Harvard: William James and Others.* New York: Norton, 1996.

Truman, David. *The Governmental Process: Political Interests and Public Opinion.*
New York: Knopf, 1951.

Twenge, J. M. "College Students and the Web of Anxiety." *Chronicle of Higher Education.* July 13, 2001, 44.

Verba, Sidney, Kay Lehman Schlozman, and Henry Brady. *Voice and Equality: Civic Volunteerism in American Politics.* Cambridge, Mass.: Harvard University Press, 1995.

Vitz, Paul C. *Censorship: Evidence of Bias in Our Children's Textbooks.* Ann Arbor, Mich.: Servant Books, 1986.

Vonnegut, Kurt. *A Man without a Country.* New York: Random House, 2007.

Votaw, C. W. "Courses in Religion." *Religious Education* 5, no. 4 (1910): 295–302.

Walzer, Michael. "Moral Education and Democratic Citizenship." *To Restore American Democracy: Political Education and the Modern University*, edited by Robert Calvert. Lanham, Md.: Rowman and Littlefield, 2006.

———. "Nation and Universe." Tanner Lectures on Human Values, Brasenose College, Oxford University, May 1–8, 1989.

Warch, R. *School of the Prophets: Yale College, 1701–1740.* New Haven, Conn.: Yale University Press, 1973.

Waters, Mary. *Black Identities.* Cambridge: Harvard University Press, 1999.

Weber, Max. "Science as a Vocation." *From Max Weber*, edited by H. H. Gerth and C. Wright Mills. New York: Oxford University Press, 1958.

Weinrib, E. J. "Legal Formalism: On the Immanent Rationality of Law." *Yale Law Journal* 97, no. 6 (1988): 949–1016.

Weissbourd, Richard. "Moral Teachers, Moral Students." *Educational Leadership* 60, no. 6 (March 2003): 6–11.

Welch, C. *Religion in the Undergraduate Curriculum: An Analysis and Interpretation.* Washington: Association of American Colleges, 1972.

Wheeler, Benjamin Ide. "An Address to Freshmen, 1904." *The Abundant Life*, edited by Monroe Deutsch. Berkeley: University of California Press, 1926.

Whitehead, Alfred North. *The Aims of Education and Other Essays.* New York: Macmillan, 1929.

Whitehead, J. S. *The Separation of College and State: Columbia, Dartmouth, Harvard, and Yale, 1776–1876.* New Haven, Conn.: Yale University Press, 1973.

Wilde, Oscar. "Phrases and Philosophies for the Uses of the Young." *The Chameleon*, 1894.

Williams, Bernard. *Ethics and the Limits of Philosophy.* Cambridge: Harvard University Press, 1985.

———. *Truth and Truthfulness.* Princeton, N.J.: Princeton University Press, 2002.

Willimon, William H. "Old Duke—New Duke: A Report to the President." 2000. http://collegiateway.org.

Wilson, Andrew. *World Scripture: A Comparative Anthology of Sacred Texts*. New York: Paragon House, 2003.

Wilson, John K. *The Myth of Political Correctness: The Conservative Attack on Higher Education*. Durham, N.C.: Duke University Press, 1995.

Winch, Peter. *The Idea of a Social Science and Its Relation to Philosophy*. New York: Humanities Press, 1958.

Winchester, Elhanan. *A Plain Political Catechism Intended for the Use of Schools in the United States of America*. Greenfield, Mass.: Dickman, 1796.

Winthrop, J. "A Model of Christian Charity." *The Norton Anthology of American Literature*, edited by Ronald Gottesman et al. New York: Norton, 1989.

Wolfe, Alan. *One Nation after All: What Middle-Class Americans Really Think about God, Country, Family, Racism, Welfare, Immigration, Homosexuality, Work, the Right, the Left, and Each Other*. New York: Penguin, 1999.

——. *The Transformation of American Religion: How We Actually Live Our Faith*. New York: Free Press, 2003.

Wong, David B. "Is There a Distinction between Reason and Emotion in Mencius?" *Philosophy East and West* 41, no. 1 (1991): 31–44.

Zagzebski, Linda. *Virtues of the Mind*. Cambridge: Cambridge University Press, 1996.

Zeitlin, Froma I. "Thebes: Theater of Self and Society in Athenian Drama." *Nothing to Do with Dionysus? Athenian Drama in Its Social Context*, edited by John J. Winkler and Froma I. Zeitlin. Princeton, N.J.: Princeton University Press, 1990.

Zernike, Kate. "Lesson Plans for Sept. 11 Offer a Study in Discord." *New York Times*, August 31, 2002, 1.

Zolo, Daniolo. *Democracy and Complexity*. University Park: Pennsylvania State University Press, 1992.

Zook, G. F. *Higher Education for American Democracy: A Report of the President's Commission on Higher Education*. Washington: United States Government Printing Office, 1947.

CONTRIBUTORS

Lawrence Blum is a professor of philosophy and the Distinguished Professor of Liberal Arts and Education at the University of Massachusetts, Boston. He is the author of *"I'm Not a Racist, But . . .": The Moral Quandary of Race*, which was named social philosophy book of the year (2002) by the North American Society for Social Philosophy; *Moral Perception and Particularity*; and many articles on moral philosophy, race theory, moral education, and multicultural education.

Romand Coles is the Frances B. McAllister Chair and Director of the Program for Community, Culture and Environment at Northern Arizona University, where he works to cultivate theories and practices of democratic engagement and stewardship of place. Some recent books include *Beyond Gated Politics: Reflections for the Possibility of Democracy*; and *Christianity, Democracy, and the Radical Ordinary: Conversations between a Radical Democrat and a Christian* (with Stanley Hauerwas).

J. Peter Euben is Research Professor of Political Science and Classical Studies and the Kenan Distinguished Faculty Fellow in Ethics at Duke University. He is the author of *The Necessity of Utopia* and also a coeditor of *When Worlds Elide: Political Theory, Cultural Studies, and the Effects of Hellenism*.

Stanley Fish is the Davidson-Kahn Distinguished University Professor and Professor of Law at Florida International University. He also writes the online column "Think Again" for the *New York Times*. One of his recent books is *Save the World on Your Own Time*.

Michael Allen Gillespie is the Jerry G. and Patricia Crawford Hubbard Professor of Political Science and Professor of Philosophy at Duke University. He is the author of *Hegel, Heidegger and the Ground of History*, *Nihilism before Nietzsche*, and *The Theological Origins of Modernity*. He is coeditor of *Nietzsche's New Seas: Explorations in Philosophy, Aesthetics, and Politics*; *Ratifying the Constitution*; and *Homo Politicus, Homo Economicus*. He has published numerous articles on the history of political philosophy and various topics in American political thought and public philosophy as well as on the relation of religion and politics. He has received grants from the National Endowment for the Humanities, the German Academic Exchange Service (DAAD), the Templeton Foundation, the Liberty Fund, the Earhart Foundation, the National Humanities Center, and the Jack Miller Foundation, and Searle Foundation. He is the director of the Gerst Program in Political, Economic, and Humanistic Studies, and the codirector of the Duke Program in American Values and Institutions.

Ruth W. Grant is a professor of political science and philosophy at Duke University and a senior fellow at the Kenan Institute for Ethics. She specializes in early modern political thought and political ethics. She has recently edited a volume of essays, *Naming Evil, Judging Evil* and is at work on a companion volume, *In Search of Goodness.*

Stanley Hauerwas is the Gilbert T. Rowe Professor of Theological Ethics at Duke University. His work cuts across disciplinary lines as he is in conversation with systematic theology, philosophical theology and ethics, and political theory, as well as the philosophy of social science and medical ethics. Two of his numerous publications include *With the Grain of the Universe: The Church's Witness and Natural Theology* and *The State of the University: Academic Knowledges and the Knowledge of God.*

David A. Hoekema is a professor of philosophy at Calvin College, where he served formerly as academic dean and as interim vice-president for student life. He was previously executive director of the American Philosophical Association. His books include *Campus Rules* and *Moral Community.*

Elizabeth Kiss served as the founding director of Duke's Kenan Institute for Ethics from 1997 to 2006. In 2006 she became the eighth president of Agnes Scott College, a national liberal arts college for women located in Atlanta. She has written on moral judgment and education, human rights, the application of rights theories to issues of ethnic conflict and nationalism, feminist debates about rights and justice, and justice in the aftermath of human rights violations. At Agnes Scott she led a strategic planning process that identified, as one of six major goals for the college, an effort to become "a living laboratory of campus-wide commitment to justice, courage, integrity, respect and responsibility through policies and practices designed to model these values and to provide the campus community with ongoing opportunities for ethical reflection, deliberation and action."

Patchen Markell teaches political theory at the University of Chicago. He is the author of *Bound by Recognition,* as well as articles in such journals as *Political Theory* and *American Political Science Review*. He is currently working on a book-length study of Hannah Arendt's *The Human Condition*.

Susan Jane McWilliams is an assistant professor of politics at Pomona College. She is the author of "Thoreau on Body and Soul," in *A Political Companion to Henry David Thoreau*, edited by Jack Turner.

J. Donald Moon is the Ezra and Cecile Professor in the College of Social Studies and dean of the social sciences and interdisciplinary programs at Wesleyan University. His interests include contemporary liberal theory, democratic citizenship, the moral basis of the welfare state, and civic education. His writings include *Constructing Community: Moral Pluralism and Tragic Conflict*.

James Bernard Murphy is a professor of government at Dartmouth College. He has received grants and fellowships from the NEH, the ACLS, the Earhart Foundation, the Manhattan Institute, and the Pew Charitable Trusts. He is the author of two books and the editor of two. His work on intellectual virtues in education has been published in the *New York Times*, *Education Next*, and the journal *Philosophy and Social Policy*.

Julie A. Reuben is a professor at the Harvard Graduate School of Education. She is the author of *The Making of the Modern University: Intellectual Transformation and the Marginalization of Morality* as well as numerous articles on the relation of colleges and universities to politics and civic education in schools.

George Shulman teaches at the Gallatin School of New York University. He is the author of *American Prophecy: Race and Redemption in American Politics*.

Elizabeth V. Spelman is a professor of philosophy and the Barbara Richmond Professor in the Humanities at Smith College. The author of *Repair: The Impulse to Restore in a Fragile World*, she currently is at work on a book tentatively titled *Philosophy and Waste: The Garbagio Seminars*.

INDEX

Association for Moral Education, 3

Association for Practical and Professional Ethics, 3

Athletics. *See* Sports

Baldwin, James, 136, 206; on moral beliefs, 222 n. 12; on power, 218; on protest novels, 217–18; on racism, 213–217; tragic view of life in work of, 220

Barber, Benjamin, 166, 182 n. 14

Bellah, Robert, 134

Benjamin, Walter, 232

Bennett, William J., 49–50, 165

Blake, William, 206, 211–13, 220

Bloch, Ernst, 233–240

Bok, Derek, 8, 12, 24 n. 20, 116

Bourdieu, Pierre, 118–21, 245 n. 6

Bowling Alone (Putnam), 182 n. 24, 281 n. 7

Brooks, David, x-xi, 68, 115

Burke, Edmund, 225, 284–89; on "just prejudices," 290

Bush, George W., 86, 131, 138 n. 25

Campus Compact, 3, 25 n. 43, 50, 53 n. 35

Camus, Albert, 298

Capitalism. *See* Political economy

Caputo, John, 4

Careerism of university students, 297

Carter, Stephen, 71

Catholic colleges and universities. *See* Roman Catholic universities

Center for Academic Integrity, 3

Character. *See* Moral character

Cheating, 261

Chesterton, G. K., 133

Christianity, and university education, 105–7

Chronicle of Higher Education, 93

Citizens: as deliberative agents, 10; education for, 10, 24, 40–43, 268; Tocqueville on, 209. *See also* Political engagement

Citizenship: intellectual and political skills for, 57–62, 306; preparing students for, 65–68, 71; university education and, 108 n. 4, 159 n. 7

Civic apathy, 23

Civic education, 179–81; civic knowledge and, 166–68; civic virtue and, 167; through extracurricular activities, 170

Civic engagement, 50, 220

Civic responsibility, 57

Civics curriculum (high school), 168–71

Civility, 166, 190

"Civil listening," 71

Civil rights movement, 8, 61, 211

Civil society, 195–98, 201, 241

Cohen, Randy, 255–56

Coles, Robert, 12

College of William and Mary, 30

College students. *See* University students

Communicative culture, 268–70

Community colleges, 6, 67, 88

Connolly, William, 201 n. 3, 277

Consumerism. *See* Materialism

Core curriculum, 3, 267

Cortez, Ernesto, 241

Critical thinking, 50, 100, 289; citizenship and, 17; doubts about, 80; facilitation of, 65, 191

Crito, 128–29

Culture wars, 164–66

Curriculum: "core," 3, 267; ethics, 6, 27–35, 186–87

Dahl, Robert, 281
Day, Jeremiah, and Yale Report (1928), 31–32
Declaration of Independence, 133
Democracy: grassroots, 241–44; higher education and, 18, 40; moral education and, 16, 208, 213; presuppositions of, 270; re-imagining meaning of, 208; risks of relativism for, 278; skepticism necessary for, 278; training of citizens for, 314 n. 29. *See also* Citizenship
Democratic citizenship. *See* Citizenship
Derrida, Jacques, 230
Dewey, John, 38, 174, 188
DiFranco, Ani, 245 n. 12
Dissertation on the Poor Laws by a Well-Wisher to Mankind (Townsend), 225–26
Diversity. *See* Affirmative action; Multiculturalism
"Doonesbury," 252
Douglass, Frederick, 214
Duke University, x, 246 n. 20, 303
Durr, Virginia Foster, 61–66, 80

Eagleton, Terry, 99, 108 n. 8
Educating Citizens (Colby, Ehrlich, Beaumont, and Stephens), 26 n. 53, 61–62
Eichmann in Jerusalem (Arendt), 18, 32
Eliot, George, 288
Empathy, 11, 118, 172; multiculturalism and, 157
Endowments, 86
Equality, and inclusion, 152–56
Erikson, Erik, 296
Ethical training, as habituation of desires, 297

Ethics: athletic training and, 298–308; expertise and, 16; historical examination of, 250; "macro" and "micro," 9; political economy and, 224–225; in professional schools, 252–254; teaching of, 229
Ethnic identities, 141–43
Extracurricular activities, 89, 170

Faculty. *See* Professors
Foucault, Michel, 225; enlightenment as "limit attitude," 230, 276
Freedom, as core university value, 33–34
Friedman, Thomas, 165

Geertz, Clifford, 298
Giamatti, Bartlett, 303
Gilgamesh, 299
Global warming, 269
Gramsci, Antonio, 96
Gratz v. Bollinger, 151
Great books movement, 41–42, 189
Greek tragedy, 193
Grutter v. Bollinger, 151
Gutmann, Amy, 166, 188

Habermas, Jürgen, 282 n. 20
Habits of the Heart (Bellah), 134
Harry Potter stories, 135
Harvard University, 27; Congregational Churches of Massachusetts and, 29; core curriculum of, 190, 202 n. 17
Hastings Center, 9, 12
Health care, debates on, 279
Higher education: American history of, 27–52; church control of, 29–31; democratic principles in, 81; in eighteenth-century Scotland, 105–6;

Moral deliberation, 5, 19, 25, n. 43, 117

Moral education: aims of, 21; assumptions about, 286; concerns of social scientists about, 14; disagreement over, 10; as dialogical, 20; history of, 27–40; imperialism and, 271–272; mandatory instruction in, 249; moral judgment and, 17–18; necessary for democratic citizenship, 280; possibility of, 267; purposes of, 21, 275; removal of impediments to, 288; role of professors in, 287; suspicions of, 186–89, 223, 267, 270–71; worries about indoctrination in, 63–64, 81

Morality: conservatism and, 164; as ideology, 211; liberalism and, 164; relation to politics, 206

Multiculturalism, 50, 140–45; fear of, 158

National Council for Social Studies (NCSS), 164

National Education Association (NEA), 164

National Public Radio, 255

"New England's First Fruits," 27–28

Nicomachean Ethics (Aristotle), 304

Nietzsche, Friedrich, 277

"On the Jewish Question" (Marx), 195–98

Open-mindedness, 174

Ordinary goodness, 283

Parable of the Sower, 125

Patriot Act, 86

Patriotism, 10, 165–66, 178

Pavela, Gary, 12

Pedagogy, 11, 63, 64

Philosophy, introductory courses in, 284

Pianist, The, 283

Pietism, 32

Plato, 180; on education of guardian class, 170–71, 284; on possibility of teaching virtue, 251

Pluralism: cultural, 22, 143; moral relativism and, 10; religious, 129, 146; values of, 152

Polanyi, Karl, 224, 226–27

Political advocacy, dangers of, 76–78

Political economy, 224–25

Political education, differentiated from "politicized" education, 59, 65

Political engagement: as medium of moral education, 220; service learning and, 50

Political theory, 104

Politics: as agonistic struggle, 207; as "who gets what, when, where, and how," 279

Postmodernism, 13

President's Commission on Higher Education, 40

Princeton University, 127

Professors: ethical character of, 11; moral instruction and, 257–58; political advocacy of, 76–78, 81, 90

Public schooling (United States), history of, 163

Putnam, Robert, 131, 182 n. 24

Radical democracy, 13, 223

Rationalization, dangers of, 291–292

Rawls, John, 132

Relativism, 10, 273–274; fear of, 140

Religion: anti-Catholicism in American education, 178; Christian community and university education,

Wages, at American universities, 72,
82–84
Walzer, Michael, 275
Weber, Max, 273
Wilde, Oscar, 8
Williams, Bernard, 4, 274

Willimon, Will, 19
Winch, Peter, 15
Winthrop, John, 135
Wright, Richard, 217–18

Zolo, Danilo, 282 n. 22

Elizabeth Kiss is the president of Agnes Scott
College. J. Peter Euben is Research Professor of
Political Science and Kenan Distinguished Faculty
Fellow in Ethics at Duke University.

Library of Congress Cataloging-in-Publication Data
Debating moral education: rethinking the role of
the modern university / edited by Elizabeth Kiss and
J. Peter Euben.
p. cm.
Includes bibliographical references and index.
ISBN 978-0-8223-4620-3 (cloth : alk. paper)
ISBN 978-0-8223-4616-6 (pbk. : alk. paper)
1. Moral education (Higher)—United States.
I. Kiss, Elizabeth. II. Euben, J. Peter.
LC311.D43 2009
370.11′4—dc22   2009032837